The Documentation
of the
European Communities

The Documentation
of the
European Communities:
A Guide

Ian Thomson

Mansell

First published 1989 by
Mansell Publishing Limited, *A Cassell Imprint*
Artillery House, Artillery Row, London SW1P 1RT, England
125 East 23rd Street, Suite 300, New York 10010, USA

British Library Cataloguing in Publication Data
Thomson, Ian
  The documentation of the European Communities: a guide.
  1. European community. Publications
  I. Title
  070.5'95

  ISBN 0–7201–2022–5

Library of Congress Cataloging-in-Publication Data
Thomson, Ian, 1953–
    The documentation of the European communities: a guide/Ian Thomson.
      p.   cm.
    Includes index.
    ISBN 0–7201–2022–5
    1. European communities—Bibliography. 2. European Economic
  Community countries—Bibliography. I. Title.
  Z7165.E8T47 1989
  [JN 15]
  015.4'052—dc20   89–32114
                              CIP

This book has been printed and bound in Great Britain:
typeset in Compugraphic Plantin by Colset (Private) Ltd,
Singapore, and printed and bound by Biddles Ltd,
Guildford and King's Lynn on Onslow Book Wove paper.

Contents

CONTENTS

Tables

1 Numbers of publications, in all languages, handled by OOPEC (excluding *Official Journal*)

2 Breakdown of institutional input in the *Official Journal* by number of pages in 1982

3 Trends in the number of pages (per language version) of the *Official Journal* ('L', 'C', 'S' series)

4 *Official Journal* 1987 breakdown by part

5 EC legislative acts

6 EC legislative proposals following the Single European Act

7 EC legislative procedure – related documentation

Preface

As the research and writing of this book comes to an end during the summer of 1988 it is possible to claim that the European Community (EC) is in the middle of one of its most significant periods of evolution. After a period in the 1970s and 1980s of institutional, budgetary and policy stalemate the EC has seemingly shaken itself out of this state of paralysis and launched upon a dynamic campaign to create a genuine single market within its borders by 1992. The date itself has assumed almost mystical and inspirational proportions. Whether all the detailed elements of the programme to complete the internal market will be achieved – the elimination of all physical, technical, legal and fiscal barriers which impede the free movement of people, services, capital and goods between the member states – by the chosen date is almost irrelevant. What is clear is that there is a definite commitment to move forward in the integration process and that the governments of the member states, many sectors within the member states, and many outside interests believe significant changes are taking place.

The need to know about the European Community – how it operates, what are its policies and how to influence its decision makers – becomes ever more necessary. There has been an explosion of organizations providing EC information services in the last few years. There is also a mass of printed sources of information about the EC. A particularly important proportion of those information sources comprise the documentation produced by the various organs of the European Community itself.

The aim of this book is to describe the current range of publicly available printed documentation produced by the EC. This ranges from the text of primary and secondary legislation to explanatory and background sources from the plethora of Community institutions, organizations and departments that exist today.

Upon embarking upon this venture I was keenly aware of the challenge – partly due to the elusive nature of much of the material, but even more due to the authoritative and highly respected existing source in this area: John Jeffries, *A guide to the official publications of the European Communities* (Mansell, 2nd edition, 1981). Having used that pioneering book consistently over a number of years I was aware of its value and scholarship.

Nevertheless, my regular need to refer to a manual of EC documentation also indicated that considerable developments were taking place. There was a need for a new book to describe the position as at the end of the decade to bring the situation up to date and to introduce the subject to people new to the world of EC information.

I would hope that the book will help two complementary categories of user of EC information. First, those librarians and information specialists who are in contact with EC documentation and its organization on a regular basis and need a comprehensive history of EC documentation practices. For these people I have not attempted to duplicate much of the historical information in the book by Jeffries. Rather I have sought to carry on the history from where Jeffries stops and bring the story comprehensively up to date.

Second, I hope that the book will also be a useful descriptive introduction to current EC documentation for that much wider range of people whose interests – whether academic, professional or personal – bring them into contact with the EC and who would like to find out the range of information available from the bewildering range of material that is published by the Communities.

The book essentially describes the situation as in early 1988. Much of the research for the book was undertaken from a thorough investigation of the resources of the European Documentation Centre at the University of Wales, College of Cardiff. I am grateful to that institution for granting me a period of study leave during the summer of 1988 to bring the project to completion.

I am also grateful to the host of people who have helped me by answering specific questions over the last year or two. These include Giancarlo Pau (London Office, European Commission); Rohan Bolton (London Office, European Parliament); Tom Kennedy (Information Office, Court of Justice); Norman Wood and colleagues (Documentation, Information and Dissemination, European Foundation for the Improvement of Living and Working Conditions); J. Michael Adams (European Centre for the Development of Vocational Training); A. Buick (European Coal and Steel Community Consultative Committee); Adam McDonaugh (European Investment Bank); Margot Bollinger (Court of Auditors); T. Barry-Braunthal (Economic and Social Committee); Eric Gaskell (Commission Library, Brussels); Henri P. Legros (SCAD); Michael Berendt (Spokesman's Service); Annette E. Bosscher (DG V, Commission); Mr Witt (DG IV, Commission); F. Devonic (DG V, Commission); W. Hunter (Steel Industry Safety and Health Commission); Edward Phillips (DG XIII, Commission); M. P. Charreton (DG XVII, Commission); Rose Doyle (DG XXII, Commission); F. Tonhofer and Ursula Kollar (Office for Official Publications of the European Communities); R. Schneider (DG III, Commission); David Millar (DG IV, European Parliament); Jill C. Dixon, (DG XVI, Commission) and Mike Cooper (Reading University EDC).

Thanks also to the many colleagues and friends in the Association of EDC Librarians who have spurred me on with frequent comments as to the need for the book and to many of the students at the University of Wales, College of Cardiff whose enquiries have forced me to delve so deeply into the European Documentation Centre to discover its riches. Above all my sincere thanks go to David Perry, Senior Manager at the Office for Official Publications of the European Communities. David has been the patient recipient of a succession of long and demanding letters requesting information and has never let me down. He has always replied promptly and comprehensively in a style all his own, which was informed, wise, humorous and detached all at once. His assistance has been invaluable.

Any errors of fact or interpretation remain my own responsibility.

Ian Thomson
European Documentation Centre
University of Wales, College of Cardiff
September 1988

Abbreviations and Acronyms

ACP	African, Caribbean and Pacific States
AGREP	A database of current agricultural research projects in the EC
BCR	Community Bureau of Reference
BRITE	Basic Research in Industrial Technologies for Europe
CCP	Consultative Committee on Publications
CCT	Common Customs Tariff
CELEX	Communitatis Europeae Lex (database of EC law and legislation)
CEDEFOP	European Centre for the Development of Vocational Training
CN	Combined Nomenclature
COM Documents	A series of working documents from the Commission
COMEXT	Eurostat database of external trade statistics
COREPER	Committee of Permanent Representatives
COST	Committee on European Cooperation in the Field of Science and Technology
CRONOS	Eurostat statistical database
DEP	EC Depository Library
DG	Directorate-General
E Numbers	Code numbers for preservatives, colourings and antioxidants in foodstuffs
EABS	The *Euro Abstracts* database
EAGGF	European Agricultural Guidance and Guarantee Fund
EBIC	European Business Information Centre
EC	European Community
ECDIN	Database of environmental data and information network on chemicals
ECHO	European Commission Host Organization
ECOSOC	Economic and Social Committee
ECR	European Court Reports
ECSC	European Coal and Steel Community
ECTS	European Community Course Credit Transfer Scheme

ECU	European Currency Unit
EDC	European Documentation Centre
EEC	European Economic Community
EIB	European Investment Bank
EIS	European Information Service
ELISE	European Network for the Exchange of Information and Experience on Local Employment Initiatives
EMS	European Monetary System
ENDOC	Database of environmental information and documentation centres
ENREP	Database of environmental research projects
ENTECH	Energy Technology
EPC	European Political Cooperation
EP Reports	Committee reports of the European Parliament
EPOS	European Pool of Studies and Analyses
ERASMUS	European Community Action Scheme for the Mobility of University Students
ERC	European Reference Centre
ERDF	European Regional Development Fund
ESA	European System of Integrated Economic Accounts
ESC	Economic and Social Committee
ESF	European Social Fund
ESPRIT	European Strategic Programme for Research and Development in Information Technologies
ESSPROS	European System of Integrated Social Protection Statistics
ETUC	European Trade Union Confederation
EUR Reports	Series of scientific and technical reports
EURATOM	European Atomic Energy Community
EURISTOTE	Database of academic research on European integration
EURODICAUTOM	Terminological database of scientific and technical terms
EUROSTAT	Statistical Office of the European Communities
EUROVOC	Multilingual thesaurus compiled by OOPEC for indexing purposes
FADN	Farm Accountancy Data Network
FAST	Forecasting and Assessment in Science and Technology

FORMEX	Formalized Exchange of Electronic Publications
GSP	Generalized System of Preferences
HS	Harmonized System
IES	Database of publicly funded IT R & D projects, research sites and electronic mail addresses
ILO	International Labour Organization
JET	Joint European Torus
JRC	Joint Research Centre
JSP	Joint Study Programme
MEDREP	Database of biomedical and healthcare research projects
MEP	Member of the European Parliament
MISEP	Mutual Information System on Employment Policies
NACE	General Industrial Classification of Economic Activities within the European Communities
NARIC	European Community Network of National Academic Recognition Information Centres
NCI	New Community Instrument
NET	Next European Torus
NIMEXE	Nomenclature of Goods for the External Trade Statistics of the Community and Statistics of Trade between Member States
NUTS	Nomenclature of Territorial Units for Statistics
OECD	Organisation for Economic Co-operation and Development
OJ	*Official Journal of the European Communities*
OOPEC	Office for Official Publications of the European Communities
PABLI	Database of current EC development projects
REGIO	Eurostat database of EC regional statistics
SAD	Single Administrative Document
SCAD	Automated Central Documentation Service; also a bibliographical database of EC documentation
SEA	Single European Act
SEC Document	Internal document from the Secretariat-General of the Commission
SEM	Single European Market

SESAME	Database of hydrocarbon technology and energy demonstration projects
SIGLE	Database of European grey literature
SITC	Standard International Trade Classification
SME	Small and Medium-sized Enterprise
SOEC	Statistical Office of the European Communities (EUROSTAT)
SPRINT	European Programme for Innovation and Technology Transfer
STIMULATION	Action to Stimulate the Efficacy of the EEC's Scientific and Technical Potential
STRIDE	Science and Technology for Regional Innovation and Development in Europe
TARIC	Integrated Customs Tariff
TED	Tenders Electronic Daily
UNICE	Union of Industries of the European Economic Community

Introduction

THE EUROPEAN COMMUNITIES

History

The horror and devastation of the Second World War have inspired a number of attempts to bring together European states in cooperative enterprises. The most significant has been the development of the European Communities.

In 1950 Robert Schuman, Foreign Minister of France, presented a plan to pool French and German coal and steel production in one organization. Other European countries were invited to participate in the venture. On 18 April 1951 Belgium, the Federal Republic of Germany, France, Italy, Luxembourg and the Netherlands signed the Treaty of Paris which set up the *European Coal and Steel Community* (*ECSC*). The organization began operating in 1952.

In 1955 at Messina the Foreign Ministers of the countries belonging to the ECSC came together to pursue further opportunities for economic cooperation. Negotiations during the next year led to the signing of two Treaties in Rome on 25 March 1957. One set up the *European Economic Community* (*EEC*) and the other set up the *European Atomic Energy Community* (*Euratom*).

At first the three organizations maintained separate institutions. In 1965, by the so-called *Merger Treaty*, a single executive was established for the ECSC, the EEC and Euratom. The Merger Treaty came into force on 1 July 1967. The term European Communities thus describes the coming together of the institutions of these three organizations, although each remains an independent legal entity.

The first increase in the number of member states within the European Communities took place in 1973. In that year Denmark, Ireland and the United Kingdom became members. This was further extended to ten with the accession of Greece in 1981 and to twelve with the accession of Spain and Portugal in 1986.

The most significant legal amendment to the founding Treaties took place with the signing of the *Single European Act* in February 1986. This altered the legislative procedure in a number of ways, brought the system of political cooperation in the field of foreign policy (the concept known as European Political Cooperation) within the formal framework of the European Communities, and extended expressly the objectives of the Communities to include policy areas that in the past had had a dubious legal basis in the founding Treaties. The Single European Act came into force on 1 July 1987.

1

Institutions

The principal institutions in the decision-making processes in the European Communities (hereafter abbreviated to EC) are:

1. The European Commission
2. The Council of Ministers
3. The European Parliament
4. The Economic and Social Committee
5. The European Court of Justice
6. The Court of Auditors.

The structure and functions of these institutions are briefly described at the beginning of the chapters on the documentation of each of the institutions (Chapters 2 and 8–12). How the institutions interrelate in terms of the legislative process is described in Chapter 1. The functions and documentation of other EC organizations such as the European Centre for the Development of Vocational Training (CEDEFOP), the European Foundation for the Improvement of Living and Working Conditions, and the European Investment Bank are described in Chapter 13.

Activities

The power and authority of the EC is confined to the areas of responsibility assigned to it by the founding Treaties, and subsequent amendments. Many areas of policy remain matters of decision by national authorities.

The progress towards European unity has always had a major political element – there still are people who see a federal United States of Europe as the long-term outcome of the integration process. The term 'European Union' is still a key phrase in Community nomenclature. Nevertheless the nature of the EC can be misunderstood by overemphasizing the political element at the expense of the economic.

The founding Treaties emphasize economic and social objectives, albeit within a political framework, and with the perspective of the founding member states. So the EC has a fully developed policy in the areas of agriculture, coal, iron and steel, for example, because they were the pressing areas of concern of countries like France and Germany in the aftermath of the Second World War. If economic barriers were to be dismantled between member states then rules for fair competition had to be established. The standard of living between one part of the Community and another should be similar so there was a need for policies to eliminate regional disparities. Efforts were made to encourage the movement of trade, people, and services between member states.

With the accession of new members with their differing policy perspectives and traditions, the worsening economic situation in the 1970s, and the increasing complexity and interrelationship of policy areas, the interests of the EC have now widened considerably. Nowadays you hear of EC education, energy, environment policies, for example. That is not to say that the EC has the final say in all aspects of these policy areas – simply that the Communities have a viewpoint on, or interest in, particular aspects.

The importance of the economic objectives of the EC have been re-emphasized in the latter half of the 1980s with the renewed commitment to 'complete the internal market' by 1992. Certain features of a 'common market' such as customs-free trade between member states, common competition laws, and a common external tariff are already in place. The current campaign aims to extend these to create a single integrated European market whereby goods, services, capital and people will move freely between member states. The EC will be dominated by this issue for the next few years, the economic impact of a Single European Market having parallel important political and social implications as well.

THE DOCUMENTATION OF THE EUROPEAN COMMUNITIES

Quantity

The aim of this book is to describe the current documentation available from the institutions and organizations of the European Communities. The question might well be asked, why is there so much published or issued? In 1984 it was estimated there were about 2500 documents a year issued in connection with the legislative and regulatory processes of the European Communities. In addition a further 5000–7000 items comprising one-off studies, annuals, periodical and series issues and pamphlets were published.[1] In 1982 it was estimated that, including internal working documentation, £40 million was spent on the publishing, printing and reproduction activities of the various institutions of the EC. This added up to approximately 2000 million pages of text printed.[2]

In 1987 the Office for Official Publications of the European Communities (OOPEC) received over 720 000 pages of text from the institutions for publishing. This included the *Official Journal* and other EC publications/documents in all language editions.[3]

Internal documentation

Some of the pages received by OOPEC, or otherwise issued, comprise internal working documentation, such as the preliminary draft of the budget and other draft documentation. The whole question of the disclosure of information from the Community institutions has been raised in a number of resolutions and reports of the European Parliament during the 1980s. In particular there have been calls for greater openness in the consultative phase of Commission activities, in the work of the numerous advisory and consultative committees that exist in the EC framework, and in the deliberations and decisions of the Council of Ministers.[4] It is beyond the scope of this book to discuss this material. However, it should be noted that certain categories of internal working documentation, such as COM Documents, EP Reports and ESC Opinions and Reports are systematically made available to the public and are described in the appropriate chapters in the book.

Categories of documentation

To understand the reason why there is so much it is useful to divide EC documentation into four categories of material:

Legislation
The EC has a legal obligation to publish its law. This ranges from the founding Treaties laying down the aims of the EC and setting up the means to carry them out to the latest Regulation and Directive.

Documentation of the legislative process
The complex process of creating legislation in the EC (described in Chapter 1) generates considerable working documentation, much of which is now made publicly available.

Research
There are two distinct elements to documentation resulting from research activities. First, in the course of policy-making the institutions, and in particular the Commission, need to study a mass of evidence before undertaking policy initiatives. The Commission will, for example, carry out research itself, will suggest lines of enquiry for its satellite organizations such as CEDEFOP and the European Foundation for the Improvement of Living and Working Conditions, or commission research from outside organizations. Many of the results of this research activity are available in documentary form. The activities of Eurostat, the Statistical Office of the European Communities, fit into this category. Second, the EC undertakes and commissions external research into a range of subjects to help Europe maintain a competitive economic position in the world and to allow Europe to remain amongst the leaders in scientific and technological advance.

Explanatory and background documentation
The EC has a need, and a duty, to inform the citizens of the Community, and elsewhere, of what it is doing and why. This ranges from explaining in layman's terms EC policies and activities to the 'man in the street' to providing information to specialized groups and sectors.

Problems of EC documentation

The EC is in many ways a very open organization and makes a

considerable effort to inform and consult. Publications form a significant contribution to that effort. Nevertheless such features as poor bibliographical control, decentralized and informal distribution methods, and the sheer quantity of the material issued have posed problems over the years for the user of EC documentation. It has to be recognized that governments and intergovernmental organizations are not first and foremost publishers. The documentation made available to the public is usually a byproduct of its functions, albeit an important one. Documentation patterns have often evolved according to the apparent needs of the moment and not to any coherent laid-down plan. As recently as 1981 the Court of Auditors in a report on the publishing, printing and reproduction practices of the institutions of the European Communities noted that, apart from the Commission, none of the institutions had a publications committee or an annual publications programme.[5] Since then internal coordination within and between EC institutions has considerably developed in documentation matters.

Availability and distribution of EC documentation

It is true that the EC has undertaken a number of initiatives in the 1980s to improve the documentation produced, its availability and its bibliographical control. Many of these improvements will be referred to throughout the book. In the introduction the means whereby EC documentation is made available and distributed is discussed.

People talk of 'European Communities documentation' or 'European Communities publications', but the ultimate origin of a document or publication is a specific EC institution, organization or department within an institution. The Commission is the major source of documentation. In Chapter 2 the publications programme of the Commission is studied. The other EC institutions and organizations also add to the documentation mountain and each has a publications budget.

The Office for Official Publications of the European Communities (OOPEC) is the primary, but not exclusive, 'publisher' and distributor of EC documentation (see p. 7 below). In the 1980s OOPEC has assumed greater responsibility but certain categories of EC documentation are still available through other means. The major such categories are:

1. Publications of the Information Offices in the member states and elsewhere are available only from those offices.
2. A proportion of scientific and technical research material is published by specialist commercial publishers (see DG XIII in Chapter 5, p. 137). There is some evidence that commercial publication may become more common outside this specialist field in the future. One example is *Higher education in the*

European Community, which is jointly published by OOPEC and a host of commercial publishers (see DG V in Chapter 5). In 1988 the Cecchini report on 1992 was published by Gower Publishing in a volume called *The European challenge - 1992 - the benefits of a single market*, rather than by OOPEC. The European Foundation for the Improvement of Living and Working Conditions is also investigating the use of commercial publishers.

3. Some EC institutions and organizations retain either total (European Investment Bank) or partial control over distribution of their publications. In the latter case material available direct from the institutions is usually free or intended for limited distribution.

The source of individual titles and categories of material is given throughout the book.

Pricing

The pricing policy for EC documentation has evolved over the years. In the period up to 1980 it was undoubtedly the case that the majority of EC documentation was freely distributed. Up to 1975 it was estimated that only 5–10 per cent of global print runs became genuine sales.[6] Most institutions had massive manually maintained mailing lists for publications. In 1980 it was estimated that there were 297 400 addresses on mailing lists.[7]

Efforts have been made in the 1980s to amend this situation. Most mailing lists have been computerized and partially revised. Free distribution has been somewhat reduced to relevant organizations such as government departments and EC depository libraries. A more realistic pricing structure has been attempted. Material such as COM Documents, which had been available free on a haphazard basis, became formally available on subscription. Publications were somewhat more effectively promoted.

Document/Publication

The EC makes a distinction between what it calls a 'document' and what it calls a 'publication'. In 1975 the Consultative Committee of Publications (see Chapter 2) made the distinction:

1. Publication – aimed for distribution outside the institution.
2. Document – aimed for internal distribution.[8]

There are a number of riders to these definitions which somewhat diminish the basic premise. Essentially a publication designates a work the contents of which are considered to be of sufficient importance to justify publication in a high-quality printing, in all or most of the official Community languages, and with effective promotion. Documents are the internal working documentation of the institutions.

However, it would be wrong to draw from this the implication that documents are not publicly available. In fact during the 1980s a proportion of 'documents' have become publicly available on a systematic basis – these comprise COM Documents, EP Reports, and ESC Opinions and Reports. They are 'published', distributed and promoted by OOPEC. In that respect they are no different from a traditionally defined 'publication', OOPEC does however maintain the distinction in that it issues a *Catalogue of Publications* and a *Catalogue of Documents* (see Chapter 3). It is also true that there is much internal working documentation which is not made publicly available.

Further confusion has arisen through the use of the word 'document' to describe a new category of EC 'publication' issued in the 1980s (this is explained in Chapter 4). Overall it is doubtful whether people seeking EC information through documentation find the distinction very meaningful.

OFFICE FOR OFFICIAL PUBLICATIONS OF THE EUROPEAN COMMUNITIES (OOPEC)

OOPEC came into being in 1969 and is generally thought of as the official publisher of EC documentation. However, it is not a traditional publisher in the accepted sense. It does not commission work, for example. Rather it is a coordinating organization that deals with the printing, selling and distributing of material from the EC institutions. OOPEC is part of the Commission for administrative and budgetary purposes, but in effect is an interinstitutional body serving all the Community institutions, who all supply a representative to its Management Committee.

It has already been mentioned that OOPEC does not handle all EC documentation. Nevertheless the role of OOPEC has expanded considerably since 1969 and it has been instrumental in many of the improvements that have taken place in EC documentation policy.

In the 1980s OOPEC has arranged for the formal sale and distribution of COM Documents, EP Reports, and ESC Opinions and Reports. Similarly many of the publications of such bodies as the European Foundation for the Improvement of Living and Working Conditions and CEDEFOP are now handled by OOPEC. It has been involved in the setting up of the Document categorization. It has brought together various units working on indexes and catalogues to improve their output and quality. In 1983 OOPEC became responsible for the distribution of material to the EC Depository Library network. All these moves towards a more centralized publishing operation have led to a more efficient system of distribution, promotion and bibliographical control of EC documentation.

OOPEC maintains its own printing units at its headquarters in Luxembourg but it does not itself print all the material it publishes. In 1978, for example, 85 per cent of all 'publications' published by OOPEC were printed externally. The balance were either printed internally by OOPEC or by printing units within the institutions. In the case of 'documents' the balance was reversed, with the bulk of material printed internally, mainly within the institutions themselves.[9] While from a purely commercial viewpoint outside printing is probably more economic, it is felt that OOPEC and the institutions should maintain their own printing capacity to deal with confidential material, or unexpected demands for rapidly needed material, as an insurance against failure by a commercial contractor and, in some cases, for pure convenience.

The role of OOPEC with 'documents' is largely confined to their sale and distribution. The appropriate institution prints them and OOPEC simply arranges for an additional cover before publicly distributing them. OOPEC does however print the Community preliminary draft and draft budget, which are not made publicly available.

The bulk of OOPEC's work at the *printing* stage is with EC 'publications', which is divided into two broad categories:

1. *Official Journal*
2. Material other than the *Official Journal*

The role of OOPEC in the production of the *Official Journal* is unique. It is a work comprising items submitted by all the Community institutions. OOPEC thus acts as both coordinator and printer. It does not decide what should go in the *Official Journal*, but oversees its publication in a more detailed way than is the case with other publications.

To publish all the language versions of the *Official Journal* at the same time is a considerable undertaking. With the accession of new members in the 1980s there were particular problems, especially with the Greek language versions. Additional personnel were needed to carry out the necessary tasks such as proofreading the new Greek, Spanish and Portuguese language editions. The material received by OOPEC from the institutions for inclusion is not always in a condition suitable for easy publication. The bunching of information to be published at certain times of the year also causes problems – particularly at the very end of each year. (Further details regarding the *Official Journal* are given in Chapter 1.)

In the case of other publications OOPEC does not have this coordinating role. It receives the material from the institutions and arranges its printing, sale and distribution.

The number of publications, other than the *Official Journal*, in all languages, handled by OOPEC since 1981 is shown to Table 1.

Table 1 Number of publications, in all languages, handled by OOPEC (excluding *Official Journal*)

Number of texts		Number of proofread pages	Number of Non-proofread pages
1981	1956	155 421	97 884
1982	2056	147 556	74 083
1983	2224	155 907	86 310
1984	2402	183 576	94 056
1985	2414	171 310	132 000
1986	2130	165 807	124 623
1987	2493	187 213	137 522

Source: *Annual management reports*, 1982–87 (OOPEC, unpublished internal documents not publicly available).

A proofread page indicates that OOPEC prepares manuscript for press, while a non-proofread page indicates that camera-ready copy is supplied by the author.

OOPEC has been actively involved in taking advantage of the new techniques in printing technologies in order to cope with the increasing complexity of publishing rapidly so much documentation in a range of languages. A number of such initiatives include:

1. *Bulletin of the European Communities*: an experiment started in 1982 linking author departments, the printer and OOPEC in an integrated production sequence of text processing, on-screen preparation, proofreading and photocomposition from magnetic tape.
2. Bibliographic databases have been used to produce catalogues.
3. Increasing attention has been given to the retrieval – for photocomposition purposes – of texts produced in word processors.
4. Utilization of programs developed for interactive graphics creation, paging etc.

It is predicted that the OOPEC internal database of references may become publicly available in the future.

AVAILABILITY OF EC DOCUMENTATION

Publications which are priced for sale and published by OOPEC are available from OOPEC or its sales agents in all the member states plus some other countries (addresses are given in Appendix 4). These sources can also give details of all items available on subscription.

Other EC documentation is available direct from the issuing institution or organization; addresses are given at the end of each appropriate chapter.

Notes and references

1. *EC Index*, vol. 0, no. 0 October 1984, p. 1
2. European Parliament: *Interim report ... on the budgetary control aspects of the publishing, printing and reproduction practices of the institutions of the European Communities*, Rapporteur: Mr E. Kellett-Bowman, PE DOC 1–425/82, p. 6
3. This information has been obtained by interpreting a number of tables from: OOPEC, *Nineteenth annual management report*, 1987 (internal document not formally published, pages unnumbered)
4. The latest report on the subject, which also lists earlier reports and resolutions, is: European Parliament: *Report ... on the compulsory publication of information by the European Community*, Rapporteur: Mr Pol M. E. E. Marck, PE DOC A2–208/87
5. Court of Auditors: Special report concerning publishing, printing and reproduction practices of the institutions of the European Communities. *Official Journal* C150 19.6.81, p. 6
6. Ibid., p. 9
7. Ibid., p. 12
8. Ibid., p. 3
9. Ibid., pp. 5–6

CHAPTER 1

European Community Legislation

In this chapter a study is made of the *Official Journal of the European Communities* (hereafter abbreviated to *Official Journal* or *OJ*), the main source of European Community legislation – and a good deal more besides. Then the various categories of EC legislation as broken down in the CELEX database are studied. A brief description is given of the complex process by which a legislative proposal becomes law in the EC decision-making structure, and this is related to the appropriate documentation. Finally, sources of bibliographical assistance to EC legislation and the legislative process are discussed.

OFFICIAL JOURNAL OF THE EUROPEAN COMMUNITIES

The *Official Journal* is the authoritative source for all EC legislation – primary, secondary, supplementary and agreements with third countries. It also gives information on many of the activities of the EC institutions including various stages in the legislative and judicial processes. Finally, it gives details of calls to tender for public supply and public works contracts.

The *Official Journal* is published by OOPEC in all the official Community languages. Single copies may be purchased from OOPEC or sales agents or an annual subscription may be taken out for the constituent parts as follows:

1. 'L' and 'C' series (calendar year; hard copy or microfiche).
2. 'S' series (calendar year; hard copy only).
3. *Annex* (March–February; hard copy only).

OOPEC compiles the *Official Journal* from information it receives for inclusion from the Commission, the Council of Ministers, the European Parliament, the Economic and Social Committee, the Court of Justice and the Court of Auditors (Table 2).

The *Official Journal* is published daily and during the 1980s has been made up of distinct parts issued separately:

1. *Legislation* (the 'L' series)
2. *Information and Notices* (the 'C' series)

Table 2 Breakdown of institutional input in the *Official Journal* by number of pages (1982)

Institutions	Per cent of input
European Parliament	13
Council of Ministers	10
Commission	72
Court of Justice	1
Economic and Social Committee	1
Court of Auditors	2

Source: OOPEC, *Fourteenth annual management report*, 1982 (unpublished internal document not publicly available)

3. *Supplement* (the 'S' series)
4. *Annex. Debates of the European Parliament*
5. *Index* (see section on bibliographical aids, p. 27.

Each issue of the *Official Journal* in the 'L', 'C', and 'S' series is given a running number starting at no. 1 in January each year. The standard way to cite the *Official Journal* is, for example, *OJ* L119 7.5.1988. The Annex is numbered differently – each plenary session of the European Parliament is assigned a number and this is used to cite an issue of the *Official Journal: Annex*. For example, Annex no. 2–358 covers the debates of the European Parliament during the plenary session 16–20 November 1987.

The *Official Journal* is a massive publishing undertaking and comprises half of the total output from OOPEC. Taking all language versions together, the total print run of the *Official Journal* in 1982 was over 19 million copies[1] (Tables 3 and 4).

Legislation

The 'L' series of the *Official Journal* consists of the texts of enacted legislation divided into two categories:

1. Acts whose publication is obligatory – these include EEC/Euratom Regulations, ECSC Decisions and ECSC Recommendations, and primary legislation.
2. Acts whose publication is not obligatory – these include the remaining legislative acts such as EEC/Euratom Directives, Decisions, Opinions and Recommendations, and also Agreements, the budget, Conventions, Financial regulations, Protocols, Resolutions, exchange rates and rules of procedure.

In effect this means that the text of *all* primary and secondary

Table 3 Trends in the number of pages (per language version) of the *Official Journal* ('L', 'C', 'S' series)

Year	Number of pages	Year	Number of pages
1974	21 964	1981	32 556
1975	23 606	1982	32 672
1976	24 224	1983	35 341
1977	23 668	1984	35 474
1978	26 392	1985	42 296
1979	28 650	1986	39 907
1980	32 940	1987	44 612

Source: OOPEC *Nineteenth Annual Management Report*, 1987 (unpublished internal document not publicly available)

Table 4 *Official Journal*: 1987 breakdown by part

	Number of issues	Number of pages
'L' series	400	20 260
'C' series	358	10 807
'S' series	250	13 545

Source: OOPEC *Nineteenth annual management report*, 1987 (unpublished internal document not publicly available)

legislation is published in the *Official Journal*. The legal distinction of the two categories of Act is maintained both in the *Official Journal* itself and in the *Index to the Official Journal of the European Communities* (hereafter called the *Official Journal: Index*).

The size of each issue can vary from 20 pages to over 1000. The larger issues contain such items as the adopted general budget of the European Communities and the Integrated Customs Tariff of the European Communities (TARIC).

The contents of each issue are listed on the front cover extended on occasion to the inside front cover and even to the inside back cover. The majority of EC legislative acts are concerned with the day-to-day management of agricultural matters and the customs union and are valid only for a limited period. Such acts are listed in light type in the contents. All other acts are listed in bold type and preceded by an asterisk.

Information and Notices

The 'C' series of the *Official Journal* consists of a diverse range of information from the various EC institutions:

1. Commission – the text of proposed legislation, rates for the European Currency Unit, job vacancies and miscellaneous notices such as calls for tenders or expressions of interest to EC funded research schemes and membership of EC organizations or committees.
2. Council of Ministers – miscellaneous Decisions, Assents and Resolutions, other notices and job vacancies
3. European Parliament – minutes of the plenary sessions, including the text of EP Resolutions, written questions and job vacancies.
4. Economic and Social Committee – Opinions of the ESC, membership and job vacancies
5. Court of Justice – lists of new actions brought, and orders and judgments delivered. Only the operative part of a judgment is given – for the full judgment it is necessary to go to other sources (see Chapter 11)
6. Court of Auditors – annual report accompanied by the replies of the institutions, and selected special reports on aspects of EC policy and organizations
7. Other EC organizations such as the European Investment Bank and the European University Institute occasionally place notices.

The contents of each issue are listed starting on the front cover, broken down into two divisions:

1. Information – further divided by institution.
2. Preparatory Acts.

Supplement

The 'S' series contains details of supply and work contracts placed by public authorities.

EC Directives exist which lay down requirements for public authorities to give companies in all member states equal rights to tender for works and supply contracts. The existing Directives are 71/305/EEC covering public works contracts and 77/62/EEC covering public supply contracts. These Directives require summary notices to be published in the *Official Journal*.

Since 1984 contracts have been divided into four categories:

1. Works contracts
2. Supply contracts
3. Notices of contracts whose publication is not obligatory pursuant to the Community Acts cited in Parts I and II

4. Notes of public supply contracts published by non-EC countries pursuant either to the Agreement on government procurement concluded within the framework of GATT or to other relevant agreements.

In addition contracts for work in developing countries when the finance for the work is coming from the European Development Fund are also listed starting on the front page of each issue. A model notice is printed in each issue as contract information is printed in a highly summarized form.

There has been considerable dissatisfaction with the public procurement operation in recent years. Suppliers from one country still find many difficulties in securing contracts in another. Plans to amend the present Directives thus form an important part of the plan to 'complete the internal market'.

The information contained in the 'S' series is also available online in the TED (Tenders Electronic Daily) database. This allows more rapid notification of contracts than is available through the printed source (see Appendix 2).

Annex. Debates of the European Parliament

Each issue of the *Annex* contains the full text of the debates held during a plenary session of the European Parliament and oral questions submitted. The minutes of the plenary sessions are contained in the 'C' series of the *Official Journal* (further details are given in Chapter 9).

Official Journal of the European Communities. Special Edition

This special English and Danish language edition appeared between 1972 and 1973 and printed the text of EC secondary legislation enacted between 1952 and 1972 that was still in force at the time of the accession of Ireland, Denmark and the United Kingdom in 1973. This edition only printed those 'Acts whose publication was obligatory'. A second series of the special edition was published in 1974 in ten issues, which listed 'Acts whose publication was not obligatory' still in force on 1 January 1973.

PRIMARY LEGISLATION

The primary legislation of the European Communities consists of the three founding Treaties:

1. Treaty of Paris, 1951 – European Coal and Steel Community (ECSC)
2. Treaty of Rome, 1957 – European Economic Community (EEC)

3. Treaty of Rome, 1957 – European Atomic Energy Community (Euratom).

In addition there have been a number of revising Treaties, for example the so-called Merger Treaty establishing a Single Council and a Single Commission of the European Communities, Brussels, 1965. The most significant amendment to the founding Treaties is the Single European Act (SEA). This was signed in 1986 and came into force on 1 July 1987.

The documents concerning the accession to the EC of Denmark, Ireland and the United Kingdom in 1973, Greece in 1980 and Portugal and Spain in 1986, are also counted as primary legislation.

The authoritative source of the texts of all these treaties is the *Official Journal*. For example, the texts for the accession of Greece are printed in the *Official Journal* L291 19.11.79, for the accession of Portugal and Spain in the *Official Journal* L302 15.11.85, and the Single European Act in the *Official Journal* L169 29.6.87.

For reasons of convenience the texts of the primary legislation of the EC are brought together in various consolidated editions published by OOPEC. The latest complete edition was published in two volumes in 1987–88 called *Treaties establishing the European Communities*: volume I was subtitled *Treaties establishing the European Communities. Treaties amending these Treaties. Single European Act*; volume II was called *Documents concerning the Accessions*. It is available in all official Community languages including Irish.

The previous consolidated edition was published in 1978 in a single volume. A supplement incorporating the Greek accession documents was published in 1982.

In addition OOPEC publish a convenient pocket-sized shortened version of the above, called *Treaties establishing the European Communities: abridged edition*. The first edition was published in 1979, the second in 1983 and the third in 1987. These give the main texts of EC primary legislation but leave out most of the associated annexes and protocols. The abridged edition is available in all official Community languages (but not Irish).

The text of an important new piece of primary legislation is often available before its publication in the *Official Journal*. The text of the Single European Act, for example, was published as an one-off publication called *Single European Act and Final Act* by the Council of Ministers through OOPEC soon after its signature in early 1986; it was also published as *Bulletin of the European Communities: Supplement*, no. 2, 1986.

The text in these sources is not authoritative. The relative importance of a piece of primary legislation will affect whether the text is formally published before its ratification.

AGREEMENTS WITH NON-EC COUNTRIES

A considerable corpus of EC legislation arises from the external relations of the European Communities which comprise the text of agreements between the EC and non-EC countries. The EC is a legal entity which can negotiate and conclude agreements with third countries on matters that fall within the responsibilities conferred on it by the founding Treaties. The EC has responsibility for external trade policy and has agreements with over 120 countries as well as around thirty multilateral agreements. In addition to trade agreements with individual countries and groups of countries, and agreements on international trading rules, the EC is involved in the international arena in such matters as the environment, help for developing countries, transport matters, research and development, agriculture and fisheries.[2]

The authoritative source for the text of agreements with non-EC countries is to be found in the *Official Journal.* For example, the Third ACP–EEC Convention was signed at Lomé (Togo) on 8 December 1984. The text of the Convention, plus various agreements on the entry into force, financing, administration and implementation of the Convention, was published in the *Official Journal* L86 31.2.1986. Publication in the *Official Journal* only takes place at the time of deposit of the instruments of ratification. The negotiations for the fourth Lomé agreement began in 1988.

As with primary legislation the EC will sometimes publish the text of an important agreement before its formal publication in the *Official Journal.* The text of the third Lomé Convention, and related documents, was published in an one-off publication by the ACP–EEC Council of Ministers through OOPEC in early 1985. The text, with additional commentary and background information, was also printed in *The Courier* no. 89, January–February 1985.

The texts of all agreements between the EC and non-EC countries are brought together in a series called *Collection of the agreements concluded by the European Communities.* The first five volumes in this series cover the texts of all the agreements in force on 31 December 1975. Thereafter annual supplements have been published. At the back of volume 10, covering the agreements of 1980, published in 1984, and volume 11, covering the agreements of 1981, published in 1985, there was a cumulative index covering all volumes so far published. The index in volume 11 was also published separately in 1986. Access to the index is through titles, subject matter and names of the contracting parties. Volume 12, covering the agreements of 1982, published in 1986, has only an index to its own contents.

Further documentation giving the text of certain categories of legislation linking the EC and non-EC countries emanates from the

Council of Ministers (see Chapter 8). DG I of the Commission are responsible for bibliographical publications in this area (see Chapter 5).

SECONDARY LEGISLATION

The secondary legislation of the European Communities is that created by the institutions of the European Communities in carrying out the powers granted to them in the founding Treaties. In French the term used is *droit derivé*, which can be translated as derived law or consequential legislation (Table 5).

Table 5   EC Legislative Acts

EEC/Euratom	ECSC
Regulations Directives Decisions Recommendations Opinions	Decisions (general) Recommendations Decisions (individual) – Opinions

Regulations (or ECSC General Decisions) are addressed to all member states, are to be applied in full, and are directly applicable without the intermediate creation of national legislation. Directives (or ECSC Recommendations) are, in contrast, indirect forms of legislation which lay down an objective to be achieved within a specified time but leave it to the member states to legislate the details of implementation. Decisions (or ECSC individual Decisions) are the means whereby the Communities implement the Treaties or Regulations. They can be intended for member states, individuals, groups of individuals or companies. Recommendations and opinions are not legally binding and merely suggest a line of action or opinion.[3]

The text of EC secondary legislation can be found in the 'L' series of the *Official Journal*. The distinction between the various legislative acts is not always very clear to the layman. It is important to be aware of the distinction when searching for secondary legislation in the *Official Journal: Index* for the various legislative acts are divided into two separate lists (see the section on the *Official Journal* above (p. 12) for further details).

The formal citation of an EC legislative act is made up of the following elements:

1. The institutional origin of the act (Commission or Council)
2. The form of the act (Regulation, Directive, Decision, etc.)

3. An act number
4. The year of the enactment
5. The institutional treaty basis (EEC, ECSC, Euratom)
6. The date the act was passed.

The sequence of these elements can vary as is shown in the following examples:

1. Commission Regulation (EEC) no. 1220/88 of 4 May 1988 on the opening supplementary quotas for imports into the Community of certain textile products originating in Yugoslavia for the 1988 Berlin Trade Fairs
2. 88/279/EEC Council Decision of 11 April 1988 concerning the European strategic programme for research and development in information technologies (Esprit).

The features to note are the order of the act number and the year. This point should be remembered when using the Methodological Table volume of the *Official Journal: Index* to trace the text of an EC legislative act in the *Official Journal*.

There is no other comprehensive source for the text of EC secondary legislation. The one partial exception is *Recueil des actes agricoles*, a multivolume set of the text of agricultural legislation broken down by product. This is maintained by DG VI of the Commission for internal purposes. Since 1986 it has been made publicly available in a series with the Document categorization (see the section on DG VI in Chapter 5).

SUPPLEMENTARY LEGISLATION

There is a relatively small corpus of supplementary legislation consisting of a diverse range of material. It includes decisions of representatives of the governments of the member states meeting within the Council and certain non-binding acts considered by the institutions to be important.[4] These can include Conventions, Protocols and Resolutions. Some recent examples include:

1. 87/353/ECSC Decision of the representatives of the governments of the member states, meeting within the Council of 25 June 1987, extending the term of validity of a zero-duty tariff quota for laser-irradiated, grain-oriented electrical sheet and plate (*OJ* L192 11.7.87, p. 42).
2. Resolution of the Council and of the ministers responsible for cultural affairs, meeting within the Council of 9 November 1987 on the promotion of translation of important works of European culture (*OJ* C309 19.11.87, p. 3).
3. Convention setting up a European University Institute (*OJ* C29 9.2.76, p. 1).

4. 86/127/EEC Internal Agreement on the measures and procedures required for implementation of the Third ACP–EEC Convention (*OJ* L86 31.3.86, p. 221).

The text of supplementary legislation is printed in the *Official Journal*. Note that items such as Resolutions and Conventions are printed in the 'C' series.

THE LEGISLATIVE PROCESS

It helps to understand the function of much EC documentation if one has a clear idea of the EC legislative process – how decisions are reached in the EC (Table 6).

Table 6   EC legislative process following the Single European Act (adapted from a personal paper by David Millar, DG IV, European Parliament)

Legislative stages	Related documentation
1. Commission sends *proposal* to Council	1.
2. Council seeks *Opinion* of European Parliament (EP) and, where appropriate, the Economic and Social Committee (ESC)	
3. EP considers legal base of proposal	
4. EP Committee adopts *report*, with or without amendments	2.
5. EP in plenary session considers report on *first reading* and (a) rejects Commission proposal, or (b) agrees to proposals with amendments (Opinion in legislative resolution), or (c) agrees to proposal without amendment (Opinion in legislative resolution)	3.
6. ESC gives *Opinion*	4.
7. Commission considers amendments, and may within one month accept or reject them or withdraw proposal and resubmit it including some or all amendments	5.
8. Within no time limit Council adopts *Common Position*, and can accept EP amendments, or	

Table 6 *Continued*

Legislative stages	Related documentation
reject them, unless Commission has submitted a modified proposal. The Common Position is sent to EP*	
9. At *Second Reading* Council's Common Position is referred to the EP Committee which made the first report	
10. EP Committee recommends to the EP Plenary Session (a) rejection of Common Position, or (b) acceptance of Common Position with amendments, or (c) acceptance of Common Position without amendments	6.
11. Within three months of receiving Common Position EP adopts one of these recommendations	7.
12. Commission may, within one month, re-examine the Common Position and include some or all EP amendments; it then forwards the re-examined proposal to Council	
13. Within three months the Council must adopt the re-examined proposal by qualified majority. Unanimity is required to amend the re-examined proposal	
14. Proposal becomes law	8.

*Certain legislative proposals are outside the remit of the Single European Act. Such proposals reach stage 6 and await a final decision of the Council.

Essentially the process works as follows. The Commission puts forward a legislative proposal and the Council of Ministers decides on the proposal after consulting the European Parliament and, in certain circumstances, the Economic and Social Committee. This is a very simplified description and gives no conception of the degree of consultation that takes place, the considerable amendment of proposals, and the time scale involved. Some decisions are taken quickly but others can take many years. Some proposals do not become law at all.

During the 1980s there was increasing dissatisfaction and frustration with the delays in the decision-making process. The Single European

Act, which came into force in 1987, made a number of amendments to the legislative process. In particular it introduced a new cooperation procedure between the institutions. One notable feature of this was the new right of the European Parliament to a second reading of a Commission proposal following the reaching of a 'Common Position' by the Council. Following the Parliament's amendments, and the possible acceptance of these by the Commission, the Council must take a decision on the revised proposal within a certain time period. It may accept the revised proposal by qualified majority or reject it unanimously.

The documentation noted in Table 7 is the publicly available documentation of the legislative process. All other stages are not easily traceable through standard documentation. The chapter numbers listed refer the reader to a full description of the documentation concerned.

Table 7   EC legislative procedure: related documentation

---

1. COM Document (text of proposal and explanatory memorandum) or *Official Journal* 'C' Series (text of proposal only) (Chapter 4)

2. EP Report: Series A (European Parliament Session Document) (explanatory section and proposed text of Opinion) (Chapter 9)

3. *Official Journal: Annex* (debates of the EP in Plenary Session). *Official Journal* 'C' series (text of Opinion) (Chapter 9)

4. CES opinions and reports or *Official Journal* 'C' series (Chapter 10)

5. As no. 1

6. As no. 2 (Opinion on Common Position)

7. As no. 3

8. *Official Journal* 'L' series

The following example illustrates the working of the EC legislative process and the related documentation.

1. Proposal for a Directive on procedures for informing and consulting the employees of undertakings with complex structures, in particular transnational undertakings.

This proposal first surfaced in the public arena with the issuing of the Commission document COM(80)423 final of the 23 October 1980. It was transmitted to the Council of Ministers on the 24 October 1980 and was published in the *Official Journal* C297 15.11.80, p. 3. The text of the initial proposal is thus available in two sources but the explanatory document accompanying the proposal is only printed in the COM Document.

On 31 October 1980 the Council activated the necessary consultation phase by sending the proposal to the European Parliament and the Economic and Social Committee for their respective opinions.

In the European Parliament the proposal was referred to the Committee on Social Affairs and Employment for its opinion. The Committee appointed Mr Tom Spencer to be the rapporteur on 27 January 1981. In this instance, because the proposal had overlapping implications, it was also sent to the Committee on Economic and Monetary Affairs and the Legal Affairs Committee for their opinions.

At a meeting of the Committee on Social Affairs and Employment on 27 May 1982 the Committee accepted the motion for a resolution contained in the report compiled by Mr Spencer. The report was issued as European Parliament Working Document (now known as EP Reports) 1–324/82/A & B. Not all reports take so long to compile and be adopted by a Committee. The controversial nature of this particular proposal led to it being discussed at many meetings of the Committee and to the rapporteur visiting the OECD in Paris and the ILO in Geneva to discuss the proposal. In addition a hearing was organized in October 1981 with representatives of employers (UNICE), and trade unionists (ETUC). The European Parliament Working Document contains the motion for a resolution, an explanatory statement, plus the opinions of the Committee on Economic and Monetary Affairs and the Legal Affairs Committee.

The Spencer report – such reports are invariably known by the name of the rapporteur – was presented to the plenary session of the European Parliament in September 1982 for debate on 13–14 September 1982. The text of the debate can be found in *Official Journal: Annex. Debates of the European Parliament* no. 1–288, p. 18. Owing to the controversial nature of the proposal and the large number of amendments tabled the vote on the resolution contained in the report was not taken in the September plenary session. Votes on the amendments tabled, and a vote on the whole of the amended proposal, were taken in the plenary session of 11–15 October 1982. Details of these votes can be found in the *Official Journal* C292 8.11.82, p. 29.

The amendments so significantly changed the proposed Directive that the Commission had to study carefully the revisions to see if they could support the revised text. At the November plenary session the Commissioner responsible, Ivor Richard, announced that most of the amendments would be accepted. His statement is printed in the *Official Journal: Annex. Debates of the European Parliament* no. 1–291, p. 134. The Commission announced that it would submit a revised text of the proposal to both the Council of Ministers and the European Parliament in early 1983.

It was only at the December 1982 plenary session that the European Parliament finally voted on the resolution contained in the Spencer Report. The text of the resolution can be found in the *Official Journal* C13 17.1.83, p. 25.

The consultative phase in the Economic and Social Committee (ESC) was considerably shorter. The proposal was delegated to the Section for Social Questions, and Mr Gerd Muhr was appointed as rapporteur. His report was presented to the 194th plenary session of the ESC in January 1982 and the Opinion adopted as CES(82)82. Note that in 1982 the CES Opinions and Reports series was not publicly available – since 1984 this has been the case. The Opinion however was published in the *Official Journal* C77 29.3.82, p. 6.

The process continued with the issuing by the Commission on the 8 July 1983 of COM(83)292 final – Amended Proposal for a Council Directive on procedures for informing and consulting employees. This proposal was transmitted to the Council of Ministers on 13 July 1983 and was printed in the *Official Journal* C217 12.8.83, p. 3.

What then took place is a vivid example of how opaque the decision-making process can be in the European Communities. The amended proposal was discussed by the Council of Ministers' Working Party on Social Questions, within the Committee of Permanent Representatives (Coreper) framework during the rest of 1983 and early 1984, but little progress was made. The Irish Government on assuming the Presidency of the Council in mid-1984 set up an *ad hoc* working group to try to resolve the points of conflict. This reported in November 1984 to the Working Party on Social Questions. The Council of Social Affairs Ministers meeting in December 1984 began an examination of the amended proposal and the new suggestions but came to no agreement. None of the above deliberations are traceable through the official documentation.[5]

It was only in 1986 that a clear reference to the subject could be found again. On 21 July 1986 the Labour and Social Affairs Council adopted a set of Conclusions on the subject and these were published in the *Official Journal* C203 12.8.86, p. 1. In effect the Council said that the issue should be shelved until 1989 when it would resume discussion of the amended proposal for a directive or any subsequent proposal.

This is an interesting example and shows graphically the difficulties of following developments through the publicly available documentation. There were long periods when it was impossible to find out exactly at what stage the proposal had reached.

BIBLIOGRAPHICAL AIDS

Finding the text of proposed and enacted legislation, and other documentation of the legislative process, through bibliographical aids has for a long time posed many problems. This has been partly due to a lack of such sources and partly due to deficiencies in what did exist. In a number of ways the situation is improving. New titles have been issued, methods of compilation enhanced, and online services made available to the public. In summary form the following list covers the important bibliographical sources:

1. *Annex to the Index of the Official Journal of the European Communities: Eurovoc.*
2. To trace documents in the legislative process (COM Documents, EP Reports and CES Opinions and Reports)
   (a) *Catalogue of Documents* (see Chapter 3)
   (b) *List of Pending Proposals*
   (c) *SCAD Bulletin* (see Chapter 3)
   (d) SCAD Database (see Appendix 2)
   (e) CELEX Database (see Appendix 2)
3. To trace the text of EC legislation
   (a) *Index* to the *Official Journal of the European Communities.*
   (b) *Directory of Community legislation in force.* . . .
   (c) CELEX Database (see Appendix 2).
   (d) *European Communities legislation: current status* (see Appendix 5)
   (e) *Encyclopaedia of European Community law* (see Appendix 5).

Annex to the Index of the Official Journal of the European Communities: Eurovoc

Eurovoc is a multilingual thesaurus comprising a list of standardized terms covering the various fields of EC activity in a controlled vocabulary. A number of EC organizations and departments – notably the European Parliament Secretariat, DG XIII of the Commission, OOPEC, the Commission Library, and the Integrated Information Systems division and the Terminology and Computer Applications Service of DG IX – cooperated on the creation of the *Eurovoc* thesaurus.[6]

The first edition of *Eurovoc* was published in the official Community languages by OOPEC in 1984. A second, extended edition started appearing from OOPEC in 1987 in all Community languages. *Eurovoc* is available in printed copy and on magnetic tape. At the time of writing the following volumes had been published:

1. Alphabetical thesaurus: terms used as descriptors and non-descriptors in alphabetical order showing hierarchical relationships.
2. Subject-oriented thesaurus: here the thesaurus is divided into fields and hierarchical units – in essence in a classified order.
3. Multilingual thesaurus: this is an alphabetical list of all

descriptors used with their equivalent terms in other Community languages.

A further two volumes to the second edition are planned:

4. Permuted thesaurus: an alphabetical list of all significant words in descriptors and non-descriptors.
5. Terminograms: a diagrammatic display of descriptor relationships.

It is evident that a lot of work has gone into the compilation and continuing evolution of *Eurovoc*. Users of the English language version do still find problems when using EC bibliographical sources that use *Eurovoc* as a basis for their indexing. This seems to be due not so much to the use of non-standard English words and phrases, which was the initial accusation against *Eurovoc*, as the need to know and understand very clearly EC policy concepts and their context as expressed in EC phraseology before being able to make full and productive use of *Eurovoc*. In other words you need to have a good idea of what you want to find and the words or phrases the EC favour before being able to make full use of *Eurovoc*-derived indexes. This is acceptable for regular users of EC documentation but is not really satisfactory for infrequent users.

A thesaurus is not an end in itself. In the context of this chapter *Eurovoc* has been used as the basis for terms used in the *Index to the Official Journal of the European Communities* and the *Catalogue of Documents*. It is also used as the basis for indexation of the European Parliament database EPoque, which may be made publicly available in the future. It may also be used in the future as the basis of indexation for the *Catalogue of Publications* (see Chapter 3).

List of Pending Proposals

This title is issued as a COM Document at irregular intervals. Even though the title has existed as an internal document for a number of years it has only systematically been made publicly available from 1985. The following COM Documents have so far been made available:

1. COM(85)379 final *List of Pending Proposals* at 1 June 1985
2. COM(86)412 final *List of Pending Proposals* at 1 June 1986
3. COM(86)604 final *List of Pending Proposals* at 1 October 1986
4. COM(87)106 final *List of Pending Proposals* at 1 February 1987
5. COM(87)346 final *List of Pending Proposals* at 1 June 1987

List of Pending Proposals lists all Commission proposals under headings corresponding to the Commission Directorate-General sponsoring the proposal. The title of the proposal is given with a COM Document reference. Other pieces of information listed, if available, are the dates of transmission of the proposal to the Council and the opinions of the

European Parliament and the Economic and Social Committee with the *Official Journal* reference to these features.

List of Pending Proposals has no index but nevertheless is an important tool for tracing legislative proposals and their current status. The title should be published more regularly and distributed more rapidly to increase its value.

A rather similar publication called *Commission proposals on which the European Parliament has delivered an opinion, now pending before the Council* is also periodically issued as a COM Document (for example, COM(87)309 final).

Index to the Official Journal of the European Communities (hereafter called Official Journal: Index)

The need for a comprehensive and high-quality index to the contents of the *Official Journal* is obviously an important requisite. The *Official Journal* contains the text of EC legislation plus many other items of information concerning EC activities. Unfortunately, the *Official Journal: Index* has not served its role at all well. However, during the 1980s there are signs that the problems are being addressed – both in terms of indexing terms and the information indexed.

Until 1983 the *Official Journal: Index* was arranged with a structure which made access extremely difficult for all but the most dedicated and experienced. From 1984 there has been a considerable improvement as *Eurovoc* is now used to compile the index.

The *Official Journal: Index* is published monthly with an annual cumulation. It is divided into two parts:

1. Methodological tables.
2. Alphabetical index.

The Methodological Tables list, and give the *Official Journal* reference to, all the legislative acts for the period covered in numerical order. It also lists the cases brought and the judgments of the European Court of Justice. To find the text of Council Directive 86/457/EEC, for example, would require finding the reference in the Methodological Tables for 1986. In these tables there are two separate sequences: 'Acts whose publication is obligatory'; and 'Acts whose publication is not obligatory'. In the example quoted of a Directive this would be listed in the latter category. This leads to the *Official Journal* reference.

The problems of the *Official Journal: Index* arise when the Alphabetical Index has to be used. Until 1983 it was arranged in a way that conformed 'generally to the structure of the Treaties and the organization of Community institutions'.[7] In no realistic way could it be seen as an alphabetical subject index. Since 1984 the Alphabetical Index has been compiled using the *Eurovoc* multilingual thesaurus.

By using the thesaurus as a guide to terms to search for in the index there is a much better chance of finding references to Community legislation. However, while the Alphabetical Index is now very detailed it cannot be said invariably to use words and phrases in standard everyday English. For example if you were looking for the text of the EC budget for the year 1985 it might be thought reasonable to expect a reference under the word 'budget' in the Alphabetical Index. However, no such reference would be found, although *Eurovoc* does suggest that 'budget' is an acceptable word. In fact, in this instance in the 1985 *Official Journal: Index* the term 'budget' does lead you to two other references for the budget of two minor EC organizations. But to find references to the overall EC budget you would have to find phrases like 'adoption of the budget' and 'European Communities'. A considerable awareness of EC nomenclature and phraseology is required to make proficient use of the *Official Journal: Index*. These problems are recognized by the compilers of *Eurovoc* and efforts are being made to alleviate them by the proposed publication of Volume 4 of *Eurovoc* (see above). The compilers can also argue that there is a limit to the user-friendliness of a necessarily complicated tool such as *Eurovoc*.

Another major criticism of the *Official Journal: Index* is that it is only, in essence, an index to *one part* of the *Official Journal*. Effectively it indexes the 'L' series and only the part relating to the Court of Justice from the 'C' series. It is acceptable perhaps that the 'S' series is not indexed as it is a title of generally limited life. The 'C' series is another matter. The contents of this series urgently need indexing comprehensively – most notably such features as European Parliament resolutions and written questions. It is rumoured that just such a development might happen in the near future. Even if public access to the various EC databases becomes more widespread many people will continue to use the *Official Journal: Index* and so continued investment to improve its usefulness is essential.

Directory of Community legislation in force and other acts of the Community institutions (hereafter called the Directory)

From the first edition in 1980 until the fourth edition in 1983 the title was *Register of current Community legal instruments*. The current more self-explanatory title began with the fifth edition. The *Directory* was an annual publication until the seventh edition in 1986, each edition describing the situation as on 1 January of the year. An updating supplement covering the situation up to 1 July was issued also up to 1986. From 1987 a completely new edition of the *Directory* is published twice a year describing the situation as on 1 June and 1 December.

The *Directory* is a bibliographical listing of the current legislation of the European Communities – that is, it lists the titles of legislative acts currently in force and gives the *Official Journal* reference to those acts.

The *Directory* is compiled from the CELEX database, the interinstitutional computerized documentation system for Community law. It does not include Sector 1 of CELEX – the primary legislation. The *Directory* thus lists:

1. Agreements between the EC and non-EC countries
2. Secondary legislation
3. Supplementary legislation.

The *Directory* is published in two volumes. Volume 1, called the Analytical Register, consists of seventeen chapters broken down by policy area, and then further subdivided – here the legislative acts are listed. Volume 2 contains a chronological and alphabetical index; the latter is not very extensive and it is as necessary to use the analytical structure at the beginning of volume 1 to make productive use of the *Directory*.

Notes and references

1. OOPEC, *Fourteenth annual management report,* 1982, p. 11 (unpublished internal document).
2. The European Community in the world. *European File*, no. 16, 1986.
3. Further details on EC legislative Acts can be found in a range of introductory EC publications and commercially produced textbooks. One example is: the ABC of Community law, *European Documentation*, no. 2, 1986.
4. European Communities: *Directory of Community legislation in force and other Acts of the Community institutions*, 10th edition, EC, 1987, p. v.
5. The information in this paragraph has been obtained from *European Industrial Relations Review*, no. 133, February 1985, p. 10.
6. The publications policy and programme of the European Communities, by Walter Verheyden, in *European Communities information*, edited by Michael Hopkins, Mansell, 1985, p. 22.
7. Wording used in the Introduction to the *Official Journal: Index* until 1983.

CHAPTER 2

European Commission

It is not possible in the EC institutional structure exclusively to assign legislative, executive, administrative and political functions to a particular institution. The Commission, the Council of Ministers and the European Parliament have an overlapping and interrelating range of functions.

STRUCTURE AND FUNCTIONS OF THE COMMISSION

A number of key functions of the Commission can be noted. It is:

1. The guardian of the founding Treaties.
2. The formal initiator of Community policy, including legislative proposals.
3. The executive implementer of Community policy.

To carry out these functions the Commission is headed by a group of Commissioners. The number of Commissioners has changed over the years as additional countries have joined the European Community. With the accession of Spain and Portugal the number has grown to seventeen. A Commissioner owes his first loyalty to the EC and not to his country of origin. Practice has ensured that each member state nominates one Commissioner; the larger states (France, Germany, Italy, Spain and the United Kingdom) have an additional Commissioner. They are appointed by an agreement between the member states for a period of four years, which can be renewed. The Commission is headed by a President.

The Commissioners take decisions as a collegiate body. Nevertheless it has become standard practice to assign a range of policy or departmental responsibilities to each Commissioner. From 1985 until 1988, for example, Lord Cockfield, one of the Commissioners nominated by the United Kingdom, was assigned the internal market, the Customs Union Service, taxation and financial institutions. The current responsibilities of each Commissioner are shown in the latest edition of the *Directory of the Commission of the European Communities* (see below).

Each Commissioner has a private office or *cabinet* to help him. Below that are the so-called Eurocrats. In 1987 there were 15 055 staff working for all the departments of the Commission. Of these 1564 were linguists and 3053 were involved in activities at the Joint Research Centre at Ispra.[1]

The Commission is based in Brussels, although certain departments are based partly or wholly in Luxembourg (notably DG XIII, DG XVIII and Eurostat). In addition there are the Joint Research Centre (JRC) staff at Ispra and elsewhere, plus the officials working in Information Offices and External Delegations throughout the world.

Departmental structure of the Commission

In 1988 the departmental structure of the Commission was as follows:

1. Secretariat-General (Chapter 4)
2. Legal Service
3. Spokesman's Service (Chapter 7)
4. Joint Interpreting and Conference Service
5. Statistical Office (Eurostat) (Chapter 6)

Directorates-General (Chapter 5)

1. DG I: External Relations
2. DG II: Economic and Financial Affairs
3. DG III: Internal Market and Industrial Affairs
   Task Force: Small and Medium-sized Enterprises
4. DG IV: Competition
5. DG V: Employment, Social Affairs and Education
6. DG VI: Agriculture
7. DG VII: Transport
8. DG VIII: Development
9. DG IX: Personnel and Administration
10. DG X: Information, Communication and Culture
11. DG XI: Environment, Consumer Protection and Nuclear Safety
12. DG XII: Science, Research and Development
    Joint Research Centre
13. DG XIII: Telecommunications, Information Industries and Innovation
14. DG XIV: Fisheries
15. DG XV: Financial Institutions and Company Law
16. DG XVI: Regional Policy
17. DG XVII: Energy
18. DG XVIII: Credit and Investment
19. DG XIX: Budgets
20. DG XX: Financial Control

21. DG XXI: Customs Union and Indirect Taxation
22. DG XXII: Coordination of Structural Instruments
23. Euratom Supply Agency
24. Security Office
25. Office for Official Publications of the European Communities
26. European Foundation for the Improvement of Living and Working Conditions (Chapter 13)
27. European Centre for the Development of Vocational Training (CEDEFOP) (Chapter 13)

(The documentation of each department is described in the chapters noted.)

Directory of the Commission of the European Communities

This title is published irregularly by OOPEC as a priced publication available in all official languages. Since 1980 either one or two editions a year have been published. The *Directory* contains the following features:

1. Names of the Commissioners and their private office
2. Policy and Departmental responsibilities of each Commissioner
3. List of Directorates-General and other Commission departments with names of all senior officials and their specific responsibilities
4. Contact addresses for all departments
5. Alphabetical index of all named officials
6. List of Information Offices and their Head of Office
7. List of External Delegations and Head of Delegation.

DOCUMENTATION

The Commission is the EC institution from which the majority of Community documentation originates. In all four categories of documentation outlined in the Introduction – legislation, documentation of the legislative process, research, and explanatory and background material – the Commission is the primary 'author'. In 1981 it was estimated that the Commission accounted for 86 per cent of EC publications other than the *Official Journal*.[2] This is understandable in the light of the functions of the Commission as formal initiator and implementer of Community policies, and guardian of the Treaties. In addition to the documentation generated in the process of carrying out its formal functions the Commission also has the task, and duty, of explaining Community policies to the population at large.

The Commission has an annual programme of publications. To talk about the Commission as 'author' of a publication is sometimes convenient but needs to be explained. A publication will emanate from a Directorate-General, or other Commission department. In the following chapters on the documentation of the Commission titles and series are ascribed to individual Directorates-General. However, before a publication from a Directorate-General is allowed there is a process of vetting.

The overall publishing programme of the Commission is broken down into four elements, each headed by a *service ordonnateur* or 'authorizing service'. They comprise:

1. DG IX: general publications
2. DG X: information publications
3. DG XIII: scientific publications
4. Eurostat: statistical publications.

The Secretariat-General can also be classified as an authorizing service. Each of the authorizing services has a budget and an annual publishing programme into which all publications from individual Directorates-General must be accepted. Above the authorizing services there is a further coordinating forum called the Consultative Committee of Publications. This was set up in 1973 to express opinions on, and establish criteria and standards for, Commission publications, as well as to coordinate the Programme administratively. The CCP comprises representatives from the authorizing services and OOPEC.

It is not important for a user of EC documentation to know which authorizing service has authorized a particular publication. In the case of Eurostat the range of titles is confined to those compiled within Eurostat itself. However DG IX, DG X and DG XIII all authorize material for publication which originates in another Directorate-General or *service auteur* ('author service'). EUR Reports, for example, are authorized for publication through DG XIII but many originate from other Directorates-General. This is illustrated in the section on the documentation of DG XIII in Chapter 5. Similarly DG IX is the authorizing service for a number of titles such as the *Bulletin of the European Communities, European Economy, Social Europe,* and other policy journals, *Investment in the Community coalmining and iron and steel industries* and the *General report on the activities of the European Communities,* and its supplements, for all of which the author service is another Directorate-General or the Secretariat-General. Series such as European Perspectives and European Documentation are also coordinated by DG IX, although individual titles may be compiled by officials from other Directorates-General, or even individuals from outside the Communities. DG IX, DG X and DG XIII are all author services in their own right.

Each authorizing service has an annual programme of publications.

This will comprise a list of titles and series that it is proposed to publish. The precise structure of the programme will differ from one authorizing service to another but the type of information given includes:

1. The author service of a proposed publication
2. The priority of the publication
3. Copyright status
4. How many issues in the year if a periodical or series
5. The anticipated number of pages or average number of pages
6. Format
7. Number of copies printed and in which language.

Budgetary details are also covered and in the case of regularly produced titles features such as the desired period of the month for publication and the anticipated period of validity for the title are indicated.

The range of documentation produced by divisions of the Commission is considerable. There is no entirely satisfactory system of categorizing the material. Documentation can be divided by subject or function. In this book, however, the documentation of the Commission is broken down by departmental origin. This includes each Directorate-General that is an author service with, in addition, the Euratom Supply Agency, Eurostat, the Spokesman's Service and the Information Offices. Bibliographical material is treated separately as is the documentation of the European Centre for the Development of Vocational Training and the European Foundation for the Improvement of Living and Working Conditions. To an extent this does allow for material to be grouped together by subject. However, to trace EC documentation by a subject approach also use Appendix 1.

Some Commission Directorates-General do not produce many publications in the sense of being a 'service auteur'. All Directorates-General are nevertheless the origin of a certain amount of EC documentation in that all are involved in generating Commission proposals and reports which are issued as COM Documents. Similarly material in such publications as the *Bulletin of the European Communities* and the more popular series such as European Documentation can be submitted by officials from a wide range of Commission departments.

The many individual documentation developments of the Commission during the 1980s are discussed in detail throughout the following chapters. Some of the broad developments can be observed here:

1. The decision systematically to make available COM Documents, and other elements of the legislative process (see Chapter 4).
2. The demise of the Studies and Dossiers series (see below).
3. The rise of the Document categorization (see Chapter 4).
4. The growth of policy area journals: alongside the well-established titles such as *European Economy* and *The Courier* new

titles have been created such as *Social Europe* and *Energy in Europe* (see Chapter 5).

5. The continuation and consolidation of such series as European File, European Documentation and European Perspectives (see Chapter 5).
6. The rationalization of Eurostat titles into themes and series (see Chapter 6).
7. Improvements in OOPEC-produced catalogues and bibliographies (see Introduction and Chapter 3).
8. The rationalization of many periodicals produced by the Information Offices (see Chapter 7).

Up to the 1980s a number of policy areas had a Studies and/or a Dossiers series. The two terms were used interchangeably. Examples included:

1. Economic and Financial series (DG II)
2. Commerce and Distribution series (DG III)
3. Evolution of Concentration and Competition series (DG IV)
4. Competition – Approximation of Legislation series (DG IV)
5. Social Policy series (DG V)
6. Education series (DG V)
7. Transport series (DG VII)
8. Development series (DG VIII)
9. Regional Policy series (DG XVI)
10. Energy series (DG XVII).

Publications in the series usually consisted of the results of research undertaken by the Directorates-General or commissioned from outside bodies. The series has not formally been discontinued but its place has been effectively supplanted by the creation of the Document categorization. It is not true to say that the Document has explicitly taken over the Studies series, as the *raison d'être* of each is different. The Document was created to enable the faster, more economical and less administratively cumbersome publication of EC information. In practice, alongside many other types of information now published with the Document categorization is material that up to 1984 would have been issued in the Studies series.

FURTHER INFORMATION

There is no single contact point for further information about the documentation of the Commission. For information relating to prices and availability you are recommended to contact the Sales Offices as listed in Appendix 4. For information regarding the categories and content of Commission documentation and advice on whom to contact in the Commission you are recommended to approach first the Information Offices of the Commission as listed in Appendix 3.

Notes and references

1. Great Britain: House of Lords: Select Committee on the European Communities, *Staffing of Community institutions*, 11th Report (1987/88) HL Paper 66 HMSO, 1988, p. 11
2. Court of Auditors, Special Report concerning publishing, printing and reproduction practices of the institutions of the European Communities, *Official Journal* C150 19.6.1981, p. 5.

CHAPTER 3

Commission – Bibliographical Documentation

INTRODUCTION

In a work of non-fiction indexes of one form or another will usually be provided to help you gain access to its contents. Similarly it is accepted that most academic journals will provide a volume index. On a larger scale there exist a wide range of bibliographies, indexes, abstracts, catalogues and computer-based services to enable people to access information from a wide variety of printed sources. Bibliographical control is, however, uneven. Some subjects are less adequately covered than others, as are sources from certain geographical areas and in different forms.

The documentation of official organizations has traditionally been poorly served by bibliographical services. The European Community is no exception to this. In this chapter a study is made of the many sources from the Commission which can be used to trace EC documentation and, in some cases, the information contained within. For the sake of completeness mention will also be made of Commission bibliographical sources which cover non-EC material.

In terms of quantity and declared aims the bibliographical coverage may seem impressive. On the whole that impression is only partially fulfilled. There is no overall authority within the EC whose task is to instil bibliographical order on its documentation. The titles described in this chapter originate from a wide variety of sources within the Commission. These sources have differing reasons for compiling their bibliographical works. Some are sales catalogues, some are the products of library catalogues, while others were initially produced for use primarily within the institution and have only subsequently been made available to a wider audience.

An organization with the influence and power of the European Community has a responsibility to make its activities known through a range of means including its documentation, which can only be used effectively if high-quality bibliographical control is available. While acknowledging, and discussing in this chapter, some of the improvements that have taken place in the last few years in EC bibliographical control it has to be said that overall much remains to be done.

The development of a number of EC bibliographical titles from non-EC publishers is testimony both to the inadequacy of existing EC sources and the demand for assistance. Some of the key non-EC bibliographical sources are briefly mentioned in Appendix 5.

The other major feature to note is the slow onward march of computerized bibliographical services. It is sometimes said that the relevant authorities do not have the will to deal radically with the bibliographical control problems of EC documentation through traditional means, preferring to look ahead to the enhanced computerized services that can be provided. These services do indeed offer a prospect of improved bibliographical control. The initial experiences with the publicly available CELEX and SCAD databases suggest, however, more that we simply exchange one set of problems with another set. EC databases, bibliographical and otherwise, are listed in Appendix 2.

OOPEC PUBLICATIONS: CATALOGUES/BIBLIOGRAPHIES FROM THE OFFICE FOR OFFICIAL PUBLICATIONS OF THE EUROPEAN COMMUNITIES

A look at the developments in the catalogues produced by OOPEC over the last decade does indicate that efforts have been made to respond to customer requirements. Primarily such publications are intended as sales catalogues, but in the absence of alternatives information specialists and others have to make continuing use of them as major bibliographical sources.

One definite improvement has been the abolition of multilingual catalogues, which were never popular with readers, and their replacement by separate catalogues for each Community language. In the English language catalogue, for example, if an EC publication exists in that language an entry only appears for the English version. It is possible, however, to tell if the publication appears in other languages, for a code is printed alongside the entry to indicate other language editions and their location in the equivalent catalogue for that language.

If a publication has not been published in an English version an entry appears for a version in another language in the following order of choice: French, German, Italian, Spanish, Portuguese, Dutch, Danish and Greek.

Another improvement has been the appearance of indexes and a clearer structure for the contents of the catalogues. However, the most significant development has been the attempt to produce a catalogue which lists the documents relating to the legislative process of the EG.

This development mirrors the more systematic public availability of these documents.

1. COM Documents
2. EP Reports
3. ESC Opinions and Reports.

Publications of the European Communities – Catalogue

The last multilingual annual *Catalogue* covered the publications of 1979. In 1981 OOPEC issued the first of the new-format monolingual annual catalogues listing the publications of 1980. This was called *Publications of the European Communities – Catalogue*. This was also the first edition to use the new structured headings and to have a series and an alphabetical index. The latter is in essence a title index using one or more keywords in the title.

The use of keywords is not entirely consistent as the following example from the 1981 *Catalogue* indicates. There are two entries close to each other in the alphabetical index:

1. Social Europe – Supplement: Recent progress in introducing new information technologies into education
2. Social Europe – Supplement: Youth initiatives in the European Community – 'Info-Action 1985' Conference.

In the second example, among other keywords used in the alphabetical index is the obvious one of 'Youth initiatives'. However, in the first example the equally obvious terms 'information technologies' and 'education' are not used.

The precise title of the catalogue has changed somewhat over the years. The 1985 and 1986 annual catalogues were called *Catalogue (1985, 1986): Part A: Publications*. The 1987 catalogue was called *Publications of the European Communities 1987*. On the cataloguing information page of the 1986 edition the title was given as *Catalogue of Publications 1986*, and this is the title used whenever it is referred to throughout the book.

It is difficult to indicate precisely what publications are listed in *Catalogue of Publications*. The catalogue itself says it comprises the monographs and series published during the 'period in question by the Institutions of the European Communities as well as the yearly periodicals'.

The catalogue is divided into three parts:

1. The classified list – a listing of all entries under broad subject headings: within each heading first are listed monographs and individual titles within series, second are listed the titles of periodicals (headings used can be seen in Appendix 1)

2. Periodicals: an alphabetical list of EC periodicals
3. Title and series indexes

For each entry the following information is given in addition to the title:

1. Author (usually the originating institution and/or Directorate)
2. Publication year
3. Pagination
4. Language
5. Catalogue number
6. ISBN
7. Price in all relevant currencies
8. Other information such as series title and volume number is given when appropriate.

A note is given on obtaining publications.

As OOPEC has widened the scope of the material it publishes and distributes on behalf of EC institutions and organizations undoubtedly its *Catalogue* becomes a more useful tool for tracing EC documentation. However, as a 'sales' catalogue for OOPEC the *Catalogue* cannot be seen as a comprehensive listing of EC documentation. For example, EUR Reports published by OOPEC are listed, but EUR Reports published by commercial publishers are, quite naturally, not. On the whole free items are not listed in the *Catalogue* although to confuse matters there are exceptions – titles in the European Documentation series *are* listed, for example. As the *Catalogue* is clearly used as more than a sales catalogue it would be helpful if as many as possible of the free publications of the EC institutions were listed. If OOPEC could also combine the *Catalogue of Publications* with the *Catalogue of Documents* (see below) into a single publication we would be a considerable way along the path to creating a really useful bibliographical publication of EC documentation.

The indexes in the *Catalogue of Publications* need to be improved – perhaps by using the *Eurovoc* thesaurus as used in the *Catalogue of Documents*.

Catalogue of Documents – year . . .

The first annual volume of this title covering the documents of 1985 was published in 1987, quickly followed by the volume covering 1986 titles. On the cover the title is given as *Catalogue (year): Part B: Documents*. The volume covering 1987, published 1988, was given the title *Documents 1987* on the title page and *Catalogue 1987* on the cataloguing page. Throughout this book this source is referred to as *Catalogue of Documents*. The long-delayed publication of this title marked a clear step forward in the bibliographical control of the documentation of the EC legislative process.

The *Catalogue of Documents* comprises references to the publicly available titles in the following series, collectively known as documents:

1. COM Documents
2. EP Reports (comprising the Committee Reports of the European Parliament known as Series A of European Parliament Working/ Session Documents)
3. ESC Opinions and Reports

The *Catalogue* is divided into three parts:

1. The classified index: entries are listed under subject headings similar to those used in the *Catalogue of Publications* and the *Directory of Community legislation in force*. Full entries appear only once but there is a certain amount of cross-referencing.
2. The alphabetical index: this is based on keywords or key expressions appearing in the document. The index is compiled using the *Eurovoc* thesaurus. Each document may have up to five index terms.
3. The numerical index: this is a numerical listing of all the documents listed. For subscribers who take these documents on microfiche this list directs you to the corresponding microfiche number.

Many users probably find the distinction between 'publications' and 'documents' in these catalogues confusing – a single catalogue is the answer. It would still be possible to designate each entry a 'publication' or a 'document' if OOPEC felt the designation was necessary. Note that the EC publications which are issued with the Document categorization (see Chapter 4) are listed in the *Catalogue of Publications*. The Document categorization should not be confused with the range of material listed in the *Catalogue of Documents*.

It is important that OOPEC produce their catalogues quickly. Ideally the annual catalogues should appear in the first quarter following the year they are covering. In addition there should be regular monthly or quarterly listings of new publications/documents.

There is some evidence that OOPEC is attempting to provide this type of service. Traditionally there had been a monthly booklet called *Publications of the European Communities* issued on yellow pages. Until 1984 this was incorporated at the back of each issue of the *Bulletin of the European Communities*. In 1985 six numbers were issued as a separate publication and none in 1986. From 1987 an edition appeared covering the publications issued during the period January–March 1987. This stated that the publication would henceforth be issued quarterly with non-cumulative classified lists but with a cumulative title index. This title index cumulates into the annual *Catalogue of Publications*.

Similarly since 1987 there has appeared a monthly list of recently published titles of documentation of the legislative process called *Documents*. The monthly list contains no indexes.

For the sake of completeness it is necessary to mention the existence of certain short-lived catalogues issued in the 1980s which were the precursors of the *Catalogue of Documents*.

COM Documents led the way in the 1980s in the documentation of the legislative process that were made publicly available on a systematic basis. Annual catalogues covering the COM Documents of 1983 and 1984 were issued called *Documents – annual catalogue*. A number of 'monthly' catalogues called *Documents – periodic catalogue* were also issued covering 1983 and 1984. The format of these catalogues is as in the *Catalogue of Documents, 1985–*.

Similarly a catalogue covering the opinions of the Economic and Social Committee issued in 1984 was published. This was called *Opinions – annual catalogue*. No such parallel publication was issued for the Committee Reports of the European Parliament (EP Reports). Perhaps this was because the European Parliament made available a publication called *Numerical list of Working Documents*. Each issue covered the Working Documents issued during a period of time. It simply listed them in numerical order. There was no index and was available only in French. It has not been publicly available since the session 1985/86.

It has been suggested that, at some stage in the future, the *Catalogue of Documents* will incorporate references to items in the *Official Journal* 'C' Series which relate to references already in the *Catalogue of Documents*.

The European Community as a publisher

This strange little publication is, in essence, a 'popular' catalogue of EC publications. Until the 10th edition, 1985–86, the phrase 'extract from our *Catalogue of Publications*' was on the cover and it claimed to be an abridged version of that catalogue comprising:

1. The main official publications of the previous five years
2. The most common publications for general information.

From the 1986–87 edition the opening phrase was changed to 'extract from our publications catalogues', which is probably a better description, although still not really the truth. In the introduction there is still talk of the 'annual multilingual catalogue', which, in fact, ceased in 1979. Also it is ironic that in the 'abridged version' of the full catalogue are listed many titles not listed at all in the *Catalogue of Publications*. For example, many individual titles in the European File and Europe Information series are listed.

Nevertheless *The European Community as a publisher* remains a useful general introduction to current EC documentation. It lists titles under approximately the same subject headings as the full catalogues. In addition to individual titles it discusses major series and categories of EC documentation. An English language edition of this title has appeared every year since 1976. It does not appear every year in all Community languages.

Traditionally the catalogues from OOPEC have been available free of charge as primarily they are sales catalogues or promotional literature. However, the *Catalogue of Documents* is in a different category. It is a serious bibliography intended primarily for those who subscribe to the documents it lists. Indeed it is not generally possible to buy individual copies of these documents. The original intention in 1985 was to charge for the *Catalogue of Documents*, but in the event the delayed publication of the first edition led it to be given away free of charge. This practice has continued with subsequent editions.

SCAD PUBLICATIONS: THE CENTRAL DOCUMENTATION SERVICE

SCAD stands for Service Central Automatisé de Documentation or Central Documentation Service. It is a department within Directorate E (personnel and administration in Luxembourg and general services) of Directorate-General IX (Personnel and Administration) of the Commission.

The principal function of SCAD is to service officials within the Commission by distributing documents and by manning an information desk. SCAD maintains a file of references to EC documentation and periodical articles relating to subjects of interest to the EC. From this file various printed source and an online bibliographical database are made available to EC officials and the general public.

SCAD Bulletin

This title has been used since 1985. From 1977 to 1984 the title used was *Documentation Bulletin: Series A. SCAD Bulletin* is a weekly publication listing a wide range of EC documentation and also articles from non-EC periodicals. The articles listed refer to the activities of the European institutions, to the policies of the member states and to issues of international law. Only articles of a substantial length are included. Articles in EC periodicals such as *Social Europe* and *The Courier* are thus usually not covered by SCAD. Commercially published books about Europe are not included.

The EC documentation covered is extensive. It includes the publicly available documentation of the legislative process and legislative acts. In the case of legislative acts SCAD only records those whose titles are printed in bold in the table of contents of the *Official Journal*. SCAD also notes a large range of other EC publications. In some ways it is more comprehensive than other EC bibliographical sources. For example, in the case of the European Parliament not only are references given to Committee Reports of the European Parliament (EP Reports) there are also *Official Journal* references given to the text of Parliament Resolutions, which relate to those reports. Another useful feature is that below a reference to a document of the legislative process are listed other related references.

Entries are noted under broad subject headings. In 1987 these were:

1. Industry
2. Social affairs
3. Agriculture
4. Budget, financial control
5. Trade, tertiary services
6. Competition
7. Cooperation, development
8. Customs
9. Law
10. Economy
11. Energy
12. Education, training, culture
13. Environment
14. Taxation
15. Administration, civil service
16. Information services, press
17. Community institutions
18. Internal market, free movement of goods, persons and services
19. Money, finance
20. International organizations, integration movements
21. Fisheries
22. Internal policy of states
23. Regional policy
24. Protection of consumers
25. Research, science
26. External relations, international trade
27. Statistics
28. Transport.

Since the publication of this title by computerized means in 1983 a French language subject index has been provided in each issue. This uses terms taken from the ECLAS thesaurus in the Commission Library. At present there is no English version of this subject index. It is rumoured that an author index may be provided in the future.

SCAD Bulletin is most useful when used as a current awareness service by someone interested in a clearcut subject area that fits neatly into one of the subject headings used.

Like all EC bibliographical tools it has its drawbacks. The subject headings are not always helpful. The publication is not easy to read owing to its poor printing and its multilingual nature. The index is only in French. Above all it does not cumulate in any systematic way. It would be a dedicated person who would go through all the individual issues covering a substantial period of time.

To be fair the last objection can be overcome if you access the SCAD database, which was launched in September 1983. In July 1986 it contained 38 500 references and was growing by 15 000 references annually.

SCAD Bulletin, like its offshoots described below, is a priced publication available from OOPEC. During the 1980s its price rose substantially.

During 1987 a *SCAD Bulletin: Supplement* was issued. This listed the contents of the audiovisual library which the Commission's Audio-Visual Production Division could offer to radio and television networks. It was the follow-up volume to *Documentation Bulletin - Supplement*, nos 1, 2 and 3 issued in 1983.

SCAD Bibliographies

This title has been used since 1985. From 1977 until that year the title was Documentation Bulletin: Series B.

Both titles consist of occasionally published bibliographies on a particular subject. They list references taken from issues of *SCAD Bulletin* (or its predecessors) over a period of time. Periodically the bibliographies are updated and the usual practice is for a new edition to cancel and replace the previous edition. All titles are published in French language editions, while a selection are also issued in English language editions.

In the period 1977–87 the following titles were issued:

1. *Community legislation on the elimination of technical barriers to trade in industrial products,* 1983
2. *Energy,* 1981
3. *Transport,* 1985 (S)
4. *Women's work,* 1979
5. *Taxation,* 1981
6. *Community legislation relating to the removal of technical barriers to trade in foodstuffs,* 1986 (S)
7. *Legislation in the veterinary and animal feeding stuffs sectors,* 1980
8. *Approximation of legislation on plant health, seeds and forestry,* 1977
9. *Education,* 1977
10. *Promotion of consumer interests,* 1978

11. *Protection of the environment,* 1980
12. *Competition policy,* 1978
13. *Regional policy,* 1981 (also F, 1987)
14. *Community relations with the Mediterranean countries,* 1983
15. *Company law,* 1983
16. *Economic, monetary and financial matters,* 1979
17. *Free movement of persons and services,* 1979
18. *North–South dialogue,* 1979 (F)
19. *EC external relations with the developing countries,* 1979 (F)
20. *EC external relations with state-trading countries,* 1979 (F)
21. *Multinational companies,* 1979 (F)
22. *Basic regulations concerning the common organization of agricultural markets,* 1980
23. *Agricultural structure policy,* 1980 (F)
24. *Investment,* 1980
25. *Public contracts,* 1984
26. *Employment–unemployment,* 1986 (S)
27. *Community relations with industrialized countries,* 1980 (F)
28. *Law of the Sea,* 1980 (F)
29. –
30. *Community agricultural policy by product,* 1981–83, 9 volumes (F)
31. *Small and medium-sized enterprises in the EC,* 1983 (F)
32. *Enlargement of the EC,* 1986 (F) (S)
33. *Condition féminine,* 1988 (F) (S)

(F) French language version only   (S) SCAD Bibliographies

If an up-to-date bibliography is available for a subject in which you are interested, SCAD Bibliographies are very useful. It is to be hoped that new editions are more systematically issued in the future and more subjects covered. On the other hand increasing promotion of the SCAD database will probably lead to the eventual demise of the series altogether.

SCAD Bibliographic File

This title has been used since 1984. It would appear to be the successor to Documentation Bulletin: Series C, five issues of which appeared in 1979–80 with the titles:

1. *Les mouvements d'intégration*
2. *Les organismes internationaux*
3. *Les marchés agricoles*
4. *Le droit communautaire*
5. *La politique intérieure des états.*

SCAD Bibliographic File consists of one-off bibliographies on particular topics. The following have been published:

1. *Les innovations technologiques,* 1985
2. *L'Espagne,* 1985
3. *Le Portugal,* 1985
4. *Dumping,* 1985
5. *Relations CEE–ACP,* 1985
6. *Countertrade/barter,* 1985.

Generally the references consist of relevant EC legislative acts and related documentation, other EC publications and periodical articles. In the case of the SCAD Bibliographic File on countertrade/barter there is simply a section of definitions and a list of periodical articles divided by language.

SCAD News

This title began in September 1984 and is issued monthly with occasional supplements. It is in essence a sales catalogue or promotional pamphlet discussing a selection of, usually recently issued, EC publications. Each issue discusses approximately twenty titles. Since July 1986 these titles have been listed on the inside cover under the following headings:

1. Economic affairs
2. Internal market
3. External relations
4. Agriculture – fisheries
5. Social affairs – employment
6. People's Europe
7. Research
8. Descriptive publications.

A brief description is given of each title and sales details. Titles listed can include documents of the legislative process, 'public documents', and explanatory publications. Precisely how a title gets chosen for inclusion is not at all clear – the selection is so limited and the range of categories of documentation so wide that altogether it comprises a strange little publication. Titles listed have not necessarily been recently published. Each issue consists of a separate English and French section, not necessarily the same.

In addition to the regular monthly issues there are occasional extra issues. Since 1986 there have been a number of special issues listing all published EC publications which have been given the Document categorization.

PUBLICATIONS OF THE COMMISSION LIBRARY

The first function of the Commission Library service is to provide assistance to the officials working in that institution. The Library is also open to external readers interested in matters relating to all aspects of European integration. Having a comprehensive collection of the documentation of the EC, plus a mass of related material from other sources, makes the Commission Library a particularly significant centre for research in this field.

The Central Library is based in Brussels with a branch in Luxembourg. There are also a number of specialized libraries in individual Directorates of the Commission.

Automated cataloguing came to the Library in 1978. The Library database, thus created, is available online internally to Commission officials and library staff. There are plans to make the database externally available. The database has allowed the creation of a number of printed bibliographies. These and the other publications described below are produced nowadays primarily for users from outside the EC institutions.

List of additions to the Library

This title was a list of the new items in the Commission Library arranged from October 1978 in classified order based on the OECD *Macrothesaurus* (3rd edition, 1978). The publication was monthly. Coverage included EC publications, a selection of publicly available EC documents, books and a selection of periodical articles. In 1985 the title was replaced by *Recent publications on the European Communities received by the Library* (see below).

In addition to the monthly volumes, *List of additions to the Library: Supplement* was also issued. Examples included:

1. 1981/1 Bibliography on the European Communities
2. 1981/2 Selection of bibliographies available in the Library
3. 1981/3 Selection of thesis [*sic*] available in the Library
4. 1982/1 Publications of international organizations (EC excluded) received by the Library
5. 1983/1 Statistical publications available in the Central Library
6. 1983/2 Selection of bibliographies available in the Library
7. 1983/3 Selection of dictionaries available in the Library.

A further issue to note is *List of additions to the Library*, 10/11/12, December 1979. This has the subheading *Catalogue of European Community Publications and Documents received at the Commission Library, 1978–79*. This was the precursor of one of the most useful new titles issued in the 1980s: *Publications and Documents of the EC received by the Library* (see below).

Publications and Documents of the EC received by the Library   *Z 2000. C 61*

The first edition of this title covering the years 1978–80 was issued in 1981. The following year a modified edition covering the years 1977–80 was issued on a limited distribution basis to Commission offices, European Documentation Centres and Depository Libraries. This edition had the distinct and useful feature of self-contained language sections. Later editions have reverted to an integrated multilingual format. The next edition was published in 1983 and covered the years 1978–82. The 1984 edition covered the years 1978–83. This pattern of publication has continued so that the volumes have got larger and larger each year. The edition covering the years 1978–85, for example, was issued in two volumes totalling over 1000 pages.

The ever-larger size has now prompted a significant change of publication policy. A supplement covering the publications of 1986–87 was published in 1988. The intention of the Library is to publish annual cumulating supplements over a quinquennium ending with a supplement for 1986–90. It is hoped to then publish a 'grand consolidated edition' covering 1978–91 and subsequently follow with annual cumulative supplements over five-year periods.

The references are classified by a modified version of the OECD *Macrothesaurus*, in French. The publication could do with a more substantial introduction explaining the precise criteria for inclusion of references and guidance on use.

As the years covered in one edition increase, *Publications and Documents of the EC received by the Library* becomes one of the more important EC bibliographical tools. It lists a large selection of EC documentation as received in the Commission Library. In the area of 'publications' it is unrivalled in its scope, covering items not easily traceable elsewhere such as:

1. Non-confidential but not formally published Commission items such as Economic Papers and many one-off commissioned research reports
2. European University Institute publications
3. CEDEFOP publications
4. EUR Reports including those published by commercial publishers
5. Titles in such series as European Perspectives and supplements in such periodicals as *Bulletin of the European Communities* and *Women of Europe*
6. Substantial articles in EC periodicals.

In the area of 'documents' the position is not quite so clear. Only a selection of such titles are noted. The main categories included would seem to be:

1. COM Documents: those which consist of major introductions or reviews of subjects are included rather than specific legislative proposals
2. EP Reports: a substantial proportion of Committee Reports of the European Parliament.

Each reference may be assigned up to four 'classification numbers'. A full entry is listed under each of these numbers. A reference is given a full classification number – for example, 09.01.02. The arrangement of the entries is alphabetical by title under a simpler version of the classification – for example, 09.01.

There are two indexes – title and author. The title index refers you to a classification number. To use the author index is a two-stage exercise. The author entry refers you to a title which then refers you to a classification number. The author index is an individual author, editor, rapporteur, or chairman index, and does not include corporate authors such as 'European Parliament'. The 1986–87 Supplement also contains an index using French language subject headings.

The information given with entries would be sufficient to order or check if a library contains the items. Prices are not given. All language versions of 'publications' are noted but only the English and French versions of 'documents'.

Recent publications on the European Communities received by the Library

This title began in 1985 and replaces *List of additions to the Library*. It is published monthly, the December issue being an annual cumulation.

The annual cumulation for 1985 arranged its entries in country and regional grouping order. Within these headings entries were arranged by French language descriptors from the OECD *Macrothesaurus*. Even though the headings are all in French there is a section giving English terms for all headings used. The 1986 cumulation was issued in two volumes with the entries grouped under broad subject headings from the OECD *Macrothesaurus*. A list of the headings used is given in French and English. Volume 1 contains the entries. Volume 2 contains the following indexes:

1. Author
2. Title
3. Country/region including the term 'Communautés Européennes'.

All the index entries direct you to a classification number; in addition, author and country indexes direct you to the relevant title(s).

Material included in *Recent publications on the European Communities received by the Library* covers:

1. EC publications and documents
2. Books from commercial and learned presses
3. A selection of periodical articles and chapters from annuals, Festschriften, etc.

If you are looking only for EC documentation references it is preferable to use *Publications and Documents of the EC received by the Library*. *Recent publications on the European Communities received by the Library* does, however, allow you to trace more recent EC documentation, and does give you many references from non-EC sources from all the member states. Many such references are not directly on matters relating to the European Communities – they are simply items that have been acquired by the Commission Library. In this sense *Recent publications on the European Communities received by the Library* is a major general bibliography. From 1987 the annual cumulation does not contain references to EC documentation.

The monthly issues of *Recent publications on the European Communities received by the Library* broadly follow the arrangement of the annual cumulation, although there are some differences. In the monthly issues during 1987, for example, author indexes were not given. The monthly issues continue to include EC documentation.

Recent publications on the European Communities received by the Library: Supplement

A number of *Supplements* have been issued since 1985:

1. 1985/1 Bibliography on monetary and financial matters
2. 1985/2 Bibliography on technological innovation
3. 1985/3 Bibliography on the external relations of the European Communities
4. 1985/4 Bibliography on European Community law
5. 1986/1 Selection of thesis [*sic*] available in the Library
6. 1987/1 Bibliography on Spain and Portugal.

These titles contains references on these subjects taken from the Commission Library catalogue since 1978.

All the titles described above from the Commission Library are priced publications available from OOPEC.

SCIENTIFIC BIBLIOGRAPHICAL PUBLICATIONS

Many of the titles already mentioned in this chapter do list EC publications of a scientific nature. However, there are some additional bibliographical sources which concentrate on this important area of EC documentation.

Euro Abstracts

Euro Abstracts is a major bibliographical source which can be used to trace documents issued in the EUR series. These are reports published on the completion of research programmes and scientific and technical studies funded by the Commission. (For further details of EUR Reports see the section on DG XIII in Chapter 5.) Unlike the *Catalogue of Publications* from OOPEC, which only lists EUR Reports published by itself, *Euro Abstracts* also covers EUR Reports published by commercial or other publishers. The aim of *Euro Abstracts* is to cover the results that emanate from all EC-supported research; EUR Reports are only one form of dissemination. Other common forms of dissemination include papers presented at conferences and papers published in commercially produced journals and monographs. *Euro Abstracts* seeks to cover all these various forms of dissemination.

Euro Abstracts is published by OOPEC on behalf of DG XIII of the Commission (Telecommunications, Information Industries and Innovation). It is a priced publication, and divided into two sections, obtainable separately.

Section I had the subtitle 'Euratom and EEC research, Scientific and technical publications and patents' until the end of 1983. Since 1984 the subtitle has been 'Euratom and EEC R & D and Demonstration Projects. Scientific and technical publications and patents'. It is published monthly with an annual index. The latter is divided into two parts – publications and patents. For publications the following indexes are given:

1. Subject
2. Author
3. Programme – either 'Direct actions' carried out by the Joint Research Centres, or 'Indirect actions' carried out under research contracts or in the context of association
4. Keywords
5. EUR Reports and books.

The patent index is divided into two parts:

1. Subjects
2. Inventors.

Instructions on how to use *Euro Abstracts* and how to obtain the publications and patents listed are given in all Community languages but the titles and abstracts of items are only given in the original language and English. *Euro Abstracts: Section I* is a high-quality service although the value of the annual index is somewhat diminished by its delayed publication.

It is worth stressing the broad nature of EC-supported research that is listed in *Section I*. In the annual index for 1984, for example, the following broad subject headings were used:

1. General and miscellaneous (including agriculture, information science, economics, law and the social sciences)
2. Chemistry
3. Earth sciences
4. Engineering and technology
5. Energy production, conversion and conservation
6. Life sciences
7. Materials
8. Mathematics and computers
9. Nuclear technology
10. Physics.

Section II lists the documentation relating the output of EC-supported research in the areas of coal and steel and 'research of a social nature'. The last category includes industrial hygiene, safety and medicine. The contents are divided into the following parts:

1. Research programmes
2. Research agreements
3. Scientific and technical publications
4. Patents
5. Training courses, seminars, conferences and symposia in preparation.

Not every part is used in each issue. *Section II* is again published monthly with an annual index. The latter has the following indexes:

1. Subject
2. Personal authors
3. Contractors
4. Research contract.

Until 1980 there was also a cumulative list of EUR Reports that had been listed in *Euro Abstracts: Section II* since 1975. This information can now be found in *Catalogue EUR Documents* (see below).

All the entries in Section II are listed in French, German and English. The value of this section is enhanced by the rapid appearance of the annual index.

The information that is listed in *Euro Abstracts* can also be accessed online in the EABS database available from ECHO (European Commission Host Organization).

Catalogue EUR Documents

The first edition of this title was issued in 1983 and covered EUR Reports issued between 1968 and 1979. A supplement covering the EUR Reports 1980–82 was issued in 1985. Both publications were published as an EUR Report (EUR 7500) in the information management series. They are divided into four sections:

1. Main entries and subject index
2. Alphabetical index of titles and series
3. Index of EUR numbers
4. Index of authors.

The catalogue lists titles in both the original language and English, the number of pages, price, form and availability. Both volumes are priced publications available from OOPEC.

Publications Bulletin

This title lists all the publications of the Joint Research Centre (JCR) – the generic name given to the four research establishments of the Commission. These centres initially undertook research into nuclear problems but have diversified into other areas.

The first edition of the *Publications Bulletin* appeared in April 1981, the second in July 1982 and henceforth it has appeared annually listing the publications of the previous year. By 'publications' a very broad range of material is included. The Joint Research Centre (JRC) categorizes material as follows:

1. Topical reports – these become EUR Reports
2. Contributions to conferences
3. Scientific or technical articles – these appear in non-EC scientific periodicals
4. Technical notes – interim information on current activities with a restricted distribution
5. Communications – confidential documents from the Commission on the activities of the Joint Research Centre distributed only to governments and other selected groups
6. Programme progress reports – confidential reports communicating the scientific or technical progress of a programme during a reporting period
7. Reports on special activities
8. Special publications – bulletins, documentation reports, manuals, reference catalogues, newsletters, etc.
9. Miscellaneous.

The references in the *Publications Bulletin* are divided into the broad areas of Joint Research Centre interest such as industrial technologies, fusion, fission, non-nuclear energies and the environment, with further subdivisions. There is an author index and a diagram of statistics relating to the publications of the Joint Research Centre for the year in question. In 1985, for example, there were 919 Joint Research Centre publications, and the statistical tables break this down further by category of publication and subject.

OTHER EC BIBLIOGRAPHICAL SOURCES

In addition to the titles mentioned above a number of further EC bibliographical titles are described elsewhere in the book, and include:

1. *Official Journal: Index* (see Chapter 1)
2. *Directory of Community legislation in force* (see Chapter 1)
3. *List of Pending Proposals* (see Chapter 1)
4. Bibliographical publications from the Library of the Council of Ministers (see Chapter 8)
5. Bibliographical publications from the Library of the Court of Justice (see Chapter 11)
6. Other EC institutions such as the European Parliament, and organizations such as the European Foundation for the Improvement of Living and Working Conditions, produce bibliographies or catalogues relating to their own documentation. These are listed in the chapters on those institutions or organizations.

Sources and references

1. The library and documentation services of the Commission of the European Communities, by Eric Gaskell, in *European Communities information*, edited by Michael Hopkins, Mansell, 1985, pp. 91–101
2. Disseminating the results of European Community research, by John Michel Gibb and Edward Phillips, in *European Communities information*, edited by Michael Hopkins, Mansell, 1985, pp. 59–75.

CHAPTER 4

Commission – General Documentation

This chapter looks at titles from the Commission in which the Secretariat-General is the 'author department', or in which there is no clearcut departmental affiliation. The following titles/series are covered:

1. *General report on the activities of the European Communities* [and its supplements]
2. *Programme of the Commission*
3. *Bulletin of the European Communities* [and its supplements]
4. COM Documents
5. The Document categorization.

GENERAL REPORT ON THE ACTIVITIES OF THE EUROPEAN COMMUNITIES

The major annual account of the activities of the European Communities. Each volume covers a calendar year. Article 18 of the Treaty establishing a Single Council and a Single Commission in 1965 instructed the Commission to produce a *General report* to be submitted to the President of the European Parliament not later than one month before the opening of the Parliamentary session in March of each year. This means that the *General report* is usually published annually by OOPEC in February. This rapid publication of a major report is a considerable achievement.

The first such *General report* was published in February 1968 covering the activities of 1967. The structure and size of the volumes have remained remarkably constant with an average size of around 400 pages.

The *General report* account is broken down into chapters and sections. The broad headings in the volume covering 1986 were as follows:

1. The Community in 1986
2. Chapter I : Community institutions and financing
   Section 1 : Institutions and other bodies
            2 : Information for the general public and specific audiences

This is then further broken down into detailed headings. This substantial contents section is necessary because the *General report* has no index. It is also useful because it helps to place a topic within the overall EC policy context in which the topic is looked at. It is worth studying the contents section closely to gain full advantage from the *General report*. For example, the phrase 'removal of physical frontiers' is mentioned twice in the contents of the 1986 report. First it is listed under the section heading 'Completing the internal market', and second it is listed under the section heading 'A people's Europe'.

The contents gives page references, but it is a feature of the *General report* that each paragraph, or 'point', is also numbered. It is worth noting that references within the text to other sections refer to paragraph numbers not pages. The considerable value of the *General report* lies in its references. While the description of the activities in a policy area is necessarily limited the *General report* gives you systematic references. This is either for further information in such sources as the *Bulletin of the European Community*, or to the text of a Commission proposal, European Parliament Resolution, Economic and Social Committee Opinion or EC law in the *Official Journal*. Reading through a series of the *General report* is a rapid means of following EC activities in a policy area over a period of time, and building up references for further information.

A feature that would make the *General report* more useful would be tables of the major legislative proposals and achievements with parallel bibliographical references, covering the year in question.

The *General report*, while covering the activities of the European Communities as a whole, is written from the perspective of the Commission. Differing perspectives can be gained from study of the annual reports from the Council of Ministers, *Review of the Council's work* (see Chapter 8), and the European Parliament, *Progress towards European integration* (see Chapter 9). The former covers the calendar year, the latter covers the rather strange period July to June.

In addition to the *General report* a number of parallel publications are issued annually. These comprise:

1. *The agricultural situation in the Community* (DG VI)
2. *Report on social developments* (DG V)
3. *Report on competition policy* (DG IV)
4. *Community law.*

The first three comprise more detailed expositions of developments in the particular policy areas than can be found in the *General report*. These are prepared in the relevant Directorates-General but finalized and approved through the Secretariat-General. The last named is a reprint, as a separate volume, of the chapter on Community law from the *General report*.

The agricultural situation in the Community

Agriculture being the most developed EC policy area it is only appropriate that there is a detailed annual report in addition to the chapter on agriculture to be found in the *General report*.

The first edition of this report as an OOPEC published title was in 1975. In the foreword to that edition it was said that the report was an abridged version of COM(75)601 final 'The agricultural situation in the Community – 1975 report'. An annual report with this title had been issued in earlier years as a COM Document. For example, in 1974 it was COM(74)2000. As COM Documents the reports were considered to be internal working documents from the Commission to the Council.

Over the years the OOPEC published report has developed and is no longer simply a reprint or abridgment of a single COM Document. It has become a comprehensive account of agricultural developments during the year in question and includes descriptions or summaries of a whole range of internal working documents. It is unfortunate therefore that, unlike the *General report*, *The agricultural situation in the Community* does not give many bibliographical references for further information.

The detailed structure of the report has changed a little over the years but generally there are three distinct sections:

1. Main events of the year are arranged with headings such as the general economic and political context, developments in the agricultural markets, in particular products, the economic situation for farmers and consumers, the Community's external relations and agriculture, policy on agricultural structures, the financing of the Common Agricultural Policy, and the harmonization of national agricultural legislation within the Community framework.

2. Special chapters on subjects of particular interest in a year: in the 1985 report, for example, there was a chapter on agricultural aspects of Community enlargement to include Spain and Portugal. In the 1986 report there was a chapter on twenty years of European agriculture.

3 Statistical section: this is a substantial section comprising rather more than half the report. While many of the tables are derived from Eurostat this section is not a reprinting of a single Eurostat title. There are tables on the agricultural economy, the farm accountancy data network (FADN), prices and production costs, structures, trade, and products.

Each volume has a detailed contents section but no index. The detailed contents for the statistical section is at the beginning of that section in the middle of the volume. The report is published at the beginning of each calendar year and is often available a little before the parallel *General report*.

Report on social developments

This title has been used since the report covering the year 1979 was published by OOPEC in 1980. From 1958 until the report covering 1978 the title was *Report on the development of the social situation in the European Community*.

Like the *General report* this report is published annually as a result of a treaty obligation. Article 122 of the Treaty of Rome setting up the European Economic Community calls for a chapter on social developments in the annual report the Commission makes to the European Parliament. In practice this has led in addition to the stated chapter in the *General report*, to a separate volume being published.

Until the volume covering developments in 1982 the size and layout of the *Report on social developments* resembled those of its parent *General report*. Since the volume covering 1983 was published in 1984 the format has changed and it is now issued with the Document categorization (see below). There is probably some reason known to Community officials for this change. However, as the sister reports on agriculture and competition, and the *General report* itself, have retained their original standard format, it is somewhat difficult for the outsider to explain the transformation. One of the reasons for the development of the Document categorization was to shorten the internal procedures for the publication of a document. It is nonetheless the case that the agriculture report, which is formally published, is available considerably earlier than the *Report on social developments* with the Document categorization.

Since the 1983 report the layout has been as follows:

1. Introduction
2. Social developments in the Community in 'year'
   a. Employment (including migrant workers)
   b. Education
   c. Vocational training
   d. Social dialogue and industrial relations
   e. Working conditions and labour law
   f. Wages and incomes
   g. Living conditions and family affairs
   h. Social security
   i. Safety and health at work
   j. Health protection.
   (These headings are from the 1986 report. There are minor changes from year to year. Within each heading there is a description of the situation in each member state)
3. Statistical appendix: brief tables on
   a. Population
   b. Education
   c. Employment

d. Unemployment
e. Working conditions
f. Wages – labour costs
g. Standard of living
h. Social protection.

The *Report on social developments* has no detailed contents section nor index. Like all the annual reports described in this chapter it is available in all Community languages as a priced publication from OOPEC.

Report on competition policy

The first report was published in 1972 following a resolution from the European Parliament in 1971. This asked the Commission to make a special report each year on the development of competition policy, which was considered an integral element in the means to achieve the aims of the Treaties establishing the European Communities. The report is published in conjunction with the *General report*.

The layout of the *Report on competition policy* has remained fairly constant, although there have been some detailed changes. Since the report covering 1983 was published the headings have been as follows:

1. General competition policy
   a. EC competition policy and the contribution from socio-economic and political circles
   b. EC competition policy and international contacts
   c. EC competition policy and small and medium-sized enterprises
2. Competition policy towards enterprises
   a. Main developments in Community policy
   b. Main decisions and measures taken by the Commission
   c. Main cases decided by the Court of Justice
   d. Application of national and Community competition law in the member states
3. Competition policy and government assistance to enterprises
   a. State aids
   b. Public undertakings
   c. Adjustment of state monopolies of a commercial character
   d. Main decisions of the Court of Justice in aid cases
4. The development of concentration, competition and competitiveness
5. Annexes – these list the Decisions and Rulings made by the Commission and Court of Justice during the year. Bibliographical references are given for certain categories. A list of studies commissioned from outside research institutes published during the year is given.

PROGRAMME OF THE COMMISSION

Alongside the formal presentation of the *General report* the President of the Commission gives an address to the European Parliament reviewing the past year and outlining the Commissions programme for the coming year.

Both the address and the programme have traditionally been published in a small volume called *Programme of the Commission*, a priced publication from OOPEC. The last edition of this title in this format was 1984.

In addition to this official version a prepublication version is issued by the Spokesman's Service. This is intended solely for the accredited press and the Information Offices of the Commission and is not available through OOPEC. Copies are sometimes available from the Information Offices upon request soon after the programme has been announced.

From 1985 the *Programme of the Commission* has been published as part of the series *Bulletin of the European Communities: Supplement*. For 1985 it was *Supplement 4/85*. For 1986–88 it has been *Supplement* no. 1; for 1989 no. 2. At the beginning of the Commission Presidency of Jacques Delors in 1985 he gave an additional speech to the European Parliament called 'The thrust of Commission policy'. This is available as *Bulletin of the European Communities: Supplement 1/85*.

It should also be mentioned that the address to the European Parliament by the President of the Commission can also be found in the issue of the *Official Journal of the European Communities: Annex: Debates of the European Parliament* for the appropriate part-session. Interestingly the text is similar but not identical to that found in the *Programme*.

BULLETIN OF THE EUROPEAN COMMUNITIES

A monthly bulletin which reports on the activities of the Commission and the other Community institutions. It is edited by the Secretariat-General of the Commission and published in all official Community languages as a priced publication by OOPEC.

The *Bulletin* is sometimes said to bring up to date the developments noted in the *General report*. Formally, however, there is no connection between the two titles. The *General report* is issued as a treaty obligation to be presented to the European Parliament. The *Bulletin* is issued as a means of informing the public of EC developments in a comprehensive but concise form. Although compiled by the Commission it does outline explicitly the activities of the other EC institutions month by month. The *Bulletin* is divided into three parts:

1. Special features

2. Activities in 'month, year'
3. Documentation.

In the 'Special features' section are highlighted three to four events of the month in question considered significant by the Commission.

Part 2 is structured as follows (headings from 1987 issues):

1. Building the Community
   a. Economic and monetary policy
   b. Internal market and monetary policy
   c. Businesses
   d. Steel
   e. Research and technology
   f. Telecommunications, information industries and innovation
   g. Customs union and indirect taxation
   h. Competition
   i. Financial institutions and company law
   j. Employment, education and social policy
   k. Culture
   l. Regional policy
   m. Environment and consumers
   n. Agriculture
   o. Fisheries
   p. Transport
   q. Energy
   r. Nuclear safety
2. External relations
   a. Multilateral trade negotiations
   b. Commercial policy
   c. Relations with industrialized countries
   d. Relations with other countries and regions
   e. Development
   f. International organizations and conferences
   g. Diplomatic relations
3. Financing Community activities
   a. Budgets
   b. Financial operations
4. Political and institutional matters
   a. Political cooperation
   b. Other intergovernmental cooperation
   c. Institutions and organs of the Communities.

As mentioned above the style of report is concise. However, the *Bulletin* does give copious references to both previous *Bulletin* issues to trace earlier developments, and to the *Official Journal* and other EC documentation to trace further detail to that given.

The third part 'Documentation' combines some standard features, such as the value in national currencies of one ECU (European Currency Unit) on a set date during the month covered and a listing of the infringement procedures initiated by the Commission against member states, and some special features.

In *Bulletin* no. 1, 1987, for example, there was the text of a statement given by the Belgian Prime Minister to the European Parliament in January 1987 marking the period of the Presidency of the Council by Belgium. In *Bulletin* no. 2, 1987 there was a special report on the application of the Code of Conduct by Community companies with subsidiaries in South Africa. In the last *Bulletin* for each year there is a useful listing under broad subject headings, such as 'Economic and monetary policy' and 'European policy', of all the features of the *Bulletin* that have been noted in Parts 1 and 3, plus the *Supplements* (see below), during the year.

A final feature to note in Part 3 is called 'Additional references in the *Official Journal*'. This section seeks to fill in bibliographical gaps from earlier issues of the *Bulletin*. Particularly conscientious people would thus be able to amend earlier issues of the *Bulletin*.

Until the end of 1984 each issue of the *Bulletin* contained a yellow insert called *Publications of the European Communities* (see Chapter 3).

The *Bulletin* is an impressive record of Community activities. However, as a means of keeping up to date with those activities it has its drawbacks. The issue of the *Bulletin* covering a particular month is often issued a considerable number of months later. For example, the issue covering January 1987 was only publicly distributed in July 1987. Ironically the *General report* covering a whole year is often available long before the final monthly issues of the *Bulletin* covering the same year. A reasonable annual *Index* to the *Bulletin* is produced but at a very long time after the year in question.

Bulletin of the European Communities: Supplement

This is a separate series published at irregular intervals. Each *Supplement* covers a single topic. The aim of the series would seem to be to give greater publicity to a Commission initiative, programme, report or proposal than would be the case if only summarized in the *Bulletin* or available in the COM Document series. The numbers published in a year vary between one and eight.

Since 1980 the following *Supplements* have been issued:

1980
1. *Report on the scope for convergence of tax systems in the Community*
2. *Council and Commission Committees*
3. *Employee information and consultation procedures*
4. *European Union – annual reports for 1980*
5. *A new trademark system for the Community*
6. *Reflections on the common agricultural policy.*

1981
1. *Report from the Commission ... to the Council pursuant to the mandate of 30 May 1980*
2. *The European automobile industry*
3. *European Union – annual reports for 1981*
4. *A new impetus for the common policies.*

1982
1. *A new Community action programme on the promotion of equal opportunities for women, 1982–85*
2. *Draft of a convention on bankruptcy, winding-up arrangements, compositions and similar proceedings – draft convention and report*
3. *The institutional system of the Community – restoring the balance*
4. *A Community policy on tourism – initial guidelines*
5. *Memorandum on the Community's development policy*
6. *Stronger Community action in the cultural sector*
7. *European Union – annual reports for 1982*
8. *Problems of enlargement – taking stock and proposals.*

1983
1. *Commission opinion on the status of Greenland*
2. *Employee information and consultation procedures*
3. *Increasing the effectiveness of the Community's structural funds*
4. *Adjustment of the Common Agricultural Policy*
5. *Prospects for the development of new policies: research and development, energy and new technologies*
6. *The structure of public limited companies; amended proposal for a fifth directive.*

1984
1. *Unfair terms in contracts concluded with consumers*

1985
1. *The thrust of Commission policy*
2. *Consumer redress*
3. *Proposal for a tenth Council Directive ... concerning cross-border mergers of public limited companies*
4. *Programme of the Commission for 1985*
5. *Progress towards a common transport policy: maritime transport*
6. *Advanced manufacturing equipment in the Community*
7. *A people's Europe: reports from the* ad hoc *Committee*
8. *A general system for the recognition of higher education diplomas*
9. *Guidelines for a Community policy on migration.*

1986
1. *Programme of the Commission for 1986*
2. *Single European Act.*[1]
3. *Equal opportunities for women*

4. *Community action in the field of tourism*
5. *The Community's broadcasting policy*
6. *A new impetus for consumer protection policy*
7. *Voting rights in local elections for Community nationals*

1987

1. *The Single Act: a new frontier; Programme of the Commission for 1987*
2. *25 March 1987: thirtieth anniversary of the signing of the treaties of Rome*
3. *European Economic Interest Grouping (EEIG)*
4. *A fresh boost for culture in the European Community.*

1988

1. *Programme of the Commission for 1988.*

Individual issues of the *Supplement* are listed in the *Catalogue of Publications* from OOPEC. They are priced items although it is often possible to obtain a free copy from an Information Office of the Commission.

COM DOCUMENTS

COM Documents form one of the largest and most important categories of EC documentation. As their popular and universally known title suggests, COM Document is the generic name given to a range of working documents of the Commission. As the initiator and implementer of EC legislation the Commission issues a large amount of documentation in carrying out those functions.

At the early stage of its existence a COM Document is not a public document. It may go through various drafts as it is discussed by Commission officials from the relevant Directorate-General(s) and the Secretariat-General. After this stage the Secretary-General places the item on the agenda of a meeting of the Commission. If the document is then accepted it becomes a public document and is known as a COM Document final. These documents are cited with the following elements:

1. COM
2. (Year)
3. Running number, final.

An example: *Communication from the Commission – making a success of the Single Act: A new frontier for Europe* is known as COM(87)100 final.

There is no significance in the running number but it is interesting to note that some of the more important COM Documents, such as the example above, and others in the agricultural field as well, do tend to have easily remembered numbers.

COM Documents can be divided into three broad categories:

1. Proposals for legislation
2. Broad policy documents
3. Reports on the implementation of policy.

Proposals for legislation

Only the Commission can formally propose EC legislation. In practice the Commission is often acting on instructions from the Council, or after a long period of wide consultation with other interested parties. Nevertheless the Commission role as initiator of EC legislation is clearcut. The majority of COM Documents issued fall into this category, and the majority of those are detailed proposals for action within the Common Agricultural Policy and the Customs Union. The others comprise the legislative proposals in all the other areas of Community competence and are usually of most interest to outsiders. An example is:

1. COM(87)166 final: Proposals for Council Regulations (EEC) establishing a Community system of aids to agricultural income; establishing a framework system for national aids to agricultural income; establishing a Community system to encourage the cessation of farming.

COM Documents in this category comprise two elements:

1. Explanatory memorandum
2. Text of the legislative proposals(s).

At a later stage the text of the legislative proposal will be reprinted in the *Official Journal: Information and Notices* (the 'C' series). The explanatory memorandum is not reprinted. So, for example, COM(87)313 final: *Proposal for a Council Regulation concerning the European strategic programme for research and development in information technologies [ESPRIT]* was issued on 23 July 1987. The text of the legislative proposal was published in the *Official Journal* C283 of 21 October 1987.

A small number of COM Documents in this category are given wider currency by being formally published as *Supplements* to the *Bulletin of the European Communities*.

It should also be noted that COM Documents also surface in other Community institutions as part of the consultative phase in the legislative process. In the European Parliament, for example, COM Documents circulate as issued by the Commission but with the addition of a European Parliament cover. From 1985 to 1987 within the European Parliament they were included in the 'C' series of European Parliament Working Documents, and from 1987 they have been included within the 'C' series of European Parliament Session Documents. Similarly COM Documents also circulate, as part of the working documentation, where appropriate, in the Economic and Social Committee and the European Coal and Steel Community Consultative Committee. In all these forms, however, COM Documents are not formally available to the public.

Broad policy documents

This is the second category of COM Document. Before the stage is reached where the Commission is ready to issue a specific legislative proposal it sometimes issues a Communication or Memorandum to solicit the views of interested parties and to signify its initial thinking on the policy area concerned. Some of these documents are the EC equivalent of the United Kingdom consultative document known colloquially as a 'Green Paper', or government statement 'White Paper'. Indeed these phrases have actually been used on the title pages of a small number of COM Documents. For example, COM(85)310 final: *Completing the internal market. White Paper from the Commission to the European Council* (Milan, 28 and 29 June 1985).

COM Documents that fall into this category often form substantial reports of considerable interest to both academics and policy-makers outside the EC. An example is:

1. COM(87)376 final: *Reform of the structural funds – Commission Communication; comprehensive proposal pursuant to Article 130d of the EEC Treaty.*

Article 23 of the Single European Act 1986 stated that a new Article 130d should be added to the Treaty of Rome setting up the European Economic Community. This article requested the Commission to submit a comprehensive proposal to the Council amending the operational rules and structure of the existing structural Funds: COM(87)376 final is part of the Commission response.

A selection of COM Documents in this category are also then issued in other formats to achieve greater publicity. Some are published as *Supplements* to the *Bulletin of the European Communities* and with the Document categorization (see below). Important agricultural COM Documents tend to be also issued within the series *Green Europe: Newsflash*. This category of COM Document is not published in the *Official Journal*.

Reports on the implementation of policy

This is the third category of COM Document. Sometimes in the text of EC legislation an explicit obligation is placed upon the Commission to issue formally a regular (usually annual) report on the workings of the Community instrument in question. On other occasions the Council or the European Parliament may subsequently request a regular or special report. An example is:

1. COM(87)203 final: *Second report from the Commission to the Council and the European Parliament on the implementation of the Commission's White Paper on completing the internal market.*

Many of these COM Documents contain a wealth of factual information. A selection of regular such reports are noted in Appendix 1. This category of COM Document is not reprinted in the *Official Journal*. A selection do reappear in other formats mainly now with the Document categorization.

COM Documents comprise a substantial collection. Since 1980 the following numbers have been issued:

1980	926
1981	826
1982	898
1983	799
1984	776
1985	859
1986	785
1987	731

The majority of these are non-confidential and made publicly available. In 1985 only 143 out of the 859 COM Documents issued were not circulated publicly. The availability of COM Documents has undergone a major change during the 1980s. As working documentation of the EC there had traditionally not been any systematic attempt to make publicly available, nor bibliographically to control, COM Documents. Equally however they were not generally considered confidential. European Documentation Centres and Depository Libraries have received them since 1974, and it was possible for others to receive individual copies from Information Offices or indeed some Directorates-General. As public awareness of the value of these documents has widened the EC has set up a method to make them systematically available. The principle of wider availability of COM Documents extends also to the series containing the Committee Reports of the European Parliament (EP Reports) and to the series containing the Opinions of the Economic and Social Committee (ESC Opinions and Reports).

From 1983 COM Documents have been available on subscription from OOPEC. It is possible to subscribe to the whole series or to a selection by subject in hard copy and to the whole series in microfiche. It is not possible to purchase an individual COM Document, although Information Offices sometimes maintain stocks of important COM Documents and will supply one upon request. In the United Kingdom, Alan Armstrong, an official subagent for EC documentation, will supply photocopies of individual COM Documents.

Alongside the systematic public availability of COM Documents OOPEC has attempted to improve their bibliographical control. For the full saga of the *Catalogue of Documents* see Chapter 3. In effect since 1985, the Catalogue has listed COM Documents, EP Reports, and ESC Opinions and Reports.

From 1981 until 1984 Giancarlo Pau, the Documentalist at the London Office of the European Commission, compiled an annual *Index to COM Documents*, which was published by Eurofi. From 1982 to 1984 the precise title was *Index to Documents of the Commission of the European Community*. Eurofi have continued to publish this title since 1985 but as a private venture.

COM Documents are covered in two of the major EC bibliographical sources: *SCAD Bulletin* (see Chapter 3) covers them comprehensively in its weekly issues; *Publications and Documents of the EC received by the Library* (see Chapter 3) lists a proportion of COM Documents, mainly non-legislative proposals.

The *Weekly Information Bulletin* compiled by the Public Information Office of the House of Commons Library lists recently received COM Documents. As such it is of some value as a current awareness service. Since 1985 Eurofi have produced *EEC update*, which is a looseleaf summary of COM Documents with a brief indication of the likely timetable for progress and implications. It is updated every two months. *European Access*, published bimonthly by Chadwyck-Healey, covers the majority of COM Documents which are not legislative proposals, and a minority which are.

The subject categories that OOPEC created in 1983 for COM Documents were unique to this series. From 1985 however the categories were rearranged so that the subjects that can be chosen in the selective subscription scheme coincide with the subject headings in the *Catalogue of Documents* and *Catalogue of Publications*. These subject headings are listed in Appendix 1.

SEC Documents

These are another category of internal working document. 'SEC' is an abbreviation used to denote the office of the Secretary-General of the Commission. These documents represent an earlier stage in the working processes of the Commission than COM Documents. SEC Documents are not made systematically available and EC Depository Libraries no longer receive even a small proportion of them. Those circulated prior to 1983 sometimes were issued as a COM Document at a later stage.

Occasionally an EC publication will refer to a SEC Document in a list of references. However, it will not be officially available and there is no point in contacting OOPEC. Sometimes a direct approach to the appropriate Directorate-General will elicit the document. SEC Documents are not covered in any of the standard bibliographical sources.

THE DOCUMENT CATEGORIZATION

The development of this 'series' has been one of the major EC documentation developments in the 1980s. It is called a 'series' for convenience – in effect each title published is a one-off publication that can be attributed to a specific Directorate-General. There is no numbering system to link titles together. The first titles with the categorization began to appear in 1984. The one common visual link is the word 'Document' that appears on the cover. The design of the cover itself has changed three times between 1984 and 1987.

As is often the case with EC documentation, it is difficult to come up with a concise definition and description of what the Document series comprises. In 1985 Walter Verheyden, the Director of OOPEC, wrote about 'public documents', which OOPEC intended to call those documents that were released for public distribution.[2] This could mean material like COM Documents and EP Reports as well as the material to be discussed in this section. Verheyden also says that these 'public documents' would henceforth be listed in the *Catalogue of Publications*. In the event it is only the category of document which has been listed in that particular catalogue that is being discussed in this section. The other 'documents' (COM Documents, etc.) are listed in the new and quite separate *Catalogue of Documents*.

In another chapter in the same book David Perry, Senior Manager at OOPEC, makes this distinction explicit. COM Documents and the like he calls 'official documents'. The other category he calls 'departmental documents'. His definition of this second group is: 'studies of compilations commissioned by or produced within the departments of the institutions in the process of information gathering and assessment prior to decision-making'.[3] This would seem to be the best definition for the wide variety of material that has been published with the Document categorization. This has included titles in series that previously were issued in other forms:

1. *Report on social developments.* Prior to 1983 this was published through OOPEC in the normal 'Publications' method in connection with the *General report on the activities of the European Communities*. Since 1983 it has been issued with the Document categorization.
2. Titles that would previously have been published in the category of publication called Studies would seem to now be published with the Document categorization. A clear example of this is the Studies series 'Evolution of concentration and competition', which stopped in 1984. Since then titles in this field have been published with the Document categorization.
3. *Euratom Supply Agency: annual report.* Prior to 1983 this was

published through OOPEC in the normal publications' way. Since 1983 it has been published as a Document.

4. *European Regional Development Fund: annual report.* This is the same as the title above. Note that this report is also available as a COM Document.

5. *Completing the Internal Market. White Paper from the Commission to the European Council.* This title was first issued as a COM Document (COM(85)310 final). The usual practice to ensure the wide circulation for a COM Document is to issue it as a *Bulletin of the European Communities: Supplement.* This example is thus rather an exception to a standard practice.

However, of more significance are the majority of other titles that have been published with the Document categorization since 1984. It is possible that a proportion of these would have become publicly available in one form or another anyway. For example a number of reports in the series Programme of Research and Actions on the Development of the Labour Market had been distributed to EC Depository Libraries prior to 1983 and were available upon request to the relevant Directorate-General. However, the subsequent publication of these titles with the Document categorization has ensured that knowledge of their existence is much improved.

It is also true that many titles now published with the Document categorization would not have been formally published in any format prior to 1984. It is clear that there has been a definite increase in the amount of material issued since the creation of the Document series. The majority of this increase comprise reports which have been commissioned by the Commission, in the course of carrying out their executive functions, from external research/consultancy organizations or academics. Prior to 1984 most of this material would not have been published in any way, although copies of reports might have been distributed to people known to the relevant Directorate-General. Much of this material is of considerable interest and the Commission clearly felt that it deserved a wider circulation. The creation of the Document series was really due to this feeling. Titles published in this series do not go through the same lengthy processes prior to formal publication. They remain in typescript form and OOPEC simply puts a standard cover on them. Most titles are published only in a very limited number of language versions, English and/or French being the most favoured. In those reports from external agencies the statement is always made that 'This document has been prepared for use within the Commission. It does not necessarily represent the Commission's official position.'

Titles with the Document categorization are priced publications available from OOPEC. As mentioned above they are listed in the OOPEC *Catalogue of Publications.* Since 1986 there have been occasional special issues of *SCAD News* (see Chapter 3) which list all the titles with the Document categorization issued since 1984.

Appendix 1 lists many of the main groups of material published with the Document categorization. The majority of titles published with the Document categorization that can be attributed to a particular Directorate-General are listed in the following pages.

Notes and references

1. The authoritative text can be found in the *Official Journal* L169 29.6.87, p. 9
2. The publications policy and programme of the European Communities, by Walter Verheyden, in *European Communities information*, edited by Michael Hopkins, Mansell, 1985, pp. 13–23
3. The role of the Office for Official Publications of the European Communities, by David Perry, in *European Communities information*, edited by Michael Hopkins, Mansell, 1985, pp. 35–36.

CHAPTER 5

Commission – Directorate-General Documentation

INTRODUCTION

This chapter looks at titles which are compiled from within the Directorates-General of the Commission. It is not possible to include every individual item that has been issued. Rather the chapter seeks to draw attention to important categories of documentation that are currently available.

DG I EXTERNAL RELATIONS

The following series are covered:

1. *Corps Diplomatique Accrédité auprès des Communautés Européennes*
2. *Agreements and other bilateral commitments linking the Communities with non-member countries*
3. *Multilateral conventions and agreements: signatures and/or conclusions by the European Communities*
4. *Practical guide to the use of the European Communities' scheme of generalized tariff preferences*
5. Miscellaneous.

Corps Diplomatique Accrédité auprès des Communautés Européennes

This title is issued twice a year as a priced publication from OOPEC. It is a directory to the diplomatic corps accredited to the European Communities. The directory is arranged alphabetically by country. Under each country the address of the embassy is given along with the names, rank and addresses of the key staff, and the date of their accreditation. Note that in the case of some of the smaller countries the accredited embassy may not be in Brussels.

There are two other features in this publication. First, there is a list of accredited countries in order of formal diplomatic precedence. This seems to be largely based on the date of accreditation of the ambassador. Second, there is a list of national days for the accredited countries.

In the tradition of diplomacy this title is in French only.

Agreements and other bilateral commitments linking the Communities with non-member countries

This title began in 1981 and has been published since then at six-monthly intervals. The edition which covers the situation as at the end of June each year is in English, while the edition which covers the situation as at the end of December each year is in French. It is issued by the Treaties Office of DG I and is available direct from them.

In the foreword to the English 1986 edition it says that this Directory of international legal commitments linking the European Communities to third countries or groups of third countries has two purposes:

1. To provide a complete list of Community agreements in force
2. To give exact references to these agreements so that the texts of documents can easily be found.

The publication is arranged by regional groupings:

1. Northern Europe
2. Southern Europe
3. State-trading countries
4. MMI [Maghreb, Mashreq and Israel] and Middle East
5. North America
6. Latin America
7. Asia
8. ACP [African–Caribbean–Pacific]
9. Australasia
10. Quotas for handicraft and handloom products
11. Generalized preferences scheme.

Within each regional grouping individual countries are listed alphabetically and then any appropriate grouping of countries (for example, the Andean group, ASEAN group). At the front of the publication is an alphabetical listing of countries with page references.

For each agreement listed the following information is given:

1. Title of agreement
2. Bibliographical reference
3. Legal basis
4. Period of validity
5. How the agreement is administered
6. Summary of the agreement.

The European Community international organizations and multilateral agreements

This title was first issued in 1977. A second edition (called an 'amending supplement') was issued in 1980 and a third revised edition in 1983. All three editions were priced publications available from OOPEC.

These sources are a mixture of historical account and directory. The European Community, being a unique organization in international law, has had to develop its relations with other international bodies very carefully and in a piecemeal fashion. This title outlines the history of that development and lists in a systematic way the agreements between the EC and other international organizations.

Multilateral conventions and agreements: signatures and/or conclusions by the European Communities

This title was first published in 1987 and was issued with the Document categorization. It is a priced publication available from OOPEC. It would seem to be a replacement for the title described above – some parts of the text are the same and much of the information is similar. The structure of the contents is, however, quite different.

In an explanatory note the structure of the 1987 title is clarified:

1. Part I lists the multilateral conventions and agreements in which the EC participates, and regroups them according to different criteria (chronological, geographical breakdown of depositories, other international organizations, breakdown by sector, agreements in which the EC has exclusive competence and agreements in which the EC has mixed competence
2. Part II consists of conventions which have been signed by the EC
3. Part III consists of conventions which the EC have accepted or to which they have acceded
4. Annex: provides for each agreement the basic elements and conditions of participation of the EC as well as the date of entry into force and the complete listing of signatures, ratifications and accessions. Bibliographical references to the *Official Journal* are given.

In essence Parts I–III are indexes to the Annex, which forms the greater part of the publication. In the explanatory section it is said that the publication is to be in looseleaf format and will be updated. Certainly there are holes punched in the pages, but it is also true that the 1987 edition came fully bound! The introductory pages are in English and French, but the main body of the text is only in the former language.

Practical guide to the use of the European Communities' scheme of Generalized Tariff Preferences

This title has been issued annually since 1977, with the exception of 1985. It is a priced publication available from OOPEC. In the first years it was available in all Community languages; it is now available in English, French and Spanish editions only.

The Generalized System of Preferences (GSP) is an international scheme that allows developing countries to send products to the industrialized countries and not incur customs charges. The first Community GSP was introduced in 1971 and it has been maintained ever since with revisions.

This title is a guide to the workings of the EC GSP. The bulk of the work are the details of the scheme for the year in question, arranged systematically, following the classification of the Common Customs Tariff (until 1987) or TARIC (from 1988). It is stressed in the introduction that it is important when using the *Practical guide* that you have access to the Common Customs Tariff or TARIC. The CCT was usually published in November or December in the *Official Journal* 'L' series for the following year. For example the CCT for 1986 was published in *OJ* L331 9.12.1985. The Community's Generalized Tariff Preferences Scheme for each year is also published in the *OJ* 'L' series. In 1985 it was published in *OJ* L352 30.12.85, for example. The structure in the *OJ* is quite different from the layout in the *Practical guide*.

A simple introduction to the concept of the GSP can be found in *European File* no. 16, October 1987.

Miscellaneous

1. *Japan and the European Community: a stocktaking*, 1984
2. *Japan: the first step*, 1985. This is a directory of facilities and services for European companies considering entry into the Japanese market
3. *The European Community and the Mediterranean Basin*, 1984 (published with the Document categorization)
4. *Industrial cooperation and investment in Yugoslavia*, 1986 (published with the Document categorization).

DG II ECONOMIC AND FINANCIAL AFFAIRS

The following series are covered:

1. *European Economy* + Supplement A, B, C
2. *Results of the business survey carried out among managements in the Community*

3. Economic Papers
4. *Report on the activities* (Monetary Committee)
5. *Report on the activities* (Economic Policy Committee)
6. Miscellaneous

European Economy

This title began in 1978 with a single issue. Three issues were published in each of the years 1979–81 and four issues a year thereafter, although not at regular intervals. It is a priced publication available on subscription from OOPEC.

European Economy is the key journal for disseminating to the general public information regarding the economic policy of the EC and the member states. The contents are a mixture of regular annual features and a small number of special articles. Regular annual features include:

1. Borrowing and lending activities of the Community. This is usually published in an issue in the first half of the year. The report is also issued as a COM Document. It is compiled by the Commission specifically for the European Parliament to aid that institution's 'monitoring of the Community's borrowing and lending activities'. Thus it reviews the activities of Euratom, the New Community Instrument (NCI), the ECSC and the European Investment Bank
2. Annual Economic Report. This is usually published in an issue in the latter half of the year. This report is also issued first as a COM Document. The report is divided into two main parts. Part 1 covers the Community economy and outlines the analysis by the Commission of the past year and future prospects highlighting particular policy needs. Each Annual Economic Report is usually given a subtitle: the 1985–86 report was subtitled 'A cooperative growth strategy for more employment', while for 1986–87 it was called 'Reduction of unemployment in a more dynamic European economy'. Part 2 of the Annual Economic Report contains a brief description and analysis of the economic policy of each of the member states.

Other articles are substantial one-off features, mainly written by officials of DG II. The two such articles in issue 31, March 1987, were, for example:

1. The determinants of investment
2. Estimation and simulation of international trade linkages in the QUEST model.

A brief list of the contents of all past issues of *European Economy* appears at the back of each issue.

European Economy: Supplement A – Recent economic trends

This eight-page title appears monthly, a single issue covering August and September. It is available as a priced publication from OOPEC. Issues covered include:

1. Consumer price index
2. Economic outlook and forecasts
3. National accounts
4. Labour costs
5. European Monetary System (EMS)
6. Inflation
7. Trade balances
8. Interest rates
9. Exchange rates
10. Value of ECU.

European Economy: Supplement B – Business and consumer survey results

Until 1984 a separate *Supplement C - Consumer survey results* was published three times a year. Since then the consumer survey results have been included in *Supplement B*, although the subtitle *Business and consumer survey results* has only been used from issue 3, March 1985.

Supplement B is published monthly with a single issue covering August and September. It is a priced publication available from OOPEC. It reports the main results of the opinion surveys carried out among businessmen and consumers in the Community. Features in 1986–87 issues included:

1. Industrial investment
2. Capacity utilization in industry
3. Industry plans
4. Orders
5. Employment expectations
6. Situation in the retail trade
7. Export expectations
8. Consumers' financial situation
9. Labour market flexibility
10. Consumer incomes
11. Consumer climate.

European Economy and its supplements can be obtained on a combined subscription.

Results of the business survey carried out among managements in the Community

The EC business surveys are carried out by national institutions on the basis of the Commission's harmonized questionnaires. In 1987 all member states except Spain and Portugal took part. In the United Kingdom the Confederation of British Industry carried out the manufacturing industry survey, the Business Statistics Office the investment survey, and the Building Employers Confederation the construction survey.

The surveys are carried out monthly and published in this publication on that basis, except for a single issue covering August and September. It is a priced publication available from OOPEC. There is one edition in French and English, although the introduction appears in all the languages of the participating countries.

Questions asked in the industry survey cover:

1. Production trends
2. Order books
3. Export order books
4. Stocks of finished products
5. Production expectations
6. Selling price expectations
7. Employment expectations
8. Limits to production
9. Production capacity
10. Duration of assured production
11. New orders in recent past
12. Export expectations in the months ahead
13. Capacity utilization
14. Stocks of raw materials.

In addition there is a half-yearly investment survey and a building survey. The latter covers the following features:

1. Trend of activity
2. Limits to production
3. Order-books or production
4. Employment expectations
5. Price expectations
6. Months of assured production.

European Economy: Supplement B gives a monthly selection of the most recent survey results. Articles containing more detailed analyses occasionally appear in *European Economy*.

Economic Papers

These are a series of highly technical academic papers on subjects of interest to this Directorate-General. They are written either by officials working in DG II, often as papers to be presented at conferences, or by academics from outside the Commission who have presented them at seminars held within DG II.

The series is regarded as an internal series and can only be obtained direct from DG II. The series began in 1981 and an irregular number is issued each year, varying between five and sixteen. Economic Papers are not listed in OOPEC catalogues but they can be traced in *Publications and Documents of the EC received by the Library*.

To give an indication of the subjects covered in the Economic Papers the following is a list of some titles published in 1987:

1. *Internal and external liberalisation for faster growth*
2. *Regulation or deregulation of the labour market: policy regimes for the recruitment and dismissal of employees in the industrialized countries*
3. *Causes of the development of the private ECU and the behaviour of its interest rates, October 1982–September 1985*
4. *Capital/labour substitution and its impact on employment*
5. *The determinants of the German official discount rate and of liquidity ratios during the classical gold standard: 1876–1913.*

Papers are only issued in one language edition, in the vast majority of cases English.

Monetary Committee

While there is now a plethora of advisory and consultative committees in the EC system, the Monetary Committee is one of the few to have been specifically set up as a result of a treaty obligation. Article 105 of the Treaty establishing the European Economic Community set up the Monetary Committee in an advisory capacity:

1. To keep under review the monetary and financial situation of the member states and of the Community and the general payments system of the member states and to report regularly thereon to the Council and to the Commission
2. To deliver opinions at the request of the Council or of the Commission or on its own initiative, for submission to these institutions.

The Member States and the Commission each appoint two members of the Monetary Committee. DG II officials comprise the Commission representatives and provide the secretariat for the Committee.

Report on the activities

This is an annual report on the activities of the Monetary Committee. It is a priced publication available from OOPEC. It is currently available in French, German and English editions.

Regular features that appear are:

1. Report on the general situation
2. Report on activities of the Committee and the EC
3. List of members and alternates of the Monetary Committee (this feature did not appear in the *Report* ... for 1985 published in 1986).

In addition there are annexes which contain special reports by working parties and various own-initiative Opinions.

Compendium of Community monetary texts

A new edition of this title is produced irregularly as a priced publication from OOPEC. The latest edition was published in 1986 and gathers together all the legal texts that are of most relevance to the work of the Monetary Committee up to early 1986. These are listed under the following headings:

1. Extracts from the Treaty founding the European Economic Community (including the Single European Act, 1986)
2. Coordination of economic policies
3. Economic and monetary union
4. European Monetary System (EMS)
5. Capital movements
6. ECU and agricultural unit of account
7. Committees (including the decision setting up and rules of procedure of the Economic Policy Committee – see below). Editions were published in English, French and German.

Economic Policy Committee

A Council Decision of 18 February 1974 [74/122/EEC] set up the Economic Policy Committee to replace three separate advisory committees. Its function is to promote coordination of member states' short- and medium-term economic policies. The Committee consists of four representatives from the Commission and four from each of the member states.

Report on the activities

Even though the Economic Policy Committee has been in existence since 1974 it was only in 1986 that an annual report (covering 1985) was published for the first time. It was published in the same format as the parallel *Report* ... for the Monetary Committee, as a priced publication from OOPEC in French, German and English editions.

The report surveys the main activities of the Committee, lists its members, and gives the text of various statements, opinions and reports made during the year under review.

Miscellaneous

The following miscellaneous titles have been published since 1980:

1. *The Danish economy*, 1980 (published as no. 14 in the Economic and Financial Series in the Studies collection)
2. *The European Monetary System: origins, operation and outlook*, 1985 (published in the European Perspectives series)
3. *Money, economic policy and Europe*, 1985 (published in the European Perspectives series)
4. *The Fourth Company Accounts Directive of 1978 and the accounting systems of the Federal Republic of Germany, France, Italy, the United Kingdom, the United States and Japan*, 1986 (published with the Document categorization).

DG III INTERNAL MARKET AND INDUSTRIAL AFFAIRS

DG III is one of the key Directorates-General in the Commission. With the drive to complete the internal market by 1992 now underway it is this Directorate-General which shoulders the major burden of producing the appropriate legislative proposals to achieve the barrier-free circulation of people, goods, capital and services within the Community.

DG III is also responsible for the management of the EC policy towards the steel industry (see also DG XVIII). From 1984 to 1986 it contained a special task force on information and telecommunications technologies. This was then transferred to DG XIII but was replaced by a new task force on small and medium-sized enterprises.[1]

DG III is not, however, a major producer of publications of which it is the 'author department'. In this section the following series are covered:

1. *Catalogue of Community legal acts and other texts relating to the elimination of technical barriers to trade for industrial products; nomenclature for iron and steel products (EURONORM)*
2. *EURO-info*
3. Studies – Commerce and Distribution series
4. Miscellaneous.

Catalogue of Community legal acts and other texts relating to the elimination of technical barriers to trade for industrial products; nomenclature for iron and steel products

Editions of this title were published annually by OOPEC from 1980 until 1984 as a priced publication. The two parts noted in the title were quite separate. In the part containing bibliographical references to the elimination of technical barriers for industrial products the following tables were given:

1. Texts of a general nature
2. Directives adopted by the Council
3. Directives adopted by the Commission
4. Proposals for directives that have been sent by the Commission to the Council but have not yet been adopted
5. Directives adopted by sector.

A new edition of this section alone was published with the Document categorization in 1988. It listed the progress of EC legislation in the following:

1. Lifting appliances and lifts
2. Gas appliances
3. Pressure vessels
4. Cosmetics
5. Motorcycles and mopeds
6. Measuring instruments
7. Fertilizers
8. Prepackaged goods
9. Electrical material
10. Construction plant and equipment
11. Dangerous substances
12. Agricultural tractors
13. Motor vehicles
14. Other sectors.

This edition takes into account the Commission White Paper on the Completion of the Internal Market by 1992 and the 'New Approach' to technical harmonization and standardization launched in 1985.

The second section comprises simply a list of EURONORMS – a series of technical specifications for iron and steel products.

EURO-info

This title is issued by the Task Force on Small and Medium-Sized Enterprises of DG III.[1] It is an irregular bulletin which aims to keep small businesses and the craft trade informed of EC developments of interest to them. It is free but only available to business organizations, associations and groups. The first issue was dated December 1985.

Studies – Commerce and Distribution Series

This was a series of numbered reports published by OOPEC as priced publications in a selection of languages. The reports in this series were compiled from within the Commission. From 1978 to 1985 the following titles (nos 6–10) were published:

1. (6) *Preliminary study on competition in the retail trade (developments, problems, measures)*, 1978
2. (7) *Measures taken in the field of commerce by the member states of the European Communities* (2nd updating), 1981
3. (8) *Changes in the structure of the retail trade in Europe*, 1982
4. (9) *Competition in the distributive trades*, 1983
5. (10) *Measures taken in the field of commerce by the member states of the European Communities* (3rd updating), 1985.

Miscellaneous

The subject of industrial competitiveness has been of central concern to DG III during the past few years. In 1982 a title in the Dossiers series called *The competitiveness of the Community industry* was published by OOPEC. Basically the same document also circulated informally with the title *The competitiveness of European Community industry* (III/387/82). The latter listed some internal documents not listed in the formally published title.

Another interesting feature to note is how the text in what is originally a working document of the Commission is changed slightly when it is formally published. COM(81)639 final (A Community strategy to develop Europe's industry) has a section called 'Europe needs to counter-attack'. In the reprint of this COM Document in the 1982 title published by OOPEC, *The competitiveness of the Community industry*, this section is refined to 'Europe must take positive action'!

A further title in this field was published with the Document categorization in 1987. This is called *Improving competitiveness and industrial structures in the Community* and is a reprint of COM(86)40 final.

The phrase 'completing the internal market' became one of the key EC policies in the late 1980s. It was not a new idea. The original Treaty of Rome setting up the EEC had talked about the need for a common market and the free movement of goods, services, capital and people. While progress had been made it was equally clear that in the 1980s many obstacles remained to creating a common market and that as a result Europe was continuing to lose out to its competitors. Discussion on removing barriers in such areas as health and safety standards, environmental regulations and technical specifications had often got hopelessly bogged down.

'Completing the internal market' thus was a major new initiative by the Commission to try and create a new impetus to the process. The following COM Documents outline the basic strategy to the new approach, and the progress of the initiative:

1. COM(85)310 final, Completing the internal market. White Paper from the Commission to the European Council (Milan, 28

and 29 June 1985). This was then also published in the Document series in 1985 with the same title.
2. COM(86)300 final, First report from the Commission to the Council and the European Parliament on the implementation of the Commission's White Paper on completing the internal market.
3. COM(87)203 final, Second report. . . .
4. COM(88)134 final, Third report. . . .

Published with the Document categorization in 1986 was a report by the Netherlands Scientific Council for Government Policy called *Completing the internal market for industrial products.*

For an introduction to the overall concept of 'completing the internal market' you are referred to *European Documentation,* 3/1988.

Subcontracting terminology metal sector

The first edition of this title was issued in 1981 in six languages. In 1984 a second edition was published by OOPEC in a single nine-language volume. The aim of the volume is to aid contractors and subcontractors who wish to establish contacts across national boundaries by producing a multilingual technical guide. The guide also serves as a basic classification of products and operation and production machinery in the subcontracting sector.

The Terminology Department of the Council of Ministers, it should be noted, produced in 1984 the first part of a glossary to harmonize Community terminology in the field of technical barriers to trade (see Chapter 8).

Operations of the European Community concerning small and medium-sized enterprises and craft industry: practical handbook

The first edition of this title was issued in 1983, the 'Year of the Small and Medium-Sized Enterprises'. It was compiled by the Permanent Office of the French Organization of Chambers of Commerce, with support from the Commission. It was issued under the imprint of the Commission but not published by OOPEC. A second edition was issued in 1984 under the same arrangements. A third edition, revised by the same author, was published with the Document categorization by OOPEC in 1986. A fourth edition was published in 1988.

It lives up to its brief of being a 'practical handbook' as it is up to date and written clearly and concisely. While it is specifically aimed at the small and medium-sized enterprises sector the information it contains would be of interest to a much wider group of people.

The *Practical handbook* has the following sections:

1. Grants and subsidies

2. The lending instruments
3. Research and innovation
4. The internal market of the European Community
5. Community action on external markets
6. Traineeships, scholarships and exchanges in the Community.

In the foreword to the 1986 edition Abel Matutes, the Commissioner responsible for small and medium-sized enterprises, says that the *Practical handbook* is 'only the first part, albeit the cornerstone, of a new policy of communication and information directed at SMEs in the Community'. An integral part of this initiative was the setting up in 1987 of thirty-nine pilot 'Centres for European Business Information' in member states. The first four United Kingdom centres are in London, Birmingham, Glasgow and Newcastle. COM(88)161 final suggests that there should be a progressive extension of the project. In the United Kingdom they are generally known as European Business Information Centres (EBICs). They are designed to provide information on the EC likely to be of interest to small and medium-sized enterprises, and to communicate to the Commission the views of this sector. It remains to be seen whether the Task Force: Small and Medium-sized Enterprises in DG III will produce a range of documentation especially for the centres, or whether they will rely on existing print-based and computer-based sources.[1]

It has already been mentioned that the EC designated 1983 as 'European Year of Small and Medium-Sized Enterprises'. In association with that an internal document (III/396/83) circulated widely called *Small and medium-sized enterprises and the craft industry in the EEC*. The reports of the inaugural and closing conferences that marked the year were issued in publications from the Economic and Social Committee but in association with the Commission and the European Parliament.

A brochure called *Business in Europe* outlining the commitment of the EC to small and medium-sized enterprises and the work of the Task Force was issued by OOPEC in 1987.

In addition to the DG III titles with the Document categorization already referred to the following titles should be noted:

1. *The Community fertilizer industry*, 1985
2. *Notice to applicants: For marketing authorizations for proprietary medicinal products in the member states of the European Community on the use of the new multi-state procedure created by Council Directive 83/570/EEC*, 1986.

DG IV COMPETITION

The following series are covered:

1. Reports on Concentration and Competition
2. Studies: Competition – Approximation of Legislation series

Reports on Concentration and Competition

This is a generic title given to a collection of reports which have been commissioned by officials of DG IV as part of a programme of study of the evolution of concentration and the competitive process in the member states of the EC.

Evolution of Concentration and Competition series

The first reports commissioned by DG IV were issued as limited-distribution documents from 1973. From 1975 reports were issued as sales publications, but it was only in 1978 that the reports published were given a number placed in the Evolution of Concentration and Competition series. The last title in this series was published in 1983 (no. 51). Titles in this series can be found in the *Catalogue of Publications* and are priced publications from OOPEC available only in the language of the author.

Evolution of Concentration and Competition series: Working Papers

This series began in 1980, and essence contains reports similar to those included in the series above but which were not formally published. They were also numbered, so for the period 1980–83 there were two parallel numbered series with very similar titles. The Working Papers were not listed in the OOPEC *Catalogue of Publications* but were listed in an annex in the annual *Report on competition policy* from 1980 until 1985. Between 1980 and 1985 eighty-four titles were issued in this series, available directly from DG IV.

Document categorization

Since 1983 reports have been issued with the Document categorization as priced publications by OOPEC and listed in the *Catalogue of Publications*. They are no longer given a number and are not explicitly part of a series. However, it is usually made clear in the preface that these reports are part of the continuing series on concentration and competition. Since 1983 the following titles have been published:

1. *Concentration, competition and competitiveness in the automotive components industries of the European Community*, 1983
2. *Entwicklung von Konzentration, Wettbewerb und Wettbewerbs-fähigkeit in den Sektoren Papiererzeugung und -verarbeitung in der Europäischen Gemeinschaft*, 1983
3. *The textile machinery industry in the EEC*, 1984
4. *Concentration, competition and competitiveness in the beverages industries of the European Community*, 1984

5. *L'Industrie européenne du matériel optique: concentration-concurrence–compétitivité*, 1985
6. *The European consumer electronics industry*, 1985
7. *The Community's pharmaceutical industry*, 1985
8. *The insurance industry in the countries of the EEC; structure, conduct and performance*, 1985
9. *The tourism sector in the Community: a study of concentration, competition and competitiveness*, 1985
10. *Die Aussenhandels unternehmen in der Europäischen Gemeinschaft: Funktionen, Strukturen, Wettbewerb*, 1985
11. *Comparaison de la situation concurrentielle des enterprises privées et publiques dans trois secteurs industriels de la CEE*, 1986
12. *Kriterien zur wettbewerbspolitischen Beurteilung der Grundung von Gemeinschaftsunternehmen: eine Analyse aus der Sicht der Wettbewerbsregeln der Europäischen Gemeinschaft*, 1986
13. *Minority share acquisition: the impact upon competition*, 1986
14. *Definition of the relevant market in Community competition policy*, 1986
15. *Compétition européenne et coopération entre enterprises en matière de recherche–développement*, 1986
16. *Franchising in ausgewählten Bereichen des Handels in der gemeinschaft-wettbewerbspolitische Analyse*, 1986
17. *Die Konzentration der Konsumgüterdistribution in der Gemeinschaft und ihre Auswirkungen auf die Nachfragemacht*, 1986
18. *Analyse des politiques de contrôle des prix dans certains secteurs sous l'angle de la concurrence et des échanges intra-communautaires*, 1986
19. *Kollektive Marktbeherrschung. Das Konzept und seine Anwendbarkeit für die Wettbewerbspolitik*, 1986
20. *La prise en compte de l'élément aide des prêts à taux réduits aux entreprises de la Communauté*, 1987
21. *The EEC telecommunications industry. Competition, concentration and competitiveness. The adhesion of Portugal and Spain*, 1987
22. *The measurement of the aid element of state acquisitions of company capital. Evolution of concentration and competition*, 1987
23. *Predatory pricing*, 1987
24. *The likely impact of deregulation on industrial structures and competition in the Community, Final report*, 1987

Studies: Competition – Approximation of Legislation series

This was a further series of numbered reports commissioned by DG IV from outside sources, and published by OOPEC as priced publications, usually in a selection of languages. From 1978 to 1983 the following titles were published:

1. (31) *Control of securities markets in the European Economic Community*, 1978
2. (32) *Supervision of securities markets in the member states of the European Economic Community. Individual country studies. Part I: Belgium, Federal Republic of Germany, Denmark, Ireland, France*, 1978
3. (33) *Supervision of the securities markets in the member states of the European Community. Report on the national systems of control. Part II: United Kingdom, Italy, Luxembourg, Netherlands. Annex: USA*, 1980
4. (34) *Les problèmes résultant de la responsabilité extra-contractuelle concomitante de la Communauté et d'un Etat membre*, 1980
5. (35) *The suitability of concentration measures for EEC competition policy*, 1983.

Competition law in the EEC and in the ECSC

The first edition of this title was published in 1972 to coincide with the first *Report on competition policy*. Replacement editions have been published in 1981 and 1986. It is a priced publication available from OOPEC in all Community languages.

The book contains all the EC regulations in the area of competition in force at the time of compilation.

A related title was published with the Document categorization in 1987 called *Competition rules in the EEC and the ECSC applicable (in)to state aids*.

Note: The annual *Report on competition policy* is compiled within DG IV but finalized and issued through the Secretariat-General. It is described in Chapter 4.

DG V EMPLOYMENT, SOCIAL AFFAIRS AND EDUCATION

The following series are covered:

1. *Social Europe/Social Europe: Supplement*
2. Studies – Social Policy series
3. *InforMISEP*
4. *ELISE News*
5. Programme of Research and Actions on the Development of the Labour Market
6. *Higher education in the European Community – student handbook*
7. *Directory of higher education institutions*
8. *ERASMUS newsletter*
9. Studies – Education series

10. *Information Bulletin of the Steel Industry Safety and Health Commission*
11. *Comparative tables of the social security schemes in the member states of the European Community*
12. *Compendium of Community Provisions on Social Security*
13. Social Security for Migrant Workers
14. Titles with the Document categorization.

Social Europe

This journal began in 1983 as a means whereby DG V could convey to the general informed public its current areas of concern. It is a priced publication available in single issues or on subscription from OOPEC and is published in English, French and German editions.

In 1983 there were two sample issues published. From 1984 there have been three issues a year. The subjects covered in articles include:

1. Employment and the labour market
2. Education
3. Vocational training
4. Industrial relations
5. Social measures
6. Social impact of new technologies
7. Equal treatment for men and women
8. European Social Fund
9. ECSC readaptation
10. Social security
11. Young people
12. Migrants
13. Handicapped.

Social Europe is divided into three parts:

1. Actions and guidelines
2. Analyses, debates and studies
3. Recent developments.

Actions and guidelines
These are short articles giving an overview of developments and current events, which can include the decisions of recent relevant Council meetings and Commission initiatives. The citing of any related bibliographical references is somewhat erratic, although by 1987 it was usually possible to deduce how to gain further information. The individual named author of an article is given in some cases.

Analyses, debates and studies
These are short articles reporting on recent conferences and commissioned research studies. Many of the latter are now published within the Document categorization series.

Recent developments

This reports on two distinct topics. First, there is a section on employment policy initiatives in the member states covering regularly such topics as aid to the unemployed, training, job creation, special categories of workers and placement. The information in this section comes from MISEP, a mutual information system set up by the Commission to circulate news of national employment initiatives around the EC. A selection of the information submitted to MISEP is reprinted in *Social Europe* (see *InforMISEP* below). Second, there is a section on recent developments in the area of new technology and social change in the member states. This covers recent national government initiatives, the attitudes of the two sides of industry, recent research studies, and experiences in specific sectors such as banking and retail. The information is prepared by the Commission on the basis of information provided by the EPOS network of correspondents. EPOS stands for European Pool of Studies and Analyses, and is made up of one expert per member state, who send in national reports to the Commission. Summaries of these reports appear in *Social Europe*. The full reports can be made available on request to the editor of *Social Europe*.

In addition there is an occasional statistical section in *Social Europe*. This is claimed to be an annual feature although it did not appear in 1987. It did appear however in nos 1/84, 1/85 and 2/86, containing statistics derived from Eurostat in the areas of population, education, employment, unemployment, industrial relations, working conditions, incomes, labour costs, standard of living and social protection.

Individual articles in *Social Europe* are not generally long enough to be indexed in EC bibliographical publications. *European Access* (see Appendix 5) does index all the articles.

Social Europe: Supplement

A number of supplements to the journal *Social Europe* are issued each year. Each *Supplement* deals with a subject in depth and can be purchased individually from OOPEC. Alternatively *Social Europe* and *Social Europe: Supplement* can be purchased in a joint subscription. Each *Supplement* is listed in the OOPEC *Catalogue of Publications* and indexed in *Publications and Documents of the EC received by the Library* and *SCAD Bulletin*. They are published in English, French and German editions. *Social Europe: Supplement* began in 1984 and issues have been numbered from 1986. Since 1984 the following have been issued:

1984

1. *Education, vocational training and youth policy. Policies for transition*
2. *Technological change and social adjustment*
3. *New technologies and social change*. Special issue 1983/84
4. *Education, vocational training and youth policy. Informatics and*

education – Report of the European Seminar of Marseille, 7–9 December 1983

5. *Education, vocational training and youth policy. Girls and transition.*

1985

1. *Education, vocational training and youth policy. Education for transition – the curriculum challenge*
2. *New technologies and social change. Office automation*
3. *Education and vocational training within the European Community. Activities of the Commission of the European Communities in 1983 and 1984*
4. *New technologies and social change. Telecommunication*
5. *Programme of research and actions on the development of the labour market: studies during 1981–1983*
6. *New information technologies and the school systems*
7. *Vocational guidance in the European Community*
8. *Youth pay and employers' recruitment practice for young people in the Community. Report of a conference held at Farnham Castle, Surrey, UK, June 1985.*

1986

1. *New technology and social change – manufacturing automation*
2. *New technology and social change – ten years of Community policy on equal opportunities for men and women*
3. *Youth training in the European Community*
4. *Recent progress made in introducing new information technologies into education*
5. *Youth initiatives in the European Community – 'Info-Action 1985' Conference*
6. *The software industry*
7. *The social integration of disabled people.*

1987

1. *Information technology and social change in Spain and Portugal*
2. *Developments in the introduction of new information technologies in education*
3. *Activities of the Commission of the European Communities in the fields of education and training during 1985 and 1986*
4. *Education and vocational guidance services for the 14–25 age-group in the European Community*
5. *Transition of young people from education to adult and working life.*

Studies – Social Policy series

A series of one-off titles published by OOPEC as priced publications covering a wide range of subjects of interest to DG V. They were mainly the results of commissioned research from people outside the Commission. Since 1978 the following Studies have been published:

1. (39) *The cost of hospitalization: micro-economic approach to the problems involved,* 1979
2. (40) *Problems and prospects of collective bargaining in the EEC Member States,* 1979
3. (41) –
4. (42) *The European labour market. Recent studies on employment issues in the European Community,* 1980.

Reports on general subjects were published in several language editions, while reports relating to a particular country were published in only a small number of language editions. No new titles in this series have been published since 1980.

InforMISEP

MISEP stands for Mutual Information System on Employment Policies. National correspondents in each of the member states send in details of new initiatives and developments in the field of employment policy, to aid their counterparts and Commission officials in their decision-making. The correspondents are usually civil servants from the employment ministries in the Member States.

The Secretariat for MISEP is based at the European Centre for Work and Society, who undertake the work on behalf of DG V. The address of the MISEP Secretariat is:

> MISEP Technical Secretariat
> European Centre for Work and Society
> PO Box 3073
> NL-6202 NB Maastricht
> The Netherlands
> Telephone: 043–216724

The public manifestation of MISEP is the quarterly periodical *InforMISEP*. This started publication in 1983, and is free and available direct from DG V (V/A/1) or the Secretariat.

Each issue covers developments as reported by the correspondents under headings such as:

1. Overall developments
2. Employment maintenance
3. Aid to the unemployed
4. Training/retraining/occupational mobility
5. Job creation
6. Placement
7. Special categories of workers
8. Working time.

Bibliographical references to national publications are not given. Some of the reports listed in *InforMISEP* are reprinted in Part 3 of *Social Europe* (see above).

MISEP has also compiled a Basic Information Report for most member states. These reports were published with the Document categorization in 1985. The countries covered were Ireland, the Federal Republic of Germany, the United Kingdom, France, Italy, The Netherlands, Greece, Luxembourg and Belgium. These were English, French and German editions published in all cases. Updated reports, and reports for Denmark, Spain and Portugal, were planned for 1988.

Each existing Basic Information Report describes the structure and content of employment policy in the Member States as in 1983. Each volume follows the same structure and contains the same basic information:

1. Institutions
2. Procedures
3. Legal framework
4. Measures.

InforMISEP and the report in *Social Europe* are thus updatings of the information in the Basic Information Report.

There was an index of articles published in *InforMISEP* from 1983 to 1987 (nos 1–18) in no. 19, September 1987. The information generated by the MISEP system is now available on an online database through the EC host organization (ECHO).

ELISE News

ELISE stands for European Network for the Exchange of Information and Experience on Local Employment Initiatives. As part of their work to stimulate employment prospects DG V set up the ELISE network in 1985 as a coordinating centre on local employment initiatives. The network operates a library and information service and seeks to bring together specialists and organizations with an interest in new initiatives in employment creation.

The first issue of *ELISE News* was Issue 0, October–December 1985. Quarterly issues appeared in 1986. At first it was available free of charge from DG V but as the network became established this was changed. From 1987 the title was changed to *Feedback-Elise* and it became a priced publication only available from:

ELISE
38 rue Vilain XIII
B-1050 Brussels
Belgium
Telephone: 02/6472400

The employment creation potential of local employment initiatives was the subject of considerable study by DG V during the 1980s. Some of the research conducted was issued in the series Programme of Research and Actions on the Development of the Labour Market (see below).

Programme of Research and Actions on the Development of the Labour Market

The Commission has undertaken a large programme of research in the area of employment and the labour market since 1975. Much of the research is undertaken by outside individuals or organizations on behalf of DG V. Until the development of the Document categorization these research reports were not formally published.

In the Studies – Social Policy series, no. 42 was called *The European labour market. Recent studies on employment issues in the European Community*, 1980. This contained review articles and summaries of many of the research projects undertaken in the first years of the Programme. From this source it was possible to obtain the full reports direct from DG V.

It was not until the development of the Document categorization that it became possible to track down these reports systematically in EC bibliographical sources. Since 1984 those reports which are published in the Document categorization are listed in the *Catalogue of Publications*. Most are only issued in one language edition.

The following reports have been published since 1984:

1. *New types of employment initiatives especially as relating to women*, 1984
2. *Prospects for workers' cooperatives in Europe*, 1984, 3 vols
3. *Local employment initiatives. Local enterprise agencies in Great Britain. A study of their impact, operational lessons and policy implications*, 1985
4. *Local employment initiatives. A manual on intermediary and support organizations. Main report*, 1985
5. *Local employment initiatives. Report on a series of local consultations held in European countries, 1982–83*, 1985
6. *Local employment initiatives. An evaluation of support agencies*, 1985
7. *Initiatives locales en matière d'emploi. Problèmes et opportunités des petites enterprises nouvellement créées*, 1985
8. *Development of new growth areas – 'Workers' cooperatives and their environment: comparative analysis with a view to job creation'. Support for worker cooperatives in the United Kingdom, Ireland and the Netherlands*, 1985
9. *Développement de nouveaux domaines de croissance de l'emploi*

- *'Les coopératives de production et leur environnement: analyse comparative en vue de la création d'emplois'*, 1985
10. *Rôle des coopératives de production dans le maintien et la création d'emplois*, 1985
11. *Comparative follow-up and evaluation of current employment measures*, 1985
12. *Wage differential between young and adults and its relation with youth unemployment*, 1985
13. *Inflation, employment and income distribution in the recession*, 1985
14. *Developing support structure for workers' cooperatives*, 1985
15. *Les difficultés d'emploi des jeunes: des solutions possibles – Le différentiel des salaires entre jeunes et adultes et la chômage des jeunes – étude monographique de la situation française*, 1985
16. *The extent and kind of voluntary work in the EEC. Question surrounding the relationship between volunteering and employment*, 1985
17. *Costs of unemployment. Main report*, 1986
18. *The quantitative and qualitative significance of the emergence of local initiatives for employment creation*, 1986
19. *Forms of organization, type of employment, working conditions and industrial relations in cooperatives, any collectiveness or other self-managing structures of the EEC*, 1986
20. *The role of local authorities in promoting local employment initiatives. Main report*, 1986
21. *The viability of employment initiatives involving women*, 1986
22. *Relevé des expériences de création d'emplois non-conventionnelles*, 1986
23. *Cooperation in the field of employment. Local employment initiatives. Report on a second series of local consultations held in European countries, 1984–1985. Final report*, 1986
24. *Job creation in small and medium sized enterprises. Main report*, 1987, 3 vols
25. *Report on a third series of local consultations held in European countries, 1986. Final report*, 1987
26. *Le marché de l'emploi au Portugal*, 1987
27. *Costs of unemployment. Main report. Annex on social costs of unemployment*, 1987
28. *Technique d'intervention des agents de développement local pour la promotion des initiatives locales de création d'emplois (IIe). Rapport final*, 1987, 2 vols
29. *New forms and new areas of employment growth. A comparative study*, 1987 (Also separate reports for Germany, The Netherlands and Italy)
30. *Analysis of the experiences of and problems encountered by worker*

take-overs of companies in difficulty or bankrupt, 1987

31. *Analysis of the dynamics of the job creation process in the United States and an evaluation of medium and long-term prospects*, 1987, 3 vols

32. *Very-long-term unemployment. Main report*, 1988

33. *Chômeurs créateurs. Analyse des origines et motivations des créateurs d'entreprises bénéficiaires de programmes publics de soutien à la création d'emplois dans la Communauté européenne. Rapport final*, 1988

34. *Youth unemployment policies*, 1988.

It should be noted that some reports commissioned by DG V in the Programme are still not formally published. As a guide it is said that those which feature in an article in *Social Europe* are subsequently published.

Higher education in the European Community – student handbook

The first edition of this title was published in 1977. Further editions were published in 1979, 1981 and 1985. The fifth edition was published in 1988 with the title *Higher education in the European Community – student handbook: a directory of courses and institutions in twelve countries*. The first three editions were published exclusively by OOPEC as a priced publication. The fourth and fifth editions were co-published by OOPEC and a number of publishing houses in the member states. In the United Kingdom the publisher was Kogan Page. The aim of the co-publication was to ensure effective distribution to a wide audience. The fourth edition was available in English, Danish, German, Greece, French, Italian and Dutch editions, the fifth also in Spanish and Portuguese.

The work of compiling this large directory of courses and institutions in the member states is undertaken by the Deutscher Akademischer Austauschdienst on behalf of DG V.

The aim of the *Student handbook* is to help students locate and plan study on other member states. National correspondents from each country supply the information. In the United Kingdom information is supplied by the British Council.

The bulk of the *Student handbook* is made up of similarly structured accounts for each member state. The following headings are used:

1. Organization of higher education
2. Admission and registration
3. Knowledge of the language of instruction
4. Financial assistance and scholarships
5. Entry and residence regulations
6. Social aspects (social security and health insurance; advisory

services; student employment; student organizations; cost of living; accommodation; services for students; facilities for disabled students)
7. Sources of information
8. Appendices (addresses; bibliography; survey of courses of study at higher education institutions; glossary).

In addition to the information above, the later editions of the *Student handbook* also contain information about:

1. European University Institute, Florence
2. College of Europe, Bruges
3. Grants from the EC for the development of joint study programmes
4. Information centres for the academic recognition of diplomas and of periods of study in the European Community.

Directory of higher education institutions

The first edition of this title was published by OOPEC as a priced publication in 1984, available in the seven official Community languages at the time. It is seen as a sister publication to the *Student handbook*. Again the information was prepared by national correspondents designated by the Ministries of Education in the member states. The task of coordinating this information was undertaken by the Office for Cooperation in Education, on behalf of the Commission.

The aim of the *Directory* is to encourage contacts between academic institutions of higher education in the member states. In essence it is a directory of addresses of higher education institutions. For each member state the following information is given:

1. Organization of higher education
2. List of individual institutions with their contact address and the main academic subjects covered
3. Other useful addresses
4. Bibliography.

A new edition is expected in 1988 or 1989.

ERASMUS Newsletter

For a number of years the Commission has been actively promoting the development of Joint Study Programmes between institutions of higher education in the member states. To help promote the joint Study Programme concept DG V, with the help of the Office for Cooperation in Education, issued a newsletter called *DELTA: the Joint Study Programme Newsletter of the Commission*. The first issue of this appeared in August 1982; subsequent issues appeared in June 1983 and thereafter two issues a year until 1/87. With no. 2/87 the title was changed to

ERASMUS Newsletter. This now appears twice-yearly as a priced publication from OOPEC.

In 1987 the Education Ministers of the EC agreed to the setting up of the ERASMUS Programme (European Community Action Scheme for the Mobility of University Students). ERASMUS brought together and expanded some of the schemes already existing, and also established new programmes under the following headings:

1. European University Network. Grants to be paid to encourage the development of joint programmes between institutions of higher education to encourage academic staff mobility, and to help establish contacts
2. Student grants. Grants to help students work in other member states for a recognized period of study. The grant is intended to cover 'mobility costs' and not to replace any existing grant they might receive
3. Academic recognition. Grants to aid ECTS (European Community Course Credit Transfer Scheme) and NARIC (EC Network of National Academic Recognition Information Centres)
4. Additional measures.

The function of *ERASMUS Newsletter* is to report on the developments in this field. This involves news articles, case studies of existing programmes, reports and announcements on conferences and practical advice on the setting up and sustaining of contacts amongst academic institutions in the member states. An *ERASMUS handbook* is planned.

Studies – Education Series

Since 1978 the following titles have been published in this series, as priced publications from OOPEC, and available in most Community languages:

1. (7) *Joint programmes of study. An instrument of European cooperation in higher education,* 1979
2. (8) *Inservice education and training of teachers in the European Community,* 1979
3. (9) *Equality of education and training for girls (10–18 years),* 1979
4. (10) *Academic recognition of diplomas in the European Community. Present state and prospects,* 1979
5. (11) *Special education in the European Community,* 1980
6. (12) *Pre-school education in the European Community,* 1980
7. (13) *The child between,* 1984.

Since 1985 the Document categorization has been used to publish one-off reports in the education field (see below).

Information Bulletin of the Steel Industry Safety and Health Commission

The first issue of the *Bulletin* appeared in 1982. Issues 2, 3 and 4 appeared in 1983, issue 5 in 1984, a joint issue 6–7 in 1985 and issue 8 in 1986. It is published by OOPEC but would seem to be available free of charge from DG XIII, which is the authorization service for the title. DG V is the author service.

The Steel Industry Safety and Health Commission was set up in 1965 to allow for the exchange of experiences in the field of occupational health and safety in the steel industry, and to draw up recommendations for future codes of good practice. The *Bulletin* is issued to further the aims of the Commission. It contains details of research projects set up, reports the results of some of these projects and discusses accidents which have taken place in steelworks in member states and action taken to prevent the accident recurring.

Other SISHC reports are published as EUR Reports (see the section on DG XIII in this chapter). The annual publication *Report of the Steel Industry Safety and Health Commission,* which was published by OOPEC until 1978, is now an internal publication, and not publicly available.

Comparative tables of the social security schemes in the member states of the European Communities: general scheme (employees in industry and commerce)

This title is published every two years as a priced publication from OOPEC. The thirteenth edition, covering the situation at 1 July 1984, was published with the Document categorization in 1985. Earlier editions were available in all Community languages, but the thirteenth edition was only published in English and French editions. The fourteenth edition covering the situation at 1 July 1986 was published with the Document categorization in 1988.

The volume is divided into the following sections:

1. Introduction
2. Organization
3. Financing
4. Health care
5. Sickness – cash benefits
6. Maternity
7. Invalidity
8. Old age
9. Survivors
10. Employment injuries and occupational diseases

11. Family benefits
12. Unemployment.

It should be noted that the tables list the principles and details of social protection provision, not the amount of finance involved.

Compendium of Community provisions on social security

The first edition of this title was published in 1981 (cover date 1980). The first updating of that edition covered the situation as at 30 June 1981 (published 1982) and the second updating as at 31 December 1981 (published 1983).

A second edition of the *Compendium* was published in 1984 (cover date 1983), with an updating supplement, covering the situation as at 30 June 1985, published in 1986. All editions and updatings have been priced publications from OOPEC available in all Community languages. A third edition was expected in 1988.

The *Compendium* replaces the title *Practical handbook of social security for employed persons and their families moving within the Community*, which was a looseleaf publication first issued in 1973 and kept up to date until 1979.

The *Compendium* brings together the official texts, with commentary, relating to social security for migrant workers. It contains the details of the basic EEC Regulations 1408/71 and 574/72 and subsequent amendments, the judgments of the Court of Justice and the decisions and recommendations of the Administrative Commission with regard to social security for migrant workers. It is worth pointing out the meaning of the term 'migrant workers'. In the English language it is often meant to indicate workers from countries outside the EC who enter the EC to work. In the EC meaning of the term it means also nationals from one member state who go to work in another member state.

In addition to the information mentioned above the *Compendium* also includes:

1. List of model forms drafted by the Administrative Commission on social security for migrant workers. This includes the well-known EIII – certificate of entitlement to benefits in kind during a stay in a member state
2. Alphabetical subject index
3. Table of Council and Commission regulations, with *OJ* references
4. Table of decisions of the Administrative Commission, with *OJ* references
5. Table of case-law of the Court of Justice, with *OJ* and ECR reference.

Social Security for Migrant Workers

These are a series of practical guides giving social security advice to nationals from one member state who go to work in another. There is a separate guide for each member state. During the 1980s the following guides were issued:

1. *Greece*, 1982
2. *Belgium*, 1985
3. *Denmark*, 1985
4. *France*, 1985
5. *Germany*, 1985
6. *Ireland*, 1985
7. *Luxembourg*, 1985
8. *The Netherlands*, 1985
9. *United Kingdom and Gibraltar*, 1986.

Editions for Italy, Portugal and Spain are planned. In addition, more specialized guides are published occasionally. For example, in 1984 there was a guide for persons staying temporarily in another member state. Titles are published by OOPEC but are unpriced.

Titles with the Document categorization

Since 1984 the following English language titles have been issued with the Document categorization of which DG V is the 'author service' (the list does not include titles issued in the subseries Programme of Research and Actions on the Development of the Labour Market which are noted above):

1. *Report on the social implications of introducing new technology in the banking sector*, 1984
2. *Cost containment in health care: the experience of twelve European countries (1977–1983)*, 1984
3. *New information technologies and small-scale job creation. Final report*, 1984
4. *Day-care facilities and services for children under the age of three in the European Community*, 1984
5. *Women and job desegregation in banking: the status of women, their roles, change*, 1984
6. *The law of collective agreements in the countries of the European Community*, 1984
7. *Work-sharing for young persons: recent experiences in Great Britain, the Federal Republic of Germany and the Netherlands*, 1984
8. *The prevention and settlement of industrial conflict in the Community member states*, 1984
9. *Overview – disability and employment*, 1984

10. *Teaching and training the handicapped through the new information technology*, 1984

11. *The economic integration of the disabled: an analysis of measures and trends in member states*, 1984

12. *Efforts to equalize opportunities for young women – case studies on the impact of new technologies on the vocational training for technicians*, 1984

13. *Office automation and work for women*, 1984

14. *European women in paid employment 1984 – do they feel discriminated against and vulnerable at work? Are they equipped to take up the challenge of technology?*, 1984

15. *Work-sharing and the reduction and reorganization of working time at firm level: Anglo-Italian-French case studies. Final report*, 1985

16. *Disabled people and their employment*, 1985

17. *MISEP – mutual information system on employment policies*, 1985 (separate publications for Ireland, Germany, United Kingdom, France, Italy, the Netherlands, Greece, Luxembourg, and Belgium)

18. *Microcomputers in the administration and management processes in smaller business – the emerging experience in EEC countries*, 1985

19. *Employment in retail trade in EC countries*, 1985

20. *Health care professions in the member states of the European Community: education and training*, 1985

21. *Literacy training in Europe. A comparative analysis of the most effective and innovatory literacy schemes being implemented in member states by the authorities or private agencies*, 1985

22. *Medicine: statistics of smoking in the member states of the European Community*, 1985

23 *Legal and administrative barriers to youth exchange in the European Community*, 1985

24 *Analysis of current needs and initiatives in the field of adaptation of vocational training for young handicapped people to the new employment realities. Final report*, 1986

25 *The extent and kind of voluntary work in the EEC*, 1986

26 *Employment and housing renovation in Europe*, 1986

27 *Higher education in the European Community, Recognition of study abroad in the European Community*, 1986

28 *The social aspects of technological developments relating to the European machine tool industry. Final report*, 1986

29 *The Greek education system*, 1987

30 *Higher education in the European Community. Study abroad in the European Community*, 1987

31 *Non-salaried working women in Europe*, 1987

32 *The re-insertion of women in working life*, 1987

33 *The specific training needs of immigrant women. Existing and recommended measures to fulfil them,* 1987

34 *Diversification of vocational choices for women,* 1987

35 *Implementation of the equality directive,* 1987

36 *Employment and positive action for women in the television organizations of the EEC member states,* 1987

37 *How women are represented in television programmes in the EEC: Part one: Images of women in new, advertising and series and serials,* 1987; *Part two: Positive action and strategies. Evaluation of and lessons to be learned from alternative programmes,* 1987; *Part three: EEC television and the image of women,* 1987

38 *A social survey in maritime transport,* 1987

39 *Educational and vocational guidance services for the 14–25 age group,* 1988, 4 vols.

Note: The annual *Report on social developments* is compiled within DG V but finalized and issued through the Secretariat-General. It is described in Chapter 4.

DG VI AGRICULTURE

The following series are covered:

1. Information on Agriculture
2. Titles with the Document categorization
3. Recueil des Actes Agricoles
4. *Farm accountancy data network*
5. Green Europe: Newsletter on the Common Agricultural Policy
6. Green Europe: Newsflash
7. *Agricultural markets: prices.*

Information on Agriculture

This was a series of studies on a wide range of topics undertaken by outside organizations and researchers on behalf of the Commission. Between 1976 and 1984 eighty-nine titles were published by OOPEC in this irregular series. The majority were only published in a single language edition. From 1980 until 1984 the following titles were published (English titles are given but note of the language is made if the single-language edition is other than English).

1. (71) *Water content of frozen or deep-frozen poultry – comparison of methods of determination,* 1980
2. (72) *The problems of oriental tobacco production in the EC,* 1980
3. (73) *Factors influencing ownership, tenancy, mobility and use of farmland in Denmark,* 1980

4. (74) *Factors influencing ownership, tenancy, mobility and use of farmland in the United Kingdom,* 1980
5. (75) *Potato products: production and markets in the EC,* 1980
6. (76) *Factors influencing ownership, tenancy, mobility and use of farmland in France,* 1980 (French language)
7. (77) *A systematic approach to agricultural forecasts 1985 for the European Community of Nine,* 1980
8. (78) *Factors influencing ownership, tenancy, mobility and use of farmland in Belgium and Luxembourg,* 1980 (Dutch language)
9. (79) *Cold storage warehousing in the EC – an inter-country comparison,* 1980
10. (80) *A prognosis and simulation model for the EC cereals market. Part II: conception of the model and quantification of factors determining the demand for cereals,* 1980
11. (81) *Factors influencing ownership, tenancy, mobility and use of farmland in Italy,* 1980 (Italian language)
12. (82) *Factors influencing ownership, tenancy, mobility and use of farmland in the Netherlands,* 1980 (Dutch language)
13. (83) *Factors influencing ownership, tenancy, mobility and use of farmland in the Federal Republic of Germany,* 1980 (German language)
14. (84) *Factors influencing ownership, tenancy, mobility and use of farmland in Ireland,* 1980
15. (85) *Energy consumption per tonne of competing agricultural products available in the EC,* 1981
16. (86) *Factors influencing ownership, tenancy, mobility and use of farmland in the member states of the European Community,* 1982
17. (87) *Comparative analysis of the regional agricultural structure of Spain, France, Greece, Italy and Portugal in the light of the enlargement of the EEC II: structure and factors: land labour and capital and results of the production system. A: general report,* 1983 (French language)
18. (88) As (87) *B: Annexes to the general report,* 1983 (French language)
19. (89) *Integrated regional development programmes,* 1984

After 1984 titles from this series were assigned to the Document categorization (see below).

Titles with the Document categorization

Since 1984 the following titles have been issued with the Document categorization of which DG VI is the 'author service':

1. *Synthèse – les coûts de production du vin de table en Espagne, France*

et Italie – analyse au niveau régional. Première partie: la production du raisin, 1985

2. *Development strategy for the agro-food industries in the Mediterranean regions of the European Community,* 1985
3. *The Farm Accountancy Data Network. Farm accounts results 1981/82–1982/83,* 1985
4. *The production and use of cereal and potato starch in the EEC,* 1986
5. *Réseau d'information comptable agricole. Résultats comptables agricoles – 1982-1983/1983-1984,* 1986
6. *Study of outside gainful activities of farmers and their spouses in the EEC,* 1986
7. *Farm Accountancy Data Network. Handbook of legislation instructions – notes for guidance,* 1987
8. *Les coûts de production des principaux produits agricoles dans la Communauté européenne,* 1987.

Recueil des actes agricoles

In 1985 OOPEC began the publication of this series with the Document categorization. The series consists of thirty-four titles. Essentially it is a reprinting of the secondary legislation of the EC in the agricultural field broken down into such areas as:

1. Cereals
2. Rice
3. European Agricultural Guidance and Guarantee Fund
4. Agricultural statistics
5. Structures
6. Fruit and vegetables
7. Veterinary legislation
8. Legislation on plant health
9. Animal feed
10. Seeds and plants
11. Tobacco and hops
12. Oils and fats
13. Dairy products
14. Beef and veal
15. Sheepmeat, pigmeat, etc.
16. Wine
17. Sugar.

As its title suggests, it is a French language publication. It is possible to use a volume to trace references to a particular product and then trace the text of the legislation in the *Official Journal* of another language. A second edition of the series began in 1987.

These volumes covering agricultural secondary legislation are the only part of a former series *Recueil d'actes* that still exist in a publicly available format. *Recueil d'actes* (Collected acts) was a looseleaf set of all the secondary legislation of the EC kept up to date until 1972 in the official Community languages. DG VI decided to maintain the agricultural acts collection internally and it is this which has now been published.

Farm Accountancy Data Network (FADN)

The network was established in the 1960s to gather farm accounts from a sample of individual holdings in member states on a yearly basis.

The detailed results of the annual survey were published until the 1979–80 accounting year. After that the detailed figures have only been available on microfiche. *The agricultural situation in the Community* (see Chapter 4) gives an abbreviated set of the FADN results.

Midway between these two extremes of details is a publication called *The Farm Accountancy Data Network*. The first edition was published in 1984 and covered the accounting years 1978/79–1981/82. An edition covering 1981/82–1982/83 was published in 1985, and since then it has been annual. Since the edition published in 1985 the title has been given the Document categorization.

There is also a *Handbook of legislation instructions – notes for guidance*. The third edition of this title was published in 1981 and a fourth edition was issued in 1984 (although dated 1983). The fourth edition is divided into five sections:

1. (1) Foreword and contents
2. (2) The legislation
3. (3) The farm return
4. (4) The Community typology for agricultural holdings
5. (5) Miscellaneous information (map of FADN, diagram of the organization of the farm accountancy network, Community committee on the FADN, national FADN committees, staff of the Commission and distribution of FADN results).

Revisions of Section 2 have been issued. The first revision, dated November 1984, was published in 1985. A further revision was issued in 1987 with the Document categorization.

Green Europe: Newsletter on the Common Agricultural Policy

The Agricultural Information Service of DG VI first produced the Newsletter in November 1963; 164 issues were published between 1963 and 1978. What was called a 'renovated series' began with no. 165 in 1979, which was, in fact, an index to all the previous issues. Until no. 193, published in 1982, the title stated 'published by the Agricultural Information Service of the Directorate-General for Agriculture'. From 1983 the Agricultural Information Service became part of DG X

Information. Thus *Green Europe: Newsletter on the Common Agricultural Policy* is now strictly a DG X title, although the compilers of a number of the titles in the series are stated as officials in DG VI.

Titles in the series are issued irregularly. Technically *Green Europe: Newsletter* is a free publication although single-copy prices are often printed on issues. This is probably in order to encourage readers to 'value' the publication. In addition, to subscribe to the Newsletter postage has to be paid. The same system applies to *Green Europe: Newsflash* described below.

Each issue is devoted to a single topic relating to the common agricultural policy. A number of issues contain articles reprinted from *The agricultural situation in the Community*. At the back of recent issues is a complete list of all the titles in the series. All are published in all of the official Community languages at the time of publication. Below is a list of titles published in the 'renovated series':

1. (165) *15 years of Green Europe*, 1979
2. (166) *Milk: problem child of European agriculture*, 1979
3. (167) *EEC agriculture: the world dimension*, 1980
4. (168) *European agriculture 1979*, 1980
5. (169) *European agriculture into the nineteen-eighties*, 1980
6. (170) *Agriculture and the problems of surpluses*, 1980
7. (171) *EEC food imports: the New Zealand file*, 1982
8. (172) *Wine in the eighties*, 1980
9. (173) *The agricultural aspects of enlargement of the European Community – Greece*, 1980
10. (174) *The agricultural aspects of enlargement of the European Community – Spain*, 1981
11. (175) *The Common Agricultural Policy and world food shortages. Food aid*, 1981
12. (176) *Aspects of the Common Agricultural Policy of concern to consumers*, 1982
13. (177) *Policy for animal feeding stuffs: the case of cereal 'substitute'*, 1982 (French language only)
14. (178) *The enlargement of the Community*, 1982 (French language only)
15. (179) *The Community's agricultural and food exports*, 1982 (French language only)
16. (180) *A new organization of the markets in sugar as from 1 July 1981*, 1982
17. (181) *A new common agricultural structure policy*, 1982
18. (182) *Financing the market side of the Common Agricultural Policy: EAGGF-Guarantee*, 1982
19. (183) *Coordination of agricultural research in the Community*, 1982
20. (184) *Community food aid*, 1982

49. (213) *Community imports of food and other agricultural products,* 1985
50. (214) *Agricultural aspects of Community enlargement to include Portugal and Spain,* 1986
51. (215) *Food surpluses: disposal for welfare purposes,* 1986
52. (216) *The European Community's food aid,* 1987
53. (217) *Twenty years of European agriculture,* 1987
54. (218) *Cheaper raw materials for Europe's industries: sugar and starch,* 1987
55. (219) *Environment and the CAP,* 1987
56. (220) *Changes to the EEC market organization for milk and milk products,* 1987
57. (221) *Competition policy in agriculture,* 1987.

Green Europe: Newsflash

This title began as *Green Europe: Newsletter in Brief.* The title changed to *Green Europe: Newsflash* with no. 26 in 1984. Up to no. 17, 1982 the title was said to be 'published by the Agricultural Information Service of the Directorate-General for Agriculture'. From no. 18 it has been 'published by the Agricultural Information Service of the Directorate-General for Information'. *Green Europe: Newsflash* is thus, at present, a DG X title.

Each issue of this irregularly produced title is devoted to a topic of current concern in European agriculture. The distinction between the two *Green Europe* titles is not entirely clear, but the impression is that the *Newsletter* generally tends to the reflective, while *Newsflash* covers the latest developments. In some instances the latter comprise reprinting of COM Documents. The annual farm price proposals and eventual settlement are usually printed in *Newsflash.*

Since 1980 the following issues have been published:

1. (12) *A new market organization – mutton and lamb,* 1980
2. (13) *A new start for the common agricultural policy,* 1980
3. (14) *Common agricultural prices 1981/82. Commission proposals,* 1981
4. (15) *Common agricultural prices 1981/1982 – Council's decisions,* 1981
5. (16) *Monetary adaptations and their implications for the common agricultural policy,* 1981
6. (17) *In view of enlargement. Proposals for adaptation of regulations concerning * fruit and vegetables * citrus fruit * wine * olive oil,* 1982
7. (18) *Common agricultural prices 1982/1983. Commission's proposals,* 1982
8. (19) *Agriculture and foreign policy,* 1982

9. (20) *Common agricultural prices 1982/1983 – Council's decisions*, 1982
10. (21) *European Community Commission proposes agricultural prices for 1983/84*, 1982
11. (22) *The political and economical influences affecting the Common Agricultural Policy*, 1983
12. (23) –
13. (24) *European Community Commission proposes agricultural prices for 1984/85*, 1984
14. (25) *The outlook for Europe's agricultural policy*, 1984
15. (26) *Agricultural incomes in the Community in 1983*, 1984
16. (27) *Agricultural prices 1984/1985 and rationalisation of the CAP – Council decisions*, 1984
17. (28) *European Community Commission proposes agricultural prices for 1985/1986*, 1985
18. (29) *1984: Agricultural incomes in the European Community*, 1985
19. (30) *Agricultural prices 1985–1986*, 1985
20. (31) *EEC–USA relations . . .*, 1985
21. (32) *Agricultural incomes in the European Community in 1985 and since 1973*, 1986
22. (33) *Perspectives for the Common Agricultural Policy. The Green Paper of the Commission*, 1985
23. (34) *A future for Community agriculture. Commission guidelines*, 1985
24. (35) *Agricultural prices 1986/1987. Commission proposals*, 1986
25. (36) *Memorandum forestry. Discussion paper on the Community action in the forestry sector*, 1986
26. (37) *Agricultural prices 1986–1987*, 1986
27. (38) *The agreement on agriculture of 16 December 1986*
28. (39) *Agricultural prices 1987/1988 proposals*, 1987
29. (40) *Social aids in agriculture*, 1987
30. (41) *Agricultural prices 1987/1988. Decisions from the Council*, 1987
31. (42) *EAGGF. The European Community's expenditure on the Common Agricultural Policy*, 1988.[2]

Agricultural Markets: Prices

In addition to the statistical titles published by Eurostat there is this title from DG VI which list prices and levies on the following items:

1. Cereals
2. Rice
3. Oils and fats
4. Wine
5. Sugar
6. Isoglucose

7. Pigmeat
8. Eggs
9. Poultry
10. Beef and veal
11. Milk and milk products
12. Sheepmeat.

Until 1980 there were two separate publications covering:

1. Livestock products
2. Vegetable products.

These combined into a single publication from 1981. From 1981 until 1984 it was published ten times a year. Since 1985 it has been a quarterly publication available on subscription from OOPEC. There is also an annual special issue giving a summary of prices from 1973 until the date of publication.

Note: *The agricultural situation in the Community* is an annual account of EC agricultural developments, largely compiled by DG VI but issued through the Secretariat-General. It is described in Chapter 4.

DG VII TRANSPORT

The following series are covered:

1. Europa Transport
2. Miscellaneous.

Europa Transport

This is the title given to a series which is divided into three parts:

1. *Market Developments*
2. *Analysis and Forecasts*
3. *Annual report*.

Together these publications are products of a system for observing transport markets set up in 1978. This covers the carriage of goods by rail, road and inland waterways between member states. The publications giving the results of the observations began in 1981.

Europa Transport: Observation of the Transport Markets – Market Developments

This title is published on a quarterly basis, although only two issues were issued in 1981 and 1984. From no. 1, 1981 until no. 14, 1984 separate language editions were available with a considerable amount of text. From no. 15, 1985 the title became trilingual (English, French, German) and primarily a statistical title.

Europa Transport: Observation of the Transport Markets – Analysis and Forecasts

This has been an annual publication since 1981, although no edition was published in 1986. Up to the 1985 edition the reports gave a description of general trends in transport activity for the past and current year including detailed analysis by mode of transport, goods categories and geographical relations.

The 1987 edition was in a different format – it only related to road transport and, in particular, the share of the Community quota in international intra-Community transport.

Europa Transport: Observation of the Transport Markets – Annual Report

This has been published each year since 1981 and is primarily a statistical publication broken down into forms of transport.

Europa Transport is a priced publication from OOPEC. The whole series of publications are available on subscription and it is also possible to purchase individual parts.

Miscellaneous

Since 1980 two titles have been published in the series Studies – Transport Series. They are:

1. (6) *Reference tariffs for goods transport,* 1982
2. (7) *Road freight transport between EEC member states. A feasibility study for a system of prices indices,* 1982

No further titles in this series have been published and neither have any titles appeared with the Document categorization of which DG VII is the 'author service'.

In 1984 the following one-off title was published by OOPEC as a priced publication in all the official Community languages: *Guide to the provisions applying to the international carriage of passengers by road by means of occasional coach and bus services.*

Also worth mentioning is the title *Transport and European integration* published in 1987 in the series European Perspectives. This is a major academic study of European transport policy.

DG VIII DEVELOPMENT

The following series are covered:

1. *The Courier*
2. Titles with the Document categorization
3. Miscellaneous.

The Courier

A journal concerned with the relations between the EC and the African–Caribbean–Pacific (ACP) countries that make up the signatories to the Lomé Conventions.

The Courier is one of the most impressive policy area periodicals published by an EC body, in terms of content, style and professionalism. This is perhaps not surprising when it is realized that on its staff *The Courier* has experienced professional journalists with considerable background knowledge of Third World affairs and from a variety of EC and ACP backgrounds. The journal has a circulation of around 80 000 in English and French editions and is distributed to over 130 countries.

The periodical in its current form began in 1970 as *Courrier de l'Association*. An earlier irregularly produced leaflet with the same title began in 1963. In 1973 an English edition called *Association News* appeared. *The Courier* began in 1975. It is published six times a year and is available on free subscription from DG VIII.

The following features appear in most issues:

1. Meeting point: an interview with a person eminent in the development field or the third world
2. ACP–EEC: news of the latest developments in ACP–EEC relations (the full texts of the Lomé Conventions were first made widely available in this source, for example)
3. Country reports – each issue takes, usually, two countries in the ACP region and gives an in-depth description of its current position, including interviews with government leaders
4. Europe: EC developments of interest to ACP countries
5. Dossier: each issue devotes approximately 20–40 pages to a particular topic and studies it in depth. Dossiers in 1987 were: roots and tubers; investment in ACP states; population and development; development NGOs; the media and development; the life of a project
6. Developing world: non-EC-related news involving developing countries
7. CTA Bulletin: information from the Technical Centre for Agricultural and Rural Cooperation
8. CDI: industrial information opportunities
9. Operational summary: details of EC-funded development schemes prior to their implementation (this information is also available online using the PABLI database).

Titles with the Document categorization

Since 1984 the following title has been published of which DG VIII is the 'author service':

1. *Euro–Arab dialogue. Commentaries and guidelines for contracting in industrial projects, October 1984*, 1985

Miscellaneous

Four titles have been published in a Development series. No. 1 in the series was headlined Studies while nos 2–4 were headlined Dossiers but it would seem that all titles are part of the same series:

1. (1) *Integrated rural development projects carried out in Black Africa with EDF aid. Evaluation and outlook for the future*, 1979
2. (2) *Europe and the Third World: a study on interdependence*, 1979
3. (3) *How to participate in contracts financed by the European Development Fund*, 1981
4. (4) *European Development Fund procedures*, 1981.

Two further one-off titles from DG VIII are:

1. *The European Development Fund. Education–training 1958–1980*, 1983
2. *Europe, the developing countries and energy*, 1986.

Another title worth noting is:

3. *Ten years of Lomé. A record of EEC–ACP partnership 1976 to 1985*, 1986.

This is a report on the implementation of financial and technical cooperation under the first two Lomé Conventions. It was compiled by officials within DG VIII, although issued as a special issue within the series Europe Information: Development of which DG X is the author service (see below).

DG IX PERSONNEL AND ADMINISTRATION

DG IX is one of the four authorizing service in the Commission (see Chapter 2). In addition to that function in the overall publishing programme of the Commission it is also a author service in its own right. The following series and titles are compiled or coordinated from within DG IX:

1. European Documentation
2. European Perspectives
3. Publications from the Translation Directorate
4. Historical archives
5. Titles with the Document categorization
6. Directory of the Commission of the European Communities (see Chapter 2)

7. Publications from the Commission Library (see Chapter 3)
8. Publications from SCAD (see Chapter 3)
9. Treaties establishing the European Communities. Abridged edition (see Chapter 1).

European Documentation

A series of explanatory publications intended for the general public. Approximately five to seven titles annually are published in the series, the aim being to explain EC policies in straightforward language. Most titles in the series comprise a mix of text, diagrams, drawings and photographs. Titles in the series are published by OOPEC but are free of charge. Copies can usually be obtained from the Information Offices of the Commission. Versions in all Community languages are available. Most titles in the series contain a bibliography for further reading.

Since 1980 the following titles have been published.

1980
1. *The Community and its regions*
2. *The European Community and the energy problem*
3. *Cultural action in the European Community*
4. *The Customs Union*
5. *The European Community's research policy*
6. *The European Community and vocational training.*

1981
1. *The Court of Justice of the European Communities*
2. *The European Community's transport policy*
3. *The social policy of the European Community*
4. *European economic and monetary union*
5. *The European Community's budget*
6. *The European Community's legal system*
7–8. *Grants and loans from the European Community.*

1982
1–2. *The economy of the European Community*
3. *Freedom of movement for persons in the European Community*
4. *An education policy for Europe*
5. *The European Community's industrial strategy*
6. *The agricultural policy of the European Community.*

1983
1. *The European Community and the energy problem*
2–3. *Wine in the European Community*
4. *The Court of Justice of the European Communities*
5. *The social policy of the European Community*
6. *The Customs Union*
7. *Europe as seen by Europeans – ten years of European polling, 1973–1983.*

1984

1. *The European Community's environmental policy*
2. *The ABC of Community law*
3. *The European Community's transport policy*
4. *Women in the European Community*
5. *The European Community's legal system*
6. *The ECU*
7–8. *The economy of the European Community.*

1985

1. *The European Community's fishery policy.*
2. *The European Community's research policy.*
3–4. *The European Community and the Mediterranean*
5. *Nuclear safety in the European Community.*

1986

1. *The European Community's budget*
2. *The ABC of Community law*
3. *European unification: the origins and growth of the European Community*
4. *Europe as seen by Europeans – European polling 1973–86*
5. *The Court of Justice of the European Community.*

1987

1. *The Common Agricultural Policy and its reform*
2. *European unification: the origins and growth of the European Community*
3. *The European Community and the environment*
4. *Europe without frontiers – completing the internal market*
5. *The ECU.*

1988

1. *Wine in the European Community*
2. *Research and technological development policy*
3. *Europe without frontiers – completing the internal market*
4. *The audio-visual media in the Single European Market.*
5. *Jean Monnet, a grand design for Europe*

As can be seen, some titles in the series are periodically updated. In addition to titles in the numbered sequence there are further titles which are part of the series European Documentation but which are not numbered.

First, there is a subseries called Brochures for Businessmen. The titles published since 1980 in this subseries are:

1. *Public supply contracts in the European Community, 1982*
2. *Government procurement in Japan – the way in, 1983*
3. *EEC competition rules – guide for small and medium-sized enterprises, 1983*

4. *The European Commission's powers of investigation in the enforcement of competition law,* 1985
5. *Grants and loans from the European Community,* 1985.
6. *Public procurement and construction – towards an integrated market,* 1988.

Second, there are further miscellaneous unnumbered titles that are not given the standard European Documentation cover but are part of the series. These include:

1. *A journey through the EC. Information on the member states and the development of the European Community,* 1982; 1986
2. *The European Community and its regions. 10 years of Community regional policy and of the European Regional Development Fund (ERDF),* 1985
3. *Steps to European unity, Community progress to date: a chronology,* 1979; 1981; 1982; 1983; 1985; 1987
4. *Working together: The institutions of the European Community.*

The last-named title was written by Emile Noël, the Secretary-General of the Commission from its founding until 1987. The title has gone through many editions and series. Since 1980 new editions have been published in 1982, 1985 and 1988.

European Perspectives

While it is not unusual for publications of international organizations to have been written by people from outside the organization the titles published in the series European Perspectives are still rather different. They comprise substantial academic studies on EC related subjects commissioned by DG IX.

Titles are not published regularly in this series and are not available in all Community languages. They are priced publications available from OOPEC and are listed in the *Catalogue of Publications.* European Perspectives is managed by DG IX through an editorial board made up of representives from DG IX and other DGs.

Since 1979 the following English language titles have been published:

1. *The European Community: how it works,* by Emile Noël, 1979
2. *The challenges ahead: a plan for Europe,* by a group of independent experts under the chairmanship of Claude Gruson, 1979
3. *The Community legal order,* by Jean-Victor Louis, 1980
4. *The Customs Union of the European Economic Community,* by Nikolaus Vaulont, 1981
5. *The Old World and the new technologies,* by Michel Godet and Olivier Ruyssen, 1981
6. *The finances of Europe,* by Daniel Strasser, 1981

7. *The professions in the European Community: towards freedom of movement and mutual recognition of qualifications*, by J.-P. de Crayencour, 1982
8. *Thirty years of Community law*, by numerous writers coordinated by an editorial committee, 1983
9. *The European Monetary System: origins, operation and outlook*, by Jacques van Ypersele, 1985
10. *The European Communities in the international order*, by Jean Groux and Philippe Manin, 1985
11. *Money, economic policy and Europe*, by Tommaso Padoa-Schioppa, 1985
12. *An ever closer union: a critical analysis of the Draft Treaty establishing the European Union*, by Roland Bieber, Jean-Paul Jacqué and Joseph H. H. Weiler, 1985
13. *The rights of working women in the European Community*, by Eve C. Landau, 1985
14. *The European Community: the formative years. The struggle to establish the Common Market and the Political Union (1958–66)*, by Hans von der Groeben, 1987
15. *Transport and European integration*, by Carlo degli Abbati, 1987
16. *Lawyers in the European Community*, by Serge-Pierre Laguette and Patrick Latham, 1987.

Some of the titles in the series are published in other Community languages in different years. European Perspectives is an impressive series and many of the titles are the product of very high quality academic research and become standard monographs on the subjects concerned.

Publications from the Translation Directorate

Within this Directorate of DG IX there is a Terminology and Computer Applications section which is responsible for the periodical *Terminologie et Traduction* (*Translation and Terminology Bulletin*). Two to three issues a year are published. The first issue was no. 1, 1985. In the introduction to that issue it is noted that the title is the product of the merging of *Bulletin de la Traduction* and *Bulletin de Terminologie*.

The periodical, which is available on subscription from OOPEC, comprises articles on terminological and translation issues. The majority of articles are in either French or English, although there are occasional features in other Community languages.

At the back of most issues is a list of special publications available from the Terminology and Computer Applications section. One of these publications is called *Committees* and appeared in 1986. This is a major reference source in addition to its specifically terminological function. Within the EC there has been a considerable proliferation of advisory, management and regulatory committees set up. There are a number of other EC publications which partially list these committees but this new title is a welcome addition. It lists all the committees set up by the Commission under the Treaties or subsequent secondary legislation.

The primary function of *Committees* is to give the authoritative version in all the Community languages of the titles of these committees. They are listed by the Directorate-General which supplies the chairman or secretary. This allows an approximate breakdown by subject. Equally, however, there is a keyword subject index in each of the Community languages at the back of the book. Finally a brief bibliographical reference is given after the entry for each committee detailing the setting up of the committee. This is useful because it enables clarification of the function of each committee to become a straightforward task. This title does not list the membership of the committees nor give contact addresses.

Other titles from the Terminology and Computer Applications section include:

1. *Glossary of labour and the trade union movement*, 1983. This glossary was prepared by the European Trade Union Institute in collaboration with the Commission. It contains approximately 400 terms in ten languages
2. *European Treaties vocabulary, Part 1*, 3rd edition, 1983
3. *Alternative energy sources*, 1984. 2 volumes
4. *Fishing gear*, 1987
5. *Vocabulary of Community primary law*, 1985. Separate provisional French–English–Portuguese and French–English–Spanish editions were published with the Document categorization in 1985. A further French–English–Spanish edition was published in 1986.

Historical archives

In 1983 the historical archives of the European Communities were opened to the public for the first time in accordance with the thirty years rule. In that year the earliest records of the European Coal and Steel Community were opened to the public. In 1989 this will be extended to the early records of the EEC and Euratom.

In 1983 to mark the opening of the ECSC archives the Commission published a commemorative book called *Opening of the historical archives of the European Communities to the public*. This book, in addition to describing the setting up and development of the EC, gives details of the existing archives services of each of the institutions of the EC, the text of the legislation relating to the opening up of the archives to the public and various addresses from international archivists.

The intention is to transfer the archives to the European University

Institute at Florence when they are made public. It is also hoped to make available three microform sets of the archives in each member state. In the United Kingdom the first such designated centre is the National Library of Scotland in Edinburgh.

Following on from the opening of the archives the first in a series of inventories was published in 1985 by OOPEC. This is called *Inventory of the historical archives*. Vol. 1, *Records of the High Authority of the ECSC 1952. Speeches 1952–67*. Separate indexes are provided in this publication for records and speeches.

Titles with the Document categorization

The following titles, of which DG IX is the 'author service', have been published in the Document categorization:

1. *Ellimikes symtomografies*, 1984
2. *Vocabulary of Community primary law*, 1985
3. *Vocabulary of Community primary law*, 1985
4. *Guidelines for an informatics architecture 1986–1991*, 1986
5. *Guidelines for an informatics architecture*, 3rd edition, 1988.

The other four series are dealt with in the following chapters:
Chapter 2: *Directory of the Commission of the European Communities*.
Chapter 3: Publications from the Commission Library; Publications from SCAD. Chapter 1: *Treaties establishing the European Communities* (abridged edition).

DG X INFORMATION, COMMUNICATION AND CULTURE

DG X is another of the four authorizing services in the Commission. In addition to that function DG X is an 'author service' in its own right to a range of titles and series. These are issued as part of the function of DG X to increase understanding of the EC amongst the citizens of the member states and elsewhere. The following titles are covered:

1. European File
2. *Eurobarometer: public opinion in the European Community*
3. *Women of Europe/Women of Europe: Supplement*
4. *Trade Union Information Bulletin*
5. Europe Information: Development
6. Europe Information: External Relations
7. *European University News*
8. *University research on European integration*
9. Miscellaneous
10. *Green Europe: Newsletter on the Common Agricultural Policy/ Green Europe: Newsflash* (see section above on DG VI).

European File

A series of small pamphlets outlining various aspects of EC developments and policies. They are free and available direct from DG X or from Press and Information Offices as long as stocks remain. They are useful introductions to subjects for students and the like. No bibliographical references are given for further reading, and approximately twenty a year are issued. The last European File issued in December each year is invariably a catalogue of all issues for the past few years that are still available and relevant.

To indicate the range of subjects covered here is a list of the titles in the European File series issued in 1987:

1. *The external trade of the European Community*
2. *The European energy policy*
3. *Europe and nuclear fusion*
4. *The Community combats poverty*
5. *The European Community and enviromental protection*
6. *European identity: symbols to sport*
7–8. *EUR 12: daily life in diagrams*
9. *The European Community and tourism*
10. *Equal opportunities for women*
11. *New rights for the citizens of Europe*
12. *The European Community and consumers*
13. *Europe, our future, a European Community – Why?*
14. *European regional policy*
15. *The European Community and the Third World*
16. *Generalized preferences for the Third World*
17. *Europe without frontiers: towards a large internal market.*
18. *Nuclear energy in the European Community*
19. *Research and technological development for Europe*
20. *European file: catalogue 1979–87.*

Eurobarometer: public opinion in the European Community

Since 1973 public opinion polls have been carried out in the member states of the Communities to find out the views of the people on European concerns. The polls are carried out by professional polling organizations twice a year in the spring and autumn. The results of these polls are issued in the publication *Eurobarometer: public opinion in the European Community*. The first issue appeared in July 1974. Note that from no. 3, 1975 until no. 26, 1986 the spelling of the first word in the title of the English language version was *Euro-barometre*.

This title is formally an internal document of the Commission and is classed as having 'restricted distribution'. Primarily the document is for use within the EC and for the media. EC Depository Libraries receive copies and it is sometimes possible to obtain copies from DG X or the Information Offices. It is not available from OOPEC.

The questions asked in the polls vary in detail over the years but there are basic themes:

1. The mood of Europeans – general feeling of satisfaction, fear of war, economic expectations, living standards, views on democracy
2. A people's Europe – European identity, relations between member states, for example
3. Attitudes towards Europe and the European Community
4. The European Parliament – public awareness and impressions.

A 'Special Thirtieth Anniversary Edition' of *Eurobarometer* was issued in March 1987 to mark the thirtieth anniversary of the signing of the Treaty of Rome. This issue had the following sections:

1. Of birthdays and anniversaries
2. Striking a balance of thirty years
3. Ten scenarios for January 2000
4. The citizens of Europe want political union
5. Europe and the young: which future?
6. European unity and national identity.

In addition to the regular series of polls various Directorates-General have commissioned special one-off polls over the years. A selection of these include:

1. *European consumers* (DG X, 1976)
2. *Science and European public opinion* (DG XII, 1977)
3. *The perception of poverty in Europe* (DG V, 1977)
4. *The attitude of the working population to retirement* (DG V, 1978)
5. *The European public's attitude to scientific and technical development* (DG XII, 1979)
6. *European men and women in 1978* (DG X, 1979)
7. *The Europeans and their children* (DG V, 1980)
8. *Europeans and their regions* (DG XVI, 1981)
9. *Public opinion in the European Community: energy* (DG XVII, 1982)
10. *The European and their environment* (DG XI, 1983)
11. *European women and men in 1983* (DG X, 1983)
12. *Public opinion in the European Community on energy in 1984* (DG XVII, 1985)
13. *Europeans and the ECU* (DG X, 1985)
14. *The European and their environment in 1986* (DG XI, 1986).

Women of Europe

A periodical produced approximately five times a year by the Women's

Information Service of DG X. It started in 1978 and reached no. 51 at the end of 1987. Its aim is to inform women in all of the member states of the European Community and other developments of interest to them. News items and other features tend to be short. The format of the journal has changed slightly over the years but regular features include:

1. The changing European Community – recent EC developments of interest to women
2. European Parliament
3. Economic and Social Committee
4. Court of Justice of the European Communities
5. Facts, institutions, laws and militant activities from the member states. *Women of Europe* maintains correspondents in all the member states
6. Europe and the world
7. Research, meetings and books.

Women of Europe is available free of charge from the Women's Information Service.

Women of Europe: Supplement
This title is published irregularly by the Women's Information Service of DG X and is available free from that unit to 'relevant' organizations such as women's associations, trade unions, journalists, libraries, research centres and ministerial departments.

Each issue of the *Supplement* is devoted to a specific topic. Below is a list of titles so far:

1. *Women and the European Social Fund*, 1978
2. *The European Community and work for women*, 1979
3. *Women and men of Europe in 1978*, 1979
4. *Women in the European Parliament*, 1980
5. *European women in paid employment*, 1981
6. *Women and the European Social Fund*, 1981
7. *Women at work in the European Community. 50 questions; 50 answers*, 1981
8. *Women in Spain*, 1981
9. *Equal opportunities: action programme 1982–1985*, 1982
10. *Women in statistics*
11. *Women in Portugal*, 1982
12. *Community law and women*, 1983
13. *Women in agriculture*, 1983
14. *Women in statistics*, 1984
15. *Women at work in the European Community. 50 questions; 50 answers*, 1984
16. *Women and men of Europe in 1983*, 1984
17. *Women and development*, 1984

18. *Women's studies – women and research in the ten member states of the European Community,* 1984
19. *Community law and women,* 1985
20. *European women in paid employment: their perception of discrimination at work,* 1985
21. *Elections to the European Parliament: women and voting,* 1985
22. *Women and music,* 1985
23. *Equal opportunities. 2nd action programme 1986–1990,* 1986
24. *The Nairobi World Conference,* 1986
25. *Community law and women,* 1987
26. *Men and women of Europe in 1987,* 1987

Trade Union Information Bulletin

Published four times a year by the Trade Union Division of DG X in English, French and German editions, *Trade Union Information Bulletin* began in 1985, replacing *Trade Union Information.* The aim of the periodical is to keep people in the trade union movement informed of EC developments of relevance to them. In no. 1, 1987, for example, there were short features on the European shipbuilding industry, a CEDEFOP conference on continuing education, the European Social Fund, a European Trade Union Institute research report on flexibility of work time and a Commission publication on microcomputers and small firms.

Trade Union Information Bulletin is edited by a non-Commission official. A disclaimer is placed in each issue: 'The views expressed in the Bulletin are those of the Editor and are not necessarily those of the European Commission.' The *Bulletin* is free of charge from DG X but will only be sent to trade unions and their members. It is sometimes possible to obtain copies from the Information Offices of the Commission.

The Trade Union Division of DG X also produces occasional one-off publications. Two recent examples are:

1. *European Community institutions and publications,* 1983
2. *The European Trade Union Confederation,* 1984.

Europe Information: Development

A series of irregularly published titles from DG X. Each title is devoted to an aspect of EC relations with the developing countries of the world. To get on a mailing list for this series contact DG X direct.

The series began in 1978, replacing a series called Information: Cooperation – Development. Some issues had been called Information: Cooperation and Development, or Information Development Cooperation. There had also been a series called Information: Development Aid.

Europe Information: Development has not had a consistent numbering system. Since 1978 the following titles have been published:

1978

1. *The European Community and the textile arrangements*
2. *EEC–ACP trade relations*
3. *EEC–Syria cooperation agreement*
4. *EEC–Egypt cooperation agreement*
5. *Ivory Coast and the Lomé Convention. Tremendous opportunities*
6. *Industrial cooperation and the Lomé Convention.*

1979

1. *Mauritius and the Lomé Convention*
2. *Europe–Third World rural development*
3. *Solar energy: a new area of ACP–EEC cooperation*
4. *Sudan–EEC relations*
5. *The EEC and the developing countries: outside the Lomé Convention and the southern Mediterranean.*

1980

1. *Implications of the second enlargement for the Mediterranean and 'ACP' policies of the European Community*
2. *EEC–Morocco cooperation agreement*
3. *EEC–Lebanon cooperation agreement*
4. *EEC–Algeria cooperation agreement*
5. *The EEC–Israel cooperation agreements*
6. *Community wine imports*
7. *Relations between the European Community and Africa*
8. *Implications for the southern Mediterranean countries of the second enlargement of the European Community*
9. *The question of commodities in the North–South dialogue*
10 *Tanzania–EEC relations* (DE 29).

1981

1. *Photovoltaic energy as a development aid* (DE 28)
2. *The EEC and the Caribbean* (DE 31)
3. *The European Community and Southern Africa* (DE 32)
4. *Kenya–European Communities cooperation* (DE 33).

1982

1. *Coffee, cocoa, bananas* (DE 34)
2. *The outlook for Community policy on cooperation with the developing countries in the light of changing North–South relations and the future development of the Community* (DE 35)
3. *Cooperation agreements between the EEC and the Maghreb countries* (DE 36)
4. *EEC–Tunisia cooperation agreement* (DE 37)
5. *The European Community and the Arab world* (DE 38)
6. *Development of the Senegal River Valley* (DE 39)
7. *Food strategies: a new form of cooperation between Europe and the countries of the Third World* (DE 40)

8. *EEC food aid to Zimbabwe* (DE 41)
9. *Food aid from the Community: a new approach* (DE 42)
10. *Europe's relations with the Third World at a time of recession* (DE 43)

1983
1. *EEC–Jordan cooperation agreement* (DE 5)
2. *Sugar, the European Community and the Lomé Convention* (DE 19)
3. *Trade between the European Community and the Arab League countries* (DE 24)
4. *A Community research policy for development* (DE 44)
5. *Ethiopia–EEC relations* (DE 45)
6. *Problems of enlargement: taking stock and proposals* (DE 46)
7. *The EEC and the Pacific* (DE 47)
8. *Commodities and Stabex* (DE 49).

1984
1. *The EEC and industrial cooperation with the developing countries* (DE 50)
2. *Summary of EEC–ACP cooperation*

1985
1. *The EEC's trade relations with the developing countries* (DE 48)
2. *Lomé III: analysis of the EEC–ACP convention* (DE 51)
3. *Ethiopia–EEC relations* (DE 52)

1986
1. *EEC assistance to Third World media* (DE 53)
2. *The EEC and the Caribbean* (DE 54)
3. *Ten years of Lomé: a record of EEC–ACP partnership 1976–1985* (DE 55).

1988
1. *Community food aid: instrument of development policy or exploitation of surpluses* (DE 56)
2. *Official development assistance from the European Community and its Member States* (DE 57)
3. *Structural adjustment in sub-Saharan Africa: adjustment, development and equity* (DE 58)
4. *STABEX* (DE 59)

As mentioned above Europe Information: Development replaced Information: Cooperation – Development in 1978. However a single issue of the latter title appeared in 1983 called *The Third World today*.

Another one-off title appeared in 1984, with an updated edition in 1985, called *Europe–South dialogue*. This was a folder of four separate booklets on aspects of EC development policy:

1. Interdependence
2. History
3. Lomé
4. The Mediterranean.

Europe Information: External Relations

A series of irregularly published titles from DG X. Each title is devoted to an aspect of the external relations of the EC and is available direct from DG X or from Information Offices of the Commission.

Europe Information: External Relations replaced Information: External Relations in 1978. The list below is of all titles published in the series.

1978

1. *The European Community and Canada*
2. *The European Community and ASEAN*
3. *Latin America and the European Community*
4. *–*
5. *Spain and the European Community*
6. *List of main EEC agreements with other countries*
7. *Portugal and the European Community*
8. *Australia and the European Community*
9. *Turkey and the European Community*
10. *–*
11. *Regional policy: the start of a new phase*
12. *The European Community and the countries of Eastern Europe*
13. *The People's Republic of China and the European Community*
14. *Greece and the European Community.*

1979

15. *The European Community and the countries of EFTA*
16. *The European Community and ASEAN*
17. *The People's Republic of China and the European Community*
18. *The European Communities' scheme of generalized preferences*
19. *–*
20. *Yugoslavia and the European Community*
21. *Latin America and the European Community*
22. *Brazil and the European Community*
23. *Portugal and the European Community*
24. *Mexico and the European Community*
25. *The GATT multilateral trade negotiations*
26. *The European Community and the countries of Eastern Europe*
27. *ASEAN and the European Community*
28. *The European Communities Scheme of Generalized Preferences.*

1980

29. *Spain and the European Community*

30. *The European Community and Yugoslavia*
31. *The European Community and New Zealand*
32. *The European Community and Australia*
33. *The European Community and Japan*
34. *Portugal and the European Community*
35. *The European Community and the EFTA countries*
36. *The European Community and Brazil*
37. *List of main EEC agreements with other countries*
38. –
39. *The European Community and the United States*
40. *The Community of Ten in figures.*

1981
41. *The Generalised System of Preferences and the European Community*
42. *The People's Republic of China and the European Community*
43. *Spain and the European Community*
44. *The European Community's textiles trade*
45. *The European Community and Bangladesh*
46. *The European Community and Sri Lanka*
47. *The European Community and Japan*
48. *The European Community and Sweden*
49. *The European Community and Norway*
50. *The European Community and India*
51. *ASEAN and the European Community*
52. *The EC and the Republic of Korea*
53. *The European Community and Central America*
54. *The European Community and Canada.*

1982
55. *The European Community and Australia*
56. *The European Community and New Zealand*
57. *The European Community and the United States*
58. *Portugal and the European Community*
59. –
60. *The European Community and the People's Republic of China*
61. *The European Community and the EFTA countries*
62. *The European Community and India*
63. *New trade and economic relations between Brazil and the European Community*
64. –

1983
65. *The European Community and Yugoslavia*
66. *ASEAN and the European Community*
67. *The European Community and Australia*
68. *The European Community and Latin America*

69. *Spain and the European Community*
70. *The European Community and New Zealand*
71. *The European Community and the Peoples's Republic of China.*

1984

72. *The European Community and Sri Lanka*
73. *The European Community and India*
74. *The European Communities and the Republic of Korea*
75. *The European Community and the Yemen Arab Republic.*

1985

76. *The European Community's textile trade*
77. *The European Community and ASEAN*
78. *The European Community and Australia*
79. *The European Community and the People's Republic of China*
80. *The European Community and the Gulf Cooperation Council (GCC)*
81. *The European Community and ASEAN*
82. *The European Community and Latin America*
83. *The European Community and the People's Republic of China.*

1986

84. *The European Community and the Republic of Korea*
85. *The European Community and India*
86. *The European Community and Pakistan.*

1987

87. *The European Community and Nepal*
88. *The European Community and Yugoslavia*
89. –

1988

90. *The European Community and China*
91. *The European Community and the Yemen Arab Republic*
92. *The European Community and ASEAN*
93. *The European Community and Bangladesh*
94. *The European Community and Yugoslavia.*

European University News

The first issue of the periodical *European University News* was in 1965. In the 1980s it has been published free of charge bimonthly by the University Information section of DG X. Earlier it had been published by the Association pour la Communauté Européenne Universitaire on a paid subscription basis.

European University News aims to develop links between institutions of higher education in the member states, and elsewhere, to encourage the study of Europe. It is partly in English and partly in French. Each issue usually contains the following features:

1. News of European studies – new courses and activities of associations of EC studies, for example
2. Results of research projects
3. Reports of conferences and seminars
4. Calendar of future conferences, courses, seminars, etc.
5. Brief review of new publications.

There are occasional special features. In no. 152, October 1987, for example, there was a feature on EC databases and databanks. Since 1984 one issue in the year has been a special issue called 'Summer Courses on European Integration'. This attempts to list courses and seminars dealing with European themes that are traditionally organized during the summer months. Details such as the length of courses and conditions for admission are given. 'Summer Courses on European Integration' was published prior to 1984 in the same format but not as part of the numbered sequence of *European University News*.

As an occasional supplement to *European University News* there is a publication called *Postgraduate Degrees in European Integration*. Editions have been published in 1978, 1982 and 1985.

University research on European integration

The European Communities maintain a database called EURISTOTE, which attempts to index research in the area of European integration taking place in over forty countries in the world. EURISTOTE is maintained at the Université Catholique de Louvain but is available publicly through the ECHO network.

From this database is published *University research on European integration*. It is a priced publication available from OOPEC; no. 11 in the series was published in 1980 with the title *University studies on European integration*. The current title has been used since no. 12 in 1982, with further editions in 1985 (no. 13) and 1987 (no. 14).

This major bibliography is divided into two parts:

1. List of studies – arranged in alphabetical order of authors' names under the headings in the classification plan; a distinction is made between studies in progress, completed studies and published studies.
2. Indexes – a directory of addresses; authors; research directors.

The directory of addresses of academic institutions and departments has been additionally published as an off-print called *Register of universities, faculties and institutes*, 1987.

The University Information section of DG X also produce periodically *Addresses, European Documentation Centres – EDC; Depository Libraries – DEP; European Reference Centres – ERC*. The latest edition was published in 1984.

Miscellaneous

DG X are responsible for a number of popular-level booklets and pamphlets. Recent examples include:

1. *About Europe* (annual or biannual)
2. *The little citizens of Europe*, 1979
3. *Do you know your rights?*, 1984
4. *The European Community: value for money*, 1986
5. *European Agricultural Guidance and Guarantee Fund: significance and functioning*, 1986 (special issue of *Green Europe*)
6. *Europeans, you have rights*, 1987.

DG XI ENVIRONMENT, CONSUMER PROTECTION AND NUCLEAR SAFETY

The following series are covered:

1. *State of the environment*
2. Titles with the Document categorization
3. Miscellaneous.

State of the environment

The first report with this title appeared in 1977. The second report followed in 1979. They were attempts by the Commission to convey to the layman some of the EC initiatives with regard to the environment. The first report summarized the whole range of activity at Community level, as shown in legislative proposals and decisions. The second chose a number of topics and expanded on them in non-technical language. A list of environmental proposals, either adopted or under discussion, were given with bibliographical references in an annex. A list of EC commissioned studies of environmental matters that had been published in 1976–77 in the EUR series was also given in a further annex.

In both the first and second reports it was stated that these reports were to be part of a regular series. In the event it was 1987 before the third report was published. It was called *The state of the environment in the European Community 1986*. It was published in the EUR series as EUR 10633.

The third report is quite different from the first two reports. Rather than concentrate on EC activities it looks more at the quality of the environment itself in the Community. The following headings are used:

1. Background
   a. Introduction.
   b. The policy context.

2. Economic activities
   a. Urban and industrial activities
   b. Agriculture, forestry and fishing.
3. State of the environment
   a. The air
   b. The land
   c. Inland waters
   d. The seas
   e. Wildlife.
4. Economic implications and impacts
   a. Economic impacts of environmental policy.

Somewhat unusually for an EC publication there is a useful index. Some of the chapters list EC legislation relevant to the topic under study. There are many coloured photographs and diagrams. It is altogether a most impressive book well suited to publication during the European Year of the Environment. It is a priced publication available from OOPEC, available in English, French and German.

Titles with the Document categorization

Since 1984 the following titles have been published of which DG XI is the author service:

1. *Ten years of Community consumer policy*, 1985
2. *A new impetus for consumer protection policy*, 1985
3. *Convention on international trade in endangered species of wild fauna and flora – EC annual report, 1984*, 1986
4. *Parameters characterising toxic and hazardous waste disposal sites*, 1987
5. *Convention on international trade in endangered species of wild fauna and flora – EC annual report, 1985*, 1987.

Miscellaneous

Since 1980 there have been a number of miscellaneous titles of which DG XI is the author service. An example is:

1. *Ten years of Community environment policy*, 1984.

In addition to a substantial description of Community environmental policy in such areas as water, air, chemicals, noise, waste, land and natural resources, flora and fauna, research, and action at international level, this volume has a bibliographical listing of Community environmental measures up to 1984. This title was unpriced and available from Information Offices.

2. *The treatment of solid municipal waste. Guide for local authorities*, 1982
3. *Energy from municipal waste. 1980/1981 summary report*, 1983

4. *The European and their environment*, 1983
5. *The European and their environment in 1986*, 1986
6. *Symposium on enforcement of food law*, 1980
7. *Food additives and the consumer*, 1980 (this title includes an appendix listing the numerical codes for food additives – the E numbers)
8. *Consumer protection and information policy. Third report*, 1981
9. *Consumer representation in the European Communities*, 1983.

DG XII SCIENCE, RESEARCH AND DEVELOPMENT

DG XII is not a significant author service, in that it does not publish titles in series exclusively of DG XII origin. Like other DGs of course, it is the author service for certain COM Documents, EUR Reports and the like, but ultimately their publication is the responsibility of other DGs.

The following series/areas are covered in this section:

1. *ENTECH: Newsletter of the EC Non-Nuclear R & D Programme*
2. FAST
3. European Communities: Information: R & D
4. Joint Research Centre
5. Miscellaneous

ENTECH: Newsletter of the EC Non-Nuclear R & D Programme

The first issue of this title (*ENTECH* stands for energy technology) was dated May 1986 and its aim was to give information on the third EC Non-Nuclear Energy R & D Programme. In the first issue *ENTECH* looked at the programme in general and also at each of the subprogrammes. It was intended to follow progress in some of the subprogrammes in more detail in later issues.

A second issue was dated February 1987, the future issues were promised three or four times a year. The third issue was dated April 1988. *ENTECH* is available direct from Directorate E of DG XII.

FAST

The FAST (Forecasting and Assessment in the field of Science and Technology) Programme was launched by the EC in 1979. A second programme ran from 1983 to 1987, and COM(87)502 proposed a third programme to run from 1988. FAST is a research programme to forecast long-term changes in the field of science and technology and subsequent assessment of their implications for the future development of the EC.

The programme includes such features as research projects, conferences, workshops and network activities. A large number of publications emerged out of all these activities. In 1987 the FAST Programme issued a *List of publications*, listing:

1. FAST Documents: various miscellaneous documents relating to the Programmes
2. FAST Series.
3. FAST Occasional Papers: between 1980 and 1987 over 200 reports had been issued in this series. The range of subjects covered is very wide, and includes the food industry, information technology, alternatives uses for farmland and forestry. These reports are only available direct from DG XII. The *List of publications* can be obtained from:

   FAST Programme
   200 rue de la Loi
   B-1049 Brussels
   Belgium

European Communities: Information: R & D

Each issue in this occasional series, which began in 1976, looks at some aspect of EC research and development. Since 1984 the following titles have been issued:

1. (22) *Community science policy: new framework programme*, 1984
2. (23) *Acid rain – a challenge for Europe*, 1984
3. (24) *Energy models – instruments for exploring Europe's energy future*, 1984
4. (25) *Biotechnology – a challenge for Europe*, 1984
5. (26) *Fusion – energy source of the future?*, 1984
6. (27) *The development of 'optical computers'. A task for European research*, 1985
7. (28) *Fifteen years of successful joint research in Europe. COST research covers ten project areas*, 1986
8. (29) *In search of new high performance magnets*, 1987.

A subscription to this series is available free of charge on written request to DG XII.

Joint Research Centre (JRC)

The JRC was established under the Euratom Treaty as a nuclear research centre and became operational in 1960–61. Later it has broadened its research into other areas such as new energy techniques, environmental problems, information and consumer protection.

The JRC comprises four establishments – Geel in Belgium, Ispra in Italy, Karlsruhe in Germany and Petten in the Netherlands. JRC research results are published in a variety of formats – full details can be obtained from an annual title called *Publications Bulletin* (see Chapter 3).

The JRC, which is part of DG XII, issues a glossy introductory brochure to its activities which is available from:

> Joint Research Centre
> Commission of the European Communities – DG XII
> 200 rue de la Loi
> B-1049 Brussels
> Belgium

The annual report of the JRC for the year 1986 was published in a glossy format intended for a general readership in the EUR series (EUR 10937) in 1987. This was the first time it had been published in this format and it was not clear whether it would be continued. It was available direct from the JRC.

Miscellaneous

1. *Science and European public opinion*, 1977
2. *Vade-mecum of Community research promotion*, 1987.

The latter title is a concise introduction to EC research activities – not just those of DG XII. It is to be hoped that it is regularly updated. It is available free from OOPEC in all Community languages.

It should be noted that DG XII in the process of promoting many of its research programmes produces pamphlets and booklets. During 1985 to 1987, for example, a number of booklets outlining calls for proposals and results in such programmes as BRITE (Basic Research in Industrial Technologies for Europe), STIMULATION (Plan to stimulate European scientific and technical cooperation and interchange), the Biotechnology Programme and the Research Action Programme in Materials were issued. These booklets are not formally published and are not covered in bibliographical sources. Information Offices of the Commission maintain stocks of this sort of material.

DG XIII TELECOMMUNICATIONS, INFORMATION INDUSTRIES AND INNOVATION

DG XIII is one of the four authorizing services in the Commission (see Chapter 2). In essence this means that all publications of a scientific or technical nature that are published by the Commission, regardless from which Directorate-General they originate, are sanctioned by DG XIII. Until 1986 the Scientific and Technical Communication Service of Directorate A (New Technologies) ran the service. Since 1988 the publications programme has been run by a unit called 'Publications' within DG XIII/C·3 – Scientific and Technical Communications.

DG XIII has to select the most appropriate method for publishing the manuscripts that are submitted for publication – whether it be from the Joint Research Centre (Direct Action) or from the results of contract research (Indirect Action) undertaken and partially financed by outside organizations such as universities, commercial companies or research centres.

In addition to major reports information from EC research activities are also disseminated in papers at scientific conferences and articles in scientific journals. However, it is the major reports which will be looked at in more detail in this section under the heading EUR Reports. The point should be made that other Directorates-General in the Commission are strictly the author service of many of these reports. They are described all together under the EUR Reports heading for the sake of convenience.

On top of DG XIII's function as a authorizing service it is also a author service in its own right to a number of publications. So overall the following series are covered in this section:

1. EUR Reports
2. *Euro Abstracts* (see Chapter 3)
3. *Information Market (I'M)*.
4. *Innovation and Technology Transfer*
5. Miscellaneous.

EUR Reports

EUR Reports is a generic name given to a major series of reports which primarily comprise the published results of EC research activities. Each such published report is given a number preceded by the letters EUR – hence the commonly known name for these reports. Not all EUR Reports are published by OOPEC. DG XIII will attempt to publish such reports through commercial or specialist published channels if they feel that it is the more appropriate channel. However, it would be true to say that OOPEC remains the largest publisher of EUR Reports (approximately 85 per cent of titles). Many reports are published primarily in microfiche only and only in a very limited number of languages. EUR Reports are priced publications whether published by OOPEC or commercial publishers. The specialist nature of these Reports is such that very few libraries or organizations would attempt to obtain a comprehensive collection. EC Depository Libraries, for example, do not automatically receive EUR Reports. Nevertheless they are entitled to request particular titles of those directly published by OOPEC. Commercially produced titles would have to be purchased. The British Library does maintain a comprehensive collection of EUR Reports.

EUR Reports, whether published by OOPEC or other outlets, are all indexed in *Euro Abstracts*, which is fully described in Chapter 3, as is the cumulated guide to EUR Reports called *Catalogue EUR Documents*.

Other sources of information on selected EUR Reports are the catalogues of the UK agents for OOPEC, Her Majesty's Stationery Office (HMSO) and Alan Armstrong.

EUR Reports cover a wide range of subjects. In HMSO's *International organizations catalogue 1985*, for example, the following broad areas are distinguished:

1. Agriculture DG VI
2. BCR information (Community Bureau of Reference) DG XII
3. Biological sciences DG XII
4. Energy DG XII
5. Environment and quality of life DG XI/JRC
6. Industrial health and safety DG V
7. Industrial processes DG III
8. Information management DG XIII
9. Innovation DG XIII
10. Medicine DG V/DG XII
11. Nuclear science and technology DG XII/JRC
12. Physical sciences DG XII/JRC
13. Radiation protection DG XII
14. Research evaluation DG XII
15. Science and technology policy DG XII
16. Technical coal research DG XVII
17. Technical steel research DG XII.

The DGs noted above are the primary author service for the reports of each subject.

It would be a mistake to assume that there are no EUR Reports of general interest. The vast majority are of only specialist interest but there *are* exceptions.

A few recent titles of general interest would include:

1. *Industrial innovation: a guide to Community action, services and funding*, 1984 (EUR 9120)
2. *Individual choice and enabling structures: European directions in care of the elderly*, 1984 (EUR 9605)
3. *Developing markets for new products and services through joint exporting by innovative SMEs*, 1985 (EUR 9927)
4. *Community research and technology policy: developments up to 1984*, 1985 (EUR 10000)
5. *Venture capital in Europe 1985. Survey on venture capital in the European Community*, 1985 (EUR 10224)
6. *The state of the environment in the European Community 1986*, 1987 (EUR 10633)
7. *Joint Research Centre: annual report 1986*, 1987 (EUR 10937).

Information Market (I'M)

This title began as *Euronet News* in 1976. It was renamed *Euronet Diane News* in 1978, and was published on a quarterly basis until no. 37, October–December 1984.

From no. 38, January–March 1985, the journal became *Information Market*. The letters *I'M* are also printed on the cover of each issue. Officially *Euronet Diane News* was incorporated into rather than replaced by *Information Market*. Euronet as a physical network was phased out at the end of 1984 to be replaced by interconnected national networks.

The new title suggested more closely the range of interests of DG XIII, which publishes *Information Market*. It is available free of charge from the following address:

> Information Market
> 177 route d'Esch
> L-1471 Luxembourg
> Telephone (352) 48 80 41
> Telex: 2181

In addition to news of European databases and attempts to harmonize procedures and equipment standards in online information retrieval, *Information Market* also now covers such areas as videotex, teletex, telefax, broadband communication and knowledge systems.

Information Market is formally a supplement to *Euro Abstracts*. It is published in one edition, the majority of articles in English but with some articles in other Community languages. In January 1988 it was stated that its circulation was approaching 40 000 copies an issue.

Innovation and Technology Transfer

This title began in 1980 as *Newsletter from the Department for Scientific and Technical Communication*, published as an occasional supplement to *Euro Abstracts*. With no. 24, January 1984 it was renamed *Newsletter: New Technologies*. With no. 33 November 1984 it was further renamed: *Newsletter: New Technologies and Innovation Policy*. This title was used until no. 59, May 1988, when it was renamed *Innovation and Technology Transfer*. The first issue with this title was no. 3, 1988.

It is published at irregular intervals – in 1985, for example, it was monthly while in 1987 there were only two issues. It is available free of charge from:

> DG XIII - C
> Commission of the European Communities
> L-2920 Luxembourg
> Telephone: (352) 4301, ext. 2918/3351

The *Newsletter* aims to promote the activities of DG XIII in the field of new technologies and innovation policy. It also lists new publications in the area, forthcoming conferences and calls for proposals for related research programmes such as SPRINT: the European Programme for Innovation and Technology Transfer.

Miscellaneous

A booklet called *Innovations from community research* has been issued annually by DG XIII since 1980. Many explanatory pamphlets and booklets outlining details and operations of programmes for which DG XIII is responsible, such as FORMEX (Formalized Exchange of Electronic Publications) and ESPRIT (European Strategic Programme for Research and Development in Information Technologies), are issued – these can be obtained from DG XIII or from Information Offices of the Commission.

Sources used in this section:

1. Commission: *Vade-mecum of Community research promotion*, EC, 1987.
2. Disseminating the results of European Community Research, by John Michel Gibb and Edward Phillips, in *European Communities information*, edited by Michael Hopkins, Mansell, 1985, pp. 59–75.

DG XV FINANCIAL INSTITUTIONS AND COMPANY LAW

The following series are covered:

1. *Inventory of taxes*
2. Titles with the Document categorization.

Inventory of taxes: levied by the state and the local authorities (Länder, départements, regions, districts, provinces, communes) in the member states of the European Communities

The ninth edition of this title was published in 1979. Further editions have been produced in 1981, 1983 and 1985, although published by OOPEC the following year in each case. The latest edition states that it is the 1986 edition on the cover and the 1985 edition on the first page. The last edition has been published with the Document categorization. the title is published in French and English editions and is a priced publication from OOPEC.

Inventory of taxes . . . is a survey of the duties and taxes in force in the member states of the EC, each tax described in turn using standard features:

1. Beneficiary
2. Tax payable by
3. Tax payable on
4. Basis of assessment
5. Special provisions
6. Deductions
7. Limitation of deductions
8. Exemptions
9. Collection
10. Rates
11. Special systems.

This title is a major reference source of factual information. It does not attempt to draw comparisons or analyse the various tax systems. As this publication is on a biennial basis it is important to note that the title is never completely up to date and that there could be significant amendments to take into account.

The author service for future editions is likely to be DG XXI.

Titles with the Document categorization

Since 1984 the following titles have been published with the Document categorization:

1. *Relief from taxes granted to imports made by private persons. Situation at 1.7.1984*, 1984. An earlier edition of this title had been published in 1979
2. *First report from the Commission to the Council on the application of the common system of value-added tax, submitted in accordance with Article 34 of the Sixth Council Directive (77/388/EEC) of 17 May 1977*, 1984
3. *Inventory of taxes, 1986 edition*, 1986
4. *Propuesta modificada de quinta directiva. Basada en al articulo 54(3)(G) del Tratado CEE referente a la estructura de las sociedades anónimas y a los poderes y obligaciones de sus órganos*, 1987
5. *The fourth company law directive. Implementation by member states*, 1987

DG XVI   REGIONAL POLICY

The following series are covered:

1. Studies – Regional Policy Series
2. *European Regional Development Fund. Annual report*
3. *The regions of Europe. Periodic report*
4. Regional Development Programmes
5. *ERDF in Figures*

6. Titles with the Document categorization
7. Internal Documentation on Regional Policy in the Community
8. Miscellaneous.

Studies – Regional Policy Series

This series began in 1973 and continued until 1985. A total of twenty-three titles were published, comprising mainly one-off studies of various aspects of regional policy developments in the member states. Many of the reports of the first generation of Regional Development Programmes (see below) were issued in this series. They were priced publications available from OOPEC. Since 1980 all reports were published in English and French and, on occasion, other languages as well.

Since 1980 the following titles have been published:

1. (18) *Deglomeration policies in the European Community. A comparative study,* 1981
2. (19) *The role of the tertiary sector in regional policy: report of a comparative study and summaries of the nine national reports on which it is based,* 1980
3. (20) *Integrated development of mountain areas. The alpine region,* 1981
4. (21) *Study of the regional impact of the common agricultural policy,* 1981
5. (22) *Study of the regional impact of the Community's external trade policy,* 1983
6. (23) *The effects of new information technology on the less-favoured regions of the Community,* 1984.

One-off titles published since 1985 have been published with the Document categorization (see below).

European Regional Development Fund. Annual report

The annual report of the ERDF is first issued as a COM Document each year. Since 1980 the references are as follows:

1. Sixth 1980 COM(81)370 final
2. Seventh 1981 COM(82)586 final
3. Eighth 1982 COM(83)566 final
4. Ninth 1983 COM(84)522 final
5. Tenth 1984 COM(85)516 final
6. Eleventh 1985 COM(86)545 final
7. Twelfth 1986 COM(87)521 final.

The *Annual report* has always, in addition, been formally published by OOPEC as a priced publication. Until the eighth report for 1982 (published 1984) these were in a distinct series. From the ninth report for

1983 (published in 1984) and *Annual report* has been published with the Document categorization. The title is published in all the Community languages.

The structure of each report changes from year to year but the standard features of recent reports include:

1. Coordination of regional policies
2. ERDF operations in 'year'
3. Specific Community regional development measures
4. The ERDF from 1975 to 'year'
5. Statistical data
6. Bibliography.

From 1976 until 1985 it was possible to trace through the *Official Journal* 'C' series lists of individual investment projects granted aid from the ERDF. A new process of compiling these lists has prevented their publication in this source since then. The 1986 *Annual report* suggests that these lists will be produced again in the future.

In the United Kingdom Offices of the Commission issue press releases listing United Kingdom projects.

The regions of Europe. Periodic report

The first report in this series, compiled from within DG XVI, was issued as COM(80)816 final. It was also formally published by OOPEC as a priced publication in all Community languages in 1981. In this format its precise title was *The regions of Europe. First periodic report on the social and economic situation of the regions of the Community.*

The second report was initially issued as COM(84)40 final and subsequently published the same year by OOPEC with the Document categorization.

The third report was initially issued as COM(87)230 final and subsequently published by OOPEC during 1987 in English, French and German editions with the Document categorization. The precise title of this report is *The regions of the enlarged Community. Third periodic report on the social and economic situation and development of the regions of the Community. Summary and conclusions.*

The aim of the reports is to give a comprehensive description of the disparities between regions in the Community and their characteristics. Among the features covered in the *Third periodic report* are:

1. Income and employment disparities
2. Labour costs
3. Regional migration
4. Infrastructure endowment of Community regions
5. Regions lagging behind
6. Declining industrial, agricultural, urban, frontier and peripheral regions

7. Problems of convergence and cohesion in the enlarged Community
8. Community and national spending on regional policy
9. Regional aspect of other selected Community policies
10. Statement by the Regional Policy Committee on the *Third periodic report*.

The volume is divided into a 'main report' and an 'annex', the latter containing maps, tables and special analyses on specific topics. The contents pages for the annex are after the main report and have a separate numbering sequence.

Regional Development Programmes

In the *Third periodic report* the point is made that it does not seek to present a detailed description of the situation in each individual region of the member states – that is the function of the separate Regional Development Programmes prepared by the Member States for the Community.

The first series of Programmes were published in the Studies – Regional Policy Series in 1978–79. The aim was to give a description of the seventy-five regions in the Community that were eligible for ERDF assistance in order to give background information on their needs.

The second series (or 'second generation') of Regional Development Programmes were submitted to the Commission by all the member states by 1983. They took the years 1981–85 as their years of reference. The aim of the reports was to give the Commission an opportunity to coordinate national regional policies and Community regional policy more effectively. The Regulation setting up the European Regional Development Fund (Council Regulation (EEC) no. 724/75 of 18 March 1975) makes clear that all schemes submitted for ERDF assistance must 'fall within the framework of a regional development programme'.

The reports of the second generation were published during 1984–85 with the Document categorization. A volume called *The Regional Development Programmes of the second generation for the period 1981–1985* (1985) summarized the reports from all the member states. Editions were published in all Community languages. In addition, separate national reports were published for Germany, Luxembourg, Belgium, the Netherlands, Denmark, Greenland, Italy, Greece and Ireland. Most reports were only published in a limited number of languages. English language editions only exist for the reports for Denmark, Greenland, Greece and Ireland. The reports for France and the United Kingdom were not published.

The third generation of programmes cover the years 1986–90. At the time of writing the only reports published, with the Document categorization, are those for Denmark and the United Kingdom. The latter is in six volumes:

1. *General*
2. *England – North-East, Whitby, Bradford, Humberside*
3. *England – South Yorkshire, Workington, Greater Manchester, Greater Merseyside*
4. *England – West Midlands, Corby, South-West, Cinderford*
5. *Wales*
6. *Scotland and Northern Ireland.*

ERDF in figures

This is a small booklet summarizing the key activities of the European Regional Development Fund for the most recent year that statistics are available. The title is issued annually and was first published in 1983. There are also some tables giving overall ERDF figures from its creation in 1975 to the most recent year.

Titles with the Document categorization

In addition to those titles mentioned above the following titles have been published with the Document categorization of which DG XVI is the author service:

1. *Regional imbalances and national economic performance,* 1985
2. *Main texts governing the regional policy of the European Communities,* 1985
3. *Sectoral productivity and regional policy,* 1985
4. *The contribution of infrastructure to regional development. Final report (with appendix),* 1985
5. *The contribution of infrastructure to regional development. Annex,* 1985
6. *Regional policy and urban decline. The Community's role in tackling urban decline and problems of urban growth. Urban problems in Europe. A review and synthesis of recent literature,* 1986
7. *Agriculture and the regions: the situation and developments in the enlarged Community. The regional impact of the common agricultural policy in Spain and Portugal,* 1987
8. *Impacts régionaux (EUR 10) des deux chocs pétroliers: les liaisons entre politiques énergétiques et politiques de développement régional,* 1987
9. *Research and technological development in the less favoured regions of the Community (STRIDE),* 1987
10. *STRIDE: Science and Technology for Regional Innovation and Development in Europe,* 1988
11. *Urban problems and regional policy in the European Community,* 1988

Internal Documentation on Regional Policy in the Community

Fourteen titles were published in this series between 1978 and 1983. They comprise one-off reports on various aspects of regional policy and are available, if still in stock, from the library of DG XVI. The following is a complete list:

1. *Cross-border communications study for the Londonderry and Donegal area. Summary report*, 1978
2. *Research study into provision for recreation and leisure in areas affected by oil industry in the Highlands and Islands of Scotland. Summary report*, 1978
3. *Stratégie de développement et région rurale. Le cas du Sud-Est de la Belgique. Rapport de synthèse*, 1978
4. *The transfrontier commuters in Europe. Summary report*, 1978
5. *Relocation of economic activities traditionally located in the Copenhagen area. Final report*, 1978
6. *La desserte aérienne interrégionale en Europe. Résumé du rapport 1ère phase*, 1978
7. *Le rôle des activités tertiaires dans la politique régionale. Résumés des études nationales et de leur étude comparative*, 1980
8. *La desserte aérienne interrégionale en Europe. Résumé du rapport*, 1980
9. *Europeans and their regions. Public perception of the socioeconomic disparities: an exploratory study*, 1980
10. *The mobilization of indigenous potential*, 1981
11. *An appreciation of regional policy. Evaluation studies. A comparative study*, 1981
12. *The enlargement of the European Community. The impact of the accession of Spain on certain French regions*, 1981
13. *Repercussions of the enlargement of the EEC on the regions of Italy*, 1981
14. *Analysis and projection of regional labour market balances in Europe (Labeur)*, 1983.

Miscellaneous

1. *Regional development atlas*, 1981: this booklet contained tables and maps giving a regional breakdown of the differences in population, employment, productivity and gross domestic product; an earlier edition had been published in 1979.
2. *The European Community and its regions. 10 years of Community regional policy and of the European Regional Development Fund (ERDF)*, 1985: this pamphlet was published within the European Documentation series but was not part of the numbered sequence of that series.

DG XVII ENERGY

The following series are covered:

1. Studies – Energy Series
2. *Energy in Europe*
3. *Bulletin of Energy Prices*
4. *The energy situation in the Community*
5. European Community Demonstration Projects for Energy Saving and Alternative Energy Sources
6. Miscellaneous.

Studies – Energy series

The first three titles in this series were published between 1968 and 1970. The only other titles published in this series were:

1. (4) *In favour of an energy-efficient society*, 1980.
2. (5) *Energy use in EEC agriculture and food processing*, 1981.

Energy in Europe

This journal is subtitled 'Energy policies and trends in the European Community'. The first issue of *Energy in Europe* was no. 0, December 1984. No. 1 was published in April 1985 and since then it has been published three times a year. *Energy in Europe* is available on subscription from OOPEC in English, French and German editions. No. 7, July 1987 contained an index of articles from all previous issues. The following subject headings in that index indicate the range of subjects covered in *Energy in Europe*:

1. Energy demonstration projects
2. Energy forecasts, markets, statistics
3. Energy models
4. Energy policy
5. Energy savings
6. Gas
7. Nuclear
8. Oil
9. Solid fuels
10. Hydrocarbons technology projects
11. International energy organizations
12. New and renewable energy
13. Prices
14. Regions
15. Research and development.

Energy in Europe aims to help the interested layman and specialist keep abreast of EC activities and policies in the area of energy policy and to show the short-, medium- and long-term energy outlook of the

Community. The first part of the journal is devoted to articles usually summarizing major Commission studies. In the latter part there are short items relating to recent Community activities in the energy field. Each issue also contains a 'technology focus' which highlights the results of Community-sponsored or partially funded research. Some of the articles give references for seeking further information. Each issue also contains a 'Document update', which lists recent Commission Documents, Proposals and Directives in the energy field. This list sometimes includes SEC Documents (see Chapter 4), which officially are not made available to the public.

Bulletin of Energy Prices

This is subtitled 'A survey of consumer prices for oil, coal, gas and electricity in the Community'. The first issue was published in 1984 covering prices up to January 1984. A single issue has been published each year since 1984, although the 1985 issue was called no. 1–2, and the 1987 issue states that the title is published twice a year. *Bulletin of Energy Prices* is available on subscription from OOPEC in a single English–French edition. At the beginning of each issue there is a short comment section with illustrative graphs. The bulk of the work is composed of tables; in the 1987 issue the following tables were presented:

1. Average CIF value of Community supplies of crude oil
2. Average CIF value of Community imports of power station coal
3. Average CIF value of Community imports of coking coal
4. Final consumer prices of energy in January 1987 in national currencies, ECU and PPS (purchasing power standard)
5. Final consumer prices of energy in national currencies 1978–1987
6. Comparison between supplied energy prices – industrial and household sector
7. Comparison between useful energy prices – industrial and household sector
8. Incidence of taxation as percentage of price including VAT.

The energy situation in the Community

This is an annual survey published by OOPEC from 1963 until 1984. Each volume described the energy situation for the previous year and looked at the outlook for the current year. The volumes were divided into a general section plus a description of specific energy sources such as oil, natural gas, coal, electricity and nuclear fuels. The last issue published covered the situation in 1983 and the outlook for 1984.

The title was issued initially as a COM Document. For example, the 1984 edition was issued as COM(84)63 final. This form of publication also ceased after 1984. In 1985 and 1986 there were COM Documents on the situation and outlook for solid fuels (COM(85)83 and COM(86)115) but these were amongst the small proportion of COM Documents not made publicly available. In 1987 this report was issued as a SEC Document(SEC(87)959) and thus definitely to be seen as an internal document.

It should be noted that each issue of *Energy in Europe* contains a feature on the short-term energy outlook in the EC, which partially covers the information previously to be found in *The energy situation in the Community*.

European Community Demonstration Projects for Energy Saving and Alternative Energy Sources

This is a series of leaflets issued by, and only available directly from:

> Commission of the European Communities
> Directorate-General for Energy
> Demonstration Projects
> 200 rue de la Loi
> B-1049 Brussels
> Belgium

Each leaflet describes a project in the EC series Demonstration Programmes on Energy Saving and Alternative Energy Sources. The leaflets are four pages long and make use of high-quality photographs and diagrams. No. 1 in the series was issued in 1983, and over fifty-five had been published by the end of 1987. The leaflets are not dated. A number of them have been listed in the 'Document update' section of *Energy in Europe*, where they are generically called *flag brochures* – the cover of each leaflet has a photograph of all the Community member state flags.

Miscellaneous

DG XVII, like a number of DGs with research and development interests, has issued a number of newsletters over the years on various aspects of its activities. These are aimed specifically at scientists and academics in the fields of interest concerned. Such newsletters often do not have a long life and are generally not published by OOPEC. An example from DG XVII and DG XII was *Energy Saving and Alternative Energy Sources Newsletter*. No. 1 of this title was dated December 1982; no further editions were issued. Another newsletter was called *The Practical Use of Energy and Alternative Sources*. Four issues were published between 1981 and 1982.

Miscellaneous one-off titles from DG XVII since 1980 include:

1. *Public opinion in the European Community: energy*, 1983
2. *Public opinion in the European Community on energy in 1984*, 1985

3. *Evaluation of the Community Demonstration Programmes in the energy sector,* 1982
4. *Energy and development. What challenges? Which methods? Research progress and results,* 1985

DG XVIII CREDIT AND INVESTMENTS

The following series are covered:

1. *Financial report* (European Coal and Steel Community)
2. *Investment in the Community coalmining and iron and steel Industries.*

Financial report

DG XVIII conducts the financial operations of the European Coal and Steel Community from its base in Luxembourg. The *Financial report* has been published annually since 1956 recording the borrowing and lending activities of the Commission in the field covered by the ECSC Treaty. The publication is published by OOPEC and available in all Community languages. It is listed as a free publication in the *Catalogue of Publications.*

The *Financial report* is first issued as a COM Document. In this format there are no colour photographs and diagrams. The report for 1985 was issued as COM(86)473 final, for example.

Investment in the Community coalmining and iron and steel industries

This is an annual report prepared on the basis of a regular survey of investment in the EC coal and steel industries. The survey collects information on actual and forecast capital expenditure and production potential of coal and steel enterprises. Following a general introduction there are more detailed sections on:

1. The coalmining industry
2. Coking plants
3. Iron-ores mines
4. Iron and steel industry
5. Statistical annex.

The title is available from OOPEC as a priced publication. Until the report on the 1984 survey, published 1985, there was a separate version for each Community language. Since 1986 three editions have been published:

1. English/French/German
2. Spanish/Italian/Portuguese
3. Danish/Greek/Dutch.

Note: See Appendix 1, Section 13 for further documentation relating to the European Coal and Steel Community, and to Chapter 13 for the documentation of the Consultative Committee of the European Coal and Steel Community.

DG XXI CUSTOMS UNION AND INDIRECT TAXATION

DG XXI is a new Directorate-General created in 1986. It comprises a coming together of the Customs Union Service, which had been an independent Commission department outside the numbered DG structure, and the indirect taxation section of DG XV.

The customs union is one of the cornerstones of the European Community. In essence a customs union is a group of nations which abolish all customs duties between the member nations and apply a common customs tariff to the imports from all external countries.

While internal customs dues have now been abolished there are still a mass of other restrictive trade rules that impede the free movement of goods between member states. The abolition of such restrictions is an integral part of the initiative started in 1985 to 'complete the internal market by 1992'.

In the area of the external tariff since 1968, the Community, as opposed to the member states, has had the power to enact tariff regulations and amend the Common Customs Tariff (CCT). The CCT itself is a list of approximately 3000 headings representing the goods that can be imported and the rate of duty that is levied on those goods.

This is the background to the documentation of which DG XXI is the current author service. Some of the material discussed emanated from other DGs before 1986.

The following series are covered:

1. *TARIC*
2. *Explanatory notes to the combined nomenclature of the European Communities*
3. *List of authorized customs offices for Community transit operations*
4. *Customs valuation*
5. *Inventory of Taxes*
6. Titles with the Document categorization
7. Miscellaneous.

TARIC

This is the title of a two-volume priced publication issued in 1987 by OOPEC in all Community languages. Amendments will be issued as and when required and new editions will be published periodically.

TARIC stands for Integrated Customs Tariff and came into force for the first time in January 1988. TARIC is in essence an expanded Common Customs Tariff (CCT) with additional information such as preferences, quotas and duty suspensions included.

The classification of goods used in TARIC is called the *Combined Nomenclature* (CN), because it brings together both the annual Regulation modifying the Common Customs Tariff and also the nomenclature used by the EC for the statistics of trading between member states, and between the EC and the rest of the world (NIMEXE).

Until 1986 both the annual Regulation modifying the CCT and the separate annual Regulation amending NIMEXE were printed in editions of the *Official Journal* in December each year. For 1987 the CCT was printed, for example, in the *Official Journal* L345 8.12.86, and NIMEXE in the *Official Journal* L368 29.12.86. The new Combined Nomenclature was published in the *Official Journal* L256 7.9.87.

Explanatory notes to the Combined Nomenclature of the European Communities

The first edition of this title was published, with the Document categorization, in 1987. It is a priced publication from OOPEC available in all languages. It gives guidance on definitions and coverage of the headings in the Combined Nomenclature.

The volume replaces a looseleaf volume called *Explanatory notes to the Customs Tariff of the European Communities*, the last updating of which was the 24th (1 October 1986).

List of authorized customs offices for Community transit operations

This is a list of the customs offices of the member states of the EC, and of Austria and Switzerland, which are authorized to handle Community transit operations. The list is in two sections:

1. Alphabetical list of offices, country by country. For each office information is given of postal address, geographical situation, traffic dealt with, opening hours and special features.
2. Alphabetical index of all offices.

Until 1982 the list was in looseleaf format. Amendment no. 16 (1.3.82) was the last amendment to be circulated. In 1985 a new bound edition was published and this was replaced by a further edition in 1986. A single edition is published by OOPEC with notes in all Community languages.

Customs valuation

This is a looseleaf title sold as a priced publication from OOPEC. The current looseleaf volume was first issued in 1976. The latest updating is the ninth (February 1986), although only published in 1987.

Customs valuation provides those involved in international trade with a practical reference work on the texts relating to customs valuation in the Community. It is divided into five main sections:

1. International conventions concerning customs valuation
2. Community provisions concerning customs valuation
3. Conclusions of the Customs Valuation Committee
4. Judgments of the Court of Justice of the European Communities
5. Chronological compendium of the original texts of the Community provisions concerning customs valuation.

Inventory of taxes: levied by the state and the local authorities (Länder, départements, regions, districts, provinces, communes) in the member states of the European Communities

The traditional author service for this title has been DG XV (see that section in this chapter). The latest edition published in 1986 was compiled by officials in DG XV; however, any future edition will probably be the responsibility of DG XXI.

Titles published with the Document categorization

1. *Clasificación de productos químicos en al arancel de aduanas de las Comunidades europeas – en siete idiomas: danés, aleman, inglés, francés, italiano, holandés y español – repertorio alfabético (en español)*, 1984 (Customs Union Service)
2. *Temporary movement of community goods in the European Community: new rules from 1 July 1985*, 1985. (Customs Union Service)
3. *Community transit: handbook on the use of control copy T no. 5 – situation on 1 September 1985*, 1985 (Customs Union Service)
4. *Transit communautaire – manual d'utilisation de l'exemplaire de contrôle T no. 5 – situation au 15 Octobre 1986*, 1986 (Customs Union Service)
5. *Explanatory notes to the Combined Nomenclature of the European Communities*, 1987.

Miscellaneous

In 1981 OOPEC published a title in the European Perspectives series called *The customs union of the European Economic Community*.

EURATOM SUPPLY AGENCY

The Euratom Supply Agency was established by the Treaty of Rome 1957, which set up the European Atomic Energy Community (Euratom). The Euratom Supply Agency is a part of the Commission. Its function is to ensure the supply of ores, source materials and special fissile materials to all users of such materials. For further details see Articles 52 and 53 of the Treaty of Rome establishing the European Atomic Energy Community.

A brief report on the activities of the Euratom Supply Agency on a year-by-year basis can be found in the 'Energy' section of the *General report on the activities of the European Communities* (see Chapter 4).

Euratom Supply Agency: annual report

Until the 1983 report this was published by OOPEC as a priced publication in English, French and German versions. This continued after 1983 but subsequent reports have been issued with the Document categorization.

The precise structure of the report has changed slightly over the years but since the 1984 report the following features have been standard:

1. Main activities of the supply agency
2. The development of nuclear energy in the Community
3. Supply of nuclear material and enrichment services in the EC
4. Supply of other fuel cycle services
5. International agreements between Euratom and supplier states
6. Administrative report.

Notes and references

1. In 1989 the SME Task Force became part of a new Directorate-General, DG XXIII. The generic term European Business Information Centres has been replaced by the term Euro Info Centres. In May 1989 DG XXIII announced details of the setting up of a further 148 centres. Details can be obtained from Offices of the Commission.
2. In 1988 *Green Europe: Newsletter* and *Green Europe: Newsflash* merged to become *Green Europe*.

CHAPTER 6

Commission – Eurostat Documentation

INTRODUCTION

Eurostat is an acronym, understandable in all Community languages, used to denote the Statistical Office of the European Communities (SOEC). It is regarded as a Directorate-General of the Commission but unlike most other parts of the Commission, which are based in Brussels, Eurostat is primarily based in Luxembourg. Here 300 of the 320 staff establishment of Eurostat work. The balance work in a unit called the Data Shop in Brussels. This was set up in an effort to remedy the problems associated with its separation from the bulk of the Commission.

The first Community statistical service was set up in 1953 to service the High Authority of the Coal and Steel Community. SOEC itself was set up in 1958 as a joint organization for ECSC, Euratom and the EEC. The functions of Eurostat were formulated by the founding head Dr Rolf Wagenführ. They were to serve the Community institutions and monitor Community policies through the collection of statistics from member states, other states and international agencies, and to bring the national statistical systems closer together towards an integrated Community system. The public dissemination of statistical information is an important, although not primary, function of Eurostat.

Since 1973 the Commission has periodically submitted a statistical programme to the Council outlining proposed Eurostat activities for the coming years. During the 1980s the following programmes were issued:

1. Fifth Statistical Programme 1982–84 COM(81)327 final
2. Sixth Statistical Programme 1985–87 COM(84)364 final
3. Seventh Statistical Programme 1989–92 COM(88)696 final

The general lines of the proposed programme are described in a main volume while there are a number of additional volumes devoted to a detailed description of the individual projects which together make up the programme as a whole.

Eurostat is organized into the following Directorates:

1. A: Processing and dissemination of statistical information
2. B: General economic statistics

3. C: External trade, ACP and non-member countries, and transport statistics
4. D: Energy, industry and services
5. E: Demographic, social and agricultural statistics.

(Situation as in April 1988)

The statistics gathered by Eurostat relate primarily to the member states of the European Community. However, in a number of the more general sources such as *Basic statistics of the Community* and *Eurostat review* figures are often also given for the United States, Japan and other countries.

The gathering together of statistics from a large number of national statistical sources with their differing methods and traditions poses many problems. Harmonization has always been a central priority for Community statistics and much has been achieved. However, when using Eurostat statistics it is important to read carefully the introduction to a particular series to be aware of the degree of harmonization involved. If figures are not harmonized then direct comparisons cannot be made, although it is still possible to make comparative analyses of short-term and long-term trends.

EUROSTAT AND COMPUTER USE

The use of computers is integral to the operations of Eurostat. At first computers were primarily used to collect and produce aggregated tables for conventional publications. Recently computer use has developed substantially to cope with the massively increased amount of information submitted to and disseminated by Eurostat. Eurostat is the compiler of a number of databanks, three of which are at present available to the general public and can be consulted online:

1. Cronos: contains over one and a half million macroeconomic time series divided into twenty-one domains. These are grouped together into seven themes corresponding to the themes used for printed documentation described later in this chapter. The data describes the member states, and in some cases, the United States, Japan and other third world countries. Eurostatus is a part of the Cronos databank. It includes 625 time series containing macroeconomic harmonized data covering various aspects of the economy of the member states, Japan and the United States. Eurostatus, in addition to being available online, is also available on diskette
2. Regio: contains information on the main aspects of the economic life of the regions of the member states of the EC. Regional breakdown is possible at three different levels. The data includes

such features as population structure, employment, economic accounts, agricultural production, industrial structure, transport and financial aid

3. Comext: contains the statistics of external trade between the member states of the EC and other countries. Data is broken down on the basis of the European nomenclature (Nimexe) into 8000 different goods.

Access to these databanks is available through commercial online information suppliers. For further information of the databanks of Eurostat contact the address given on p. 193.

DOCUMENTATION

In Annex 1 to the Sixth Statistical Programme of the European Communities 1985–1987 (COM(84)364 final/Annex 1: Processing and dissemination of statistical information), the point is made that conventional printed publications account for a rapidly diminishing proportion of the information disseminated by Eurostat. A greater proportion is disseminated by online means, magnetic tape and microfiche.

However Eurostat still remains, and will continue to remain, a substantial publisher of conventionally printed statistical titles. In fact if one discounts the *Official Journal*, Eurostat accounts for approximately one-quarter of the official publications of the European Communities. In 1987 ninety-four titles were published, and in addition a number of 'internal' titles were made publicly available in a controlled circulation. Publications can sometimes be seen as an introduction to more detailed data available in other formats.

Users of EC statistical publications sometimes get exasperated with the seemingly frequent and arbitrary changes in titles published, patterns of publication, and the content therein. Primarily the Statistics Office produces statistics for the policy needs of the EC institutions, and at different times there are different priorities, necessitating changes in publication patterns. Nevertheless it is also clear that Eurostat are constantly working hard to improve the service they provide to outside users of EC statistics. During the 1980s, for example, there was considerable development in the area of the rapid availability of statistics and in improved analysis of these statistics. Improvements in the presentation of the publications in such features as standardized covers, the production of the tables and in the use of diagrams can also be noted.

Above all a structured classification of Eurostat publications has developed. This classification has two aspects – themes and series. Before 1980 there had been some form of colour coding of Eurostat publications. However, it was from 1980 that this was regularized and streamlined with the creation of a classification based on themes or subjects. This was further developed with the creation in 1985 of the 'series' indicating the precise nature of a publication.

CLASSIFICATION OF EUROSTAT PUBLICATIONS

Theme

1. General Statistics (dark blue cover) (grey until 1985)
2. Economy and Finance (violet cover)
3. Population and Social Conditions (yellow cover)
4. Energy and Industry (light blue cover)
5. Agriculture, Forestry and Fisheries (green cover)
6. Foreign Trade (red cover)
7. Services and Transport (orange cover)
8. Miscellaneous (brown cover).

Series

A: Yearbooks
B: Short-term Trends
C: Accounts, Surveys and Statistics
D: Studies and Analyses
E: Methods
F: Rapid Report.

From 1986 each Eurostat title has been slotted into this classification scheme and the code listed on the front cover. Thus *Basic statistics of the Community* has the classification code 1A, *Rapid reports – population and social conditions* has the code 3F, and *Agricultural income – sectoral income index Analysis 1986* has the code 5D, for example.

Individual titles published by Eurostat are discussed later in the chapter broken down into 'themes'. It is useful to discuss here in a little more detail the meaning of the various series codes. This information has been obtained from *Eurostat News*, 4, 1985.

Series A: Yearbooks

These are regarded as the most prestigious Eurostat publications. The purpose of these yearbooks is to provide broad information on the statistics of the subject concerned and to refer the reader to more rapid or detailed information to be found elsewhere. Comparative data is given for Japan and the United States. Composition or photocomposition techniques are used and there is a systematic attempt to exploit the value of diagrammatic representation. Tables are usually presented in two languages but the aim is to provide short introductions in all Community languages.

Series B: Short-term Trends

The principal feature of titles published in this series is that they deal with the short-term economic climate, which necessitates that the titles should be published as and when the information becomes available. In effect this means that titles published in this series are published monthly or quarterly and contain date that is submitted at these intervals regularly to Eurostat. These periodic bulletins are published in two or three languages, but explanatory leaflets in other languages are appended to the first issue of a title each year, or issued separately.

Series C: Accounts, Surveys and Statistics

Only small numbers of copies are published of titles in this series, which are intended for a specialist readership. In a number of instances conventional publication has ceased and the information is now only available on microfiche or floppy disks. Where conventional publication continues titles are published usually in only two languages. The majority of Series C titles are either annual or non-periodic.

Series D: Studies and Analyses

Titles in this series are mainly devoted to the analysis of specific subjects and will have a useful life of several years. Usually only one or two language versions will be published and most titles issued are non-periodic.

Series E: Methods (methodologies, nomenclatures and user guides)

A recent trend has been to cut down the length of methodological explanations in the regular Eurostat publications to a small number of pages. For specialist users of statistics the detailed methodological basis for a series is sometimes now published in a separate one-off title in all Community languages, which remains relevant for a number of years. User guides are a further extension of this concept.

Series F: Rapid Reports

Titles in this series consist of statistical bulletins a few pages long giving, with comments, the main findings of a survey for which the figures have just become available or a brief analysis (including the use of graphs, tables, comments and maps) of statistics which have just been received by Eurostat. While titles in this series give information in their own right they also serve a function of providing publicity for other Eurostat titles. Titles are non-periodic in character, usually produced in only two single-language versions or one two-language version and are usually available free of charge as a supplement to a regular Eurostat title. Being rather ephemeral in nature this series, more than others, is prone to changes in title. During the early 1980s the generic heading Statistical Bulletin often appeared on the cover, along with the subject title. Later in the decade the heading Rapid Reports took over as the generic title.

EUROSTAT TITLES

The titles described below are divided by 'theme' and the further subdivisions as used by Eurostat in 1987. Statistical sources do often change name and coverage. The list is thus probably not entirely comprehensive and reference should be made to recent issues of *Eurostat News* for the most up-to-date listing of Eurostat titles available. Internal publications are not generally listed although some are made available publicly. The Statistical Programme lists such publications.

A full bibliographical history of a title is only given when there have been changes in the 1980s. *Eurostat News* will indicate which Eurostat databank has been used to produce the publication, and the publications themselves will indicate whether more detailed information is available in other formats. With the accession of new members in the 1980s the statistical definition of the EC as a whole has changed from EUR 9 through EUR 10 to EUR 12. It is necessary to read carefully in each publication the basis of the 'EC' definition.

Theme 1: General statistics

Basic statistics of the Community (1A, annual)

This is a pocket-sized paperback comparing the most important statistical data of the European Community with a number of other European countries, Canada, Japan, the United States and the USSR. Intended primarily for the layman, *Basic statistics*, which contains a number of colour graphs as well as tables, covers the following fields:

1. National accounts
2. Regional accounts
3. Finance
4. Balance of payments
5. Prices
6. Population
7. Education and training
8. Employment
9. Social protection
10. Energy
11. Iron and steel
12. Agriculture, forestry and fisheries (production, consumption, balances, structure, prices and economic accounts)
13. Foreign trade

14. Services
15. Transport.

The 25th edition published in 1988 contains statistics up to and including 1986.

Eurostat Review (1A, annual)

This title gives EC statistics showing overall trends within the Community over a period of ten years. Comparisons are made with Japan, the United States and Sweden. In addition to tables, use is made of coloured maps and graphs. The edition published in 1987 contains data covering the period 1976–85. *Eurostat Review* is divided into seven main sections corresponding to themes 1–7 of the Eurostat classification, plus a section called European Community institutions. This gives some useful statistical information, not always easily available from other sources, concerning the institutions, the budget and the European Development Fund. For example, you can find out the number of staff in each of the EC institutions, the number of plenary sessions of the Economic and Social Committee, the number of written questions in the European Parliament and the number of Council meetings in each of the years covered by the volume.

Eurostatistics: Data for Short-term Economic Analysis (1B, monthly)

This title is a monthly report on short-term economic development, which seeks to provide information rapidly. Four kinds of information are published in *Eurostatistics*:

1. In brief: a short article in each issue looking at the latest trends in the data available
2. A visual presentation of the most important economic series for the EC, the twelve member states, the United States and Japan
3. Short-term trends: presents data harmonized by Eurostat on the basis of common criteria for the member states as a whole, with comparisons with the United States and Japan
4. Tables by country: shows a selection of the most common economic indicators used in each member state, the United States and Japan.

Tables included in the 'short-term trends' section include

1. National accounts
2. Employment
3. Unemployment
4. Industrial production
5. Opinions in industry
6. Industrial products

7. Retail sales
8. Agricultural products
9. External trade
10. Consumer prices
11. Producer prices of agricultural products
12. Wages and salaries
13. Financial statistics
14. Balance of payments.

The above describes *Eurostatistics* since 1985. Prior to that there were certain differences in the contents.

Regions: Statistical Yearbook (1A, annual)

The purpose of this yearbook is to show the main aspects of the economic and social life of the regions within the member states. The 'regions' are those as defined in NUTS, the Community's nomenclature of statistical territorial units. In the yearbook levels I and II of NUTS are used. In addition to a large pullout map of the regions and a number of other coloured maps, the tables cover the following topics:

1. Population
2. Employment and unemployment
3. Agriculture
4. Energy
5. Industry
6. Transport
7. Living standards
8. The Community's financial participation in investments.

In the 1985 *Yearbook* there is also a section analysing the European elections in 1984 by a regional breakdown. From its inception in 1981 until 1985 this title was called *Yearbook of Regional Statistics*.

Regions: The Community's Financial Participation in Investments (1C, annual)

This title gives a regional breakdown of the financial support granted by the Community under the following headings:

1. European Regional Development Fund (ERDF)
2. European Agricultural Guidance and Guarantee Fund (EAGGF), Guidance Section
3. European Investment Bank (EIB) – loans from own resources and the New Community Instrument (NCI)
4. European Coal and Steel Community
5. Euratom.

From its inception in 1975 until the volume published in 1985 (covering 1983) the title was *Regional Statistics: the Community's financial participation in investments* and it was issued in Theme 2 with pink covers.

Further statistics relating to the ERDF can be found in *European Regional Development Fund: annual report* (see Chapter 5); to the operations of the EIB in its *Annual report* (see Chapter 13); to the EAGGF in *The agricultural situation in the community* (see Chapter 4); and to the operations of ECSC in its *Financial report* (see Chapter 5).

Regional Accounts ESA: Detailed Tables by Branches (1C, annual)

This title gives main aggregates of economic accounts down up for the Community's basic administrative units. Time series are given for value-added by groups of branches (agriculture, industry, services), for population and for employment. Editions published up to 1985 (basically covering 1981) were issued in Theme 2 with pink covers.

Rapid Reports: Regions (1F, occasional)

This publication started in 1985 and is issued irregularly. The issues of 1985 and 1986 had the title *Regions*. Each issue covers a particular subject. For example, the October 1986 issue covers 'Unemployment in the regions 1986' and the January 1987 issue covers 'Community financing of regional investment in 1985'.

ACP: Basic Statistics (1A, annual)

This is a pocket-sized paperback providing basic information on the ACP and Mediterranean countries which have association agreements with the EC. The publication is divided into four parts:

1. The ACP countries in the world
2. Principal economic and social indicators by ACP state
3. The activities of the EDF and the EIB under the Lomé agreements
4. The Mediterranean countries.

The following topics are covered:

1. Population
2. National accounts
3. Industrial, mining and agricultural production
4. External trade
5. Prices
6. Finance
7. External aid
8. Standard of living.

The title began in 1981 and has appeared annually since 1984. Prior to that there had been the *ACP: Statistical Yearbook*, 1978 and 1980.

Reports on ACP Countries (1C, irregular)

The first in this important new series, covering Zaire, was published in 1988. Eurostat intend to build up a series which will give the main current statistical information for each of the ACP countries. In the volume covering Zaire there are statistical tables and substantial accompanying text on the following topics:

1. Population
2. Health
3. Education
4. Employment
5. Agriculture, forestry and fisheries
6. Manufacturing industry
7. External trade
8. Transport and communications
9. Tourism
10. Public accounts
11. Wages and salaries
12. Prices
13. National accounts
14. Balance of payments
15. Development planning.

The series is essentially a translation into English and French editions by Eurostat of an existing series called Statistics of Foreign Countries from the Statistical Office of the Federal Republic of Germany.

Statistical panorama of Europe

This is a one-off pamphlet published in 1984; it is a simple introductory guide to some basic EC statistics in diagrammatic form.

Theme 2: Economy and finance

1. National accounts
2. Prices
3. Money and finance
4. Balance of payments.
   (Regional accounts and finance titles were moved to Theme 1 in 1986)

National accounts (ESA: European system of integrated economic accounts)

Quarterly National Accounts ESA (2B, quarterly)
This title started in 1986. It gives annual and quarterly trends in the main aggregates of national accounts, in volume and in price, for the EC,

Germany, France, Italy, the United Kingdom, the United States and Japan.

National Accounts ESA – Aggregates (2C, annual)
This title gives the main national accounts aggregates of the EC countries, the United States and Japan, divided into two main sections:

1. Comparative tables
2. Tables by country.

National Accounts ESA – Detailed Tables by Branch (2C, annual)
This title gives data on transactions in goods and services for member states – gross value-added, wages and salaries, gross fixed capital formation, final consumption of households – together with a branch-by-branch breakdown of employment, structural data and figures based on purchasing power parities.

National Accounts ESA – Detailed Tables by Sector (2C, annual)
This title brings together the economic and financial accounts for the EC and its member states' institutional sectors – for example, government, households, credit institutions and insurance companies.

General Government Accounts and Statistics (2C, annual)
This title shows the total of general government transactions broken down into three subsectors:

1. Central government
2. Local government
3. Social security funds.

National Accounts ESA – Input–Output Tables (2C, occasional)
This title contains the input–output tables of the EC member states. The latest edition, covering 1980, was published in 1986. These give a detailed description of the flow of goods and services within a national economy and with the rest of the world.

Studies of National Accounts (2D, occasional)
This series of occasional titles supplement the regular national accounts publications and comprise either methodological studies or analyses of the data. The titles so far issued are:

1. *The treatment in the national accounts of goods and services for individual consumption produced, distributed or paid for by government*, 1983
2. *Stock of fixed assets in industry in the Community member states: towards greater comparability*, 1983
3. *Trends in the public finances of the member states (1970–1981)*, 1983
4. *Structural database tables by branch 1960–1981*, 1984
5. *Accounts of the institutional sectors: an initial analysis of*

companies, households and banks in the member states (1970–82), 1984

6. *The degree of similarity in the economics of the EEC countries 1975 and 1970/1981,* 1984

7. *Current international thinking and objectives for the revision of the systems of national accounts,* 1985

8. *Main indicators of economic accounts in the EC, the United States and Japan 1970–1983,* 1985

9. *Europe, United States, Japan 1970–86: main indicators of economic accounts,* 1986 .

Miscellaneous

Since 1979 a number of one-off titles have been published:

1. *European system of integrated economic accounts ESA,* 2nd edition, 1980 (2E)

2. *National accounts ESA – 1970–1978.* Detailed financial tables, 1981 (2C)

3. *Multilateral measurements of purchasing power and real GDP 1981,* 1982 (2D)

4. *Comparison in real value of the aggregates of ESA 1980,* 1983 (2C)

5. *Comparison of national accounts aggregates between Austria and the European Community,* 1984 (2D)

6. *Comparison of national accounts aggregates between Israel and the European Community,* 1985 (2D)

7. *Proceedings of the seminar on the provision and use of economic statistics, Gaborone, 6–10 April 1987,* 1987 (2D)

8. *Purchasing power parities and gross domestic product in real terms, Results 1985,* 1988 (2C)

Prices

Consumer Price Indices (2C, occasional)

This title gives monthly and annual figures for the consumer price index for the EC member states, the United States, Canada and Japan. A further breakdown into sectors such as food, clothing, transport and household goods is given for all the above countries except Canada and Japan. A volume published in 1983 covers the years 1976–82, and another in 1986 covers the year 1982–85. Both also contain a historical review of consumer price indexes from 1955. From 1987 the information contained in this title was issued in the quarterly supplement to the title *Consumer Price Index.*

Consumer Price Index (2B, monthly)

This title began in 1986 and gives the up-to-date general consumer price index for the EC member states, the United States, Japan, Canada, and a number of other West European states. A quarterly supplement to this title is issued giving a more detailed breakdown by sector.

Money and finance

Money and Finance (2B, quarterly)

This title started in 1984 and brings together various financial statistics relating to the EC, the United States and Japan. The information given includes:

1. Structural indicators: includes financial accounts, money supply, interest rates, public finance, exchange rate, foreign reserves
2. European Monetary System (EMS): includes composition of the ECU basket, central rates, realignments, intervention margins and divergence indicators
3. Current statistics: includes money supply , savings deposits, public finance, interest rates and share yields, index of share prices, exchange rates, and foreign official reserves.

ECU-EMS Information (2B, monthly)

This title started in 1987 and gives data on the European Monetary System and private uses of the ECU. This includes:

1. Daily and monthly ECU exchange rates and current central rates
2. Bilateral fluctuations of the EMS currencies
3. Consumer price indices in ECU
4. ECU denominated bond issues and their yields, together with interest rates for ECU deposits.

Balance of payments

Balance of Payments: Global Data (2C, annual)

This title gives annual balance of payments data for each EC member state, the United States and Japan over a period of years, broken down into:

1. Summary tables: trade balance; current balance; basic balance; reserves
2. Tables by heading: goods and services; unrequited transfers; current account; capital; reserves
3. Tables by country.

The last edition of this title was published in 1985 and covers global data 1972–83. Since then the information has been contained in an annex to issue no. 3 of each year's *Balance of Payments: Quarterly Data* (see below).

Balance of Payments: Geographical Breakdown (2C, annual)

This title is divided into two sections:

1. Country tables: balances by reporting country and by geographical zone
2. Tables for selected items: tables by heading and by geographical zone.

Balance of Payments: Quarterly Data (2B, quarterly)
This title contains the information included in *Balance of Payments: Global Data* but broken down into quarters for recent years. Since 1985 issue no. 3 of this title for each year has contained global data for the previous eleven years, originally published separately.

National Methodologies of Balance of Payments (2E, occasional)
This is the generic title given to a series of booklets which seek to describe the principles, definitions and methods applied by the member states to establish their balance of payments. The titles so far published are:

1. *Balance of payments methodology of the United Kingdom*, 1983 (English and French)
2. *The balance of payments statistics of the Federal Republic of Germany*, 1983 (German, English and French)
3. *Balance of payments methodology of France*, 1984 (French and English)
4. *Methodology of the balance of payments of the Belgo-Luxembourg Economic Union*, 1984 (French, Dutch and English)
5. *Balance of payments methodology of Denmark*, 1985 (Danish, English and French)
6. *Balance of payments methodology of Greece*, 1986 (Greek, English and French).

Theme 3: Population and social conditions

1. Population
2. Employment and unemployment
3. General social statistics
4. Wages and incomes
5. Education and training
6. Social protection
7. Other.

Population

Demographic Statistics (3C, annual)
This title first gives EC tables and then country tables for the following topics:

1. Population (by sex and age groups)
2. Birth and death rates
3. Marriages and divorces
4. Fertility
5. Life expectation
6. Population projection
7. Migration.

Population (3F, occasional)
From 1982 until 1985 this title appeared with the generic heading Statistical Bulletin on the cover. Usually only one issue a year was published – an updating by one year of the principal figures given in *Demographic Statistics*. It ceased publication in 1986 to be incorporated in the new title *Rapid Reports: Population and Social Conditions* from 1987.

Miscellaneous
Since 1980 the following miscellaneous titles have been produced:

1. *Comparative study of the contingents entering and leaving the population of working age 1973–1977* (3C, 1981)
2. *A study on the future of the census of population: alternative approaches* (3C, 1987)
3. *Censuses of population in the Community countries 1981–1982* (3C, 1988)
4. *Demographic and labour force analysis based on Eurostat databanks* (3D, 1988).

Employment and unemployment

Employment and Unemployment (3C, annual)
This title gives statistics on the following aspects of the labour market:

1. Population
2. Active population and employment by sex, status and sector of activity
3. Paid employment in industry and services (SITC and NACE nomenclatures)
4. Registered unemployment, and vacancies
5. Industrial disputes
6. Working hours.

Figures are given covering a ten-year timespan for the EC and the member states. Some international comparisons are given for the main series with the United States and Japan, while there are also a number of coloured charts to illustrate main trends.

Unemployment (3B, monthly)
This title shows the unemployment situation in the member states for the latest month available. The figures for one month are usually published in this title by the end of the following month. The figures are broken down by sex, and show:

1. Total number of unemployed
2. Variation (in per cent) over the previous month
3. Unemployment rate
4. Unemployed under 25 (by number and percentage)
5. Foreigners unemployed (by number and percentage)

6. Job vacancies
7. Newly registered unemployed.

Employment and Unemployment (3F, occasional)
Until 1981 this series also showed the generic title Rapid Information on the cover. Issues 2–4, 1981 and 1, 1982 had no generic title; Statistical Bulletin was used from issue 2, 1982 until 5, 1983. From then until its demise in 1986 no generic title was used. Each issue provided data and comment on a separate subject. From 1987 the information contained in this series was incorporated in *Rapid Reports: Population and Social Conditions*.

Labour Force Survey: Results (3C, annual)
The EC has conducted a series of labour force sample surveys since 1960. From 1973 until 1983 the survey was carried out biennially but since 1983 it has been annual. The survey is a harmonized and synchronized sample survey to determine the level and structure of employment and unemployment in the EC. The structure of the survey allows for comparison between countries and over a period of time, and includes figures on the following topics:

1. Population and activity rates (often broken down by age)
2. Employment (by sector and trade)
3. Working time
4. Unemployment and search for work.

The present title has been in use since the 1984 survey. Earlier it was called *Labour Force Sample Survey*.

Miscellaneous
Since 1981 the following miscellaneous titles have been published:

1. *Vacancies notified: methods and measurement in the European Community* (3E, 1982)*
2. *Multiple job holders: an analysis of second jobs in the European Community* (3D, 1982)*
3. *Industrial disputes: methods and measurement in the European Community* (3E, 1982)*
4. *Handicapped and their employment: statistical study of the situation in the member states of the European Communities* (3D, 1983)
5. *Duration of unemployment: methods and measurement in the European Community, 1982* (3E, 1983)*
6. *Working time statistics: methods and measurement in the European Community* (3E, 1984)*
7. *Definitions of registered unemployed, 1984* (3E, 1985)* (an interim edition of this title was published in 1982)
8. *Labour force sample survey: methods and definitions* (3E, 1985)
9. *Trade union membership: methods and measurement in the European Community* (3E, 1985)*

10. *Schemes with an impact on the labour market and their statistical treatment in the member states of the European Community* (3D, 1987)

11. *Definition of registered unemployed* (3E, 1987) (Replaced 1985 edition)★

★These titles form part of a series called: Studies in Labour Market Statistics. The other title in the series is *A guide to current sources of wage statistics in the European Community* (3E, 1984), (see Wages and incomes).

General social statistics

Social Indicators for the European Community: Selected Series (3C, occasional)

This title gives data on selected aspects of the social situation in the EC. An edition was published in 1980 covering the years 1960–78. A further edition was published in 1984 and covers the following topics:

Part A
1. Unemployment
2. Employment
3. The trend in employment in manufacturing industries
4. The position of women in the Community
5. Community regional indicators.

Part B
1. The European Community and the world
2. Population
3. Consumer price indices
4. Exchange rates
5. Earnings
6. Working time
7. Public holidays
8. National accounts
9. Private consumption per inhabitant
10. Means of communication and information
11. Pupils and students in full time education
12. Social protection
13. Medical services
14. Housing.

As can be seen from list above this title covers a broad field – more detailed figures on many of the subjects can be found in other Eurostat titles. With its extensive use of coloured graphs and diagrams the title is, like the titles in theme 1, particularly suited to non-experts in statistical analysis.

Miscellaneous

The following miscellaneous titles have been published since 1980:

1. *Methodology of surveys on family budgets, 1979* (3E, 1980)
2. *Pensioners in the Community, 1977* (3C, 1981)
3. *Economic and social position of women in the Community* (3C, 1981)
4. *Economic and social features of households in the member states of the European Community* (3C, 1982)
5. *Consumer prices in the EC. 1980* (3C, 1983)
6. *Family budgets: comparative tables: Germany–France–Italy–United Kingdom* (3C, 1984)
7. *Family budgets: comparative tables: Netherlands–Belgium–Ireland–Denmark–Greece–Spain* (3C, 1986).

Wages and incomes

Structure of Earnings: Principal Results 1978/1979 (3C, occasional)
This title is a ten-volume work which first appeared in 1983. Each volume is devoted to a single member state and gives thirty-four tables of data. These comprise the main results of the Community survey on the structure and distribution of earnings in industry, wholesale and retail trade, and banking and insurance for the period 1978–79. A much enlarged number of tables is available on microfiche. The volumes are as follows:

Volume 1: *Methods and definitions*
Volume 2: *France* (1983)
Volume 3: *Luxembourg* (1984)
Volume 4: *Belgium* (1984)
Volume 5: *Denmark* (1984)
Volume 6: *Netherlands* (1985)
Volume 7: *Germany* (1985)
Volume 8: *Italy* (1985)
Volume 9: *Ireland* (1985)
Volume 10: *United Kingdom* (1986).

Earnings in Industry and Services (3B, half-yearly)
This title began in 1983 and replaces *Hourly Earnings: Hours of Work*, which ceased in 1982. Although advertised as a twice-yearly publication the two issues for 1985 (published 1986) and 1986 (published 1987) were combined into a single volume for each year. This title gives detailed results of the harmonized statistics on the earnings of manual and non-manual workers in industry and certain groups of activities in the services sector. It also gives the main results of the surveys of labour costs and updated figures for the years between two surveys (see *Labour Costs*, below). The data is broken down according to NACE (General Industrial Classification of Economic Activities within the European Communities). Results are given for each member state, and are further

broken down into regions for Germany, Italy, the Netherlands, Belgium and the United Kingdom.

Labour Costs (3C, occasional)
This title forms part of the Community system of wages statistics which has the objective of showing the various aspects of labour costs and earnings. The results are broken down by branch of activity, by size classes of the establishments and by region. Labour cost surveys are held every three years – for industry they have been held in 1966, 1969, 1972, 1975, 1978, 1981 and 1984. Surveys on commerce, banking and insurance were held in 1970 and 1974 before being conducted at the same time as the industry survey.

The 1981 survey was published in two volumes in 1984 and the 1984 in two volumes in 1987:

1. Volume 1: *Principal results for all branches of activity and data on the cost structure of selected branches of activity*
2. Volume 2: *Results by size classes and by regions.*

As with most EC harmonized surveys, more detailed tables are available on microfiche and magnetic tape.

Earnings in Agriculture (3C, occasional)
This little presents the results of the occasional surveys of the earnings of permanent workers in agriculture in the member states. The 1980 survey results were published in 1983 and the 1984 survey results in 1986. In addition to earnings this title also can be used to find out the numbers working in agriculture in the member states and the hours worked. The title is broken down into:

1. General results
2. Results for each country
3. Results by region (not for all member states).

Wages and Incomes: Statistical Bulletin (3F, occasional)
This title was used from 1982 until 1986 for the bulletin which gave summary results of such EC surveys as structure of earnings, and labour costs. From 1987 this title was replaced by *Rapid reports: population and social conditions*.

Miscellaneous
Since 1980 the following miscellaneous title has been published:

1. *Guide to current sources of wage statistics in the European Community* (3E, 1984) (part of the series Studies in Labour Market Statistics).

Education and training

Education and Training (3C, occasional)
This title was published at two-yearly intervals from 1976 until 1980.

The next edition was dated 1985 (published 1986). The point is made in the introduction to that edition that the differing structures of education systems in the member states makes direct comparisons difficult. The tables in the latest edition comprise:

1. Numbers and percentage of pupils and students by level of education and age
2. Enrolment ratios by age
3. The ratio of girls to boys
4. Pupils and students as a percentage of the population
5. Foreign pupils and students by level, nationality and as a percentage of all pupils and students
6. Pupils learning a foreign language
7. Third level students by field of study
8. Pupils and students by national types of education
9. Full-time and part-time teachers
10. Public expenditure on education and training.

Education and Training: Statistical Bulletin (3F, occasional)
This title was used for the bulletin from 1982 to 1985. Until 1982 the phrase *Rapid Information* was used instead of *Statistical Bulletin*. With the long gap (1980–85) between editions of the major publication *Education and Training*, the bulletins were the main source of printed statistics in this subject area. Each bulletin was devoted to a single subject – for example, public expenditure on education and training, and numbers in full-time education. The last issue was 1985 and since 1987 the title has been formally replaced by *Rapid Reports: Population and Social Conditions*.

Social protection

Social Protection: Statistical Bulletin (3F, occasional)
This title was used from 1982 to 1986, when *Statistical Bulletin* was replaced by *Rapid Reports*.

Miscellaneous
The following miscellaneous title was published in the period after 1980:

1. *European system of integrated social protection statistics (ESSPROS) methodology Part 1 1980* (3E, 1981).

Other

Rapid Reports: Population and Social Conditions (3F, occasional)
This title began in 1987 and replaced *Wages and Incomes: Statistical Bulletin, Education and Training: Statistical Bulletin, Employment and Unemployment: Statistical Bulletin* and *Population: Statistical Bulletin*. The aim of all these publications was to publish important statistical

data, including comments and graphics, as soon as the data became available.

Miscellaneous

The following miscellaneous title was published after 1980:

1. *Statistical assessment of land use: the impact of remote sensing and other recent developments on methodology* (3E, 1987).

Theme 4: Energy and industry

1. Energy
2. Industry
3. Iron and steel
4. Raw materials.

Energy

Energy: Statistical Yearbook (4A, annual)

Until 1983 this title was called *Energy Statistics Yearbook*. The current title began with the 1984 volume, published 1986, and gives a range of date on energy supply and demand in the EC and the member states. It is divided into three main sections:

1. Base data of the energy economy from an analytical viewpoint: historical series of indicators show the development of the main energy aggregates for the Community and for each member state and these are compared with some general economic indicators and define the structural changes which have occurred during the last few years
2. 'Energy supplied' balance sheets
3. Historical series for each energy source (coal; hydrocarbons; electrical energy).

Useful energy balance sheets appears as an occasional supplement to *Energy: Statistical Yearbook*. An edition covering 1980 was published in 1983, and a further edition covering 1985 was published in 1988.

Energy: Monthly Statistics (4B, monthly)

This title began in 1986 and replaced three separate monthly bulletins: *Coal*, *Hydrocarbons* and *Electrical Energy*. The main divisions of the new title are as follows:

1. Coal
2. Hydrocarbons
3. Electrical energy
4. General data.

The first three sections deal with short-term trends in supply and consumption, while the fourth section gives the general results for energy as a whole and explains trends in energy supply and demand in terms of economic indicators, energy prices, and climatic conditions.

Rapid Reports: Energy (4F, occasional)
This title began in 1986 and replaces *Energy: Statistical Telegram*. It aims to make public information in the energy sector which has just become available. Generally issues are published in the early months of a year and give the first account of some aspect of the energy economy for the previous year.

Structural Aspects of Energy (4C, occasional)
This title began with no. 1 in June 1986 and gives up-to-date information on the structural aspects of the coal, hydrocarbons and electrical energy industry.

Miscellaneous
The following miscellaneous titles have been published since 1980:

1. *Energy balance sheets based on the input–output tables (1975)* (4C, 1982)
2. *Energy price indices 1960–1980* (4C, 1982)
3. *Useful energy balance sheets* (4C, 1983)
4. *Principles and methods of the energy balance sheets* (4E, 1988)
5. *Energy balance sheets* (4D, 1988)
6. *Useful energy balance sheets 1985. Supplement to Energy Statistics Yearbook* (1988).

Electricity Prices (4C, annual)
The first edition of this title was published in 1980 (covering electricity prices for the years 1973–78). Another edition was published in 1984 (1978–84) and thereafter it has been annual. Prices are given for all member states, Spain and Portugal being included from the 1986 edition. Electricity prices to industrial and domestic consumers are recorded in around thirty cities and conurbations, using a 'standard consumer' presentation. The accompanying text sets out the definitions and gives further details of tariff and tax systems and offers a price analysis with international comparisons.

Gas Prices (4C, annual)
The first edition of this title was published in 1977 (covering gas prices for the years 1970–76), and the second in 1980 (1976–80). From the third edition published in 1984 (1978–84) the title has become annual. The structure of the publication is the same as that of *Electricity Prices*.

Operation of Nuclear Power Stations (4C, annual)
This title gives information on the following features:

Part one
1. Principal statistics for the year in question
2. Structure of nuclear plant
3. Stations under construction
4. Evolution of net production

5. International comparison
6. Energy availability.

Part two
1. Monthly operation for the year in question of every nuclear power station in the EC.
2. Historical statistics of annual operation for every nuclear power station in the EC.

Industry

Industry: Statistical Yearbook (4A, annual)
The first issue of this publication in 1984 was called *Yearbook of Industrial Statistics*. The current title began with the second edition, 1985 (published 1986). The aim of the yearbook is to permit rapid and comprehensive analysis of the industrial structure of the EC, its member states, and, for comparison, Japan and the United States. Data shows the role of industry in the EC, the position of industry in the wider context of the European economy and in the regions of the Community. There are a number of colour graphs and maps. The *Yearbook* contains the following main sections:

1. Graphs and diagrams
2. Industry in the EC, the United States and Japan
3. Employment in industry
4. Structure and activity of industry
5. Data by size of enterprise
6. Industrial products: production and external trade
7. Index of industrial production
8. Regional industrial statistics
9. Energy and raw materials.

Many of the tables in the *Yearbook* are taken from more specialized Eurostat titles, some from titles not issued in theme 4. These are all listed in the *Yearbook*.

Industrial Trends: Monthly Statistics (4B, monthly)
Until 1985 this title was called *Industrial Short-term Trends*. It gives information, updated monthly, on industrial activity in the EC. Data is broken down by branch of industry and includes statistics for production, turnover, new orders, number of employees, wages and salaries, and imports and exports. Occasional supplements deal with methodology and retrospective series. There are numerous graphs.

Industrial Production: Quarterly Statistics (4B, quarterly)
This title began in 1982 as *Industrial Production*. Note that in 1985 only two issues were published and in that year also there was a rationalization of the contents. The words *Quarterly Statistics* have only been used on

the cover from 1986. It gives statistics of industrial production broken down as follows:

1. Man-made fibres, textiles, clothing
2. Leather and footwear
3. Pulp, paper and board
4. Data processing machinery
5. Domestic-type electric appliances
6. Mechanical engineering products
7. Miscellaneous sectors (these figures are not harmonized but include such important industries as food and drink, transport equipment, timber, glass and the chemical industry).

Structure and Activity of Industry: Annual Inquiry – Main Results
(4C, annual)

In this work Eurostat publishes the main results of the coordinated annual inquiry into industrial activity carried out by the member states. There is a considerable delay in the publication of the data for a particular year – the data for the inquiries of 1982 and 1983 was only published in 1987, for example. The annual nature of the title began in 1981 (covering the 1976 inquiry). Previously a more detailed but irregular publication had been issued. The inquiry covers all establishments in industry and handicrafts which employ twenty or more people and whose principal economic activity is listed in one of the three-digit headings of the General Industrial Classification of Economic Activities (NACE). Data includes:

1. Numbers of employees
2. Labour costs
3. Production values
4. Gross value-added at factor cost.

This is a particularly complex title to use and it is necessary to use the general methodological guide published in 1979 called *Structure and activity of industry: coordinated annual inquiry into industrial activity in the member states: methods and definitions, 1978*.

Structure and Activity of Industry: Data by Size of Enterprises
(4C, annual)

This title contains selected results of the coordinated annual survey of industrial activity broken down by the size of establishment. The sizes used are the number of employees, 20–99, 100–499, 500 +. The first edition was published in 1984 covering the survey for 1979. Data given is as for the *Annual Inquiry – Main Results* detailed above.

Annual Investments in Fixed Assets in the Industrial Enterprises of the EC (4C, annual)

This title contained detailed results of the coordinated annual survey of industrial investments and fixed assets carried out in the member states.

The first part of the bulletin contained, for each member state, the detailed results in national currencies and subdivided by NACE groups. The tables contained the following headings:

1. Machinery, plant, vehicles
2. Construction of structures and buildings
3. Purchase of existing buildings and of land
4. Disposals.

The second part was devoted to the presentation at Community level of the data. The edition published in 1985 (covering 1977–82) was the last to be published separately. From 1986 the information was to be found in the publication *Structure and activity of industry*.

Rapid Reports: Industry (4F, occasional)
This title began in 1987 and gives preliminary or summarized data that is available in more detail in another source, usually at a later date; no. 1 for 1987, for example, gave preliminary results for some member states of the coordinated annual survey of investment in industry in 1984.

Miscellaneous
The following miscellaneous titles have been published since 1980:

1. *NACE: General Industrial Classification of Economic Activities within the European Communities* (4D, 1985)
2. *Industrial production: methodology* (4C, 1987)
3. *Europe, USA, Japan. A comparison of sectoral data on production, employment and external trade, 1980–1983* (4D, 1988).

Iron and steel

Iron and Steel: Statistical Yearbook (4A, annual)
This title gives statistical data for the EC iron and steel industry and ECSC products. The sections are as follows:

1. Graphs
2. Main summary tables
3. Production basis (including employees, size of undertakings, blast furnaces, consumption and figures for the various types of ore, pyrite, residues, scrap, coke)
4. Production (divided into crude iron, crude steel, special steel, finished and end products, primary iron and steel processing and byproducts)
5. Works deliveries
6. Foreign trade
7. Steel consumption
8. Investment
9. Prices, unit values, wages
10. The levy.

Prior to the 1985 volume the title was *Iron and Steel Yearbook* and this title has remained on the spine of later editions.

Iron and Steel: Quarterly Statistics (4B, quarterly)
This title gives annual, quarterly or monthly data on the topics listed in *Iron and Steel: statistical yearbook*. Until the last issue of 1985 the title was *Quarterly Iron and Steel Bulletin*.

Iron and Steel (4B, monthly)
This title gives short-term (monthly) statistics on the production of crude steel and finished roll mill products, production indices, new orders, deliveries and orders in hand, foreign trade in ECSC products, consumption and intake of scrap, and short-time working. Prior to 1985 it was called *Iron and Steel Monthly*.

Miscellaneous
The following miscellaneous titles have been produced since 1980:

1. *Explanatory notes: iron and steel* (4E, 1981)
2. *Iron and steel, 1952–1982* (4C, 1983)
3. *Steel consumption by user branch, 1970–1984* (4D, 1987)
4. *Glossarium 1988* (4E, 1988).

Raw materials

Raw Materials: EC Supply (4C, annual)
This title was first published in 1981 (covering 1975–78) and called *EC Raw Materials Balance Sheets 1975–78*. This latter title was used for the editions published in 1983 (covering 1980 and 1981) and 1985 (covering 1979–82). The new title was first used for the 1986 edition (covering 1975–83).

This series has been produced because of the high dependency that the EC has on outside raw materials sources. The contents of each edition have varied – the following tables are presented in the 1986 edition:

1. Consolidated EC balance sheets
2. Detailed EC balances
   a. Major non-ferrous metals
   b. Iron and major alloying metals
   c. Other metals
   d. Non-metals
3. EC raw materials imports.

Note: Eurostat titles in the areas of transport, communications, tourism and commerce (retail sales) were moved from Theme 4 to the new Theme 7 in 1986.

Theme 5: Agriculture, forestry and fisheries

1. Agriculture

2. Prices
3. Forestry
4. Fisheries.

Agriculture

Agriculture: Statistical Yearbook (5A, annual)
Until the 1985 edition (published 1986) the title was *Yearbook of Agricultural Statistics*. The description that follows is of the 1986 edition (published 1987) and the 1988 edition (published 1988) of *Agriculture: Statistical Yearbook*, which differs somewhat in layout and contents from earlier years. The arrangement is as follows:

Agriculture
1. General (population, the EC in the world, agricultural external trade, etc.)
2. Land use (including crops)
3. Structure (holdings, manpower, machinery, etc.)
4. Crop production
5. Animal production
6. Prices and price indices
7. Agricultural accounts

Forestry
1. Structure, production and prices

Fisheries
1. General, catches and fleet.
(Figures are generally given for a number of years.)

Note: The annual publication *The agricultural situation in the Community* (see Chapter 4), issued by the Commission in conjunction with the *General report on the activities of the European Communities*, contains a large, and quite different, set of statistical tables.

Animal Production: Quarterly Statistics (3B, quarterly)
Until 1985 this was called *Animal Production* and this title has remained on the spine of volumes since then. It is arranged in four parts:

1. Monthly statistics on meat
2. Monthly statistics on eggs and poultry
3. Monthly statistics on milk and milk products
4. Supply balance sheets – survey results – forecasts.

Animal Production began in 1980 and replaced three publications: *Monthly Statistics of Meat*, *Monthly Statistics of Eggs* and *Monthly Statistics of Milk*.

Crop Production: Quarterly Statistics (5B, quarterly)
Until 1979 this was a monthly publication. From 1980 it became

quarterly with the title *Crop Production*. The current title has been used since 1986. It is arranged in five parts:

1. Land use
2. Areas, yields and production
3. Production statistics of vegetables and fruit
4. Data on agricultural meteorology
5. Supply balance sheets.

In 1987 a *Glossarium* was published which showed the full list of tables of plant products that are stored in the Cronos databank. A further edition of this title was published in 1988.

Economic Accounts: Agriculture, Forestry (5C, annual)
This title first appeared in 1978 (covering 1977). Further editions appeared in 1979 (1978); 1981 (1974–79); 1983 (1976–81); 1985 (1978–83), and thereafter annually. It gives tables by country presenting time series on:

1. Final production
2. Intermediate consumption
3. Value-added and fixed capital formation.

The edition published in 1988 (covering 1981–86) was called *Economic Accounts for Agriculture.* The forestry accounts were henceforth to be published separately.

Agricultural Income: Sectoral Income Index Analysis (5D, annual)
This title first appeared in 1987 (covering 1986) as a public manifestation of an existing internal publication *Sectoral income index.* It was decided to make this information more widely available as developments in agricultural incomes were becoming a central issue in the overall agricultural policy debate. The main sections in the 1988 published volume were as follows:

1. Changes in agricultural income in 1987 over 1986
2. Medium-term trends in agricultural income from 1977 to 1987
3. Level of agricultural income in the Community member states
4. Total disposable income of agricultural households.

Farm Structure (5, occasional)
This is the new title given to what had previously been called *Community Survey on the Structure of Agricultural Holdings.* These surveys have been held in 1966–67, 1970–71, 1975, 1977 and 1979–80. The last-mentioned was published in four volumes in 1984–85. For the 1983 survey the new generic title Farm Structure was used. A number of separate publications were published with this title, and then an additional subheading:

1. *Methodology of community surveys* (5E, 1986). This volume was to apply to the 1983, 1985 and 1987 surveys.

2. *1983 Survey: main results* (5C, 1986). Arranged as follows
   a. Results for 1983
      i. Results by member state
      ii. Main results by size classes of holdings
      iii. Main results by regions
   b. Historical results from 1966–67.
3. *Enquête de 1983: analyse des résultats* (5D, 1987). This volume analyses the 1983 results compared, where possible, with those of 1975. It highlights the main structural characteristics of Community agriculture by including with the tables, graphs and maps brief comments of the salient facts. The publication was only available in French, although a translation into English and German was available by contacting Eurostat.

The detailed results for the 1983 were only available on microfiche. The main results for the 1985 survey were published in 1987, with a substantial corrigendum issued the following year. A further title published in 1988 was *Farm structure, 1985 survey: analysis of results (1), Economic size and other gainful activities*.

Miscellaneous
The following miscellaneous titles have been published since 1980:

1. *Community survey of orchard fruit trees. 1982* (5C, 1984)
2. *Vines in the Community* (5C, 1985)
3. *The European orchard: 1977 and 1982 surveys – analyses and forecasts* (5D, 1986)
4. *Manual on economic accounts for agriculture and forestry* (5E, 1987).

Prices

Agricultural Prices (5C, annual)
Until the 1983 edition (covering 1971–82) this was called *Agricultural Price Statistics*. The title gives statistics covering twelve years for:

1. The selling prices of crop products
2. The selling prices of animal products
3. The purchase prices of the means of agricultural production for the member states of the EC.

From 1983 monthly agricultural prices are available in a microfiche publication also called *Agricultural Prices*. This gives figures for the preceding two years, and is published quarterly.

Agricultural Prices: Selected Series from the Cronos Databank
(5B, quarterly)
This contains the most important monthly prices that are published in the microfiche version of *Agricultural Prices*. This title began in 1983.

EC Agricultural Price Indices: Monthly and Annual Results. Half-yearly Statistics (5B, half-yearly)

From its inception in 1980 until 1985 the title was *EC Agricultural Price Indices (Output and Input).* In 1980–81 it was quarterly, but the frequency has been half-yearly since 1982. Overall the title replaces two separate publications which ceased in 1979: *EC-Index of Producer Prices of Agricultural Products* and *EC-Indices of Purchase Prices of the Means of Agricultural Production.*

This publication shows trends in monthly EC producer price indices for agricultural products and the purchase of the means of agricultural production over the last thirteen available months for the EC and the member states. The first issue of each year also includes annual results for the preceding ten years.

The Rates of Value-added Tax in Agriculture (5D, annual)

This title was first published in 1984, and is a supplement to the annual *Agricultural Prices.* It shows the VAT rates applicable to sales of agricultural products and to purchases of the means of agricultural production in the member states of the EC.

Miscellaneous

The following miscellaneous title has been published since 1980:

1. *Methodology of EC agricultural prices indices (output and input)* (5E, 1985)

Forestry

Forestry Statistics (5C, annual)

This title appeared in 1978 (covering 1970–75), 1981 (1973–77), 1982 (1975–79), 1984 (1976–80) and 1987 (1980–84). The title has the following sections:

1. Summary data
2. Structure of forests
3. Removals
4. Supply balance sheets for raw wood
5. Intra-EC trade in raw wood
6. Supply balance sheets for the major wood products
7. Pulpwood consumption by industrial product
8. Forest fires.

Data is given for the EC and for member states. Since the 1984 edition there has also been a regional breakdown.

Miscellaneous

Since 1980 the following miscellaneous title has been published:

1. *Forestry statistics: methodology* (5E, 1987).

Note: A number of forestry statistics are listed in *Agriculture: Statistical Yearbook*.

Fisheries

Fisheries: Statistical Yearbook (5C, annual)
From its inception in 1983 until 1985 the title was *Yearbook of Fishery Statistics*. This title replaced two separate publications: *Fisheries: Catches by Region* and *Fisheries: Fishery Products and Fishing Fleet*.

Fisheries: Statistical Yearbook comprises fisheries statistics for the EC member states and for other countries of importance in this sector. The title has the following sections:

1. Catches by fishing region
2. Catches by species group
3. Catch of principal species
4. Fishing fleet
5. Fishermen
6. Foreign trade.

Note: A number of fisheries statistics are listed in *Agriculture: Statistical Yearbook*.

Maps

Eurostat with the Directorate-General for Agriculture of the Commission have collaborated to publish two large colour maps. These are:

1. *The European Community: farming* (1987)
2. *The European Community: forests* (1987).

Both give a range of statistical information.

Theme 6: Foreign trade

Geonomenclature (6E, occasional)
This title gave the standard country nomenclature for the external trade statistics of the EC. There were maps of the world indicating the geo-nomenclature codes for each country, a table of countries in a classified order and an alphabetical index. The title was generally published annually but there was no edition in 1982 and none since 1984.

There are a number of classifications, or nomenclatures, existing for the breakdown of goods in EC foreign trade statistics. Primarily until 1987 there was NIMEXE – Nomenclature of goods for the external trade statistics of the Community. The latest NIMEXE code was to be found in an edition of the 'L' series of the *Official Journal* published in December of each year. The NIMEXE tables for 1987, for example, were printed in the *Official Journal* L368 29.12.86.

A further classification used in SITC Rev. 2. This is the second revision, 1974, of the Standard International Trade Classification, of the

United Nations. The SITC is used primarily for economic analysis. The United Nations published in 1986 the third revision (SITC Rev. 3), and from 1988 this has been used by Eurostat.

From 1988 NIMEXE was merged with the annual Regulations modifying the Common Customs Tariff (CCT) to form the 'combined nomenclature' (CN), the basis of TARIC (The integrated tariff of the European Communities). A two-volume set called *TARIC* was published by OOPEC at the end of 1987. The 'combined nomenclature' was also printed in the *Official Journal* L256 7.9.87. A publication called *Explanatory notes to the combined nomenclature of the European Communities* was published with the Document categorization in 1987. Note that this important change will probably produce changes in the titles and structure of publications listed below. At the time of writing these changes were not known.

Note that HMSO publish annually a *Guide to the classification for overseas trade statistics*, which has a useful alphabetical index to SITC and the Customs Co-operation Council Nomenclature, the headings of which correspond to NIMEXE. Eurostat also intend to produce comparative tables of NIMEXE and the 'Combined Nomenclature'.

External Trade: Statistical Yearbook (6A, annual)
This title began in 1985. Previously many of the tables it contains were included in an annual special issue of the *Monthly External Trade Bulletin.*

The *Statistical Yearbook* contains the main results of the statistics on trends in the EC external trade and in trade between member states from 1958 to date. The 1986 edition contained the following tables:

1. EC and world trade
2. World exports by origin and destination
3. Trends in trade of the EC with its main extra-EC trading partners
4. EC and main non-EC partners' shares in the trade of each country
5. General summary of EC trade by country
6. General summary of EC trade by commodity
7. Indices of volume, value, unit value, terms of trade and ratio of volumes
8. Trends in EC trade, total, intra-and extra-EC
9. Trends in EC trade, intra-EC by member country
10. Trends in EC trade, with major areas
11. Trends in EC trade, by SITC sections and areas
12. Trends in EC trade, by SITC sections
13. Trends in trade of main non-EC countries
14. Conversion rates.

External Trade: Monthly Statistics (6B, monthly)
Until 1985 this was called *Monthly External Trade Bulletin.*

This title provides rapid regular statistics on short-term monthly and quarterly developments in the external trade of the member states. The 1987 issues contained the following sections:

1. General summary of trade by country
2. General summary of trade by commodities
3. Trends in trade by country
4. Trends in trade by commodities
5. Trade by partner countries
6. Indices
7. Trade of main non-Community countries
8. Conversion rates
9. EC trade in agricultural products
10. EC trade in petroleum products.

Until 1984 a special issue of *Monthly External Trade Bulletin* was published each year in addition to the normal monthly issues. From 1985 this was renamed *External Trade: statistical yearbook.*

External Trade: Analytical Trade – NIMEXE (6C, annual)
Up until 1985 (covering 1984) this was called *Analytical Table of Foreign Trade: NIMEXE.*

This title gives the detailed external trade statistics of the EC and the member states in the NIMEXE nomenclature. Separate volumes of imports and exports are given in tables by value (ECU) and by weight. There are twenty-six volumes in all:

1. A   Agricultural products
2. B   Mineral products
3. C   Chemical products
4. D   Artificial materials, leather
5. E   Wood, cork, paper
6. F   Textiles, footwear
7. G   Stone, plaster, glass, ceramics
8. H   Iron and steel
9. I   Other base metals
10. J   Machinery, appliances
11. K   Transport equipment
12. L   Optical precision instruments
13. Z   Countries – products.

The information contained in this publication is also available on microfiche issued quarterly.

Analytical Tables of Foreign Trade: SITC/CTCI, Rev. 2 (6C, annual)
In twelve volumes this title gives external trade statistics of the EC and

its member states in the SITC nomenclature. It is also available on microfiche issued quarterly.

Foreign Trade: Third Countries: Statistical Yearbook (6C, biennial)
Although now called a yearbook, and in the Eurostat list of 1986 publications called a biannual, the pattern of publication seems to be irregular:

1. *ACP: yearbook of foreign trade statistics 1968-1976,* 1978
2. *ACP: yearbook of foreign trade statistics 1972-1978,* 1981
3. *Yearbook of foreign trade statistics. Third countries 1974-1981*
   Volume A - ACP countries. 1983
   Volume B - Mediterranean countries, 1983.
4. *Foreign trade: third countries: statistical yearbook 1977-1983*
   Volume A - ACP countries, 1986
   Volume B - Mediterranean countries, 1986.

This title shows the external trade statistics of the ACP countries (the African, Caribbean and Pacific signatories to the appropriate Lomé Convention at the time of publication) and, since 1983, the Mediterranean states. The following tables are shown for each country:

1. Growth and structure of imports from the world
2. Growth and structure of imports from the EC
3. Growth and structure of exports to the world
4. Growth and structure of exports to the EC
5. Imports by SITC sections
6. Exports by SITC sections
7. Exports by principal products.

Miscellaneous
The following miscellaneous titles have been published since 1980:

1. *EC-world trade: a statistical analysis 1963-1979* (6D, 1981)
2. *External trade statistics: user's guide* (6E, 1982)
3. *Analysis of the trade between the European Community and the Latin American countries 1965-1980* (6D, 1982)
4. *EC-ACP trade: a statistical analysis 1970-1981* (6D, 1983)
5. *Analysis of EC-Latin America trade: recent trends* (6D, 1985)
6. *External trade statistics: user's guide* (6E, 2nd edition, 1985)
7. *Trade: EC-developing countries. Manufactured products - analysis 1970-1984* (6D, 1987)
8. *EC-ASEAN trade: a statistical analysis 1970-84* (6D, 1987)
9. *External trade: monthly statistics. Glossarium* (6E, 1987)
10. *External trade: analytical tables - NIMEXE 1986. Glossarium* (6E, 1987).

Theme 7: Services and transport

Note: Theme 7 came into being in 1986. Titles now included in this theme were previously published in Theme 4.

Transport, Communications, Tourism: Statistical Yearbook
(7A, annual)
Until the 1985 edition this was called *Statistical Yearbook: Transport, Communications, Tourism*. In the 1980s editions were published annually, except for 1984 and 1986. The following sections are included:

1. General tables
2. Railways
3. Road
4. Inland waterways
5. Merchant shipping
6. Aviation
7. Pipelines
8. Post and telecommunications
9. Tourism.

In the transport field tables includes data on infrastructure, mobile equipment, the distances covered by the various modes and selected traffic accidents.

Carriage of Goods: Inland Waterways (7C, annual)
This title, which began in 1985 (covering 1983), gives statistics referring to the carriage of goods within the member states by inland waterways. The following sections are included:

1. Total traffic
2. International traffic
3. Transit
4. National traffic
5. Regional traffic.

Only the six original countries of the EC supply data for this title.

Carriage of Goods: Railways (7C, annual)
This title, which began in 1985 (covering 1983), gives statistics referring to the carriage of goods on the main railway networks of the member states open to public traffic. The sections are as in *Carriage of Goods: Inland Waterways*. Data is supplied by all member states.

Carriage of Goods: Road (7C, annual)
This title, which began in 1986 (covering 1983), gives statistics of goods traffic by road, carried on vehicles registered in the member states. Tables are divided into the following sections:

1. International traffic
2. National traffic
3. Regional traffic.

Data is supplied by all member states, except Italy.

Trends in Distributive Trades: Retail Sales – Registration of Cars
(7B, monthly)
This title began in 1987, replacing: *Retail Sales – Index Numbers*
(1985–86). From 1987 the title contained the following sections:

1. Volume of retail sales indices
2. Breakdown of retail sales indices into foodstuffs, clothing and household goods (every quarter)
3. Registration of new cars indices.

Data is given for the EC, its member states, the United States and Japan.

Theme 9: Miscellaneous

Eurostat News (9C, quarterly)   G.D. Int.
This title is published to give information about Eurostat activities and publications. It began in 1976 and until 1979 was published six or seven times a year. Since 1980 *Eurostat News* has become a quarterly with the occasional 'special issue' in addition.

Some of the features regularly included in *Eurostat News* are:

1. News regarding Eurostat as an organization
2. Articles on particular statistical series
3. Parliamentary questions which involve statistics
4. Database news
5. Eurostat publications (see below).

In issue 4, 1986 there is a list of all the articles that have appeared in *Eurostat News* 1976–86.

Eurostat News is useful for seeing what has recently been published by Eurostat as well as what is going to be published. In each issue there is a list of titles which have been published in the last quarter, a separate list of titles which are about to be published, and a list of periodicals. Full bibliographical details are given for each title, including price, languages available and a brief summary of contents. An order form is included in each issue.

Once a year there is an insert, usually printed on yellow pages, the 'Programme of Eurostat publications' for the following year. Since no. 4, 1981 the insert has been put in the fourth issue of a year. This list breaks down the titles by theme and series, indicates the frequency of the title and the database from which the title is created. On the whole these lists of future publications are accurate although, occasionally, the publication of a particular title is postponed or even cancelled, or there is a change of title.

In no. 2, 1980, and from 1981 to 1985 in no. 1' for each year, there was a similar insert for 'Internal documents to be published' in the year in question. This has not appeared since 1985. 'Internal publications' are not sold through OOPEC; they are officially for Community officials and statisticians in national organizations and are available direct from Eurostat. Such titles are available for inspection in the Information Offices of the Commission.

The following special issues have been published since 1980:

1. *Conclusions of the seminar on statistical databanks* (Luxembourg, 25–27 May 1981), 1982
2. *Seminar on the measurement of employment and unemployment* (Luxembourg, 7–10 December 1981), 1982
3. *1953–83: The first 30 years and beyond. A commemorative brochure,* 1983
4. *Recent developments in the analysis of large-scale data sets* (Seminar, Luxembourg, 16–11 November 1983). 1984
5. *Protection of privacy, automatic data processing and progress in statistical documentation* (Seminar, Luxembourg, December 1984), 1986
6. *Figures for food in Africa* (Workshop, Brussels, May 1986), 1987
7. *External trade indices* (Seminar, Luxembourg, November 1985), 1988 (1986 on cover)

Government Financing of Research and Development (9C, annual)
This title includes a broad analysis of developments in the public financing of R & D over a period of time, together with a detailed analysis of objectives of the financing of R & D by the member states for the latest year figures are available. From the 1983 edition 1975 has been used as the reference year. The following regular sections are listed:

1. Introduction
2. Trends in budget appropriations for R & D
3. Changes in the structure of R & D budget appropriations by objectives
4. Special features of government R & D financing in each member states
5. Multilateral cooperation.

Until the 1983 edition this title was published in Theme 2 with pink covers.

FURTHER INFORMATION

In addition to *Eurostat News* there are some other sources worth mentioning for information on Eurostat publications. In 1986 Eurostat issued a *Catalogue of Eurostat publications.* This listed, and gave details of, the latest editions of regular statistical titles, and selected recent non-periodic titles. For each title listed, format, number of pages, languages available, price and order number were given.

The annual *Catalogue of Publications* from OOPEC lists Eurostat titles published during the year in question, with bibliographical details. Until the 1984 catalogue this was called *Publications of the European Communities*.

Eurostat periodically issue a *Directory* which lists officials and their responsibilities, with contact telephone numbers. A new edition is expected following a major reorganization of Eurostat in 1988.

In 1988 Eurostat published a new title called *Europe in figures*. It is essentially a popular introduction to the statistics of Eurostat using texts and coloured diagrams and photographs as well as a few tables. *Europe in figures* is divided into the following sections:

1. The European Community
2. The environment and population
3. Economics and finance
4. Production
5. External relations.

On each page a Eurostat title is listed which gives more detailed information to that given in this source. New editions are promised annually.

Finally one cannot write an account of Eurostat activities without mentioning *Eurostat Index*. This is compiled by Anne Ramsay of the European Documentation Centre at Newcastle upon Tyne Polytechnic. *Eurostat Index* is a detailed keyword subject index to Eurostat titles available at the time of compilation, and is an invaluable source. The fourth edition was published in 1989.

Readers who have a copy of the Eurostat *Directory* should use that when making an enquiry on a particular topic or aspect of Eurostat activity. Initial enquiries can be directed to:

Statistical Office of the European Communities
Bâtiment Jean Monnet
rue Alcide de Gasperi
L-2920 Luxembourg

Telephone: 43011
Telex: COMEUR LU 3423

Sources and references

1. Eurostat *Directory*, no. 3, 1984, EC, 1984
2. *Directory of the Commission of the European Communities*, February 1987, EC, 1987
3. *Catalogue of Eurostat publications*, 1986, EC, 1986
4. Sixth Statistical Programme of the European Communities 1985–87, COM(84)364 final

5. *Eurostat Index*, by Anne Ramsay, 3rd edition, Capital Planning Information, 1986
6. *European Communities statistics: a guide to sources*, by Anne Ramsay, Association of EDC Librarians, 1984
7. *Eurostat News* Special Number, 1983; no. 4, 1984; no. 4, 1985; no. 2, 1986; no. 4, 1986.

CHAPTER 7

Commission – Spokesman's Service/Information Offices

SPOKESMAN'S SERVICE

The function of the Spokesman's Service, which is under the authority of the President of the Commission, is to supply the press and other media with news of Community and, in particular, Commission developments. While the role of the media is most apparent during the occasional European Council summits or periodic crises, nevertheless there is a permanent accredited press corps in Brussels whose members attend daily briefings and receive background and explanatory documentation. It should be stressed that the Spokesman's Service is not intended to provide either information or documentation to any group outside the press and the Commission Information Offices. It does not maintain distribution lists for public circulation of its documentation.

Nevertheless some of the documentation produced by the Spokesman's Service does reach beyond the target audience, if only unofficially, and is thus worth mentioning.

Information memos

Information memos have been issued by the Spokesman's Service since 1958 and provide a summary of COM Documents, extracts of speeches and other topical information. Approximately one hundred are issued each year. Since 1984 they have been distributed to EC Depository Libraries (listed in Appendix 6) but are generally not publicly available. They are sent in batches to this group of libraries – that is, not individually on the day of issue – so their value as rapid sources of information on EC developments is somewhat compromised. In most cases an information memo which summarizes a COM Document will indicate the appropriate reference.

For those who need to find out rapidly about developments from the Commission, and who do not have access to consultancy services and the like, the best sources are newspapers such as the *Financial Times* and the regular alerting agency publications *Agence Europe* and *European Report* (see Appendix 5).

Written questions

The public can only trace written questions of the European Parliament through the *Official Journal* 'C' Series. Usually there is a long delay before the appearance of a question, and its answer, in this source. The Spokesman's Service provides a faster service to its accredited journalists and Information Offices. This service is not available to the public. Confusion was caused during the short life of a commercially produced index to EC documentation called *EC Index*, 1984–86. This listed the reference to the service from the Spokesman's Service. This was a mistake.

Programme of the Commission

Each year the President of the Commission presents his programme for the coming year at the January or February plenary sessions of the European Parliament. The Spokesman's Service provides a prepublication version to the accredited press and to the Information Offices. Again this is not formally available to a wider audience. Since 1985 the programme has been formally published in the series *Bulletin of the European Communities: Supplement* (see Chapter 4).

Miscellaneous

Occasionally the Spokesman's Service will issue a more substantial report. These are not usually formally advertised or distributed. However, some enter the public domain and are available from Information Offices. Two examples are:

1. *The European Community budget: the facts*, 1986.
2. *Thirty years after the Treaty of Rome ... Europe at the crossroads. Making a success of the Single Act: a new frontier for Europe*, 1987.

The latter title was formally published as *Bulletin of the European Communities: Supplement* no. 1, 1987.

INFORMATION OFFICES

In all the member states of the EC there are Press and Information Offices which carry out the dual function of:

1. Informing individuals and groups in the member states of EC activities
2. Conveying the views of individuals and groups on EC activities back to Brussels.

It should also be mentioned that in non-member states where the EC maintains an External Delegation there is usually an information unit as part of the mission.

In carrying out their functions the Information Offices pursue a range of activities. Of relevance here are the documentation activities. Information Offices maintain limited stocks of much of the popular-level material of the EC for free distribution on request and also stocks of application forms and background material for EC research opportunities and other schemes.

Information Offices contain major collections of EC documentation for their own working purposes. These are used to provide an information service regarding current EC activities. These collections should not be seen as archival collections of EC documentation. For those, researchers should use the resources of EC Depository Libraries, which are listed in Appendix 6. Nevertheless the public is usually permitted to use the documentation resources of the Information Offices.

In the past it was often possible to obtain copies of EC documents from Information Offices. The trend now is for an enquirer to be given a bibliographical reference and the address of the appropriate EC documentation supplier from which to purchase an item. Budgetary cutbacks have forced the large-scale free distribution of EC documents to be curtailed.

In addition to documentation received from Brussels by the Information Offices many of the offices also produce a range of material themselves geared particularly to individuals and groups of the country in which they are based.

The OOPEC *Catalogue of publications* gives a list of all the periodicals produced by the Information Offices and External Delegations. During the 1980s cutbacks in the budgets of the Information Offices led to the cessation of a number of these titles and the development of titles produced by commercial publishers, but with a Commission contribution.

In the United Kingdom, for example, the London Office of the European Commission published from 1981 to 1985 a free monthly journal called *Europe '81, Europe '82 . . . Europe '85*. A new arrangement began from the middle of 1987 when a commercial publisher, Lawrence-Allen Publishing, in cooperation with the Commission, started publishing *Europe '87* as a priced publication on a bimonthly basis.

A similar process took place in Germany. Until 1987 the Bonn Office of the Commission had published *EG Magazin* on a monthly basis. From that year this became a joint publication of a commercial publisher and the Commission and substantially increased in price. *30 Jours d'Europe* from the Paris Office of the Commission ceased publication during 1986.

Changes also took place outside the member states. *Europe*, the quarterly periodical from the Canadian delegation of the European Communities in Ottawa, ceased publication with the winter 1986–87 issue. In this case a smaller replacement publication called *EC Newsletter* has been issued from September 1987; this is a four-page newsletter published six times a year.

For further information on the current situation regarding the publications of the Information Offices outside the United Kingdom contact the offices at the addresses given in Appendix 3. The point should be made that the distribution of titles produced by the Information Offices of one country is not always encouraged to addresses outside that country, particularly in terms of free subscriptions.

The documentation of the United Kingdom Office of the Commission (London Office)

The London Office of the European Commission is the main office of the European Commission in the United Kingdom. Documentation produced by that Office is intended to be of relevance throughout the United Kingdom. The Offices of the Commission in Cardiff, Edinburgh and Belfast are sub-offices of the London Office. Any documentation produced by the sub-offices is primarily intended for Wales, Scotland and Northern Ireland respectively.

European Community

This was a journal produced by the Information Service of the Commission in London from 1963 to 1980. (From 1958 until 1962 the title had been *Bulletin from the European Community*.) *European Community* changed in shape and format a number of times during its life although basically remaining a monthly publication pattern. The last issue was nos 11/12, November/December 1980.

Europe '81

This was the name given to the restyled periodical of the London Office of the Commission – the date changing each year. The title was nominally published monthly, although every year there were a number of joint issues – in 1985, for example, only eight issues were published. It was available free from the London Office until 1985 when cutbacks in the Office's budget forced its temporary closure.

The demise of the title was much lamented because *Europe . . .* was a well-produced journal. Stylistically it was attractive with its use of colour in photographs and texts. The articles were well written and interesting. In a readable manner *Europe . . .* sought to bring alive EC policies in a way relevant to a United Kingdom readership. It also mentioned recent books on Europe, had a letters page and a section called 'What's in the papers'. The centre pages of each issue contained *Euroforum*, a four to eight page insert of recent EC news compiled by DG X in Brussels.

Until 1980 *Euroforum* had been issued as a separate periodical from Brussels. From 1981 *Euroforum* became an insert in the periodicals of the Information Offices of the Commission.

The demise of *Europe* . . . seemed particularly ironic at the very time when the EC was discussing how to bring 'Europe' alive for the ordinary citizens in its 'People's Europe' initiative. Many people were therefore pleased when in the middle of 1987 the periodical was restarted as *Europe '87*. Three issues were published in 1987, and henceforth it is intended to be published bimonthly. The title is now published by Lawrence-Allen Publishing as a priced publication. Enquiries should be directed to:

> Lawrence-Allen Publishing
> Magazine Subscription Dept
> Gloucester Street
> Weston-super-Mare
> Avon BS23 1TB
> England
> Telephone 0934 21415

Background Reports

Background Reports are short reports, usually of two to eight pages, discussing a EC topic of current interest. Many are descriptions of EC proposals slanted to a United Kingdom audience. Bibliographical references for further information are usually given. The Background Report series is in typescript and available free from the London Office. The number issued each year varies although it is generally decreasing over the years. Sixty-six were issued in 1980 and only twenty-two in 1987.

An index to the Background Reports series is promised on the cover of each issue, but has not materialized since the early 1980s.

Some examples from 1987 are:

1. *Hopes for a more dynamic economy. Annual economic report 1986–87* (ISEC/B1/87)
2. *The modern plague – Aids: acquired immune deficiency syndrome* (ISEC/B3/87)
3. *You and the European Community: making equal opportunities work. The European Community boosts women's rights* (ISEC/B5/87)
4. *A cleaner environment with unleaded petrol* (ISEC/B7/87)
5. *Strategies against hunger* (ISEC/B10/87)
6. *Community travel: medical care and customs allowances* (ISEC/B11/87)
7. *Renaval – a strategy on shipbuilding* (ISEC/B15/87)
8. *Prevention of tragedy: child safety* (ISEC/B16/87)

9. *Perspectives on the CAP. A balance sheet* (ISEC/B17/87)
10. *Reform of the Community Structural Funds* (ISEC/B20/87).

Press release

During the 1980s between fourteen and twenty-six press releases have been issued each year by the London Office of the Commission. Four categorises of press release can be recognized:

1. Reporting general EC developments (for example, ISEC/10/87: ERASMUS adopted)
2. Reporting European Regional Development Fund grant allocations to the United Kingdom (for example, ISEC/3/87 £183 million Regional Fund grants to the United Kingdom). Other EC grants are also sometimes covered
3. Events in the United Kingdom with an EC connection (for example, ISEC/14/86 The first European Community Club Team Swimming Championships, Leeds, 11–12 April 1987)
4. Speeches in the United Kingdom by EC officials (for example, ISEC/6/88 Address by the Rt Hon. Lord Cockfield, Vice-President of the Commission of the European Communities, to the Confederation of British Industries, London, 3 March 1988)

The week in Europe

A two-page typescript weekly briefing summarizing the key EC events of the past week. There is also a short listing of the major meetings of the Council and other EC institutions to be held in the near future. It is available free from the London Office.

Women in Europe: news and views about women and the European Community

A short newsletter issued every month or so by the London Office. It contains brief features concerning EC activities of interest to women and developments in the United Kingdom in the field of women and equality with an EC perspective. *Women in Europe* is primarily intended for women's organizations and the like.

Finance from Europe: a guide to grants and loans from the European Community

The first edition of this booklet was issued in July 1982, with updated editions issued in June 1983 and May 1986. *Finance from Europe* indicates the areas in which EC finance is made available, conditions of applicability and how to apply. The standard headings in the first three editions are:

1. Employment and training grants
2. Finance for agriculture and fisheries

3. Regional grants
4. Loans for economic development
5. Finance for energy
6. Aid to coal and steel regions
7. Assistance for developing countries
8. Aid for research and development
9. Miscellaneous funds.

Miscellaneous

The London Office occasionally issues one-off publications on current subjects of interest, many in typescript form. Recent examples include:

1. *European Council: Athens, December 5 and 6 1983*, 1983
2. *The Inter-governmental Conference: Background and issues*, 1985
3. *The accession of Spain and Portugal to the European Community: a survey*, 1986
4. *The European Community and the developing countries: the growth of a policy*, 1986
5. *Britain in the European Community: the impact of membership*, 1987.

Also issued in the 1980s were a number of guides dealing with the impact of the EC on the planning regions of the European Community under the generic title *The United Kingdom and the European Community: A Survey of Planning Regions*. These dossiers are periodically updated, usually at the time of elections to the European Parliament.

In association with the 1992 campaign the London office issued in 1988 a booklet called *Europe 1992: developing an active company approach to the European Market*.

The UK sub-offices of the European Commission

The sub-offices are not substantial producers of documentation. The Cardiff Office produced a small pamphlet in 1979 called *Wales in the European Community*. In November 1982 was issued *Britain in the Community 1973–1983: Wales*, and this was updated in 1984 by a publication called *The United Kingdom and the European Community: the impact of Community policies: Wales*, also available in a Welsh language version called *Cymru a'r Gymuned Ewropeaidd*.

The main publication from Cardiff, the newsletter called *Community News*, was issued from the opening of the office in Wales in 1976 until the end of 1987. Until 1980 it was issued on a fortnightly basis; since then it had become irregular, a new edition appearing around every four to six weeks. *Community News* covered items relating specifically to Wales and the EC and other items of general interest. From the beginning of 1988 this was replaced by *The Week*. This usually contains the same information as in the London edition of the same title, although occasionally there is a substitute Welsh item. The Cardiff Office also issue press releases.

Similar regional versions of *The Week* are now also available from the Edinburgh and Belfast sub-offices. In addition the Edinburgh sub-office has published a small booklet called *Scotland in Europe*. Editions were published in 1981 and 1984. Until *The Week*, which started in 1988, the Scotland sub-office did not produce a regular newsletter but has always issued press releases.

The Belfast sub-office also issues press releases and an attractive monthly newsletter called *Europe in Northern Ireland*.

CHAPTER 8

Council of Ministers

The Council of Ministers is the primary decision-making institution of the European Community. It is composed of ministers from the member states representing their country. Many Council meetings take place in Brussels where the 1900-strong General Secretariat is based. However, a number of meetings take place annually in Luxembourg and also in whichever member state currently holds the Presidency.

STRUCTURE OF THE COUNCIL OF MINISTERS

While the Secretariat is a permanent body, the Council of Ministers does not meet in continuous session. Meetings are periodically held at which a minister from each member state appropriate to the subject under discussion attends. Foreign ministers attend meetings concerned with foreign affairs and political and institutional matters relating to the EC, agriculture ministers attend meetings relating to agriculture, and so on.

Each member state takes on the Presidency of the Council for a period of six months. This means that a representative from that member state will chair all meetings held at whatever level within the Council and act as its representative at an international level. To ensure continuity between presidencies it has become an increasing feature for close cooperation to take place between a member state which is in the Presidency and the immediate past and immediate future Presidencies.

The Council of Ministers is assisted by the *Committee of Permanent Representatives* (Coreper), which is a sort of permanently sitting meeting of the Council of Ministers. Composed of senior officials from the member states, Coreper tries to coordinate the complex negotiations that occur on policy proposals between the Council, the Commission, other Community institutions and the member states.

When the Council of Ministers takes a decision on a legislative proposal or policy proposal it is not simply a case of one member state, one vote. Some major decisions have to be unanimous, while others can be by simple or qualified majority. Depending upon their size and importance member states have a different number of votes to cast in a decision taken by a qualified or simple majority. Since the accession of Spain and Portugal the votes of member states have been weighted as follows:

1. Ten votes – West Germany, France, Italy, United Kingdom
2. Eight votes – Spain
3. Five votes – Belgium, Greece, The Netherlands, Portugal
4. Three votes – Denmark, Ireland
5. Two votes – Luxembourg.

In a qualified majority voting situation fifty-four votes are necessary for the proposal to be adopted. By the Single European Act in many instances where unanimity was previously required qualified majority voting has been substituted.

The heads of government of the member states, accompanied by their foreign ministers, meet together on two or three occasions a year in a forum called the *European Council*. It came into existence following a decision of the heads of government in 1974. Until the Single European Act the European Council was an institution which was parallel but distinct from the institutions of the EC. The heads of government could discuss issues strictly outside the competence of the EC. It was also an aim that the European Council would concentrate on the long-term development of European union. In reality the summit meetings of the European Council often became indistinguishable from Council meetings as heads of government time and time again in the 1980s became bogged down in minute details of policy matters. The European Council formally became a Community institution by the Single European Act.

The structure of the Council of Ministers and the names of the relevant ministers from the member states can be found in the *Guide to the Council of the European Communities*. In addition the *Guide* lists the Coreper representatives and their addresses, and also contains a directory to the General Secretariat, the various special and standing committees, working parties, association councils, cooperation councils, the ACP–EEC Council of Ministers, and representatives of the ACP states.

Until 1982 the *Guide* was a looseleaf publication. Since then a completely new edition has been issued twice a year. It is a priced publication available from OOPEC.

DOCUMENTATION

Unlike the Commission the Council of Ministers is not a significant originator of EC documentation. This reflects the differing functions of the institutions. On the other hand it does seem a deficiency that the deliberations, and even more the decisions taken by the Council and the European Council, are not easy to follow through their documentation. It is true that if an EC legislative act follows a Council decision it is eventually printed in the *Official Journal*. There is a need, however, for a more rapid and contextual dissemination of the decisions taken at Council and European Council meetings. One solution would be to make Council press releases more widely available either in their present format or in some other more formal publication. A press release is issued after every Council of Ministers meeting outlining decisions and conclusions reached. In addition other background reports are sent to the press offices of member state embassies and Commission Information Offices outlining Council activities. These reports are not generally made available to the public. Similarly, while there is usually extensive media coverage of European Council summit meetings there is no widely and rapidly available factual account from the EC itself.

Review of the Council's work

This is an annual review of the work of the Council of Ministers. Unlike the *General report* issued by the Commission (see Chapter 4), which is issued very quickly after the year it is describing, there is usually a long delay before the *Review* appears. The 33rd *Review* covering the work of the Council in 1985 only appeared in 1987 for example.

During the 1980s the standard chapter headings have been:

1. Introduction
2. Freedom of movement and common rules
3. Economic and social policy
4. External relations and relations with the associated states
5. Agriculture and fisheries (since 1984 split into two separate chapters)
6. Administrative matters.

While the work of the Commission is touched upon the *Review* naturally describes EC developments from a Council perspective. It pinpoints dates of Council meetings and the outcome of those meetings. Where legislation followed a Council decision the *Official Journal* reference to the text of the legislation is usually given. Within the *Review* it is possible also to discover such facts as:

1. The number of days spent on Council meetings and meetings of preparatory bodies
2. The number of instances when the Council was involved in cases brought before the Court of Justice
3. Attendance by representatives of the Council at meetings/ sessions of the European Parliament and Economic and Social Committee
4. The number of questions received by the Council from the European Parliament.

The *Review* contains a reasonable alphabetical subject index at the back of each volume. The references are to paragraphs rather to pages.

It is sometimes asked by people trying to keep track of Community developments whether the Council *Review* or the Commission *General report* should be used. It is difficult to give a clearcut answer for they serve different functions – in fact to read the two alongside each other on a particular development can be an illuminating illustration of the rather uneasy relationship existing between the two institutions. Both are arranged in a way that does not guarantee automatic access into their contents. The speed of publication of the *General report* is a distinct advantage, and its detailed contents pages with its indication of hierarchy is perhaps as effective an entry as the index in the *Review*. The value of both comes from their bibliographical references which lead you to further information or the text of a proposal or piece of legislation. With this latter point there is a distinction to be made. The *General report* is the source to use when trying to track down references to Commission proposals. The rapid publication of the *General report* does not always, however, allow for the *Official Journal* reference to be listed for a new piece of Community legislation. The *Review*, with its delayed publication, is a better source for references to Community legislation.

Annual report of the ACP–EEC Council of Ministers

Each of the ACP–EEC Conventions (the Lomé Conventions) stipulate that the ACP–EEC Council of Ministers should issue an annual report for the ACP–EEC Consultative Assembly and for general information purposes. As from 1981 the reference period for the *Annual report* became the calendar year rather than the twelve months from 1 March as had been the case. The structure of the *Annual report* has remained broadly similar during the 1980s:

1. Introduction
2. Overview of the ACP–EEC Council's work
3. Trade cooperation
4. Customs cooperation
5. Export earnings from commodities
6. Industrial cooperation
7. Agricultural cooperation
8. Financial and technical cooperation
9. Least-developed, landlocked and island ACP states.

In addition there are some special features relevant to a particular *Annual report*. For example, in the 1983 *Annual report* there is a feature on the negotiations for the third Lomé Convention; in the 1984 *Annual report* there is a feature on that Convention, while in the 1985 *Annual report* there is a feature discussing the implications of the enlargement of the EC upon the ACP countries.

In an Annex the texts of some of the resolutions adopted by the ACP–EEC Consultative Assembly are printed although the criteria for inclusion is not entirely clear. The *Annual report*, while having a proper printed cover, gives the impression of primarily being an internal working document. The 1985 *Annual report*, for example, despite having a contents page and numbered pages throughout does not link the two! The contents page also does not note the existence of the annexes in the volume.

In addition to the *Annual report* a publication called *Report of the ACP-EEC Council of Ministers (1 April 1976-29 February 1980)* was issued in 1980. All these publications are available through OOPEC.

Association and cooperation agreements

In addition to the ACP-EEC Conventions the EC has signed a number of other agreements with non-EC countries. These include EFTA countries, with other countries in the developed world such as Canada, state-trading countries such as Romania and China, and non-ACP developing countries, particularly those in the Mediterranean area, but also countries and interregional organizations in Latin America, Asia and the Middle East.

The text of these agreements is printed in various sources. The authoritative text is that found in the *Official Journal*. To trace these agreements you can use the *Index to the Official Journal* or the Commission publication *Agreements and other bilateral commitments linking the Communities with non-member countries* (see Chapter 5).

A consolidated chronological set of the texts is printed in *Collection of the agreements concluded by the European Communities* (see Chapter 1). However, in addition to these there is another source for many of these agreements. During the 1970s the Secretariat of the Council of Ministers started issuing these agreements grouped together by country or international grouping in looseleaf folders called *Collected acts*. The following series were issued:

1. First ACP-EEC Convention
2. Second ACP-EEC Convention
3. Overseas countries and territories; French overseas departments
4. EEC – Algeria
5. EEC – Cyprus
6. EEC – EASTAF (Tanzania, Uganda and Kenya)
7. EEC – Egypt
8. EEC – Greece
9. EEC – Israel
10. EEC – Jordan
11. EEC – Lebanon
12. EEC – Malta
13. EEC – Morocco
14. EEC – Syria

15. EEC – Tunisia
16. EEC – Turkey.

Invariably they comprised straightforward reprints of the *Official Journal* texts of the agreements. In 1983 the updating supplements ceased to be issued. Instead the Council now issues a number of volumes containing the texts of agreements made during a calendar year between the EC and a number of other countries. This series is called *Compilation of texts*. For example, the texts of agreements signed in 1984 within the framework of the Association Agreements between the EEC and Cyprus, the EEC and Malta, and the EEC and Turkey were printed in one volume published in 1985. Similar volumes covering later years and other Association Agreements are now published annually.

COST projects: Collected Agreements Concluded within the Framework of European Cooperation in the Field of Scientific and Technical Research

The COST project (European Cooperation on Scientific and Technical Research) was inaugurated in 1969 as an European response to the perceived technological challenge from the United States. Today it is composed of nineteen European countries – the member states of the EC plus Yugoslavia, Norway, Austria, Switzerland, Finland, Sweden and Turkey. Although COST is not an EC organization as such its secretariat is provided from within the EC. Both the Commission and the Council are involved with COST. Directorate A in DG XII: Science, Research and Development of the Commission coordinates the project. The COST Secretariat as such is to be found in the General Secretariat of the Council. Also within the Council is the Committee of Senior Officials on Scientific and Technical Research. Its function is to prepare the general strategy of COST cooperation, to select and prepare the various projects and elaborate the agreements relating to them. It is also responsible for managing the COST fund, appointing project coordinators and experts and setting up subcommittees.

The COST Secretariat has published *COST projects: collected agreements*. . . . Volume 1 covering agreements concluded between 1971 and 1980 was published in 1983; volume 2 covering 1981 and 1982 was published in 1984; volume 3 covering 1983 and 1984 was published in 1986; volume 4 covering 1985 and 1986 was published in 1988. All are available through OOPEC. An introductory brochure on COST and a pamphlet on points of contact at the national level are available from the COST Secretariat in the General Secretariat.

List of Laws and Regulations Adopted in the Member States of the Communities in Application of Acts Adopted by the Communities

This publication was issued fortnightly during the 1970s until 1977 when it seems to have become bimonthly. Later still publication became spasmodic and the last issue covered the year 1981. The title is self-explanatory and seems to suggest a useful reference source. In fact the lack of an index, the non-cumulative nature of the issues and the very broad subject headings used (in French) made for an unimpressive publication.

It will be possible at some stage for the public to trace national measures taken to implement Community provisions in Sector 7 of CELEX.

European Communities Glossary

This generic title covers a number of different volumes. The aim of the series is to enable you to find the equivalent word or phrase in different Community languages of key concepts used in EC operations and legislation. The eighth edition of a French to English glossary was published in 1984; a supplement was published in 1988. The third edition of a French to German glossary was published in 1984. The third edition of an English to French glossary was published in 1986, as was the first edition of a German to French glossary. All are compiled by the Terminology Service within Directorate IV, Translation Department, of Directorate General A of the General Secretariat of the Council.

Also compiled by the Terminology Service is *Multilingual glossary of abbreviations*, published in 1982. The same edition was republished in 1983 with a different catalogue number and ISBN. This glossary contains 3000 entries giving abbreviations and corresponding full forms to do with the internal and external activities of the EC. Included are national, Community and international terms and organizations, technical terms and everyday abbreviations. Greek, Spanish and Portuguese entries are not included in this edition. There is a French subject index and a general index listing all the abbreviations alphabetically and giving the serial numbers under which the abbreviation is to be found in the body of the work.

Two further more specialized glossaries published in the 1980s are *Technical barriers glossary 1. Administrative procedures*, 1984 and *ACP-EEC glossary (plus list of states)*, 1984. The harmonization of Community terminology is an immense undertaking and over the years many further glossaries can be expected. Certainly they can be of considerable value for non-linguists trying to translate phrases accurately. For terminological publications from the Commission see Chapter 5.

Miscellaneous publications

It is not the responsibility of the Council to publish the text of EC legislation or major agreements. However, there are a number of instances of publications which relate to important institutional developments which have been issued by the Council. An example is *Conclusions of the European Council . . . on the report on European institutions presented by the Committee of Three to the European Council*, 1981. Another is the report from the Ad hoc Committee for Institutional Affairs (The Dooge Committee) called *Report to the European Council (Brussels, 29–30 March 1985)*, 1985. Similarly in 1986 the Council issued booklets called the *Single European Act and Final Act* and *Speeches and statements made on the occasion of the signing of the Single European Act*. A commemorative brochure called *Europe 25 years after the signature of the Treaties of Rome*, containing speeches made at the official celebrations in March 1982, was issued the following month.

Over the years the Council has issued a number of publications relating to the Community patent. The Convention for the European Patent was signed in 1975 and the text plus all the documents involved can be found in *Records of the Luxembourg Conference on the Community Patent 1975*, 1981. In 1985 a further conference was held in Luxembourg with the aim of:

1. Arrranging the rapid implementation of the 1975 Convention
2. Defining the conditions governing participation in the system by countries which joined the EC after 1975
3. Finalizing a protocol setting up the judicial machinery for the settlement of litigation of Community patents.

In the event only the final aim was achieved. The details can be found in *Texts established by the Luxembourg Conference on the Community Patent 1985*, 1986. A comprehensive report on the subject can be found in a study by the (United Kingdom) House of Lords Select Committee on the European Communities (First Report [1986–87] HL 17).

In 1983 the Council issued *European educational policy statements 1974–1983*. This booklet brought together the texts of directives, resolutions and conclusions on education at EC level from the establishment of Community educational cooperation in 1974. A supplement covering 1984 developments was published in 1985 and an enlarged second edition was published in 1986. A third edition dated June 1987 was published in 1988. It should be noted that only Council actions are listed in the text, not the actions by the Commission or member states to give effect to the Council texts. A subject index of sorts is supplied.

Publications of the Library of the Council of Ministers

List of Acquisitions

List of Acquisitions is a quarterly publication listing all titles recently received by the Library arranged by the Universal Decimal Classification. Note that while the library of the Council of Ministers does receive all the publications of the European Communities these are *not* listed in *List of Acquisitions*.

Selected Articles

Selected Articles is a quarterly publication listing articles mainly on European integration which appeared in non-EC periodicals taken by the General Secretariat of the Council. The articles are classified by the Universal Decimal Classification. The list of the principal periodicals indexed are listed on the inside of the front and back covers. *Selected Articles* is a good source of recent articles – for example no. 4, 1986, published in February 1987, covers periodicals issued mainly in the period June–December 1986. It has neither index nor cumulation.

General catalogue of periodicals

This 1983 publication lists the periodicals and newspapers taken by the Library of the Council of Ministers. There is an alphabetical listing of titles and a subject breakdown according to the Universal Decimal Classification.

FURTHER INFORMATION

It is worth noting a couple of publications not of Council origin but which give information relating to the Council of Ministers. In the *Bulletin of the European Communities* (see Chapter 4) there is a section called 'Council' which lists the Council meetings that took place during the month described in that issue. The table lists the number, place and date of each meeting, the name of the Council President and Commission representative, and the main items of business. Under the last heading you are referred to the section in the *Bulletin* where you can find a more detailed account of the outcome of the meeting.

In *The Week in Europe*, issued by the London Press and Information Office of the Commission, you can find a list of provisional dates for future Council meetings in the coming weeks.

Further information on the documentation of the Council of Ministers can be obtained from:

General Secretariat of the Council of Ministers
DG A-III Information, Publications, Documentation
170 rue de la Loi
B-1048 – Brussels
Belgium
Telephone 234 61 11
Telegrams: CONSIL – Brussels
Telex: 21711 CONSIL B

CHAPTER 9

European Parliament

The European Parliament is the democratic conscience of the European Community. It has to be consulted by the Commission and the Council of Ministers on most proposals and policy initiatives and has the opportunity to question those institutions on their activities. The European Parliament has been the common term used for many years but until the Single European Act 1986 the institution was formally called 'the European Assembly'.

In June 1979 the first democratically elected European Parliament was established. Since then the Parliament has attempted, albeit with limited success, to maintain a high profile and develop its supervisory and decision-making powers. These attempts culminated in the Single European Act. This, among other provisions, gave the European Parliament the power of veto over agreements made between the Community and other countries, and to the enlargement of the EC. It also introduced into the EC decision-making process a new cooperation procedure allowing the European Parliament a second reading stage in the legislative process.

STRUCTURE

The Secretariat of the Parliament consisting of around 2900 officials is based in Luxembourg. Plenary meetings of the Parliament take place monthly in Strasbourg, while most Committee meetings take place in Brussels. It is expected that the Parliament will attempt to centralize its activities in Brussels in due course. The peripatetic existence of the Parliament, plus its severely circumscribed functions, has led to criticism of the institution. Although the budgetary powers of the Parliament are real and have been much used during the 1980s, essentially the Parliament is only *consulted* during the legislative process and its opinion can be ultimately ignored. The long-term implications of the changes brought about by the Single European Act remain to be seen.

Since the accession of Spain and Portugal the European Parliament has been composed of 518 members, who form themselves into political rather than national groupings. Elections take place every five years. The names of all Members of the European Parliament (MEPs) and key officials in the European Parliament can be found in the *Official handbook of the European Parliament* (see under Miscellaneous Publications, p. 225).

The Secretariat of the European Parliament comprises the following divisions (structure since 1986):

1. Secretariat General
2. Directorate-General 1: Registry
3. Directorate-General 2: Committees and delegations
4. Directorate-General 3: Information and public relations
5. Directorate-General 4: Research
6. Directorate-General 5: Personnel, budget and finances
7. Directorate-General 6: Administration

DOCUMENTATION

As mentioned above, the first direct elections to the European Parliament took place in 1979. The increase in the numbers of Members of the European Parliament, further increased with the accession of Greece in 1981 and Spain and Portugal in 1986, plus the enhanced status the European Parliament assumed with its democratic legitimization, led to a rapid expansion of its activities and attendant documentation in the 1980s. In 1971, for example, 281 Working Documents had been issued. By 1978 this had increased to 841 and by 1985 to 2269. Similar expansion occurred in other areas of European Parliament documentation.

DG I is responsible for the production and distribution of formal European Parliament documentation. In the case of information concerning Parliament that is published in the *Official Journal* this is sent by DG I to the Office for Official Publications of the European Communities. DG III and DG IV also issue documentation that enters the public domain. Note that until 1985 the Research and Documentation Directorate-General was DG V. Documentation from the political groups is not handled by the European Parliament or OOPEC. Some of the political groups issue a considerable degree of publicly available material. For further information contact the political groups, the addresses of which are given at the end of this chapter.

The plenary sessions of the European Parliament

Every month of the year, except August, the European Parliament meets together for a week for its plenary session. Sometimes it is called a part session ('part' of the Parliament session) or a full session (comprising the 'full' complement of MEPs).

The *Official Journal of the European Communities: Annex: Debates of the European Parliament* is the authoritative record of the debates held during a plenary session. The debates cover discussion of committee reports, topical or urgent issues, and the reaction to statements made by the Commission, the Council, the European Council and the foreign ministers meeting in political cooperation. In addition there will also be the oral questions (and subsequent answers) submitted during the various periods of question time held during a plenary session. During question time only a small number of the scheduled questions are usually dealt with but the *Official Journal: Annex* prints the full allocation with answers. It also prints the monthly Commission report to the European Parliament on the action it has taken on the opinions conveyed to it by Parliament.

The *Official Journal: Annex* is published in the nine official languages of the Communities. A summary of the contents is shown on the front cover. A slightly more detailed listing is given at the begining of each day's account – this includes the name of all the speakers and references to the committee report debated.

Plenary sessions are numbered in a straighforward numerical sequence, starting with no. 101 in 1968. From March 1980 until May 1984 a figure '1' preceded the session number and from July 1984 a figure '2' has preceded the session number. For example, the *Official Journal: Annex* for April 1986 was numbered no. 2–338, the figure '2' indicating the second directly elected European Parliament term (1984–89). Presumably from July 1989 a figure '3' will be used.

At the end of most debates a vote is taken on a resolution. The text of the resolutions plus the formal record of what took place at a plenary session is recorded in the *Official Journal of the European Communities: Information and Notices* (the 'C' series). As noted elsewhere this section of the *Official Journal* contains much information in addition to that concerning the European Parliament. However, on the inside cover of the *Official Journal: Annex* a reference can be found to which issue of the *Official Journal: Information and Notices* contains the resolutions adopted during that particular plenary session.

An alternative source for the text of resolutions can be found in *Texts Adopted by the European Parliament*. This began publication with an issue covering the plenary session of March 1985. It is published monthly while the European Parliament is sitting.

Written questions submitted by MEPs to the Commission, Council and foreign ministers meeting in political cooperation are printed in issues of the *Official Journal: Information and Notices*. Occasionally one will come across an issue headed 'Written questions without answer'. This lists questions which the Commission failed to answer within one month and the Council has failed to answer within two months. It does not preclude the question being answered at a later date.

An index to the *Official Journal: Annex* is produced for each session, broken down into three sections:

1. Index of names

2. Index of subjects
3. List of working documents.

Under the name of each MEP is listed the committees of which he or she is a member, any document to which his or her name is attached, the debates to which he or she has contributed, and the questions he or she has asked during the session.

In the subject index, which is of a reasonable standard, one can trace debates and questions, and the name of the MEPs who were involved. The third table lists in numerical order all the documents presented to Parliament during the session in question. It mentions the dates of presentation, debate and adoption.

Unfortunately the index is published a number of years after the session it is describing. The index covering the session 1983–84 only appeared in late 1987 and was not widely distributed. This is clearly not satisfactory.

Equally problematical is the indexing of the information about the European Parliament in the *Official Journal: Information and Notices*. Up to 1981 this information was indexed in the *Index to the Official Journal of the European Communities*. After that date the only information given in that source is a list of the editions of the *Official Journal: Information and Notices* in which 'Written questions with answers' are printed for the period in question. In effect that means there is no indexing of such information as written questions in a printed format (see the section on CELEX, SCAD and the databases of the European Parliament in Appendix 2).

From the Publications and Briefings Division of the Directorate-General for Information and Public Relations are issued a number of publications which preview or review each plenary session. First, there is *Briefing*. Usually issued about a week before a plenary session, it summarizes the forthcoming agenda including reports to be debated and questions to be asked. Then there is *The Week* (final edition). Issued about two weeks after a plenary session it summarizes what took place on a day-by-day basis during the week in question. From September 1986 a cumulating alphabetical subject index to all the issues of *The Week* for the calendar year has appeared at the back of each issue. This is very useful. Finally there is *EP News*, which again covers what took place during a plenary session. It is printed in a newspaper popular-level format with photographs. Although the editorial is done in Luxembourg, *EP News* is printed in the United Kingdom and is intended primarily for UK and Irish readers. Similar publications exist for other member states. All these publications are free of charge.

There is a considerable delay between a plenary session and the publication of the *Official Journal: Annex* and *Official Journal: Information and Notices* that cover the session. Obviously MEPs,

Parliamentary officials and journalists have a need for more rapid information. Thus a provisional version of the *Official Journal: Annex* is issued called *Verbatim Report of Proceedings*. Each issue covers the debates of a single day and is issued a day later. The important thing to note is that speeches are printed only in the language in which they were spoken and have not been checked by the speakers. Listed questions not answered orally are covered in an *Annex* to the *Verbatim Report*. An edition covering a full plenary session was issued from January to July 1987 on an experimental basis as a possible replacement for the *Official Journal: Annex*. The experiment would seem to have been abandoned after that period.

Similarly *Minutes of Proceedings of the Sittings of . . .* covers provisionally the information later printed, corrected and revised in the *Official Journal: Information and Notices*. Neither the *Verbatim Report* (daily edition) nor *Minutes of Proceedings* are on sale to the public. The information they contain is not confidential, however, and the information offices of the European Parliament will send photocopies of a particular section if required. A publication called *Strasbourg Notebook* is issued on a daily basis during plenary sessions. Primarily intended for MEPs and the media, it is not publicly available but the information it contains and the style of presentation is to be found in *The Week*.

European Parliament Working/Session Documents

These documents, as their name implies, are the documents that the MEPs use in carrying out their business in the European Parliament. They are numbered in a running sequence starting each session. Until the session 1984–85 no distinction was made in the numbering system between the various categories of information to be found in this series. Since the session 1985–86 the following distinction has been made:

1. Series A: Reports   JN 95. A1 A 112
2. Series B: Motions for Resolutions, Oral Questions, Written Declarations, etc.
3. Series C: Documents received from other institutions (for example, COM Documents).

The reports which comprises Series A are those from the committees of the European Parliament. The number of committees changes from time to time; at present there are eighteen:

1. Political affairs
2. Agriculture, fisheries and food
3. Budgets
4. Economic and monetary affairs and industrial policy
5. Energy, research and technology

6. External economic relations
7. Legal affairs and citizens' rights
8. Social affairs and employment
9. Regional policy and regional planning
10. Transport.
11. Environment, public health and consumer protection
12. Youth, culture, education, information and sport
13. Development and cooperation
14. Budgetary control
15. Rules of procedure, verification of credentials and immunities
16. Petitions
17. Institutional affairs
18. Women's rights.

(Committees as of February 1988)

Occasionally temporary committees are established to investigate a particular issue. An example is the Temporary Committee for the success of the Single Act, set up in 1987. Another was the Committee of Inquiry into the problem of stocks in the agriculture sector, set up in 1986.

The main work of committees is to look at legislative proposals as part of the Parliament's consultative role. A committee can also look at questions of its own choosing – these are called *own-initiative reports*. An MEP is appointed as rapporteur to write a report. Once adopted by the committee the report is presented by the rapporteur to a plenary session. If accepted here, after possibly a number of amendments, the resolution within the report becomes an Opinion of the European Parliament.

A committee report is usually made up of two sections:

1. Motion for a resolution – the text of the proposed resolution that will be voted upon at the plenary session
2. Explanatory statement – here the rapporteur gives the background to the report. This section can vary from a page or so to a substantial review of the subject of the report.

With the coming into operation of the new legislative processes introduced by the Single European Act in 1987 additional Series A European Parliament Session Documents appeared. These comprised Second Reading reports compiled by the rapporteur commenting upon the reaction of the Council and Commission to the first submission by the Parliament of its opinion on a proposal. Usually in these reports there would not be a substantial explanatory section; rather they comprised a detailed line-by-line comparison of the text as proposed by the various institutions.

From 1987 symbols appeared on the internal European Parliament cover of European Parliament Session Documents to denote their precise status:

* Consulation procedure requiring a single reading
**I Cooperation procedure (first reading)
**II Cooperation procedure (second reading) which requires the votes of the majority of Members of Parliament
*** Parliamentary assent which requires the votes of the majority of the current Members of Parliament.

The same symbols are used in the issues of the *Official Journal: Information and Notices* which contain the minutes of plenary sessions.

These reports are important for they reflect the Parliament's areas of current concern. Even though they are 'working documents' they are made available to the public on subscription. When received in this way from OOPEC an additional cover is put on the document. This has no mention of the terms European Parliament Working Document or European Parliament Session Document on the cover. Instead they are titled European Parliament: Reports – often called EP Reports. Even more confusion is caused by certain sales catalogues referring to the reports as Committee Reports of the European Parliament. You can either subscribe to the whole set of these reports or just to those within particular subject categories. In the session 1986–87 there were 257 Series A European Parliament Working Documents issued.

Series B and C documents are not publicly available, but the information they contain is often to be found elsewhere. Oral questions, for example, can be found in the *Official Journal: Annex*. Many of the documents in Series C are available from the Commission as COM Document, as items in the *Official Journal* or in other formats.

The citation for these reports is illustrated in the following example:

European Parliament: Political Affairs Committee
Report on the use of the veto in the Council, Rapporteur:
Mr Hans R. Nord
PE DOC A2-56/86

* PE: Parlement Européen (European Parliament)
* A: Series A
* 2: The second directly elected European Parliament (1984–89)
* 56/86: The 56th report of the parliamentary session 1986–87.

On many European Parliament publications you will also find a reference such as PE 103 937. This is an internal European Parliament number not used as a public citation.

During the session 1987–88 the term European Parliament Working

Document was replaced by the term European Parliament Session Document.

As mentioned above European Parliament Session Documents are listed in the *Official Journal: Annex: Index*. DG I also distributed periodically until March 1985 a *Numerical list of Working Documents* in the French language only. From the session 1985–86 these documents have been listed in the *Catalogue of Documents* from OOPEC (see Chapter 3). In this catalogue they are listed with COM Documents, and ESC Opinions and Reports, under broad subject headings.

Bulletin of the European Parliament

The *Bulletin* is aimed at keeping MEPs informed of activities within Parliament and of new documents and research papers issued. Activities include the work of the President of the European Parliament, the Enlarged Bureau, the committees, forthcoming meetings, agendas and the like. The titles of new European Parliament Session Documents are listed as are special reports, bibliographies and other publications produced by the Directorate-General for Research for MEPs. Special issues of the *Bulletin* list written questions, the work being undertaken by committees and the draft agenda for plenary sessions. Since the Single European Act the documentation received by the Parliament from the Council and Commission during the operation of the Cooperation Procedure must be listed in the *Bulletin*.

The *Bulletin* is not generally made available to the public. This is a pity, for it contains much information that someone trying to keep abreast of Parliamentary activities would find of interest. It is true that some issues contain confidential information regarding expenses and the like but it would not be difficult to break the *Bulletin* down into parts, some of which could be made publicly available. This has been done with the European Parliament Session Documents. Since 1987 the heading *Bulletin of the European Parliament* has been removed from the cover although the word *Bulletin* is still printed inside. On the cover under the words European Parliament are one of the following headings:

1. Activities (A)
2. Calendar of meetings (B)
3. Work in Committees (C)
4. Written questions (D)

SCAD News for April 1986 states that the *Bulletin* is available to the public but this is probably an example of one Community institution not knowing the policy of another. An occasional special issue of the *Bulletin* which listed MEPs was made available publicly. From the 1986–87 session, however, this has been published separately as *List of Members*. This gives an alphabetical list of all MEPs, indicating their party affiliation, committee membership, country of origin, date of birth and current address. It is available as a priced publication from OOPEC.

DG III documentation

The task of the Directorate-General for Information and Public Relations is to provide information to the public and the media. Publications are only one aspect of their work. Three of their regular publications have already been mentioned:

1. *Briefing*
2. *The Week*
3. *EP News*

DG III is also responsible for the issuing of press releases and a series called *Info Memo*, which mainly cover the work of the parliamentary committees, and are intended for journalists. In 1986 a publication called *Retrospect* was issued. This was an eleven-page summary of the work of the European Parliament during 1985. A further edition covering 1986 was issued in 1987.

Other publications from DG III tend to be one-off booklets. A selection of fairly substantial titles issued during the 1980s includes:

1. *Report on the situation of small and medium-sized undertakings in the Community*, 1982
2. *Draft Treaty establishing the European union*, 1984
3. *Programme for European economic recovery*, 1984
4. *The situation of women in Europe*, 1984
5. *A new phase in European union*, 1985
6. *Committee of Inquiry into the rise of fascism and racism in Europe: report on the findings of the inquiry*, 1985
7. *Committee of Inquiry into the drugs problem in the member states of the Community: report on the results of the Enquiry*, 1987
8. *Public hearing on security policy in Europe: situation and prospects*, 1987
9. *The budget: Parliament's case*, 1987.

Since 1987 titles have been published, with certain exceptions, as priced publications in all Community languages from OOPEC. Prior to this they were available, usually free of charge, direct from the European Parliament.

On a more popular level and often issued in connection with direct elections are various booklets periodically updated. A selection includes:

1. *The European Parliament and the world at large*, 1981
2. *Europe: a time to choose*, 1988
3. *One Parliament for twelve*; 7th edition, 1988.

The Information Offices of the European Parliament in the member states issue material appropriate to their own country. In particular this often includes regularly updated lists of addresses of MEPs for that country. At the time of the first two European elections additional material was issued. For example, for the 1984 election the United Kingdom Office published a substantial booklet called *Your Parliament in Europe: the European Parliament, 1979–1984*. A second edition of this book was published in 1985. For the 1989 European elections most of the money allocated for information purposes was spent by the political parties rather than the Information Offices. The Information Offices also issue press releases.

DG IV documentation

(Note that until 1986 the Directorate-General for Research and Documentation was DG V)

The principal function of DG IV is to provide information to MEPs – either as individuals or in groups such as committees and political groups. Documentation produced by DG IV can be a response to a specific request from an MEP or group, or it can be compiled by DG IV in the expectation that the publication will be of benefit to MEPs.

Publications from DG IV are not normally intended for the general public and are not usually distributed from OOPEC. However, the obvious usefulness of many of their titles has led to a number being made available. EC Depository Libraries receive a selection and a number are freely available from Information Offices of the European Parliament (listed at the end of this chapter).

Europe today: state of European integration

This title led the way to the greater public availability of the documentation of the Research Directorate-General. First published in 1976 in looseleaf format and later in paperback editions, *Europe today* claimed to be a 'collection of the most important legislative acts of the European Parliament ... and ... designed to give an overall picture of the latest stage reached in the political legal development of the Community'. It was essentially a bibliographical directory of Community legislation. The last edition published was the seventh in 1983. It is a great shame that the title was discontinued as it was one of the most useful and easily digestible of major EC reference sources.

Fact sheets on the European Parliament and the activities of the European Community

It has been sometimes claimed that *Fact sheets* replaces *Europe today*. *Fact sheets* was first issued in 1979 for the first European elections. A second edition emerged in late 1983 in readiness for the second direct elections the following year. A third edition, published in 1987, was the first to be properly typeset and clearly intended for a wide public readership. A fourth edition was published in 1989.

The foreword claims that the '*Fact sheets* present a concise synopsis of the Communities' achievements ... and of the part played by the European Parliament'. Broken down under headings such as taxation, social and public health policy, regional policy, and the like, *Fact sheets* outlines the legal basis of the policy objectives and achievements. It is a valuable publication but the lack of bibliographical references and index reduces its value now that *Europe today* is not published in tandem. The numbering system of sections is also unduly clumsy – even the compilers or printers found this as there are mistakes in the order of the sections in the third edition.

Progress towards European integration: survey of the main activities of the European Parliament

This has been an annual publication since 1980, and is most useful although its frequent change of title in its first years caused librarians bibliographical nightmares. Four changes of title in six years must be a record. Essentially the 'title' in question is an annual review of the activities of the European Parliament in the general context of European integration. It can be used in parallel with *Fact sheets* as the subject headings used are similar (though not identical). The big advantage of the annual review is that after a descriptive account bibliographical references are given to enable you to trace the primary texts.

The precise titles are as follows:

1. *Main aspects of European development during the period June 1979–June 1980*
2. *Development of the Community from June 1980 to June 1981*
3. *Principal developments in the European Community from June 1981 to June 1982, ... 1982–1983, ... 1983–1984*
4. *Progress towards European integration: survey of the main activities of the European Parliament July 1984–June 1985*. This title is now the standard title used in all subsequent reviews.

Research and Documentation Papers

Individual MEPs or parliamentary groups commission reports and analyses from the Research Directorate-General. When completed these will often be made available to other MEPs in the series Research and Documentation Papers. Other studies in the series are compiled on the initiative of officials in DG IV. Not all these studies are compiled for the general public, but as is often the case with such material many reach the public domain – some have been received by EC Depository Libraries over the years, others are spasmodically available from the Information Offices of the European Parliament, while it has been known for academic researchers in a particular discipline to get on a mailing list and receive all the titles published in the relevant subject series.

Research and Documentation Papers are broken down into series – examples include: environment, public health and consumer protection series; political series; economic series; regional policy and transport series; and the quaintly named action-taken series. Many are very short and of limited interest but there are also many substantial titles of more than considerable interest. Political series 4 of January 1984, for example, was called 'Transfer of responsibilities and the democratic deficit'. Behind this opaque title was an important study of the extent to which responsibilities had been transferred over the years from the member states to the European Community and the extent to which parliamentary democracy has been eroded. Another study in the same series (no. 6, February 1984) was a textual comparison of the various initiatives towards European union being taken in the 1980s. No. 10, 1987, in the environment, public health and consumer protection series was a substantial European Parliament manual on the European Year of the Environment. The President of the European Parliament, Lord Plumb, makes clear in the preface that the publication is intended for the general public. An example of a title in the action-taken series is no. 1, 1987, called 'Achievement of the internal market: action taken by the Commission and Council on Parliament's Opinions'.

It is hoped that further of these titles extend into the public domain – many are of a quality that deserve a wider readership. Research and Documentation Papers are not systematically listed in the standard EC bibliographical sources, but in the *Bulletin of the European Parliament* and also the Newsletters of the European Centre for Parliamentary Research and Documentation.

Miscellaneous DG IV documentation

There are various one-off monographs and booklets intended for the general public. Some are major works of reference – a selection would include:

1. *The effects on the United Kingdom of membership of the European Communities*, 1975
2. *Elections to the European Parliament by direct universal suffrage*, 1977
3. *The position of women in the European Parliament in the European Community*, 1981
4. *Growing together*, 1982
5. *Organization of services in the Parliaments of the EC member states*, 1980; 1983
6. *Forging ahead: thirty years of the European Parliament, 1952–1982*, 1982 (new edition 1989)

7. *Counting the cost: parliamentary control of the Community finances*, 1984; 1985.

Forging ahead: thirty years of the European Parliament, 1952-1982 is an invaluable reference source giving a comprehensive historical, organizational and statistical account of the first thirty years of the European Parliament.

Miscellaneous publications

The European Parliament publishes a booklet called *Rules of procedure*. The third edition was published in 1984 and lists the rules of procedure adopted by Parliament in 1981 and as amended in 1983 and 1984. The fourth edition, taking into account the significant changes brought about by the Single European Act, was published in 1987.

In 1980 the Secretariat of the Parliament published an *Official handbook of the European Parliament* in looseleaf format. This contained short biographies and photographs of all MEPs, extracts of the Treaties establishing the European Communities, national electoral laws, rules of procedure and committee and political group membership. A new paperback edition was published in 1985 covering the second electoral period 1984-1989. This contains biographies, committee and group membership and a directory of personnel in the Secretariat of the European Parliament.

An updated alphabetical listing of MEPs, with photographs, party affiliation and contact addresses was issued in *Vademecum* in 1986. A further edition of this title was issued in December 1987. The most up-to-date directory of MEPs is to be found in the occasionally updated *List of members* – a new edition is issued at least once a year.

In the early 1980s the Committee on Institutional Affairs of the European Parliament looked at the question of the reform of EC institutions and the further progress of European integration. They asked for the text of all previous proposals to be brought together and this resulted in the compilation of *Selection of texts concerning institutional matters of the Community from 1950 to 1982*. Hopefully a similar publication bringing together the initiatives of the 1980s will be produced in due course.

In 1979 DG V (now DG IV) produced *The European Parliament: bibliography 1970-1978*. This was primarily an index to non-EC sources of information about the European Parliament although some EC material was included. The material was indexed under such headings as procedures and rules, sessions and activities, direct elections etc. Annual supplements have been produced since 1980.

FURTHER INFORMATION

Certain EC databases available to the public can be used to find information relating to the European Parliament. Questions submitted by MEPs and resolutions of the European Parliament can be traced on CELEX. Committee reports of the European Parliament and resolutions can be found in the SCAD database.

For information regarding the documentation of the European Parliament contact:

> The Director General
> Directorate-General III
> Information and Public Relations
> The European Parliament General Secretariat
> Centre Européen
> Plateau du Kirchberg
> L-2929 Luxembourg
> Telephone: 4300-1
> Telex: 2894 EUPARL LU

In the member states contact the Information Offices of the European Parliament:

97–113 rue Belliard
B-1040 Brussels
Belgium
Telephone: (2) 234 21 11

Børsen
DK-1217 Copenhagen
Denmark
Telephone: (1) 14 33 77

2 Queen Anne's Gate
London SW1H 9AA
England
Telephone: (1) 222 0411
Telex: 894160 EP, LDNG

Bonn-Center
Bundeskanzlerplatz
D-5300 Bonn 1
Federal Republic of Germany
Telephone: (0228) 22 30 91

288 boulevard St Germain
F-75007 Paris
France
Telephone: (1) 45 50 34 11

2 Avenue Vassilissis Sophias
GR-10674 Athens
Greece
Telephone: (1) 723 34 21

43 Molesworth Street
Dublin 2
Ireland
Telephone: (1) 71 91 00

149 Via IV Novembre
I-00187 Rome
Italy
Telephone: (6) 679 05 07

European Parliament
L-2929 Luxembourg
Telephone: 4300–1

27 A Lange Voorhout
NL-2514 EB 's Gravenhage
The Hague
The Netherlands
Telephone: (70) 62 49 41

Centro Europeu
5660 Jean Monnet
50–60 Rua do Salitre
P-1200 Lisbon
Portugal
Telephone: (1) 57 82 98

Fanãn Flor
E-28014 Madrid
Spain
Telephone: (1) 429 33 53

Enquiries concerning the documentation of the political groups should be addressed to the relevant political group at:

European Centre
Plateau du Kirchberg
L-2929 Luxembourg
Telephone: 4300–1

or

97–113 rue Belliard
B-1040 Brussels
Belgium

National parties within the political groups often maintain offices in their own country. Contact the European Parliament Information Office in the country concerned for further details.

Sources and references

1. European Parliament, *Activities of the European Parliament since 1970. Key statistical data* (PE-i-0016105–84) (Internal document)
2. European Parliament information, by Anthony Reid, in *European Communities information*, edited by Michael Hopkins, Mansell, 1985, pp. 77–90
3. European Parliament, *Organisation des services du Secrétariat général et des Groupes Politiques*, June 1986 (internal document)
4. The Single European Act and the new legislative cooperation procedure: a critical analysis, by Juliet Lodge, *Journal of European Integration*, vol. XI no. 1, Autumn 1987, pp. 5–28.

CHAPTER 10

Economic and Social Committee

Since 1986 the Economic and Social Committee has comprised 189 members who represent the three distinct groups:

1. Employers (group I)
2. Workers (group II)
3. Other interest groups (group III) representing agriculture, consumers, small firms, the professions, the scientific world, family organizations, environment protection, transport etc.

STRUCTURE OF THE ECONOMIC AND SOCIAL COMMITTEE

Members are nominated by member states' governments. The function of the Economic and Social Committee (usually abbreviated to ECOSOC) is to advise the Commission and Council of the views of the interest groups involved on Community proposals and matters of its own concern. ECOSOC is not necessarily consulted on all issues and the Council is certainly not forced to follow the opinions of the Committee. The value of ECOSOC is as a means of formalized expression of the views of powerful interest groups within the Community. The Committee has also organized, or helped to organize, conferences on subjects of concern such as small and medium-sized enterprises in 1983, new technologies in 1984 and the environment in 1987.

The Bureau of the Economic and Social Committee, comprising twenty-seven members, organizes the work of the Committee. The Bureau allocates proposals from the Council or Commission, or own-initiative studies, to one of nine sections:

1. Agriculture
2. Industry, Commerce, Crafts and Services
3. Economic, Financial and Monetary Questions
4. Social, Family, Educational and Cultural Affairs
5. Transport and Communications
6. External Relations
7. Energy, Nuclear Questions and Research
8. Regional Development and Town and Country Planning

9. Protection of the Environment, Public Health and Consumer Affairs.

A section reaches an opinion on the basis of a report compiled by a member of the section. The opinion is then presented to a plenary session of all members. These are held in Brussels over a period of two days ten times a year. Plenary sessions are referred to numerically – the 239th plenary session, for example, took place on 17 and 18 September 1986.

If a section's opinion is adopted it is then sent to the Commission and Council. In the 1980s approximately 100 opinions, information reports and studies have been issued annually, and this number is slowly rising.

Since 1984 the term 'Economic and Social Consultative Assembly' has been used on the cover of certain ECOSOC documentation. The use of this term was agreed by the Bureau in December 1983. It was intended as a subtitle of the institution and is used next to the official one (Economic and Social Committee) only on non-official material such as brochures, press releases, briefings, books and posters. The idea behind the subtitle was that the official title of the Committee was misleading and gave a wrong impression, in particular to citizens of those countries which do not include an economic and social council in their legislative structure. The parallel has been made with the standard, and since 1987 the official, use of the term 'European Parliament' instead of 'European Assembly'.

DOCUMENTATION

In common with other EC institutions and organizations a greater effort has been made during the 1980s to publicize the work of the Economic and Social Committee. In the area of documentation the major development has been the distribution of the Opinions and Reports by OOPEC. Nevertheless it is still not possible to trace in detail on a regular basis the reports of the sections or the discussions at the plenary sessions. Summaries are available and these are outlined below. The relative obscurity of ECOSOC to the public at large reflects perhaps that it is an advisory body of nominees rather than a democratically elected consultative institution.

Documentation from the Economic and Social Committee is compiled by the Press, Information and Publications Division, a division of the office of the Secretary-General within the General Secretariat. In addition to the documentation issued through OOPEC, ECOSOC continues to issue publications of its own, while some titles are also issued through commercial publishers.

Annual report

During the 1980s the *Annual report* retained a standard format and contained the following information:

1. Role and influence of ECOSOC
2. Work of the sections
3. Press relations and outside reactions
4. The groups
5. Participation in meetings outside the Committee
6. Personnel changes
7. Internal affairs of the General Secretariat
8. List of opinions, studies and information reports issued
9. List of opinions drawn up by ECOSOC on its own initiative since 1973
10. Tables indicating the extent to which opinions led to proposals being amended.

There is no index or subject arrangement to the documentation referred to, but in the annex listing opinions, studies and information reports a CES reference is given. The *Annual report* is now available as a priced publication from OOPEC in all Community languages.

Bulletin

A monthly account of the activities of the Economic and Social Committee. To be accurate, in most years ten issues are published – those for June and July, and August and September being combined in single issues. Until 1984 the *Bulletin* was available directly from ECOSOC, but since 1985 it has only been available from OOPEC on a subscription basis.

The format of the *Bulletin* has remained essentially the same during the 1980s and comprises the following information:

1. Recent speeches and statements by the Chairman of ECOSOC
2. A summary of opinions adopted at the most recent plenary session
3. External relations (the relations of ECOSOC personnel with outside organizations)
4. New consultations (a list of proposals that the Council or Commission has asked ECOSOC to consider)
5. Provisional future work programme (lists the 'Opinions upon consultation', 'Own-initiative opinions' and information reports to be considered at the next and subsequent plenary sessions.
6. Members' news.
7. Publications (a list of publications obtainable from ECOSOC and other sources; does not include internal working documentation which is available).

List of members

This information is available in a number of different sources. In the past a *Directory* has been issued listing Bureau members by nationality and by group, members of the Economic and Social Committee classified by country, position and group, and composition of the sections by group and nationality. However, the *Directory* has now ceased publication; the last edition was issued in 1981.

In the *Bulletin* no. 8–9, 1982 there was a list of members as nominated for the seventh term of office of the Economic and Social Committee, 1982–86. In the *Bulletin* no. 8–9, 1986 the same information appeared for the eighth term of office, 1986–90. This information is also available in the *Official Journal* – for the term 1986–90, for example, the information was in the *Official Journal* C244 30.9.86. The composition of the sections for the same term was printed in the *Official Journal* C56 4.3.87.

However, probably the most useful source is a multilingual publication called *Index: list of members of the Bureau, Committee, groups and sections*. Issued periodically this lists:

1. Members of the Bureau
2. Alphabetical list of ECOSOC members (with their occupation, member state, Group, date of appointment and contact address)
3. Membership of the Sections
4. Composition of Groups (with breakdown by nationality)
5. The General Secretariat of ECOSOC.

Opinions

The texts of Opinions of the Economic and Social Committee are printed periodically in the *Official Journal: Information and Notices* (the 'C' series). However, the *Official Journal: Index* does not refer to them, so unless one already has an *Official Journal* reference they are difficult to track down in that source. The Commission document *List of Pending Proposals* (see Chapter 1) will direct you to an ECOSOC Opinion in the *Official Journal*, as will the preamble to the text of a piece of EC legislation in the *Official Journal: Legislation*.

Over the years ECOSOC has selected a small proportion of its opinions for wider distribution and notice. Up to the mid-1980s these publications were distributed by the Committee itself. Since then the position has become less clear. OOPEC publish and distribute a number of these 'selected Opinions' (in addition to the complete series described below), but ECOSOC continue to distribute other 'selected Opinions' themselves. An example of the latter is *Target date 1992: The Economic and Social Committee supports 'The New-Frontier Europe'*. This brought together the texts of seven Opinions of the Committee and was distributed by ECOSOC in 1988.

When Opinions are issued in this format they contain not only the text of the Opinion but also often the background report of the relevant Section. Examples of this series include:

1. *Problems of the handicapped*, 1981
2. *Prevention of marine pollution*, 1981
3. *Prospects for the '80s*, 1981
4. *The promotion of small- and medium-sized enterprises*, 1982
5. *The economic and social situation of the Community*, 1982
6. *The economic and social situation of the Community*, 1983
7. *Relations between the European Community and the United States*, 1983
8. *Youth employment*, 1983
9. *Tourism*, 1984
10. *Producer–consumer dialogue*, 1984
11. *The economic and social situation in the Community*, 1985
12. *Occupational medicine; occupational cancer*, 1985
13. *EEC air transport policy*, 1985
14. *EEC maritime transport policy*, 1986
15. *GATT: towards a new Round*, 1986
16. *Relations between the EC . . . and ASEAN*, 1986
17. *National regional development aid*, 1986
18. *Effects of the CAP on the social situation of farm workers in the European Community*, 1987
19. *Target date 1992: The Economic and Social Committee supports 'The New-Frontier Europe'*, 1988.

The background report can often be very informative. They have sometimes been compiled by study groups set up by the Section looking at the particular proposal or issue. Study groups are made up of members of the Section plus a number of experts to help the representatives of each Group, and personnel from the Studies and Research Division of the General Secretariat (see also Information Report below).

The big step forward in the availability of Opinions came in 1984 when OOPEC began to distribute them formally. They are now available on subscription as a complete collection or by selective breakdown by subject in all Community languages. The subject breakdown is shown in Appendix 1. In this format the Opinions are simply the document that circulates internally within the institutions with an additional cover put on by OOPEC. From 1984 for about a year the title on this cover said 'Opinion on the . . .'. From sometime in 1985 (it is impossible to be precise as there was a period when both titles existed) the cover title was changed to Opinions and Reports. This is the current title.

This would seem to suggest that in addition to the text of the Opinion an explanatory or background report is included. However, that is not the case. The vast majority of titles issued in this series are simply the texts of Opinions of the Economic and Social Committee. A very small minority comprise more substantial reports. A small number of Information Reports and Studies are also issued in this series.

An annual catalogue of this series was issued in 1984 called *Opinions – annual catalogue*. Since then the Opinions and Reports of ECOSOC have been listed with COM Documents and EP Reports in *Catalogue of Documents* (see Chapter 3).

The Economic and Social Committee assigns each internal working document a number in the series CES (Year) .... CES stands for the French equivalent of the Economic and Social Committee – Comité Economique et Social. For example CES(86)753 is the Opinion of ECOSOC on Community action in the field of tourism. The titles published in the Opinions and Reports series only form a small proportion of the CES series. It would be helpful for librarians if ECOSOC could follow the European Parliament in creating clear subseries in the CES series to distinguish between the various categories of material.

Information Reports; Study; Colloquy

The terms 'information report', 'studies' and 'study group' were used above in the description of Opinions. It is impossible to separate clearly in the documentation one category of material from another. In the comprehensive series published through OOPEC called Opinions and Reports, the Opinions of ECOSOC are usually printed without an accompanying Information Report. However, in the 'selected Opinions' series it is common to have the text of the Opinion and the related Information Report brought together. Just to confuse the situation still further, some titles can be published which only contain an Information Report, while the terms Study and Colloquy have also been used.

In an internal document called *Basic documents* issued in 1986 containing the Bureau's Standing Orders the following information was given. An Opinion is a document which sets out the Committee's position. They should be brief and give a 'reasoned statement of the Committee's views on the Commission proposal or the question examined by the Committee' (Part III, p. 51). Since 1974 the Committee can prepare Opinions on its own initiative as well as at the request of the Commission or Council.

'Studies' were ECOSOC's way of getting around the fact that before 1974 they did not have the right of initiative in compiling Opinions. Article 20 of the Rules of Procedure (1986) of ECOSOC states that the Committee can prepare a Study on matters which it might later be called upon to give an Opinion. However, since ECOSOC now does have the right of compiling own-initiative Opinions there is little need for the procedural device of Studies and they have been discontinued. Some examples of a Study are:

1. *Organization and management of Community research and development*, 1980
2. *Aims and priorities of a common research and development policy*, 1982
3. *The EEC's external relations – stocktaking and consistency of action*, 1982
4. *Structural changes in the textile and clothing sector*, 1982
5. *Integrated operations in the field of regional development*, 1982.

An Information Report is compiled by a Section for the information of Committee members. It is discussed at a plenary session but does not commit the Committee and would usually not be published in the *Official Journal*. In many cases an Information Report serves as the basis for preparing a subsequent own-initiative Opinion. It is in these circumstances that a number of the titles in the 'selected Opinions' series have been published. However, an Information Report can be published where there is no accompanying Opinion. Below is a selection of recent examples:

1. *The Community oils and fats sector*, 1982
2. *Development programme for the Irish border area, 1983*, 1983
3. *Integrated operation Clwyd (North Wales), 1984*, 1985
4. *The European Monetary System*, 1984
5. *Hydrocarbons exploration and production in the Community: the need for a new impetus: the role of the Community*, 1984
6. *National regional development aid, 1984*, 1986
7. *The demographic situation in the Community, 1984*, 1986
8. *Energy options: environmental constraints and their implications for Community energy policy*, 1984
9. *EC shared-cost research, development and demonstration programmes*, 1984
10. *The effect of the CAP on the social situation of farm workers in the Community, 1985*, 1987
11. *The new technologies, 1985*, 1986
12. *Stocktaking and prospects for a Community rail policy, 1986*, 1987
13. *The importance of technological research and development to small and medium-sized enterprises*, 1986.

(The first date is the date when the document was assigned a CES reference; the second is when the Information Report was formally published, sometimes with a slightly different title.)

Earlier in this chapter it was mentioned that ECOSOC occasionally organized conferences. The reports of a number of these were issued in publications with the word Colloquy on the cover. An example is *Genetic engineering*, 1981.

Miscellaneous publications

The Economic and Social Committee issues a booklet called *The other European Assembly*, which is an introduction to the organization. New editions are issued periodically, the latest being published in 1989. In 1983 ECOSOC published a twenty-fifth anniversary celebratory pamphlet subtitled *The role and contribution of economic and social interest groups in the development of the Community*. This contains the texts of the main speeches at a formal sitting of ECOSOC in May 1983. In 1984–85 ECOSOC was asked to give its views to the *ad hoc* Committees for Institutional Affairs and a People's Europe. Subsequently these were published in the pamphlet *European union, a people's Europe and the Economic and Social Committee*, 1985. The Committee also issued booklets on two conferences it helped to organize – on small businesses in 1983 and new technologies in 1984.

A number of major reference works have been issued by ECOSOC over the years:

1. *Community advisory committees for the representation of socioeconomic interests*, 1980 (with Saxon House)
2. *European interest groups and their relationship with the Economic and Social Committee*, 1980 (with Saxon House)
3. *Right of initiative of the Economic and Social Committee of the European Communities*, 2nd edition, 1981 (with Editions Delta and Nomos Verlagsgesellschaft)
4. *Directory of European agricultural organizations*, 1984 (with OOPEC and Kogan Page)
5. *The cooperative, mutual and non-profit sector and its organizations in the European Community*, 1986 (with OOPEC).

Various sections of the Secretariat have produced one-off booklets; for example:

1. *European environment policy: air, water, waste management*, 1987
2. *Community competition policy*, 1987.

Rules of procedure

Revised rules of procedure were adopted by the Economic and Social Committee in 1972 and published in the *Official Journal* L228 19.8.74. A small number of amendments were made in 1980–82, but in 1986 a major revision took place. The complete and revised Rules of Procedure, which came into force in September 1986, were published in the *Official Journal* L354 15.12.86.

During the 1970s the Economic and Social Committee was feeling its way in the development of its procedure. An interesting study was issued called *The right of initiative of the Economic and Social Committee*, 1977, which covers in considerable detail how the rules of procedure could be exploited for maximum effect. A second edition was published in 1981.

FURTHER INFORMATION

In June 1987 ECOSOC issued a small *Catalogue of publications*. This lists a selection of currently available titles from ECOSOC – some of them available direct, some sold by OOPEC, and some sold by commercial publishers. For a copy of this catalogue and for further information contact:

> Economic and Social Committee
> Press, Information and Publications Division
> 2 rue Ravenstein
> B-1000 Brussels
> Belgium
>
> Telephone: 519 90 11
> Telefax: 513 48 93
> Telegrams: ECOSEUR
> Telex: 25 983 CESEUR

CHAPTER 11

Court of Justice of the European Communities

INTRODUCTION

The Court of Justice is the legal guardian of the Treaties setting up the the European Communities and subsequent implementing legislation. It deals with cases brought by the Commission or member states against other member states, or companies for breach of Community law. In addition it hears requests for preliminary rulings from national courts. In these instances the task of the Court is to interpret Community law for the guidance of the national court. Finally the Court deals with disputes between the Community institutions and between the Community institutions and their employees.

The Court of Justice when hearing cases brought before it by a member state or Community institution sits in plenary session or full court. In addition there have been set up a number of chambers. In 1986 there were four chambers composed of three judges and two chambers composed of six judges. These courts hear cases in which it is not thought that the Court needs to decide in plenary session. The Single European Act 1986 allowed for the setting up of a Court of First Instance to be attached to the Court of Justice. The new Court began operating in 1989. This hears actions brought by Community employees, competition cases and actions for damages to relieve the pressure of increased work on the main Court.

The Court of Justice has assumed a considerable importance in the development of the European Community. By its detailed interpretation of Community legislation in its judgments it has advanced certain areas of EC policy and integration in significant ways.

STRUCTURE OF THE COURT OF JUSTICE

The Court of Justice is based in Luxembourg. It is composed of thirteen judges with at least one from each member state. The Court is assisted by six advocates-general. Their role is to comment on the main points of a case, put it in the perspective of European Community law, and suggest a solution. However, it is still the judges who make the final judgment.

The judges elect one of their number President. The judges and advocates-general are aided by an administration headed by a Registrar. In addition to his responsibility for procedural aspects of cases before the Court, carried out through the Registry, the Registrar may be regarded as the 'Secretary-General' of the Court. In this capacity the Registrar is ultimately responsible for the day-to-day management of the institution. Under the Registrar are a number of independent administrative units such as the Interpretation Division, Information Office, Administration, Library, Research and Documentation Directorate, and Translation Directorate.

The Court of Justice does not issue a regular directory as such. However, some factual information concerning the organization and personnel of the Court is contained in the publication *Synopsis of the Work of the Court of Justice of the European Communities in* ... (see below, p. 240).

DOCUMENTATION

The largest percentage of the publications budget of the Court of Justice goes on the set of law reports that comprise the judgments and opinions of the Court. While that is clearly a vital function it is a pity that more is not done to explain the workings and judgments of the Court to an informed but not necessarily legal audience. It is also to be hoped that the computerization of many of the administrative procedures of the Court that took place in the 1980s facilitates more rapid access to the work of the Court.

Reports of Cases before the Court

The Report of Cases before the Court is the authoritative source for the judgments of the Court of Justice. The series is also known as the European Court Reports and in the English language is always cited as ECR. There is now available in English a complete set of the European Court Reports from 1954. Between nine and twelve parts of the ECR are issued each year, the last being an index which is issued after a considerable delay. At the beginning of each part is a list of cases included in that part arranged alphabetically by a small number of subject headings such as agriculture, approximation of laws, free movement of goods, and social policy. The full index for the annual volume is more informative. In addition to a more detailed alphabetical subject index there are a number of other indexes and tables to help users find the text of judgments and opinions. There is an index of parties, a table of Community legislation referred to, a table of cases reported, and a table of cases classified in numerical order. The index is compiled by the Research and

Documentation Division of the Court but the European Court Reports overall are the responsibility of the Registry.

While the ECR are the only authentic source for citation of Court of Justice judgments problems are associated with them. The importance of achieving precise and accurate translation of the judgments and opinions into all the Community languages means that the publication of the judgments in the ECR is often delayed for as much as two years. In 1984–85, for example, 159 000 pages of text had to be translated – a massive undertaking. In March 1987 the latest set of the ECR published covered judgments delivered in February 1985. As mentioned earlier the annual index to complete a volume of the ECR is issued after a further delay. This means that the ECR cannot be used to trace a *recent* judgment.

Judgments or Orders of the Court and Opinions of Advocates-General

Soon after a judgment or order or opinion is given it is possible to receive the text in a roneo format. Subscribers to the European Court Reports can subscribe at the same annual subscription rate to the Judgments. . . . Alternatively it is possible to purchase the text of a single judgment, order or opinion on payment of a fixed charge. In this format the judgments are not authoritative and not all the facts and issues are given. There is no index to this series. Subscriptions to this series, and the European Court Reports should be sent to the Internal Services Division of the Court of Justice.

Proceedings of the Court of Justice of the European Communities

A weekly bulletin of the work of the Court giving a summary of the judgments and opinions delivered during the week in question. *Proceedings* . . . is produced by the Information Office of the Court from whence it can be ordered free of charge. It is primarily a current awareness service alerting those interested to what is going on in the Court. The text of the judgments given is not considered authoritative but a fair degree of detail is given. Publication of the *Proceedings* . . . covering a particular week is usually a couple of months later. Since 1985 a useful annual index has been produced. This arranges the judgments noted (but not the opinions) under a number of broad headings such as approximation of laws and free movement of persons.

Liste des audiences (List of hearings)

A calendar of public sittings of the Court is drawn up each week. This lists in date order all known future court hearings and indicates whether the case will be heard in plenary session or in chambers. The time when the hearings will begin is given and also the language of the proceedings.

It is made clear that the information contained in the *Liste des audiences* is provisional and liable to change. The publication, available in French only, is free and available from the Court Registry.

Synopsis of the Work of the Court of Justice of the European Communities in ...

This is an annual publication giving an account of the work of the Court. It is obtainable free of charge on request from the Information Office of the Court. Throughout the 1980s the information contained in the *Synopsis* ... has remained broadly the same:

1. A detailed breakdown of the case-law of the Court during the year; this includes both a description of the major cases plus a statistical section
2. A description of the work of the departments of the Court of Justice (Registry, Library, Research and Documentation Division, Translation Directorate, Interpretation Division)
3. List of the judges of the Court
4. Information and documentation on the Court of Justice and its work
5. A list of journals published in EC countries which cover Community case-law
6. A list of Press and Information Offices of the European Communities
7. Organization of public sittings of the Court, summary of types of procedure, and notes for the guidance of counsel at oral hearings.

The *Synopsis* ... is usually published at the end of the following year to which it is describing. However, in the mid-1980s there was a hiccup to this pattern; the volumes covering the activities of 1984 and 1985 were combined into a single volume published in 1987, and this volume also contained a section called *Formal sittings of the Court of Justice of the European Communities 1984 and 1985*. In the past this has been published as a separate publication (see below), but henceforth was to become part of the *Synopsis*. ...

Formal sittings of the Court of Justice of the European Communities

This publication contains the addresses given by the President of the Court on the retirement or entry into office of a judge or advocate-general, and the replies of the individuals concerned. Biographical details of new judges or advocates-general are given. Addresses on the occasion of other miscellaneous formal sittings are also included. The formal sittings for the years 1984 and 1985 were included at the back of the *Synopsis of the Work of the Court of Justice of the European*

Communities in 1984 and 1985, and this practice, it was claimed, would continue in the future.

Digest of case-law relating to the European Communities

This is sometimes referred to as *Digest of Community case-law*. The aim of this looseleaf set of volumes is to present systematically a summary of the case-law of the Court of Justice and also selected judgments of national courts arranged in a convenient easily accessible format. This is clearly a massive undertaking and publication of the complete set seems to be taking a painfully long time. However, when complete the *Digest* will be a major legal source.

The *Digest* is divided into four parts:

1. A Series: case-law of the Court of Justice excluding the matters covered by the C and D Series
2. B Series: case-law of the courts of member states excluding the matters covered by the D series (not yet published)
3. C Series: case-law of the Court of Justice relating to Community staff law (not yet published)
4. D Series: case-law of the Court of Justice and of courts of member states relating to the EEC Convention of 27 September 1968 on Jurisdiction and the Enforcement of Judgments in Civil and Commercial Matters.

A Series

In 1986 this series consisted of judgments covering the period 1977–81. Further supplements were promised to both bring up to date and, eventually, to cover the years before 1977. Note that, even though it is not always made clear, the supplements, when supplied, need to be inserted within the existing text. Series A is divided into four parts:

1. Part A : the Community legal order
2. Part B : the EEC
3. Part C : the ECSC
4. Part D : EURATOM.

Each part is then divided into chapters which are arranged according to a scheme that closely follows that of the Treaties themselves. At the beginning of the A series there is both a concise and a detailed table of contents.

Within the main body of the text a digest of the significant cases relating to the various headings is given. In addition, bibliographical references are given to enable the reader to trace the full reports of the cases.

At the end of the volume there are various indexes:

1. Table of judgments in chronological order

2. Tables of cases in numerical order
3. Alphabetical index of parties
4. Table of Community legislation whereby the cases relating to a particular provision of primary or secondary law may be found
5. Alphabetical subject index.

D Series

In 1988 this consisted of cases before the Court of Justice, 1976–84 and cases before courts of member states, 1973–82. Further supplements were promised. The D series is divided into three parts:

1. Part 1: Summaries of the decisions considered and an appendix of Treaty provisions; the structure follows that of the Convention, which is also reprinted
2. Part 2: Extracts in the original language from the decisions of courts of member states which have been summarized in Part 1
3. Part 3: Contains a number of indexes.

The D series replaces the *Synopsis of case-law* which was published in instalments by the Documentation Division of the Court but has now been discontinued.

The *Digest* ... is compiled by the Research and Documentation Division of the Court of Justice. Orders for the *Digest* ... should be sent to OOPEC, or to selected booksellers as listed in the *Synopsis of the Work of the Court of Justice of the European Communities* .... In the United Kingdom orders should be sent to:

Hammick, Sweet and Maxwell
116 Chancery Lane
London WC2A 1PP
England

It is intended eventually that the *Digest* ... will cover judgments before 1977. It is worth noting that a commercial publication already exists which covers the pre-1977 period. Called *Compendium of case-law relating to the European Communities*, this covers the period 1953–76 in separate French and German editions. An English edition only exists for the years 1973–76.

Regarding the series that have not appeared: series B will be available first of all on a computer database developed from an existing card index in the Research and Documentation Division. Future publication in a traditional format is possible. The format of series C has yet to be decided and may depend on the proposed setting up of the Court of First Instance.

Different language editions of the various supplements are issued at widely varying times. .

Information on the Court of Justice of the European Communities

This title has now ceased publication, the last issue being no. 2, 1982. It was a quarterly bulletin containing summaries of recent judgments delivered by the Court, and issued by the information office of the Court of Justice.

Miscellaneous Publications

The Information Office issues a small introductory brochure called *The Court of Justice of the European Communities*, which provides information on the organization, jurisdiction and composition of the Court of Justice. The latest edition was issued in 1984, and is available free of charge. However, prior to a new edition of the guide being published the recommended introduction to the Court of Justice, which takes into account the accession of Spain and Portugal, is the quite separate publication in the European Documentation series called *The Court of Justice of the European Community* (4th edition, no. 5, 1986).

Produced by the Registry and available from OOPEC is *Selected instruments relating to the organization, jurisdiction and procedure of the Court*. The aim is to bring together into a single volume all the provisions on the organization, jurisdiction and procedure of the Court that are contained in the founding Treaties, the protocols and conventions attached to them, and in the implementing Regulations made under these Treaties. In essence this volume contains, amongst other information, the rules of procedure of the Court. The third edition of this title was published in 1975. A new edition is said to be in preparation.

Produced by the Library Division of the Court of Justice is *Bibliographie juridique de l'intégration européenne*. This is a bibliography of monographs and articles on European integration available in the Library. It has been published annually since 1981. The title is available free of charge and can be obtained from the Library Division. References are to material in all Community languages, although the bibliography is basically a French language publication.

Another French language bibliographical title is *Notes*. This is an index of references to notes and commentaries on judgments of the Court of Justice published by the Research, Documentation and Library Directorate of the Court. *Notes* is periodically updated on a cumulative basis and is available free of charge.

One of the judges of the Court, Pierre Pescatore, has written two pamphlets. The first is called *Court of Justice of the European Communities: information for lawyers* (1984), which is basically an introduction to the Court of Justice. The second pamphlet is an introduction to the important aspect of the work of the Court involving requests for preliminary rulings. It is called *Court of Justice of the European Communities: references for preliminary rulings under article 177 of the EEC Treaty and cooperation between the Court and national courts* (1986).

Finally in this section it is worth noting some other EC publications not issued by the Court of Justice but which do relate to its work. There are a number of titles in the European Documentation series which are of interest. Examples include *The Court of Justice of the European Community* (4th edition, no. 5, 1986) and *The ABC of Community law* (2nd edition, no. 2, 1986). In the European Perspectives series is a title called *Thirty years of Community law*, published in 1983. This title surveys comprehensively the development of the Community legal order from 1950 to 1980. Of particular relevance here is a long chapter on the Court of Justice by Hjalte Rasmussen. Each year in the *General report on the activities of the European Communities* is a chapter on developments in Community law during the year in question, much of the material relating to judgments of the Court of Justice. In an annex is a statistical section on the activities of the Court during the year. This information is thus available much more rapidly in this format than the similar, if slightly expanded, information printed in the *Synopsis of the work of the Court of Justice of the European Communities in*. . . . The chapter in the *General report* . . . is also reprinted as a separate publication called *Community law* each year.

The monthly *Bulletin of the European Communities* always contains a section on the Court of Justice. This lists new cases brought and judgments delivered during the month in question broken down under broad subject headings. Only the barest details are given. In issues 4, 7/8 and 10 each year there is an analysis of judgments delivered during the previous quarter.

The *Official Journal*, as the authoritative record of the activities of the EC institutions, also gives essential information about the activities of the Court of Justice in the 'C' Series (*Information and Notices*).

FURTHER INFORMATION

Enquiries on the Court of Justice and its documentation can be directed to:

The Information Office
Court of Justice of the European Communities
L-2925 Luxembourg
Telephone: 4303–1
Telex: 2771 CJ INFO LU
Telegrams: CURIA

Sources and references

1. The Court of Justice of the European Community, 4th edition, *European Documentation*, no. 5, 1986
2. The ABC of Community law, 2nd edition, *European Documentation*, no. 2, 1986
3. *Halsbury's Laws of England*, 4th edition, vol. 51, Butterworths, 1986
4. *Synopsis of the Work of the Court of Justice of the European Communities in 1984 and 1985 and Record of Formal Sittings in 1984 and 1985*, EC, 1987
5. European Community law, by Ian Thomson, in *How to use a law library*, 2nd edition, Sweet and Maxwell, 1987.

CHAPTER 12

Court of Auditors

INTRODUCTION

The Court of Auditors is regarded formally as the sixth of the major institutions of the European Community. Its function is to audit the accounts of the Community institutions and other EC bodies such as CEDEFOP (European Centre for the Development of Vocational Training), the European Foundation for the Improvement of Living and Working Conditions and JET (Joint European Torus). It examines whether revenue and expenditure have been properly handled, checks that financial management has been sound, and reports back to the Community institutions. Its submits regular annual reports and occasional special reports.

The Court of Auditors was set up by the Treaty of Brussels 1975 and began operating in 1977. Luxembourg has been designated the provisional seat of the Court of Auditors. It comprises twelve members, one national from each member state. Each member is assigned specific sectors of activity for which he/she is responsible for the preparation and implementation of the decisions of the Court of Auditors. For example, in 1984 the United Kingdom member, Charles J. Carey, was responsible for the audit of research and investment, energy and industry expenditure, and external bodies. In 1987 there were approximately 310 permanent and fifty-six temporary staff in the Court of Auditors.

DOCUMENTATION

The documentation of the Court of Auditors is not extensive. Most material is available through OOPEC, but see below for full details.

Court of Auditors of the European Communities

This is a short introductory pamphlet to the work of the Court of Auditors. A new edition is issued periodically. The latest edition was published in 1988, and contained sections on:

1. Powers of the Court of Auditors
2. Work of the Court of Auditors
3. Principal reports of the Court of Auditors
4. Structure of the Court of Auditors
5. Responsibilities of the members of the Court of Auditors.

Annual report concerning the financial year . . . accompanied by the replies of the institutions

This is the most important of the reports of the Court and covers the entire range of the activities of the EC. After the various institutions have been informed and their replies received the *Annual report* is published in the *Official Journal* in December of the following year; for example, . . . the financial year

1977 in *Official Journal* C313 30.12.78
1978 in *Official Journal* C326 31.12.79
1979 in *Official Journal* C342 31.12.80
1980 in *Official Journal* C344 31.12.81
1981 in *Official Journal* C344 31.12.82
1982 in *Official Journal* C357 31.12.83
1983 in *Official Journal* C348 31.12.84
1984 in *Official Journal* C326 16.12.85
1985 in *Official Journal* C321 15.12.86
1986 in *Official Journal* C336 15.12.87

In addition to the result of the audit and subsequent replies from the institutions other regular features included in the *Annual report* . . . worth noting are:

1. Allocation of responsibilities among members of the Court of Auditors at the time the report was adopted
2. Financial information relating to the general budget of the EC (using diagrams and texts, this is a very good introduction to the Community budget)
3. Reports and opinions adopted by the Court of Auditors during the last five years.

The last feature is the easiest way of tracking the bibliographical references to the special reports of the Court of Auditors.

The *Annual report* . . . covers the accounts of the EC institutions. The annual reports of the accounts of other EC organizations such as JET, EURATOM, the European Schools, CEDEFOP and the European Foundation for the Improvement of Living and Working Conditions are not published. An exception is the report on the financial statement of the European Coal and Steel Community, which is published in the *Official Journal*.

Special Reports

Special Reports are compiled by the Court of Auditors at the request of another EC institution, or on the initiative of the Court itself. Most, but not all, are published in the *Official Journal*. Fifty-four Special Reports had been compiled up to the beginning of 1988. The bibliography in the *Annual report* . . . indicates those which have been published in the

Official Journal. For example, Special Report 2/86 on the ERDF's specific Community regional development measures was published in the *Official Journal* C262 20.10.86. Other Special Reports are available by contacting the Court of Auditors direct.

Opinions

The Court of Auditors has to be consulted when the Council adopts a Financial Regulation. In these cases the Court issues an Opinion. By the beginning of 1988 there had been fifty such Opinions, nearly all published in the *Official Journal*. See the list in the *Annual report . . .* for details.

FURTHER INFORMATION

A substantial study of the Court of Auditors was undertaken by the United Kingdom House of Lords Select Committee on the European Communities in 1987 (6th Report [1986/87] HL 102).

A full list, in French, of the Special Reports and Opinions, plus other information concerning the Court of Auditors can be obtained from:

> Secretariat
> Court of Auditors of the European Communities
> 29 rue Aldringen
> L-1118 Luxembourg
>
> Telephone: 4773–1
> Telegraphic address: EURAUDIT – Luxembourg
> Telex: 3512 EURAUD LU

Sources and references

1. *Working together: the institutions of the European Community,* EC, 1985
2. *Financial Times,* 19.11.86 p. IV (Supplement)
3. *Court of Auditors of the European Communities,* EC, 1986 and 1988
4. *Annual report concerning the financial year 1985 . . . (Official Journal* C321 15.12.86).

CHAPTER 13

Other EC Organizations

CONSULTATIVE COMMITTEE OF THE EUROPEAN COAL AND STEEL COMMUNITY (ECSC)

Article 7 of the Treaty of Paris 1951 establishing the European Coal and Steel Community set up the institutions to carry out the objectives of the Treaty. The executive was called the High Authority and it was to be assisted by a Consultative Committee comprising the three groups:

1. Producers
2. Workers
3. Consumers and dealers.

In 1967 the institutions of the European Coal and Steel Community, the European Economic Community and Euratom were merged. From that date the task of the Consultative Committee has been to assist the Commission of the European Communities in its policy-making. The Consultative Committee plays an analogous role in relation to the coal and steel policy areas that the Economic and Social Committee has in relation to social and economic affairs.

Today the Consultative Committee consists of ninety-six members appointed in a personal capacity for a two-year term by the Council. In the case of the producers and workers members are chosen from lists submitted by representative organizations.

The Consultative Committee meets at least five times a year – there is an organizational session and four ordinary sessions. At the latter reports from four standing subcommittees and any *ad hoc* committees that exist for specific matters are discussed. The Committee drafts resolutions and opinions which are sent to the Commission. Most meetings take place in Luxembourg but by tradition at least one meeting a year is held elsewhere. In 1986, for example, the 258th session of the Consultative Committee was held in Swansea.

The rules of procedure or 'Internal Regulations' of the Consultative Committee are published in the *Official Journal*. The seventh edition of the Internal Regulations was printed in the *Official Journal* C149 16.6.86, p. 1.

Besides the documentation noted below a general introduction to the activities, structure and workings of the Consultative Committee of the European Coal and Steel Community can be found in the *Bulletin of the European Communities*, no. 3, 1986, p. 100.

Documentation

Yearbook

This title is issued directly by the Secretariat of the Consultative Committee and contains the following standard features in each volume:

1. Consultations and exchanges of views: a list of the topics on which the Committee was asked for its opinion, divided according to the Treaty basis of the request. This can be on a wide-ranging topic such as the general objectives for steel in the forthcoming year, or on something more specific, such as the advisability of giving financial aid to a highly specialized research project.
2. Meetings of the Consultative Committee: a list of all meetings of the Bureau, the Committee, the subcommittees and the categories for the year. In the case of the sessions of the Committee an agenda for the session is given, plus a list of documents used and documents compiled. Few of these documents enter the public domain.
3. Appendix: this lists the members of the Consultative Committee and a list of references to the *Official Journal* that relate to the Consultative Committee. Personnel changes are recorded but of more importance are the text of Opinions and Resolutions passed by the Committee. The *Official Journal* is the only publicly available source for these texts. They are not traceable through the *Official Journal: Index*.

Handbook

This is issued periodically and contains the following information:

1. The text of the various treaties and regulations that relate to the Consultative Committee.
2. The composition and organization of the Consultative Committee since its formation.
3. The current organization and composition of the Consultative Committee.
4. An annex containing a list of the publications of the Consultative Committee.

Further information

The Consultative Committee does not issue any other regular publications. Brief accounts of the work of the Committee are given in the *Bulletin of the European Communities* and the *General report on the activities of the European Communities*.

It is perhaps worth making the point that the European Coal and Steel Community as such does not produce documentation. Material relating to coal and steel emanates from the *institutions* of the European Coal and Steel Community – most notably the Commission.

For further information relating to the documentation of the Consultative Committee of the European Coal and Steel Community contact:

> Secretariat of the Consultative Committee of the European
> Coal and Steel Community
> Bâtiment Jean Monnet
> Boîte Postale 1907
> Luxembourg
>
> Telephone: 43011
> Telex: 3423 COMEUR LU

EUROPEAN BUREAU FOR LESSER USED LANGUAGES

The European Bureau for Lesser Used Languages is not strictly a European Community organization. However, it owes its origin to the EC, is partially funded by the EC, and defines its primary aim in its constitution as preserving and promoting 'the lesser used autochthonous languages of the member states of the European Communities, together with their associated cultures'.

It came into being as a consequence of a seminar held in Brussels in 1982 which looked at the European Parliament Report and Resolution on a Community charter of regional languages and cultures and on a charter of the rights of ethnic minorities (The Arfe Report PE DOC 1–965/80 and *Official Journal* C287 9.11.81, p. 106).

The Bureau is an independent body but works in close cooperation with the Commission and the European Parliament and is partially funded by subventions from the Commission. The Bureau also works with the Council of Europe and other interested organizations.

Documentation

Contact Bulletin

Contact Bulletin is the journal of the European Bureau for Lesser Used Languages, which is funded by the Commission. It is free and is available direct from the Bureau. The first issue of *Contact Bulletin* was dated November 1983. Ten issues had been published up to May 1988 at irregular intervals.

Contact Bulletin reports on the activities of the Bureau, seminars and conferences, EC activities in the area of minority languages and cultures and other items of general interest.

Further information

To receive *Contact Bulletin* and to receive further information about the activities of the Bureau contact:

> The Editor, *Contact Bulletin*
> European Bureau for Lesser Used Languages
> 7 Cearnóg Mhuirfean
> Dublin 2
> Ireland
> Telephone: 353 1 763222, ext 151
> Fax: 353 1 6122205

EUROPEAN CENTRE FOR THE DEVELOPMENT OF VOCATIONAL TRAINING (CEDEFOP)

The role of vocational training has increasingly been stressed in the European Community. It has been seen as a way for workers to adjust to the radical changes taking place in the labour market, to ensure that young people are properly prepared for working life, and to promote equal opportunities for all workers with regard to access to employment. The function of the European Centre for the Development of Vocational Training (hereafter in this section referred to by its acronym CEDEFOP) has been to assist the Commission in encouraging at Community level the promotion and development of vocational training and of continuing education. In practice this means that in addition to the technical assistance CEDEFOP gives to the Commission, it organizes courses and seminars, arranges research studies, undertakes pilot projects, administers a study visit programme and maintains a considerable publications programme and documentation network.

CEDEFOP was created in 1975. It is based in West Berlin and has a staff of around forty-five. The Centre is independent of other European Community institutions but works closely with them. A Management Board administers the Centre. It is composed of twelve representatives of trade union organizations, twelve representatives of employers' organizations, twelve representatives of government, and three representatives of the Commission.

Documentation

A key function of CEDEFOP is to promote the exchange of information and experience in the field of vocational training. This involves the maintenance of close relations with national organizations and individuals concerned with vocational training; in particular, CEDEFOP has a Documentary Information Network which comprises the Centre and a network of national organizations. The latter have a dual responsibility of providing input information to CEDEFOP and distributing information from CEDEFOP to other groups in their country interested in aspects of vocational training. With the help of this network CEDEFOP has published a series of bibliographies and documentary dossiers, created a library and documentary centre, and established a catalogue of about 25 000 bibliographical references in the area of vocational training. (The members of the Documentary Information Network are listed at the end of this section.)

In addition to the above activities CEDEFOP publishes most of the studies carried out for the Centre and maintains a number of periodicals. OOPEC now handles the production and distribution of most of the documentation of CEDEFOP but there are still some free items distributed directly by CEDEFOP.

Annual report

The annual report for a particular year is adopted by the Management Board in March of the following year and published a short time afterwards. It is distributed directly by the Centre and is unpriced. The contents differ slightly from year to year but the following features have been included regularly since the mid 1980s:

1. Permanent activities – a description of the publications programme for the year, visitors to the Centre, study visit programme and other continuing activities
2. Priority area of activity – a description of the activities undertaken during the year in question in the Centre's current main areas of interest
3. CEDEFOP relations with EC institutions and other organizations
4. Manpower and financial resources
5. List of meetings held
6. Membership of the Management Board and CEDEFOP personnel
7. List of publications issued during the year, including language and number of copies printed
8. Survey of projects – this is a list of each individual project undertaken by CEDEFOP, including the production of periodical issues, and gives the name(s) of personnel involved, the objective of the project, the countries concerned, the achievements in the year in question and the documentation output. Note that for the year 1985 this section was published separately.

Vocational Training

This periodical is issued three times a year by CEDEFOP. Note that on the inside cover the title is given as *Vocational Training Bulletin*. The aim of *Vocational Training* is to promote an exchange of views and ideas within the Community on issues relating to vocational training. Most issues feature a particular theme. There has been an occasional bibliographical section over the years in *Vocational Training*. This was regularized from no. 2, 1986 when a bibliographical article on the theme of the special subject of each issue became a standard feature. *Vocational Training* is available from OOPEC on subscription.

Since 1980 the following themes have been covered:

1. 1980/1 Agriculture
2. 1980/2 Vocational training of the handicapped
3. 1980/3 Training, employment and regional development
4. 1980/4 Linking work and training for young persons in the European Community
5. 1981/5 Technological development and vocational training
6. 1981/6 Guidance, information, vocational training
7. 1981/7 Small and medium-sized enterprises
8. 1982/8 The young
9. 1982/9 Innovations in continuing education and training
10. 1982/10 Young migrants: the 'less equal'
11. 1983/11 Vocational training and new technologies: new Community initiatives
12. 1983/12 Alternance training
13. 1983/13 The trainers
14. 1984/14 Small and medium-sized undertakings
15. 1984/15 Distance learning
16. 1984/16 Training of young people in new forms of employment
17. 1985/17 Young people
18. 1985/18 CEDEFOP, ten years on . . .
19. 1985/19 Adult training
20. 1986/1 Spain, Greece, Portugal
21. 1986/2 Regional concepts of vocational training: a challenge
22. 1986/3 Continuing training and labour market policy
23. 1987/1 The factory of the future and the future of work
24. 1987/2 Models, ideas, experience
25. 1987/3 Small and medium-sized enterprises: new horizons for vocational training

CEDEFOP News

CEDEFOP News is a brief four-page newsletter published rather irregularly since 1981. There are usually between two and four issues a year. The objective of *CEDEFOP News* is to make available to a wide readership concise information on topical vocational training issues. Many of the short articles are supplied by the national organizations connected to the Documentary Information Network of CEDEFOP. *CEDEFOP News* is free and available through OOPEC.

CEDEFOP Flash

This *ad hoc* publication began with no. 1, November 1984. The aim of this series is to disseminate the Centre's research findings rapidly. It consists of A4 typescript sheets stapled together and photocopied. Each issue covers a single topic. These include reports on conferences, workshops and other meetings and on the major areas of the Centre's activities. *CEDEFOP Flash* is issued irregularly, usually in English, French and German editions only, and is free. In 1985, for example, eight issues were sent to approximately 1200 subscribers of the journal *Vocational Training*. It is available direct from CEDEFOP.

The following are a selection of titles from 1987 issues:

1. (1) London Conference on 'People and Technology – Investing in Training for Europe's Future' (London, November 1986).
2. (2) Comparability of vocational training qualifications in EC member states (information on Commission and CEDEFOP activities).
3. (7) The promotion of cooperation amongst research and development organizations in the field of vocational training (CEDEFOP Research Forum, October 1987).
4. (8) Role of the social partners in initial and continuing vocational training in the EC – interim report (CEDEFOP Workshop, Berlin, October 1987).

Other publications

It is not possible to list all CEDEFOP publications, but below are listed a number of titles of interest issued during the 1980s. The majority of titles are the results of commissioned research projects. Such reports are published by OOPEC and are listed in *Catalogue of Publications* (see Chapter 3). The *Annual report* lists all publications of CEDEFOP issued during the year.

In 1982 the Management Board adopted for the first time a programme defining the area in which CEDEFOP would concentrate its efforts in the following three years. This was published as *Guidelines for the activities of CEDEFOP 1983–1985*. This was followed in 1985 by *CEDEFOP action guidelines 1986–1988*. These three-year guidelines laid down general lines of action. The annual *Work programme* translates these general lines into detailed projects and specific time schedules. This is not formally published but is available by contacting CEDEFOP directly.

The creation of a documentation and information network has

already been mentioned. In connection with this it was felt that there had to be a common documentation language that CEDEFOP and all the national members of the network could use to analyse the contents of relevant literature. This resulted in the publication of a *CEDEFOP thesaurus* in 1979 and a successor volume called *Thesaurus of vocational training* in 1986. This was published in English, French, German and Italian, English being the common indexation language. In effect this is a multilingual dictionary of vocational training.

Among the key series of publications is one which attempts to describe the vocational training systems in the member states. In 1984 a title was published called *Vocational training systems in the member states of the European Community: comparative study*. There are also separate studies in more detail of the systems in each of the member states with the generic series title: *Descriptions of the vocational training systems*. The first editions of these studies were published in 1979–80. Revised editions began appearing in 1984. The *CEDEFOP action guidelines 1986–1988* suggests that increased priority should be given to the continual updating of these descriptions.

In addition to the bibliographical information that is regularly published in *Vocational Training*, CEDEFOP have published a number of one-off bibliographies and documentary dossiers. In 1983 a series of bibliographies on vocational training in the member states were published, and similarly in 1986 a series of the financing of vocational training. An example of a bibliography bringing together material from a number of countries in a single volume is *Distance education in Western Europe: a selective annotated bibliography of current literature*, 1985.

As mentioned above the majority of documentation from CEDE-FOP describes the results of commissioned research. In the 1980s subjects covered included:

1. Training for unemployed young people
2. Alternance training
3. Equality of training opportunities for women
4. Vocational training challenges and the new technologies
5. Innovations concerning education
6. The training of trainers
7. Vocational training and regional development
8. Vocational training for small and medium-sized enterprises
9. Vocational training in the Mediterranean countries
10. Social partners and vocational education
11. Migrants and vocational training.

CEDEFOP helps the Commission to compile the chapter on vocational training in *Report on social developments*. Results of some of the CEDEFOP studies are also reported in the periodical *Social Europe* from DG V of the Commission (see Chapter 5).

Further information

Enquiries about CEDEFOP documentation and a catalogue of current publications available can be obtained from:

> The European Centre for the Development of Vocational
> Training (CEDEFOP)
> Bundesallee 22
> D-1000 Berlin 15
> Federal Republic of Germany
> Telephone: (030) 88 41 20
> Telex: 184163 EUCEN D

Enquiries can also be directed to members of the Documentary Information Network. There have been occasional changes in membership. The list below comprises organizations noted in 1987 issues of *Vocational Training*.

Belgium

Office National de l'Emploi
11 boulevard de l'Empereur
B-1000 Brussels
Telephone: (02) 513 91 20, ext. 1001

Denmark

Statens Erhvervspaedagogiske Laereruddannelse
Rigensgade 13
DK-1316 Copenhagen
Telephone: (01) 14 41 14

France

Centre Inffo
Tour Europe
CEDEX 07
F-92080 Paris-la-Défense
Telephone: (1) 47 78 13 50

Federal Republic of Germany

Bundesinstitut für Berufsbildung
Fehrbelliner Platz 3
D-1000 Berlin 31
Telephone: (030) 86 31-1

Greece

Pedagogical Institute
Ministry of National Education and Religion
396 Messogion Street
GR-15341 Athens

Ireland

The Industrial Training Authority
PO Box 456
27–33 Upper Baggot Street
Dublin 4
Telephone: (01) 68 57 77

Italy

Istituto per lo Sviluppo della Formazione Professionale dei Lavoratori
Via Bartolomeo Eustachio 8
I-00161 Rome
Telephone: 84 13 51

The Netherlands

Pedagogisch Centrum Beroepsonderwijs Bedrijfsleven
13–15 Verwersstraat
Postbus 1585
NL-5200 BP 's-Hertogenbosch
Telephone: (073) 12 40 11

Portugal

Ministério do Trabalho e Segurança Social
Serviço de Informação Cientifica e Técnica
Praça de Londres 2 – 1. °ander
P-1091 Lisbon
Telephone: 896628

Spain

Instituto Nacional de Empleo
9 Condesa de Venadito
E-28027 Madrid
Telephone: (1) 408 24 27

United Kingdom

British Association for Commercial and Industrial Education
16 Park Crescent
London W1N 4AP
Telephone: 01 636 5351

EUROPEAN COMMUNITY ACTION PROGRAMME: TRANSITION OF YOUNG PEOPLE FROM EDUCATION TO ADULT AND WORKING LIFE (IFAPLAN)

There have been two Action Programmes:

1. 1976–83
2. 1983–87

They were set up by the Commission as part of its study of the education and training needs of young people and particularly because of the alarming rise in youth unemployment in the 1970s. The Action Programmes have been coordinated, managed and implemented for the Commission by an organization called IFAPLAN, an applied social research institute based in Cologne in the Federal Republic of Germany. Since 1983 there has been an IFAPLAN Information Office in Brussels.

Each Action Programme consisted of a number of pilot projects partially funded by the EC. There were twenty-eight projects in the first Programme and thirty in the second. An important feature of the initiative was the attempt to encourage the systematic exchange of experiences, promote grassroots transnational cooperation, and to fully evaluate the results of the projects.

Documentation: Action Programme 1976–83

Each of the individual projects taking part in the first Action Programme compiled a report. An example is:

1. Industrial training units for slow learners in Mid Glamorgan, 1982 (by Rhian Ellis, Sociological Research Unit, University College, Cardiff).

This was issued as a 'restricted working document' by IFAPLAN on behalf of the Commission.

Information publications about the pilot projects were produced by an IFAPLAN coordination group called the Central Animation and Evaluation Team (CAET). In 1980 they published *Project information as at June 1979*, which gave a general outline of the objectives and methods of each of the pilot projects, with contact addresses for the originating authority, project leader and the external EC evaluator. This was updated by *Project information II as at November 1981*, 1981, which gave descriptive accounts of the stages reached by the projects in 1981.

Interim report was published in 1981 and described the development of the programme up to 1980. In 1982 IFAPLAN published *Directory of material originating from pilot projects*, which listed many of the curriculum and general information materials produced by the personnel working in the individual projects.

IFAPLAN issued a *Newsletter* to promote its activities. The first issue was dated September 1979 and it was published quarterly until no. 15, April 1983. A final special issue was published in October 1983.

The final report of the Programme was published by the Commission in five parts in 1983. Part A was a synthesis of the main issues. This part has been summarized in a further text called *Policies for transition* (see Working Documents of the Second Action Programme below). Part BI dealt with *Experiences of work*, and Part BII summarized the main results concerning *Staff development*, Parts A and B were only available from DG V of the Commission with the internal number V/286/83.

The other three parts were issued as Working Documents (see below) and called:

1. Girls and transition, 1984
2. Education for transition: the curriculum challenge, 1984
3. New developments in assessment, 1984.

Many other reports evaluating the work of the Action Programme and discussing future actions were not formally published either at Community or national level. For further details of reports at a Community level contact IFAPLAN or DG V of the Commission. For national reports contact the relevant national coordinating authorities. In the United Kingdom full sets of all the reports in the National Dossier are kept at the Department of Education and Science, London; the Scottish Education Department, Edinburgh; the Welsh Office Education Department, Cardiff; and the British Library. Details of individual projects can be obtained from each Projects' Originating Authority.

Documentation: Action Programme 1983–87

The Second Action Programme concentrated on projects which opened up schools and which encouraged interaction between schools and their environment: industry, social partners, parents and local associations. Ten themes were highlighted:

1. Development of work experience
2. Development of equal opportunities for girls and boys
3. Improvement of information and counselling for the young
4. Staff training
5. New forms of educational assessment
6. Integration of young migrants
7. Education for enterprise
8. Schools and social action (illiteracy, rejection, delinquency, and drug abuse)
9. Development of alternative curricula
10. Cooperation and partnership in a local or regional context.

Working Documents

This was the title given to the main series of publications reporting on aspects of the Second Action Programme. Titles in the series included:

1. *Thirty Pilot Projects. Short descriptions of the 30 Pilot Projects in the European Community's Second Transition Programme*, 1984.
2. *Girls and transition*, 1984
3. *Policies for transition*, 1984 (a summary of the final synthesis report of the first Action Programme)
4. *Education for transition. The curriculum challenge*, 1984
5. *New developments in assessment*, 1984
6. *Youth Information 1985*, 1985
7. *About work experience. An inventory of published materials*, 1985
8. *Project management. Report of a workshop held in Luxembourg, June 1984*, 1985
9. *Action handbook: how to implement gender equality*, 1985
10. *Info Action '85. Youth initiatives in the European Community*, 1986
11. *Education for enterprise. An interim report*, 1986
12. *Assessment and certification: issues arising in the pilot projects*, 1986
13. *Thirty pilot projects*, 1986
14. *Teacher training. Strategies from the Second Transition Programme*, 1986
15. *The world of work as a learning resource*, 1986
16. *Guidance and the school*, 1987
17. *School–industry links*, 1987
18. *Partnership – parents and secondary schools*, 1987
19. *Strategies to combat disadvantage*, 1988
20. *Gender equality. Strategies from the Second Transition Programme*, 1988
21. *Transition education for the '90s: the experience of the European Community's Action Programme*, 1988

The final title in the list above is a report giving an overview of the complete Second Action Programme and marks the end of the overall Programme. This report is also available as *Social Europe: supplement 1/88*. A final summary report on the Second Action Programme was issued by the Commission as COM(87)705 final and summarized in *Information memo*, no. 94, 1987.

Programme News

The first issue of *Programme News* was dated October 1984. In all, six issues were published, the last dated February 1988. The aim of the title was to promote the activities of the Action Programme and, in particular, announce details of the publications issued. Each issue contained details of the latest publications plus an order form for all titles available at the time.

Information Note

Two issues of this title were issued. The first gave a short introduction to the Second Action Programme and its Pilot Projects. It was issued in 1984. The second was issued in 1985 and updated the information in the first, giving contact addresses for all the Pilot Projects.

Innovations

These were four-page profiles dealing with innovative developments in the main theme areas of the Second Action Programme. Thirty-nine titles were published in total, all in 1987. The following is a complete list grouped together by theme:

The world of work
1. *Enterprise development*
2. *School–community linking – Greece*
3. *Work experience integrated into the curriculum – Ireland*
4. *School cooperatives – Italy*
22. *Work experience for teachers*
23. *'COA': School–employment centres*
24. *School, community and environment, United Kingdom*
25. *School and 'Territorio' – Reggio Calabria*
26. *Guidance course – The Netherlands*
37. *Schools, firms and trade unions*
38. *'Arbeitslehre' – Germany*
39. *Schools, industry and curriculum.*

Guidance
5. *Work experience and guidance – Denmark*
6. *Guidance training and coordination*
7. *Field experience for guidance teachers – Greece*
8. *The 'Youth Team'*
9. *Group-work guidance materials – France.*

Provision for the disadvantaged
10. *Enterprise education in a special school*
11. *The 'Learning Place' – Venissieux, France*
12. *Youth and Culture Centre – Berlin*
18. *Classrooms for active learning – Manchester*
19. *The Outreach programmes – Dublin*
20. *Outreach Youth Centres – Luxembourg*
21. *School and vocational skills course – Strathclyde*
36. *Work Exploration Centre – Dublin*

Partnership in education and training
13. *The 'Missions Locales': local task forces*

14. *The School Contact Committee – Aalborg, Denmark*
15. *School–work agency – Modena, Italy.*
16. *'RAA' – Germany*
17. *Involving parents – United Kingdom.*

Staff development
27. *Curriculum coordinators – Manchester, United Kingdom*
28. *'Writing teams' – Manchester*
29. *Training for local needs – Belgium*
30. *School-linking – Baden-Württemberg.*

Equal opportunities
31. *The 'Why Not . . .?' Course – Ireland*
32. *Turkish girls' centre – Berlin*
33. *Widening girls' occupational choice – France*
34. *Equal opportunities programme – Manchester*
35. *The 'Girls' Programme' – Castlemilk, Glasgow.*

All publications from IFAPLAN were available in all Community languages and were free of charge. In 1988 a final *Catalogue* was published listing the majority of publications of the Second Action Programme, with an order form. Further evaluative reports on the Programme will be published in due course. The journal *Social Europe* and *Social Europe: supplement* have regularly reported on aspects of the Second Action Programme.

Further information

Enquiries about the activities and documentation of the European Community Action Programme: Transition of Young People from Education to Adult and Working Life should be sent to:

> Programme Information Office
> IFAPLAN
> 32 Square Ambiorix
> B-1040 Brussels
> Belgium
> Telephone: 02 230.71.06

or

> Eurydice European Unit
> 17 rue Archimède
> Bte 17
> B-1040 Brussels
> Belgium
> Telephone: 02 230.03.82
> Telex: 65398 eurydi b
> Telefax: 230.65.62

EUROPEAN FOUNDATION FOR THE IMPROVEMENT OF LIVING AND WORKING CONDITIONS

The European Foundation for the Improvement of Living and Working Conditions (hereafter called the Foundation) came into being as an autonomous Community organization in 1975. In the introduction to its *Catalogue of publications* it is said that the aim of the Foundation 'is to contribute to the planning and establishment of better living and working conditions through action designed to increase and disseminate knowledge. In particular, the Foundation deals with the following themes:

1. Man at work
2. Organization of work and job design
3. Problems peculiar to certain categories of workers
4. Long-term aspects of improvement of the environment
5. Distribution of human activities in space and in time.'

Organizationally the Foundation, which is based in Dublin, consists of an Administrative Board, a Committee of Experts and a staff of approximately forty-five. The Administrative Board, comprising representatives of the Commission, national governments, employers' organizations and trade unions, takes the major decisions concerning the approval of work programmes, the budget and the adoption of the annual report. The Committee of Experts comprises twelve specialists in the various activities of the Foundation appointed by the Council of Ministers. Their task is to give advice especially as regards research programmes.

The Foundation maintains close relations with Community institutions – in particular DG V and DG XI of the Commission. The Foundation plans a research programme, holds conferences and seminars, and publishes the results of its research.

Documentation

Until the middle of the 1980s much of the material emanating from the Foundation was elusive to track down and difficult to obtain. The Foundation largely organized the distribution of its own publications. A publications policy came into being in 1980 and over 160 publications were produced in the following four years. However, it was only in 1984 that a determined effort was made to pursue an efficient marketing and publications strategy. This resulted in 1985 in a number of developments. OOPEC took over the marketing and selling of Foundation publications. Thus some previously freely available research reports became priced publications. There was the development of newsletters, information booklets, and briefs. Various leaflets and catalogues describing Foundation publications were more systematically made available. All Foundation reports were microfilmed and made alternatively available in that format.

In 1987 negotiations began with various commercial publishers in the member states to bring out the results of certain Foundation research projects in the form of co-publications. Between 1984 and 1986 there had been a 478 per cent increase in the number of pages printed by the Foundation with 13½ million pages of text printed in 1986 alone.

Four-year rolling programme of the European Foundation

So far four of these Programmes have been issued. These cover the periods:

1. 1977–80
2. 1981–84
3. 1985–88
4. 1989–92.

Their aim is to set the future work of the Foundation into a context – both an economic and social context as well as a Community one. Each Programme outlines a framework of action and selects the topics to be studied. Thus in the 1985–88 Programme research activities were divided into three groups:

1. Man at work
2. Time
3. The environment.

These groups were then further subdivided into particular projects. In an Annex to this Programme the major projects undertaken in the earlier Programmes are listed.

Annual report

The format of the *Annual report* has not remained standard but the following features are always included:

1. Description of the work programme for the year
2. Breakdown of the programme into topics and description of work undertaken
3. Evaluation activities
4. Publications of the European Foundation
5. Meetings organized by the European Foundation
6. Budget
7. Directory of members of the Administrative Board, the Committee of Experts, Foundation staff and of research bodies and experts involved in implementing the work programme for the year.

Programme of work

An annual programme of work is approved by the Administrative Board and subsequently published. It covers the three basic activities of the Foundation.

1. Research activities
2. Evaluation of research work
3. Dissemination of information.

In 1986 the title given to this publication was *New research 1986,* but in 1987 it reverted to the title *Programme of work.* The point has been made that the publication is intended to help researchers identify topics on which they might wish to exchange information or become involved.

EF News

This bimonthly newsletter started in 1986 and aims to highlight the activities of the Foundation and selectively cover other work being done in Europe on themes relevant to the Foundation's aims. *EF News* is published in all Community working languages, is free, and available direct from the Foundation.

Research Reports

While each research project is managed by a member of the Foundation staff, outside organizations and individuals are commissioned to undertake the research in the various member states. Each project does not necessarily involve all member states. The results of this research are published in the series Research Reports and are usually issued only in the language of the country concerned. An example is *Commuter transport: experiences in participation,* 1986. The national studies covered Denmark, France, Ireland, Italy and the United Kingdom. The Danish study is in the Danish language only, the French study in the French language only, and so on. Many of these national studies are no longer formally published but are only available in the Working Paper Series, described below (see also Consolidated Reports below).

There are also instances where an outside research organization is responsible for the overall research project. An example is *Living conditions in urban areas: an overview of factors influencing urban life in the European Community,* 1986. This study was undertaken by the School for Advanced Urban Studies at the University of Bristol but covered all Community countries. In these instances in addition to the language of the research organization involved there are usually also versions available in a selection of other Community languages.

It should be made clear that the term Research Report is not necessarily printed on the cover of such publications. The term was used on some publications in the 1980s but it is used here more as a generic term to describe conveniently a category of material.

Some of the topics covered in the 1980s have included:

1. New technology
2. Changes in organization
3. Developments in industrial relations
4. Safety and health
5. Shiftwork
6. New forms of work and activity
7. Biotechnology
8. Hazardous wastes
9. The urban environment
10. The unemployed
11. The elderly
12. Organization of time
13. Women
14. Commuting
15. Participation.

Some of the work is into new areas of research for the Foundation, but there are also instances of reviews of previous Foundation research.

Consolidated Reports

This again is a category of document. In those instances where there have been a whole series of national studies it has become common practice to produce a Consolidated Report based on the national studies and produced in most Community languages. An example is *Meeting the needs of the elderly*, 1987. This is available in English, French, German and Italian editions. The national studies in this instance are only available in the Working Paper Series.

Evaluation Reports

Prior to the publication of the academic/professional research reports they are submitted to a political evaluation at seminars and colloquia by representatives of member states' governments, trade unions and employers' organizations. Each of these groups presents an Evaluation Report.

Until 1986–87 these reports were usually published as a separate section in the same volume as the Consolidated Report. Since 1987 Evaluation Reports have not usually been issued as a distinct entity – rather the views of the groups are incorporated in the preface to the Consolidated Report, which is written by the appropriate research manager for the project.

Information Booklet series

This series began in 1985 as a product of the renewed effort to make the research findings of the Foundation more widely and systematically available. The pilot number published in that year was called *The role of the parties concerned in the introduction of new technology*. In the preface to this pilot issue it was said that the aims were:

1. To provide a succinct summary of the key findings contained in full research reports
2. To introduce to the reader the work of the European Foundation.

The hope was that the 'less specialised reader' would find the booklets 'attractive and straightforward to read'.

The first in the series proper was published in 1986 and called *Visual display unit workplaces: emerging trends and problems*. The second in the series was called *Safety in hazardous wastes* and was published in 1987. Titles in the Information Booklet series list the full research reports from which these mini-consolidated reports are compiled. They are published in all Community languages and available through OOPEC.

Working paper series

As the volume of research undertaken by the Foundation increased during the 1980s the problems of what exactly to formally publish and in how many languages became a major concern. By 1987 there was a substantial backlog of material. The Working Paper series was a response to this. An example of the material included in this series are many national studies produced as a result of Foundation research. While the Consolidated Report bringing together the results of the national studies might have been formally published, it was not usually considered economic to publish each national study. Such studies would henceforth be available, but not published, in the Working Paper series. A Consolidated Report would refer to the 'available' national studies, which an interested reader could obtain direct from the Foundation. To confuse matters somewhat there are also some examples of Consolidated Reports issued only in the Working Paper series. It is intended that lists will occasionally be produced of titles in this series.

Miscellaneous publications

A newssheet called *In Brief* began publication in 1985. Two to three issues are published a year in a single English and French edition. Its aim is to communicate to Members of the European Parliament and others information relevant to the issues concerning the Foundation. *In Brief* is not available to the general public.

An example issued in October 1986 was entitled *Commuting needs a policy*. This two-page sheet presented some of the salient features of three major studies published by the Foundation.

The research studies which are commissioned by the European

Foundation sometimes comprise bibliographies or a study of available data sources. Examples include:

1. *An investigation of activities for the unemployed*, 1984
2. *European Foundation studies of especial interest regarding women*, 1984
3. *Working participation and the improvement of working conditions*, 1985
4. *New technology in the public service*, 1986.

Other research studies usually contain substantial bibliographical sections.

The proceedings and documentation of Foundation conferences have been occasionally published. Two examples are:

1. *Safety aspects of hazardous wastes (Proceedings of a Round Table, Dublin, November 1985)*
2. *New forms of work and activity (Colloquium, Brussels, April 1986)*

Further information

A *Catalogue of publications* was published by the Foundation in 1985 which listed all publications available in the summer of 1985. An updated *Price list of publications* was issued in 1986 and 1987. Note that although the *Catalogue of publications* says that Foundation publications are available from the Foundation, this is now true only for 'administrative documents' such as the *Annual report* and the *Programme of work*, *EF News* and the Working Paper series. Other publications are available from OOPEC.

Since 1985 European Foundation publications have been listed in the sales catalogues of OOPEC.

In 1987 the Foundation published a comprehensive *Subject guide to Foundation reports published in the English language*.

The European Foundation maintains a library and information service which is available to all organizations and individuals concerned with living and working conditions. Requests for assistance by letter or telephone are welcomed and personal visits can be arranged.

Enquiries concerning the documentation of the Foundation should be addressed to:

Head of Section
Documentation, Information and Dissemination
European Foundation for the Improvement of Living and
   Working Conditions
Loughlinstown House
Shankill
Co. Dublin
Ireland
Telephone: 01 826888
Telex: 30726 EURF EI.

EUROPEAN INVESTMENT BANK

The European Investment Bank (EIB) was established by Article 129 of the Treaty of Rome setting up the European Economic Community. Its function is to help promote the economic and social development of the countries of the EC. In practice this means that the EIB makes or guarantees loans for investment projects, particularly in the area of industry, energy and infrastructure. Loans to the less favoured regions have priority. In 1986 financing provided inside the EC totalled some 7.5 billion ECU (£5½ billion). In addition 474 million ECU was lent to countries outside the EC, mainly in the Mediterranean region and the ACP countries.

An example of an EIB loan was a £3.4 million modernization loan for British Alcan in May 1986 to assist the company's modernization schemes at Rogerstone, Gwent and Lynemouth, Northumberland. EIB loans are available in high unemployment regions to cover 50 per cent of fixed capital investment in stepping up productivity or quality or in such areas as energy-saving schemes.

Documentation

The main feature to note concerning the documentation of the EIB is that it does not use OOPEC as a source of distribution. All EIB documentation is issued and distributed directly by the institution itself. No charge is made for publications.

The one exception to direct distribution is the EC Depository Library network. EIB documentation for these centres is distributed via the EDC/DEP Section in OOPEC.

The publications of the EIB maintain a high standard of presentation and content, which manage to make the complex activities of the Bank intelligible to the layman. The publications noted below generally are introductions to aspects of the activities of the EIB or retrospective analyses of past EIB activities. To keep abreast of new loans arranged by the bank you need to be put on a mailing list for EIB press releases, for which there are two levels. Projects of particular importance are discussed in releases distributed comprehensively. Other projects are noted in releases intended primarily for the country to which they relate and are printed only in the relevant language.

Annual report

This is issued approximately six months after the financial (and calendar) year it is describing. Throughout the 1980s the *Annual report* has maintained a broadly standard format. Complete with numerous colour photographs illustrating the type of project that the EIB helps to finance, there is a complete list of EIB loans and financing operations within and outside the Community. These are broken down by country and give brief details of the nature of each project along with amount of finance involved in ECU and the national currency involved. In addition to this information the *Annual report* also contains the following regular features:

1. Directory – names and national position of the Board of Governors, the Audit Committee, Board of Directors, the Management Committee and the organizational structure of the Bank
2. Financing provided in 'year'
3. Operations within the Community
4. Operations outside the Community
5. Resources
6. Results for the year
7. Administration
8. Financial statements
9. Historical pattern of financing.

EIB Information

A small publication of about eight to twelve pages issued periodically. There are usually four or five issues a year although it is not published at regular intervals. Issue no. 50 was published in October 1986. *EIB Information* gives a wide variety of short articles on areas of current concern to the Bank and general news features.

EIB Papers

The first issue of this title was dated February 1986. *EIB Papers* contains articles that have usually been written by officials of the EIB in the course of their day-to-day information gathering and analysis. The title is published irregularly; no. 5 was dated February 1988. The articles in the single edition are either in French or English. There is a short abstract of each article in English. While the foreword claims that the papers are of 'general interest' the style of *EIB Papers* is clearly aimed for a professional or academic audience.

Miscellaneous publications

Periodically the EIB brings out a review covering the history and operations of the Bank to date. The latest edition called *European Investment Bank 25 years 1958–1983* was published in 1983. In addition, to mark its twenty-fifth anniversary, the Bank sponsored a book entitled *Investing in Europe's future*, also issued in 1983. This major monograph, published by Basil Blackwell for the EIB, contains a number of articles by leading independent figures in the world of finance on the problems of investment in the Community in the 1980s.

Another substantial monograph, published directly by the EIB in 1984, was a tribute to its retiring Chairman of the Board of Directors,

Yves Le Portz. This also consisted of a series of scholarly articles on subjects related to investment. It was entitled *Y.L.P. Bene Meritus de Europa.*

The Statute of the EIB and various other formal texts are contained in a publication called *Statute and other provisions.* The latest edition was published in 1986. Another periodically updated booklet has been an introduction to the work of the Bank called *Loans and guarantees in the member countries of the European Community.* The fifth edition was published in 1981. This would seem to be have been replaced by a booklet called *Financing facilities within the European Community,* issued in 1986.

A short leaflet called *European Investment Bank,* introducing the Bank and its operations, is issued in January of each year. The leaflet is sometimes called *European Investment Bank: key facts.* A booklet published for the first time in 1986 was called *One hundred questions and answers.*

The work of the EIB outside the member states is noted in two booklets. *Financing outside the Community: Mediterranean countries* was last published in 1983. The operations of the EIB in the overseas countries associated with the EC is recorded in a booklet the title of which has changed over the years. The latest edition, published in 1986, is called *Financing facilities under the Third Lomé Convention.*

In addition to the *Annual report* for 1987 the EIB also issued an abbreviated version of the activities of the bank for that year in 1988.

Further information

For further information on the activities and documentation of the European Investment Bank contact:

> European Investment Bank
> Information – Public Relations
> 100 boulevard Konrad Adenauer
> L-2950 Luxembourg
>
> Telephone: 4379–1
> Telex: 3530 bnkeu lu
> Telecopier: 43 77 04

There are also liaison offices in some of the member states from which information can be obtained. In the United Kingdom the address is:

> European Investment Bank
> 68 Pall Mall
> London SW1Y 5ES
> England
>
> Telephone: 01 839 3351
> Telex: 919159 bankeu g
> Telecopier: 930 9929

EUROPEAN UNIVERSITY INSTITUTE

The European University Institute (EUI) was set up in Florence in March 1975, after a long set of negotiations, by the member states of the European Communities.

The EUI is a postgraduate teaching and research institute which concentrates on work that contributes to the intellectual development of Europe. At present it has four main strands to its research.

1. History and civilization
2. Economics
3. Law
4. Political and social sciences.

In addition a European Policy Unit was set up in 1984 to coordinate research on policy related subjects covering the European Communities. In 1987 a European Culture Research Centre was set up to coordinate research in this area.

The EUI has thirty-four full-time teaching and research staff plus additional researchers for specific research projects and visiting and external professors. The Principal of the EUI is in charge of day-to-day operations. Since 1987 the Principal has been Emile Noël, formerly the long-serving Secretary-General of the Commission. Overall control of the Institute is in the hands of the High Council. This comprises representatives of the member states who are contracting participants to the Convention of the EUI. There is also an Academic Council concerned with the teaching and research activities of the Institute.

Documentation

Academic year '...'

This is the title given to the annual prospectus of the EUI. A new edition is issued in the latter half of each year intended for prospective students for the forthcoming academic year beginning the next September. Note that since 1986 the deadline date for applications is 31 January for entry in the following September.

The precise arrangement of the prospectus changes somewhat from year to year but the following features are standard:

1. Administrative organization of the EUI
2. Academic organization
3. Admission procedures
4. Work methods and organization of studies
5. Degrees offered
6. Jean Monnet Fellowships
7. Services for research students (Visiting professors, Library,

computing facilities, study travel, linguistic assistance, publications, vocational guidance, etc.)
8. Practical information
9. List of national grant-award bodies (each language version of the prospectus also has an additional section on grants relevant to native speakers of that language).

Academic year '...' is published by OOPEC but copies may be obtained free of charge from the Academic Service at the address given at the end of this section. Up to *Academic year 1982–83* the prospectus was published in English and French versions. Since then it has also been published in Dutch, German and Italian versions.

Report of activities

An annual report detailing the main activities of the EUI. At present it is published by OOPEC in English, French, Italian, Dutch and Geman versions and is unpriced. The latest report covering the activities of 1985 was published in 1987. Information is given on the following topics:

1. Officers and full-time staff of the Institute
2. Research and teaching activities (including running projects, future research, activities during the year in question and the work of the Jean Monnet Fellows)
3. The Jean Monnet Fellows
4. Activities of the Institute's authorities
5. Other activities of the Institute
6. Annexes (including the publications of research students and a full cumulative list of EUI publications).

Publications resulting from EUI research

A significant amount of academic research undertaken by the staff and researchers at the EUI is made available publicly. The EUI has published material under its own imprint since 1978. These books are usually distributed by commercial publishers. In addition since 1982 the EUI has co-published material in a series with the commercial publisher Walter de Gruyter.

There is also a series called EUI Working Papers. These comprise papers reporting the results of research undertaken at the EUI. Up to the beginning of 1988 333 EUI Working Papers had been issued in a single language edition and available free of charge from the Publications Officer at the address given at the end of this section. Only a limited number of each title is printed and many earlier papers are now out of print. A full list of EUI Working Papers is listed in each *Report of activities*. In addition the Institute issued in early 1988 a separate catalogue of the EUI Working Papers.

In 1986 OOPEC published for the EUI *Noi si mura: selected Working Papers of the European University Institute,* edited by Werner Maihofer, the Principal of the EUI at the time. This had twenty-six EUI Working Papers written by EUI staff over a number of years in English, French or German. The publication was unpriced.

European Political Cooperation Documentation Bulletin

The first issue of this journal was published by OOPEC in 1987. On the cover it was called vol. 1, no. 1, 1985. The journal is officially cited as *EPC Bulletin.* It is a collaborative effort between the European Policy Unit at the European University Institute and the Institut für Europäische Politik in Bonn. *EPC Bulletin* is a systematic compilation of all the public documentation associated with the concept known as European Political Cooperation (EPC).

EPC can be defined as an attempt by the member states of the European Communities to align their foreign policies while continuing to respect their national sovereignties. It is more an exercise in cooperation and coordination than the creation of a common foreign policy. Its early development had no foundation in the original Treaties setting up the EC. EPC was however brought formally within the EC structure by the Single European Act 1986.

EPC Bulletin is issued twice a year and can be obtained on subscription through OOPEC. The first issue covered the period January–July 1985 and listed:

1. All official statements of the European Council, of the Foreign Ministers, and speeches of the Presidency at international gatherings
2. Documents relating to the European Parliament such as written and oral questions and reports by the Presidency on EPC.

Each item is given a unique document number and there is a reasonable index using such headings as:

1. Countries
2. Regions and subregions
3. International organizations and political groupings
4. Issues
5. Document source
6. Status of document
7. EPC structure and procedure.

These headings are then further subdivided. By 1988 three further issues had been published covering the period up to December 1986. The index in each issue is cumulative of all issues. From the second issue the statements made by representatives of the EC in the General

Assembly of the United Nations are also noted. A special issue covering the activities of EPC up to 1985 is promised.

The Jean Monnet Lecture

For most years since 1977 a distinguished statesman, academic or public figure has been asked to give the Jean Monnet Lecture in memory of one of the key figures in the history of the integration process in Europe. The lectures have been published by OOPEC since 1981. The following is a complete list of the lectures published so far:

1st	Roy Jenkins:	*Europe: present challenge and future opportunity*, 1977
2nd	Emilio Colombo:	*Appointments for Europe*, 1978
3rd	Ralf Dahrendorf:	*A Third Europe*, 1979
4th	Simone Veil:	*The Community and European identity*, 1980
5th	Max Kohnstamm:	*Jean Monnet: the power of the imagination*, 1981
6th	Altiero Spinelli:	*Towards the European Union*, 1983
7th	Gaston Thorn:	*European Union or decline: to be or not to be*, 1984
8th	Giulio Andreotti:	*European Union: one character in search of an author*, 1985
9th	Jacques Delors:	*The Single Act and Europe: a moment of truth*, 1986
10th	Felipe González Marquez:	*Europe from the Community of Twelve to European Union: the objective for 1992*, 1987.

Copies can be obtained from the Academic Service of the EUI.

Further information

A publication called *Convention setting up a European University Institute* was published by the General Secretariat of the Council of the European Communities in 1975.

The Publications Officer of the EUI issued in 1988 a list of EUI Working Papers and a separate listing of *Publication of the European University Institute*, with details of commercial publishers, price and distribution arrangements. To obtain copies of these lists and for other enquiries concerning EUI documentation contact:

Publications Officer
European University Institute
Badia Fiesolana

I-50016 San Domenico di Fiesole (FI)
Italy
Telephone: (055) 477931
Telex: 571528 IUE
Telefax: 599887 ·

For copies of the prospectus *Academic Year '...'* and *Report of activities* contact the Academic Service at the address above.

YOUTH FORUM OF THE EUROPEAN COMMUNITIES

The Youth Forum of the European Communities is the political platform of national and international youth organizations in Europe, partially funded by the European Communities. It started its work in 1978. Its aims, according to Article 1 of its Statute, are:

1. To increase the activities and the actions which will ensure the greater involvement of youth in the future development of the European Communities.
2. To increase the role in the development of mutual understanding and safeguarding the equal rights of all citizens in the European Communities.
3. To increase democracy and real participation at all levels of the European Communities.

The supreme decision-making body in the Youth Forum is the General Assembly which meets periodically to lay down broad outlines of the work programme for future years, adapt new statutes, rule on membership applications and elect the Bureau, the management committee for the Youth Forum. The seventh General Assembly was held in 1987, after which the total membership of the Youth Forum was thirty-seven members, two consultative members and seventeen observers.

Documentation

The documentation produced by the Youth Forum reflect the subjects that have dominated the organization through the 1980s.

Youth Opinion

The journal of the Youth Forum was first issued in June 1982. It has been issued on an irregular basis, no. 19 being dated December 1987; no. 20, May 1988 was issued in a new more substantial format and claimed henceforth to be published quarterly, no. 20 contained the following features:

1. Youth Forum news
2. Interview: Youth Forum President

  3. Dossier: 'A woman's place ... The EC and women'
  4. Documentation
  5. Book review
  6. Features
  7. Culture
  8. Member organization.

Youth Opinion is published in English and French editions and is available free of charge from the Youth Forum.

Miscellaneous publications

The following miscellaneous publications have been issued since 1982:

  1. *Youth rights in the European Communities. A comparative study on the legal status of young people in the Ten Member States*, 1982
  2. *The fight against illiteracy in the European Community*, 1982
  3. *Youth exchanges and the European Communities*, 1982
  4. *Mobility of disabled young people*, 1983
  5. *The future of the Lomé Treaty: contribution to development*, 1983
  6. *Intercultural education: proposals for an adequate EC policy*, 1983
  7. *The need for an EC development policy*, 1984
  8. *Documentation. No EC links with apartheid*, 1984
  9. *Youth Forum Urgency Programme 1984*, 1984
  10. *Catalogue of proposals for an EC policy on equal opportunities between men and women, summarizing the position of the Youth Forum of the European Communities*, 1984
  11. *Democratization of the European Communities*, 1984
  12. *Social security: taking stock*, 1985
  13. *The future for young women*, 1986
  14. *Youth Forum statement on the Commission's memorandum on International Youth Year*, 1986
  15. *Youth Forum statement on YES for Europe*, 1986
  16. *Youth Forum*, 1986 (information leaflet)
  17. *Lomé 4 Youth. A youth contribution to dialogue and development*, 1987
  18. *A European perspective on vocational training for young people. Policy statement of the Youth Forum of the European Communities, January 1987*, 1987.
  19. *Income, status and jobs. A Youth Forum discussion document on employment*, 1987
  20. *Policy statement. A collection of Youth Forum policy, 1985–1987*, 1987.

Further information

Youth Forum of the European Communities
10 rue de la Science
B-1040 Brussels
Belgium
Telephone: 32.2.230.64.90

EC series/periodicals/ reports

Below is a list of major EC reports, periodicals, series and statistical titles that are currently published at 'regular' intervals. The list is divided into the main subject headings used by OOPEC in the *Catalogue of Publications* and *Catalogue of Documents*. The aim is to:

1. Bring together documentation from the various EC institutions/ organizations by subject/policy area
2. Highlight series which are issued within overall series such as COM Documents and the Document categorization.

SUBJECT DIVISIONS

1. General, political, institutional and budgetary matters
2. Customs union and free movement of goods
3. Agriculture
4. Fisheries
5. Employment and social policy
6. Laws and procedures
7. Transport
8. Competition
9. Taxation
10. Economic and monetary policy and free movement of capital
11. External relations
12. Energy
13. Industrial policy and internal market
14. Regional policy
15. Environment and consumers
16. Scientific and technical research
17. Education, culture
18. Tertiary sector, right of establishment and freedom of services
19. Development and cooperation
20. Statistics (subject titles listed under headings 1–19)
21. Documentation
22. Miscellaneous.

Institution

This is the author institution/organization/department of the publication. The following abbreviations are used:

EC	European Communities
OOP	Office for Official Publications of the European Communities
COM	Commission
EUR	Eurostat
COU	Council of Ministers
EP	European Parliament
ESC	Economic and Social Committee
ECJ	European Court of Justice
AUD	Court of Auditors
ECSC	Consultative Committee of the European Coal and Steel Community
LAN	European Bureau for Lesser Used Languages
CED	European Centre for the Development of Vocational Training (CEDEFOP)
IFA	European Community Action Programme: Transition of Young People from Education to Adult and Working Life
EF	European Foundation for the Improvement of Living and Working Conditions
EIB	European Investment Bank
EUI	European University Institute
JRC	Joint Research Centre
YF	Youth Forum of the European Communities

Title

In most instances the precise title of the series/periodical is given. In some cases, particularly of reports, the title is slightly rearranged or expanded to give a clearer idea of the contents – these names are shown in brackets.

Frequency

The number listed is the usual number of issues published in a year. 'i': irregular pattern; 'x': more than a hundred issues a year; 'b': biannual; 't': triannual.

Other information

If a series or report is issued within a more general series the latter is noted (for example, COM Document or titles published with the Document categorization). Information on titles that are obtained other than direct from OOPEC or its sales agents is noted. If a title has started or ceased since 1980 this is noted. Further information can be found in the chapter (Ch.) shown. Precise page references to titles can be found in the index.

1. General, political, institutional and budgetary matters

Title	Institution	Frequency	Other information
Official Journal of the European Communities 'C'; 'L'; 'S' Series; *Annex*	EC	x	Ch.1/Ch.9
COM Documents	COM	x	Ch.4
EP Reports (Committee Reports of the European Parliament/European Parliament Session Documents; Series A)	EP	x	Ch.9
Opinions and Reports (Economic and Social Committee)	ESC	x	Ch.10
Reports of Cases before the Court	ECJ	i	Ch.11
Directory of the Commission of the European Communities	COM	i	Ch.2
Corps Diplomatique Accrédité auprès des Communautés Européennes	COM	2	Ch.5
Commission monitoring of the application of Community law	COM	1	COM Doc, 1984– OJ 'C', 1986–
General report on the activities of the European Communities	COM	1	Ch.4
Programme of the Commission	COM	1	Ch.4 Bull. EC; Supplement, 1985–
Bulletin of the European Communities	COM	11	Ch.4
Bulletin of the European Communities: Supplement	COM	i	Ch.4
Guide to the Council of the European Communities	COU	2	Ch.8
Review of the Council's work	COU	1	Ch.8
Annual report of the ACP–EEC Council of Ministers	COU	1	Ch.8 1981–
Handbook of the European Parliament	EP	i	Ch.9
Progress towards European integration: survey of the main activities of the European Parliament	EP	1	Ch.9 DG IV
Texts adopted by the European Parliament	EP	12	Ch.9 1985–
Fact sheets on the European Parliament and the activities of the European Community	EP	i	Ch.9
Briefing	EP	12	Ch.9 DG III
EP news	EP	12	Ch.9 DG III
The week	EP	12	Ch.9 DG III
Research and Documentation Papers	EP	i	Ch.9 DG IV restricted distribution
Annual report (Economic and Social Committee)	ESC	1	Ch.10

Title	Institution	Frequency	Other information
Bulletin (Economic and Social Committee)	ESC	12	Ch.10
The other European Assembly	ESC	i	Ch.10
Judgments or Orders of the Court and Opinions of Advocates-General	ECJ	i	Ch.11 ECJ
Proceedings of the Court of Justice of the European Communities	ECJ	26	Ch.11 ECJ
Liste des audiences	ECJ	26	Ch.11 ECJ
Synopsis of the work of the Court of Justice of the European Communities	ECJ	1	Ch.11 ECJ
Formal sittings of the Court of Justice of the European Communities	ECJ	1	Ch.11 ECJ
Digest of case-law relating to the European Communities	ECJ	i	Ch.11 ECJ looseleaf
Annual report . . . (Court of Auditors)	AUD	1	Ch.12 OJ 'C'
(Special reports) (Court of Auditors)	AUD	i	Ch.12 OJ 'C' and AUD
(ECSC: *Financial report*)	COM	1	Ch.5 + COM Doc
Yearbook (Consultative Committee of the European Coal and Steel Community)	ECSC	1	Ch.13 ECSC
Handbook (Consultative Committee of the European Coal and Steel Community)	ECSC	i	Ch.13 ECSC
Annual report (European Foundation for the Improvement of Living and Working Conditions)	EF	1	Ch.13
Programme of work (European Foundation . . .)	EF	1	Ch.13 EF
Four-year rolling Programme of the European Foundation	EF	i	Ch.13 EF
Annual report (European Centre for the Development of Vocational Training)	CED	1	Ch.13 CEDEFOP
Annual report (European Investment Bank)	EIB	1	Ch.13 EIB
EIB information	EIB	i	Ch.13 EIB
EIB papers	EIB	i	Ch.13 EIB 1986–
European Investment Bank: key facts	EIB	1	Ch.13 EIB
Academic year . . . (European University Institute)	EUI	1	Ch.13 EUI
Report of activities (European University Institute)	EUI	1	Ch.13 EUI
European Political Cooperation Documentation Bulletin	EUI	i	Ch.13 1987–
The Jean Monnet Lecture	EUI	1	Ch.13
(The Document categorization)	COM	i	Ch.4
EUR Reports	COM	x	Ch.5
European Documentation	COM	6–7	Ch.5
European File	COM	20	Ch.5
European Perspectives	COM	i	Ch.5

1. General, political, institutional and budgetary matters *Contd.*

Title	Institution	Frequency	Other information
Eurobarometer	COM	2	Ch.5 DG X (restricted distribution)
Information memo	COM	x	Ch.7 (restricted distribution)
Background Report	COM	i	Ch.7 Commission: London
Press Release	COM	i	Ch.7 Commission: London
The week in Europe	COM	45	Ch.7 Commission: London
Basic statistics of the Community	EUR	1	Ch.6
Eurostat review	EUR	1	Ch.6
Eurostatistics: data for short-term economic analysis	EUR	12	Ch.6
Regions: statistical yearbook	EUR	1	Ch.6
Demographic statistics	EUR	1	Ch.6
Rapid reports: population and social conditions	EUR	i	Ch.6 1987–
Avrupa	COM	12	Commission: Ankara
Community Report	COM	12	Commission: Dublin
Comunità Europea – Dossier Europa	COM	2	Commission: Rome
E news	COM	12	Commission: Rome
EC Newsletter	COM	6	Commission: Ottawa 1987–
Echos de l'Europe	COM	12	Commission: Luxembourg
EF-Avisen	COM	12	Commission: Copenhagen
Eur-info	COM	12	Commission: Brussels
Europa-bericht	COM	12	Commission: Brussels
Europa van morgen	COM	52	Commission: The Hague
Europe	COM	6	Commission: Washington
Europe	COM	6	Ch.7
Euroscail	COM	12	Commission: Dublin
Télex 12	COM	6	Commission: Lisbon
(Building loans to EC officials: utilization)	COM	1	COM Doc.
(New Community instrument: rate of utilization of tranches)	COM	2	COM Doc., 1984–

2. Customs union and free movement of goods

Title	Institution	Frequency	Other information
Customs valuation (looseleaf)	COM	i	Ch.5
Explanatory notes to the Combined Nomenclature of the European Communities	COM	i	Ch.5 1987–
List of authorized customs offices for Community transit operations	COM	i	Ch.5
Practical guide to the use of the European Communities' scheme of generalized tariff preferences	COM	1	Ch.5
TARIC	COM	1	Ch.5, 1987–
(Internal market; implementation of Commission White Paper on completing the internal market)	COM	1	COM Doc 1986–

3. Agriculture

Title	Institution	Frequency	Other information
Recueil des actes agricoles (Compendium of agricultural Acts)	COM	i	Ch.5 'Document', 1985–
Agricultural situation in the Community	COM	1	Ch.4
EUR Reports (agriculture)	COM	i	Ch.5
Green Europe: Newsletter on the Common Agricultural Policy	COM	i	Ch.5
Green Europe: Newsflash	COM	i	Ch.5
Information on agriculture	COM	i	Ch.5 –1984
(Agricultural markets: situation)	COM	1	COM Doc.
(Prices: Commission proposals)	COM	1	COM Doc./ Green Europe: Newsflash
(European Guidance and Guarantee Fund: financial report—guidance section)	COM	1	COM Doc.
(European Guidance and Guarantee Fund: financial report—guarantee section)	COM	1	COM Doc.
(Hops: production and marketing)	COM	1	COM Doc.
(Co-responsibility levy funds: milk sector)	COM	1	COM Doc.
(Wine: estimates of supply)	COM	1	COM Doc.
(Wine: trends in wine-growing)	COM	1	COM Doc.
Agricultural markets: prices	COM	10 (81–84) 4 + 1 (85–)	Ch.5
Agricultural income: sectoral income index analysis	EUR	1	Ch.6, 1987–
Agricultural prices	EUR	1	Ch.6
Agricultural prices: selected series from the Cronos databank	EUR	4	Ch.6, 1983–
Agricultural price indices: monthly and annual results, half-yearly statistics	EUR	2	Ch.6
Agriculture: statistical yearbook	EUR	1	Ch.6
Animal production: quarterly statistics	EUR	4	Ch.6

3. Agriculture *Contd.*

Title	Institution	Frequency	Other information
Crop production: quarterly statistics	EUR	4	Ch.6
Earnings in agriculture	EUR	i	Ch.6
Economic accounts: agriculture, forestry	EUR	1	Ch.6
Farm Structure	EUR	1	Ch.6
Forestry statistics	EUR	1	Ch.6
The rates of value-added tax in agriculture	EUR	1	Ch.6, 1984–
Regions: the Community's financial participation in investments	EUR	1	Ch.6

4. Fisheries

Title	Institution	Frequency	Other information
(Total allowable/allowance catches: proposals (TACS))	COM	1	COM Doc.
Agriculture: statistical yearbook	EUR	1	Ch.6
Fisheries: statistical yearbook	EUR	1	Ch.6, 1983–

5. Employment and social policy

Title	Institution	Frequency	Other information
Report on social developments	COM	1	Ch.4 'Document.'
(European Social Fund: annual report)	COM	1	COM Doc.
Social Europe	COM	3	Ch.5
Social Europe: Supplement	COM	i	Ch.5
Programme of research and actions on the development of the labour market	COM	i	Ch.5 'Document', 1984–
InforMISEP	COM	4	Ch.5 DG V, 1983–
MISEP: basic information reports	COM	i	Ch.5 'Document', 1985–
Trade Union Information Bulletin	COM	4	Ch.5 DG X
Compendium of Community provisions on social security	COM	i	Ch.5
Comparative tables of the social security schemes in the member states of the European Communities	COM	b	Ch.5 'Document'
Social security for migrant workers	COM	i	Ch.5
(Social protection expenditure and financing: medium-term projections)	COM	1	COM Doc.
(Safety, hygiene and health protection at work: Advisory Committee progress report)	COM	1	COM Doc.
Information Bulletin of the Steel Industry Safety and Health Commission	COM	i	Ch.5 1982– DG XIII
(EUR Reports: industrial health and safety)	COM	i	Ch.5
(EUR Reports: medicine)	COM	i	Ch.5

Title	Institution	Frequency	Other information
(*Road transport: social legislation*)	COM	1	COM Doc.
Women of Europe	COM	5	Ch.5 DG X
Women of Europe: supplement	COM	1	Ch.5 DG X
Women in Europe: news and views about women and the European Community	COM	i	Ch.7 Commission: London
Annual report (European Foundation for the Improvement of Living and Working Conditions)	EF	1	Ch.13
Four-year rolling programme of the European Foundation	EF	i	Ch.13 EF
Programme of work (European Foundation . . .)	EF	1	Ch.13 EF
(*Research reports*) (European Foundation . . .)	EF	i	Ch.13
(*Consolidated reports*) (European Foundation . . .)	EF	i	Ch.13
(*Evaluation reports*) (European Foundation . . .)	EF	i	Ch.13
Information booklet series (European Foundation . . .)	EF	i	Ch.13 1985–
Working Paper Series (European Foundation . . .)	EF	i	Ch.13 EF 1987–
EF news	EF	5	Ch.13 1986–
Annual report (European Centre for the Development of Vocational Training)	CED	1	Ch.13 Cedefop
Work programme (European Centre for the Development of Vocational Training)	CED	1	Ch.13 Cedefop
Vocational training	CED	3	Ch.13
CEDEFOP news	CED	4	Ch.13
CEDEFOP flash	CED	i	Ch.13 Cedefop, 1984–
Programme news (IFAPLAN)	IFA	i	Ch.13 Ifaplan 1984–1988
Innovations (IFAPLAN)	IFA	i	Ch.13 Ifaplan 1987
Youth opinion	YF	i	Ch.13 YF 1982–
Demographic statistics	EUR	1	Ch.6
Earnings in agriculture	EUR	i	Ch.6
Earnings in industry and services	EUR	2	Ch.6 1983–
Education and training	EUR	i	Ch.6
Employment and unemployment	EUR	1	Ch.6
Labour costs	EUR	i	Ch.6
Labour force survey: results	EUR	1	Ch.6
Rapid reports: population and social conditions	EUR	i	Ch.6
Social indicators for the European Community: selected series	EUR	i	Ch.6
Structure of earnings: principal results	EUR	i	Ch.6
Unemployment	EUR	12	Ch.6

6. Law and procedures

Title	Institution	Frequency	Other information
Official Journal of the European Communities 'C'; 'L'; 'S' series; *Annex*	EC	x	Ch.1/9
Directory of Community legislation in force . . .	EC	1 (80–86) 2 (87–)	Ch.1
Collection of the agreements concluded by the European Communities	EC	1	Ch.5
(*Commission monitoring of the application of Community law*)	COM	1	COM Doc., 1984– OJ 'C', 1986–
Reports of Cases before the Court (European Court Reports)	ECJ	i	Ch.11
Judgments or Orders of the Court and Opinions of Advocates-General	ECJ	i	Ch.11 ECJ
Proceedings of the Court of Justice of the European Communities	ECJ	26	Ch.11 ECJ
Liste des audiences	ECJ	26	Ch.11 ECJ
Synopsis of the work of the Court of Justice of the European Communities	ECJ	1	Ch.11 ECJ
Formal sittings of the Court of Justice of the European Communities	ECJ	1	Ch.11 ECJ
Digest of case-law relating to the European Communities	ECJ	i	Ch.11 ECJ looseleaf
Community law	COM	1	Ch.4
(*Internal market: implementation of Commission White Paper on completing the internal market*)	COM	1	COM Doc.

7. Transport

Title	Institution	Frequency	Other information
Europa transport: observation of the transport markets – market developments	COM	4	Ch.5
Europa transport: observation of the transport markets – analysis and forecasts	COM	1	Ch.5
Europa transport: observation of the transport markets – annual reports	COM	1	Ch.5
(*Transport Infrastructure Committee: Triannual report on the work of*)	COM	t	COM Doc. 1981–
(*Transport infrastructure: expenditure on and utilization of rail, road and inland waterway infrastructures*)	COM	1	COM Doc.
(*Railway undertakings: economic and financial situation*)	COM	b	COM Doc.
(*Railway undertakings: transposed annual accounts*)	COM	1	COM Doc.
(*Road transport: social legislation*)	COM	1	COM Doc.

Title	Institution	Frequency	Other information
Transport, communications, tourism; statistical yearbook	EUR	1	Ch.6
Carriage of goods: inland waterways	EUR	1	Ch.6 1985–
Carriage of goods: railways	EUR	1	Ch.6 1985–
Carriage of goods: roads	EUR	1	Ch.6 1986–

8. Competition

Title	Institution	Frequency	Other information
Report on competition	COM	1	Ch.4 + COM Doc.
Competition law in the EEC and in the ECSC	COM	i	Ch.5
(*Evolution of concentration and competition*)	COM	i	Ch.5 'Document', 1984–/DG IV
(*Community anti-dumping and anti-subsidy activities*)	COM	1	COM Doc.

9. Taxation

Title	Institution	Frequency	Other information
Inventory of taxes	COM	i	Ch.5 'Document'
The rates of value-added tax in agriculture	EUR	1	Ch.6 1984–

10. Economic and monetary policy and free movement of capital

Title	Institution	Frequency	Other information
(*Annual economic report*)	COM	1	COM Doc./European Economy
(*Annual economic review*)	COM	1	European Economy
(*Economic situation in the Community*)	COM	1	COM Doc.
(*Borrowing and lending activities of the Community*)	COM	1	COM Doc./European Economy
Report on the activities (Monetary Committee)	COM	1	Ch.5
Compendium of Community monetary texts	COM	i	Ch.5
Report on the activities (Economic Policy Committee)	COM	1	Ch.5 1986–
Economic Papers	COM	i	Ch.5 DG II
European economy	COM	4	Ch.5
European economy – Supplement A: Recent Economic Trends	COM	11	Ch.5

10. Economic and monetary policy and free movement of capital *Contd.*

Title	Institution	Frequency	Other information
European economy – Supplement B: Business and Consumer Survey Results	COM	11	Ch.5
Results of the business survey carried out among managements in the Community	COM	11	Ch.5
(Internal market: implementation of Commission White Paper on completing the internal market)	COM	1	COM Doc.
Balance of payments: geographical breakdown	EUR	1	Ch.6
Balance of payments: global data	EUR	1	Ch.6
Balance of payments: quarterly data	EUR	4	Ch.6
Consumer price index	EUR	12	Ch.6 1986–
ECU–EMS information	EUR	12	Ch.6 1987–
General government accounts and statistics	EUR	1	Ch.6
Money and finance	EUR	4	Ch.6 1984–
National accounts ESA – aggregates	EUR	1	Ch.6
National accounts ESA – detailed tables by branch	EUR	1	Ch.6
National accounts ESA – detailed tables by sector	EUR	1	Ch.6
National accounts ESA – input–output tables	EUR	i	Ch.6
National Methodologies of Balance of Payments	EUR	i	Ch.6 1983–
Quarterly national accounts ESA	EUR	4	Ch.6 1986–
Studies of national accounts	EUR	i	Ch.6 1983–

11. External relations

Title	Institution	Frequency	Other information
Collection of the agreements concluded by the European Communities	EC	1	Ch.1
(Association/cooperation agreements: compilation of texts)	COU	i	Ch.8
Agreements and other bilateral commitments linking the Communities with non-members countries	COM	2	Ch.5 DG I, 1981–
Multilateral conventions and agreements: signatures and/or conclusions by the European Communities	COM	i	Ch.5 'Document', 1987–
Practical guide to the use of the European Communities' scheme of generalized tariff preferences	COM	1	Ch.5
Corps diplomatique accrédité auprès des Communautés Européennes	COM	2	Ch.5
European Political Cooperation Documentation Bulletin	EUI	i	Ch.13 1987–

Title	Institution	Frequency	Other information
(*Community anti-dumping and anti-subsidy activities*)	COM	1	COM Doc.
Europe Information: External Relations	COM	i	Ch.5 DG X
Europe Information: Development	COM	i	Ch.5 DG X
ACP: basic statistics	EUR	1	Ch.6, 1981–
Analytical tables of foreign trade: SITC, CTCI, Rev. 2	EUR	1	Ch.6
External trade: analytical trade – NIMEXE	EUR	1	Ch.6
External trade: statistical yearbook	EUR	1	Ch.6 1985–
Foreign trade: third countries: statistical yearbook	EUR	i	Ch.6

12. Energy

Title	Institution	Frequency	Other information
The energy situation in the Community . . .	COM	1	Ch.5 COM Doc (–1984)
EUR Reports (energy)	COM	i	Ch.5
Energy in Europe	COM	3	Ch.5 1984–
Bulletin of energy prices	COM	1	Ch.5 1984–
ENTECH: newsletter of the EC non-nuclear R & D programme	COM	i	Ch.5 DG XII, 1986–
European Community demonstration projects for energy saving and alternative energy sources	COM	i	Ch.5 DG XVII
Annual report (Euratom Supply Agency)	COM	1	Ch.5 'Document'
EUR Reports (nuclear science and technology/radiation protection)	COM	i	Ch.5
(*Report on the application of Article 37 of the Euratom Treaty (disposal of radioactive waste)*)	COM	i	COM Doc., 1982–
(*Coal research programme*)	COM	1	COM Doc.
(*ECSC: financial report*)	COM	1	Ch.5 + Com Doc.
Investment in the Community coalmining and iron and steel industries (ECSC)	COM	1	Ch.5
Yearbook (Consultative Committee of the European Coal and Steel Community)	ECSC	1	Ch.13 ECSC
Handbook (Consultative Committee of the European Coal and Steel Community)	ECSC	i	Ch.13 ECSC
EUR Reports (technical coal research)	COM	i	Ch.5
Electricity prices	EUR	1	Ch.6
Energy: monthly statistics	EUR	12	Ch.6 1986–
Energy: statistical yearbook	EUR	1	Ch.6
Gas prices	EUR	1	Ch.6
Operation of nuclear power stations	EUR	1	Ch.6
Rapid reports: Energy	EUR	i	Ch.6

13. Industrial policy and internal market

Title	Institution	Frequency	Other information
(*Internal market: implementation of Commission White Paper on completing the internal market*)	COM	1	COM Doc., 1986–
European economy	COM	4	Ch.5
European economy: Supplement A – Recent Economic Trends	COM	11	Ch.5
European economy: supplement B – business and consumer survey results	COM	11	Ch.5
Results of the business survey carried out among managements in the Community	COM	11	Ch.5
Newsletter: new technologies and innovation policy	COM	i	Ch.5
Catalogue of Community legal acts and other legal texts relating to the elimination of technical barriers to trade for industrial products; nomenclature for iron and steel products (EURONORM)	COM	i	Ch.5 'Document'
EUR Reports (industrial processes)	COM	i	Ch.5
(*Report, on realization of the objectives of the Community action programme for small and medium-sized enterprises*)	COM	i	COM Doc., 1987
Operations of the European Community concerning small and medium-sized enterprises: practical handbook	COM	i	Ch.5
EURO-info	COM	i	Ch.5 DG XXIII
(*ECSC: levy rate/operating budget proposals*)	COM	1	COM Doc.
(*ECSC: financial report*)	COM	1	Ch.5 + COM Doc.
Investment in the Community coalmining and iron and steel industries	COM	1	Ch.5
(*Steel industry: application of the rules on aid*)	COM	1	COM Doc., 1981–
(*Steel industry: general objectives*)	COM	1	COM Doc., 1983–
(*Iron and steel research programme*)	COM	1	COM Doc.
Information bulletin of the Steel Industry Safety and Health Commission	COM	i	Ch.5 DG XIII, 1982–
Yearbook (Consultative Committee of the European Coal and Steel Community)	ECSC	1	Ch.13 ECSC
Handbook (Consultative Committee of the European Coal and Steel Community)	ECSC	i	Ch.13 ECSC
(*Shipbuilding: report on state of industry*)	COM	1	COM Doc.
Annual investments in fixed assets in the industrial enterprises of the EC	EUR	1	Ch.6 –1985
Industrial production: quarterly statistics	EUR	4	Ch.6 1982–
Industrial trends: monthly statistics	EUR	12	Ch.6
Industry: statistical yearbook	EUR	1	Ch.6 1984–
Iron and steel	EUR	12	Ch.6
Iron and steel: quarterly statistics	EUR	4	Ch.6
Iron and steel: statistical yearbook	EUR	1	Ch.6

Title	Institution	Frequency	Other information
Rapid reports: industry	EUR	i	Ch.6 1987–
Raw materials: EC supply	EUR	1	Ch.6 1981–
Regions: the Community's financial participation in investments	EUR	1	Ch.6
Structure and activity of industry: annual inquiry, main results	EUR	1	Ch.6
Structure and activity of industry: data by size of enterprises	EUR	1	Ch.6

14. Regional policy

Title	Institution	Frequency	Other information
(*The regions of Europe: periodic report*)	COM	t	Ch.5 COM Doc./'Document'
(*European Regional Development Fund: annual report*)	COM	1	Ch.5 COM Doc./'Document'
(*Regional development programmes*)	COM	i	Ch.5 'Document'
ERDF in figures	COM	1	Ch.5 DG XVI, 1983–
Finance from Europe: a guide to grants and loans from the European Community	COM	i	Ch.7 Commission: London 1982–
Rapid reports: regions	EUR	i	Ch.6 1985–
Regional account ESA: detailed tables by branches	EUR	1	Ch.6
Regions: statistical yearbook	EUR	1	Ch.6
Regions: the Community's financial participation in investments	EUR	1	Ch.6

15. Environment and consumers

Title	Institution	Frequency	Other information
(*The state of the environment*)	COM	i	Ch.5 EUR Report
(*Environmental action programme*)	COM	i	Ch.5 COM Doc./OJ
EUR Reports (environment and quality of life)	COM	i	Ch.5
Annual report (European Foundation for the Improvement of Living and Working Conditions	EF	1	Ch.13 EF
Programme of work (European Foundation . . .)	EF	1	Ch.13 EF
Four-year rolling programme of the European Foundation	EF	i	Ch.13 EF
(*Research reports*) (European Foundation . . .)	EF	i	Ch.13

15. Environment and consumers *Contd*

Title	Institution	Frequency	Other information
(*Consolidated reports*) (European Foundation . . .)	EF	i	Ch.13
Working Paper Series (European Foundation . . .)	EF	i	Ch.13 EF 1987–
Information Booklet Series (European Foundation . . .)	EF	i	Ch.13 1985–
EF news	EF	5	Ch.13 EF 1986–
(*Convention on international trade in endangered species of wild fauna and flora: annual report*)	COM	1	Ch.5 'Document'
(*Implementation of directive on air quality limit value and guide values for sulphur dioxide and suspended particulates*)	COM	1	COM Doc., 1985–
Consumer price index	EUR	12	Ch.6 1986–
Trends in distributive trades: retail sales: registration of cars	EUR	12	Ch.6 1987–

16. Scientific and technical research

Title	Institution	Frequency	Other information
EUR Reports	COM	i	Ch.5
Euro Abstracts	COM	12	Ch.3
Government financing of research and development	EUR	1	Ch.6
European Communities: information: R & D	COM	i	Ch.5 DG XII
Newsletter: new technologies and innovation policy	COM	i	Ch.5 DG XIII
Information market (I'M)	COM	4	Ch.5 DG XIII
ENTECH: newsletter of the EC non-nuclear R & D programme	COM	i	Ch.5 DG XII, 1986–
Annual report (Joint Research Centre)	JRC	1	Ch.5 DG XII/JRC., 1986–
Publications bulletin (Joint Research Centre)	JRC	1	Ch.3 JRC., 1981–
(*CADDIA: Cooperation in Automation of Data and Documentation for Imports/Exports and Agriculture*)	COM	1	COM Doc.
(*Coal research programme*)	COM	1	COM Doc.
(*CIDST: Committee for Information and Documentation on Science and Technology – report*)	COM	i	EUR Report
COST projects. Collected agreements concluded within the framework of European cooperation in the field of scientific and technical research	COU	i	Ch.8 1983–
(*Data processing: report on the multi-annual programme*)	COM	1	COM Doc., 1987–

Title	Institution	Frequency	Other information
(*EUROTRA: Machine translation programme – report*)	COM	1	COM Doc., 1986–
FAST: Occasional Papers	COM	i	Ch.5 DG XII
(*Iron and steel research programme*)	COM	1	COM Doc.
(*MEL programme: microelectronics technology: Community action*)	COM	1	COM Doc., 1983–1987
(*SPRINT: Innovation and technology transfer programme – annual progress report*)	COM	1	COM Doc.,/ Newsletter: New Technologies and Innovation Policy, 1985–

17. Education, culture

Title	Institution	Frequency	Other information
European educational policy statements	COU	i	Ch.8 1983–
Higher education in the European Community – student handbook	COM	i	Ch.5
Directory of higher education institutions	COM	i	Ch.5 1984–
University research on European integration	COM	i	Ch.5
Academic year . . . (European University Institute)	EUI	1	Ch.13 EUI
Report of activities (European University Institute)	EUI	1	Ch.13 EUI
European university news	COM	6	Ch.5
Summer courses on European integration	COM	1	Ch.5
Postgraduate degrees in European integration	COM	i	Ch.5
(*ERASMUS programme: annual report*)	COM	1	COM Doc., 1988–
ERASMUS newsletter (formerly DELTA: The Joint Study Newsletter of the Commission, 1983–1987)	COM	i	Ch.5
Annual report (European Centre for the Development of Vocational Training)	CED	1	Ch.13 CEDEFOP
Vocational training	CED	3	Ch.13
CEDEFOP news	CED	4	Ch.13
CEDEFOP flash	CED	i	Ch.13 1984– CEDEFOP
Contact bulletin (European Bureau for Lesser Used Languages)	LAN	i	Ch.13 1983– BUR
Terminologie et traduction	COM	2–3	Ch.5 1985–
Education and training	EUR	i	Ch.6
Youth opinion	YF	i	Ch.13 YF 1982–

18. Tertiary sector, right of establishment and freedom of services

Title	Institution	Frequency	Other information
(*Internal Market: implementation of Commission White Paper on completing the internal market*)	COM	1	COM Doc., 1986–

19. Development and cooperation

Title	Institution	Frequency	Other information
(*ACP-EEC conventions of Lomé: compilation of texts*)	COU	i	Ch.8
Annual report of the ACP-EEC Council of Ministers	COU	1	Ch.8 1981–
Agreements and other bilateral commitments linking the Communities with non-member countries	COM	2	Ch.5 DG I., 1981–
Multilateral conventions and agreements: signatures and/or conclusions by the European Communities	COM	i	Ch.5 'Document', 1987–
Practical guide to the use of the European Communities scheme of generalized tariff preferences	COM	1	Ch.5
(*Generalized scheme of preferences (GSP): annual proposals*)	COM	1	COM Doc.
Collection of the agreements concluded by the European Communities	EC	1	Ch.1
(*European Development Funds: balance sheets and accounts*)	COM	1	COM Doc.
(*European Development Funds: results of invitations to tender*)	COM	1	COM Doc.
(*European Development Funds: estimate of contributions required to meet expenditure*)	COM	1	COM Doc.
(*Non-governmental organizations (NGOs): Community cooperation with NGOs in the development field*)	COM	1	COM Doc.
(*Financial and technical assistance to non-associated developing countries (NADCs)*)	COM	1	COM Doc.
The Courier	COM	6	Ch.5 DG VIII
Europe information: external relations	COM	i	Ch.5 DG X
Europe information: development	COM	i	Ch.5 DG X
ACP: basic statistics	EUR	1	Ch.6 1981–
Foreign trade: third countries: statistical yearbook	EUR	i	Ch.6
Reports on ACP countries	EUR	i	Ch.6 1988–

20. Statistics

Title	Institution	Frequency	Other information
Eurostat news	EUR	4	Ch.6

For other statistical titles see under headings 1–19

21. Documentation

Title	Institution	Frequency	Other information
(*Official Journal of the European Communities: Index*)	EC	12 + 1	Ch.1
Directory of Community Legislation in Force . . .	EC	2	Ch.1
Documents (*Catalogue of documents*)	OOP	12 + 1	Ch.3, 1985–
Publications of the European Communities (*Catalogue of Publications*)	OOP	4 + 1	Ch.3
The European Community as a publisher	OOP	1	Ch.3
Agreements and other bilateral commitments linking the Communities with non-member countries	COM	2	Ch.5 DG I, 1981–
(*List of pending proposals*)	COM	2	Ch.1 COM Doc.
Multilateral conventions and agreements: signatures and/or conclusions by the European Communities	COM	i	Ch.5 'Document'
University research on European integration	COM	i	Ch.5
SCAD bulletin	COM	52	Ch.3
SCAD Bibliographies	COM	i	Ch.3
SCAD Bibliographic File	COM	i	Ch.3
SCAD news	COM	12	Ch.3 1984–
Publications and documents of the EC received by the Library	COM	1	Ch.3
Recent publications on the European Communities received by the Library	COM	12 + 1	Ch.3
Recent publications on the European Communities received by the Library: supplement	COM	i	Ch.3
Euro Abstracts (*Section I* and *II*)	COM	12	Ch.3
Catalogue – EUR documents	COM	i	Ch.3
Publications bulletin (Joint Research Centre)	JRC	1	Ch.3
List of acquisitions	COU	4	Ch.8
Selected articles	COU	4	Ch.8
The European Parliament: bibliography	EP	1	Ch.9 DG IV
Bibliographie Juridique de l'Intégration Européenne/Legal bibliography of European integration	ECJ	1	Ch. 11 ECJ 1981–
Notes	ECJ	i	Ch.11 ECJ

22. Miscellaneous

Title	Institution	Frequency	Other information
(*European Communities glossary*)	COU	i	Ch.8
Terminologie et traduction	COM	2–3	Ch.5 1985–

APPENDIX 2

EC online services

Below is a list of EC databases/databanks available to the public, with addresses for further information.

Type: B: Bibliographical F: Factual S: Statistical

Database	Contents	Type	Host
AGREP	Inventory of current agricultural research projects in the European Community	F	Datacentralen
BROKERSGUIDE	Inventory of information brokers	F	ECHO
CELEX*	European Community law/legislation	B/F	Eurobases
COMEXT	EC external trade statistics	S	WEFA–CEIS
CRONOS	EC statistics	S	Datacentralen/ GSI-ECO/ CISI–Wharton
DIANEGUIDE	Guide to European database producers, hosts, databases and databanks	F	ECHO
EABS	References to the published results of scientific and technical research programmes	B	ECHO
ECDIN	Environmental data and information network on chemicals	F	Datacentralen
ECU	Daily ECU exchange rates	F	ECHO
ENDOC	Directory of environmental information and documentation centres	F	ECHO
ENREP	Directory of environmental research projects (linked to ENDOC)	F	ECHO
EURISTOTE	Directory of academic research on European integration	B	ECHO
EURODICAUTOM	Terminological databank of scientific and technical terms in all EC languages	F	ECHO
IES	Inventory of publicly funded IT R & D projects, research sites and electronic mail addresses	F	ECHO
INFO 92	EC 1992 information	B	Eurobases
MEDREP	Inventory of biomedical and health care research projects	F	ECHO
PABLI*	Monitor of EC development projects	F	ECHO
REGIO	EC regional statistics	S	WEFA–CEIS
SCAD*	EC documentation + non-EC periodical articles	B	Eurobases

Database	Contents	Type	Host
SESAME	Hydrocarbon technology and energy demonstration projects	F	Datacentralen
SIGLE	European grey literature	B	BLAISE
TED*	Calls for tenders for public contracts (Works and supplies)	F	ECHO
THESAURI	Inventory of structured vocabulary	F	ECHO

*CELEX

CELEX (Communitatis Europeae Lex) was created in 1969 and became operational in 1971. It is a bibliographical and factual database to the law and legislation of the European Communities produced by the institutions of the EC. It was created primarily for the officials of the EC but has been made progressively available to the public. For the public it is basically a bibliographical database and is available in French, English, German, Dutch and Italian versions, with other language versions in preparation.

CELEX is a single database from a retrieval point of view but it is possible to break the database down into files and sectors:

The legislative file

Sector 1 Treaties establishing the EC, and amending and supplementary treaties
Sector 2 Legislation arising from the external relations of the EC
Sector 3 Secondary legislation
Sector 4 Complementary legislation.

The case-law file

Sector 6 Judgments of the Court of Justice and Opinions of the Advocates-General.

The preparatory documents file

Sector 5 Commission proposals, resolutions of the European Parliament and opinions of the Economic and Social Committee and the Court of Justice
Sector 9 European Parliament written and oral questions.

Other sectors not publicly available

Sector 7 National measures to implement EC legislation
Sector 8 Decisions of national courts relating to Community law
Sector 10 Published works on Community law from a legal perspective.

The primary host for CELEX is Eurobases; CELEX is also available through other hosts in the member states. The United Kingdom host is Context (Context Ltd, Assets House, Elverton Street, London SW1P 2QG; Telephone: 01 828 2355). For the addresses of the other hosts contact Eurobases at the address given on p. 302.

SCAD

Further details of the coverage of the SCAD database can be found in Chapter 3 under the description of its print manifestation *SCAD Bulletin*.

PABLI/TED

For these two databases users can subscribe to a telex service in which the customer will regularly receive information newly added to the database according to previously designated customer profiles.

EUROPEAN PARLIAMENT DATABASES

At present the following European Parliament databases are not publicly available – but some may become publicly available in the future. SYSDOC is the name given to the European Parliament document system programme, which comprises the databases PEGASE, MIDAS and EPoque. EPoque stands for European Parliament OnLine Query System, consisting of EP Reports, debates, questions and other EP information. MIDAS stands for Management Information Dissemination Administrative System. PEGASE is the library catalogue of the European Parliament.

FURTHER INFORMATION

The periodical *I'M* (see DG XIII in Chapter 5) publishes details on new EC databases as well as other information on the information market in Europe. *ECHO News* gives news on the databases and activities of ECHO (European Community Host Organization).

Good brief introductions to the EC databases, as available in 1987, can be found in two publications from the Commission Offices in Washington and Tokyo:

1. On line to Europe: a guide to EC databases, by Elizabeth Hardt, *Europe*, no. 270, October 1987, pp. 21–27
2. *Information technology at your service (how to use EC on-line systems)*, by Giancarlo Pau, INFO/3/1987 Commission: Press and Information Service of the EC Delegation, Tokyo, 1987.

USEFUL ADDRESSES

ECHO Customer Services
BP 2373
L-1023 Luxembourg
Telephone 352 488041
Telex: 2181 eurol lu

European Information Market
  Development Group
177 route d'Esch
L-1471 Luxembourg
Telephone: 352 488041
Telex: 2181 eurol lu
Telefax: 352 488040

Blaise-Line
The British Library
Bibliographic Services Division
2 Sheraton Street
London W1V 4BH
England
Telephone: 01 3237078
Telex: 21462

Eurobases
Commission of the European
  Communities
ARL 03/04
200 rue de la Loi
B-1049 Brussels
Belgium
Telephone: 32 235 0001

Datacentralen
6–8 Retortvej
DK-2500 Valby
Denmark
Telephone: (45) 1 468122
Telex: 27122 dc dk

Eurostat
Bâtiment Jean Monnet
Plateau du Kirchberg
L-2920 Luxembourg
Telephone: (352) 4301 3526
Telex: Comeur lu 3423

GSI-ECO
45 rue de la Procession
F-75015 Paris
France
Telephone: (33) 14 566 7889
Telex: 613163 f

WEFA–CEIS
25 rue de Ponthieu
F-75008 Paris
France
Telephone: (33) 14 563 1910
Telex: 260710 F

EC Information Offices/External Delegations

INFORMATION OFFICES

Information Offices in the member states maintain Information Units which contain substantial documentation collections and provide a general information service. Similar units exist in the offices of the External Delegations, although their size and services offered will often be limited. These Offices are not generally sales agents for EC documentation but will give advice on how to obtain such documentation. Certain free titles and publications issued by the Offices themselves are available from these sources.

Belgium

73 rue Archimède, B-1040 Bruxelles
Archimedesstraat 73, B-1040 Brussel
Telephone: 235 11 11
Telex: 26657 COMINF B
Telecopy: 235 01 66

Denmark

Højbrohus
Ostergade 61
Postbox 144
DK-1004 København K
Telephone: 14 41 40
Telex: 16402 COMEUR DK
Telecopy: 11 12 03

France

61 rue des Belles-Feuilles
F-75782 Paris Cedex 16
Telephone: 45 01 58 85

Telex: Paris 611019 F COMEUR
Telecopy: 47 27 26 07

CMCI/Bureau 320
2 rue Henri Barbusse
F-13241 Marseille CEDEX 01
Telephone: 91 46 00
Telex: 402 538 EURMA
Telecopy: 90 98 07

Federal Republic of Germany

22 Zitelmannstrasse
D-5300 Bonn
Telephone: 23 80 41
Telex: 886648 EUROP D
Telecopy: 23 80 48

Kurfürstendamm 102
D-1000 Berlin 31

Telephone: 892 40 28
Telex: 184015 EUROP D
Telecopy: 892 20 59

Erhardtstrass 27
D-8000 München
Telephone: 202 10 11
Telex: 52 18 135
Telecopy: 202 10 15

Greece

2 Vassilissis Sofias
PO Box 11002
Athina 10674
Telephone: 724 39 82
Telex: 219324 ECAT GR
Telecopy: 722 37 15

Ireland

39 Molesworth Street
Dublin 2
Telephone: 71 22 44
Telex: 93 827 EUCO EI
Telecopy: 71 26 57

Italy

Via Poli 29
I-00187 Roma
Telephone: 678 97 22
Telex: 610184 EUROMA I
Telecopy: 679 16 58

Corso Magenta 61
I-20123 Milano
Telephone: 80 15 05/6/7/8
Telex: 316002 EURMIL I
Telecopy: 481 85 43

Luxembourg

Bâtiment Jean Monnet
rue Alcide De Gasperi
L-2920 Luxembourg
Telephone: 430 11

Telex: 3423/3446/3476
 COMEUR LU
Telecopy: 4301 4433

The Netherlands

Lange Voorhout 29
Den Haag
Telephone: 46 93 26
Telex: 31094 EURCO NL
Telecopy: 64 66 19

Portugal

Centre Européen Jean Monnet
56 Rua do Salitre
D-1200 Lisboa
Telephone: 154 11 44
Telex: 0404/18810
 COMEUR P
Telecopy 155 43 97

Spain

Calle de Serrano 41
5a planta
Madrid 1
Telephone: 435 17 00/435 15 28
Telex: 46818 OIPE E
Telecopy 276 03.87

United Kingdom

8 Storey's Gate
London SW1P 3AT
Telephone: 01 222 8122
Telex: 23208 EURUK G
Telecopy: 01 222 0900

Windsor House
9–15 Bedford Street
Belfast BT2 7EG
Telephone: 0232 24 07 08
Telex: 74117 CECBEL G
Telecopy: 24 82 41

4 Cathedral Road
Cardiff CF1 9SG
Telephone: 0222 37 16 31
Telex: 497727 EUROPA G
Telecopy 39 54 89

7 Alva Street
Edinburgh EH2 4PH
Telephone: 031 225 2058
Telex: 727420 EUEDING
Telecopy: 26 41 05

EXTERNAL DELEGATIONS

To countries outside the EC

Algeria

36 rue Arezki Abri
Hydra
16300 Alger
Telephone:
    59 08 22/59 09 25/59 09 42
Telex: 66067 EURAL DZ
Telecopy: 59 39 47

Angola

Rua Rainha Jinga 6
Caixa Postal 2669
Luanda
Telephone:
    39 30 38/39 12 77/39 13 39
Telex: (provisional) 3397
    PROQUIM AN

Antigua and Barbuda

2nd Floor, Alpha Building
Redcliffe Street
St John's
PO Box 1392
Telephone/Telecopy: 462 29 70

Australia

Capitol Centre
Franklin Street
PO Box 609
Manuka, ACT 2603
Canberra
Telephone: 95 50 00
Telex: AA 62762 EURCOM
Telecopy: 95 37 12

Austria

5 Hoyosgasse
1040 Vienna (Wien)
Telephone:
    65 33 79/65 34 91/65 73
    35/65 74 52
Telex: 133152 EUROPA A
Telecopy: 65 18 08

Bangladesh

Dacca Office
House CES (E) 19
Road 128, Gulshan
Dacca 12
Telephone: 60 70 16/41 18 41
Telex: 642501 CECO-BJ

Barbados

Sunset House, Fairchild Street
PO Box 654 C
Bridgetown
Telephone: 427 43 62/429 71 03
Telex: 2327 DELEGFED WG
Telecopy: 427 86 87

Belize

85 Bella Vista
Belize City
Telephone: 453 65
Telex: 106 CEC-BZ

305

Benin

Avenue Roume, Bâtiment
　Administratif
BP 910
Cotonou

Telephone: 31 26 84/31 26 17
Telex: 5257 DELEGFED-
　COTONOU

Botswana

Plot 68
North Ring Road
PO Box 1253
Gaborone

Telephone: 44 55
Telex: 2403 DECEC BD
　GABORONE

Brazil

QI 7
Bloc A, Lago Sul
Brasilia, DF

Telephone: 248 31 22
Telex: 612 517 DCCE BRE
Telecopy: 248 07 00

Burkina Faso

BP 352
Quagadougou

Telephone:
　30 73 85/30 73 86/33 55 22
Telex: DELCOMEU 5242 BF

Burundi

Avenue du 13 Octobre
BP 103
Bujumbura

Telephone: 34 26/38 92/59 30
Telex: 5031 FED BDI-
　BUJUMBURA

Cameroon

Quartier BASTOS
BP 847
Yaoundé

Telephone:
　22 13 87/22 33 67/22 21 49
Telex: 8298 DELEGFED KN-
　YAOUNDÉ
Telefax: 23 00 28

Canada

Office Tower
Suite 1110
350 Sparks Street
Ottawa, Ontario K1R 7S8

Telephone: 238 64 64
Telex: 0534544 EURCOM
　OTT
Telecopy: 238 51 91

Cape Verde

Prédio 'Galerias'
4o andat, apartamento D
CP 122
Praia

Telephone: 61 37 50/61 15 68
Telex: 6071 DELCE CV

Central African
Republic

Rue de Flandre
BP 1298
Bangui

Telephone: 61 30 53/61 01 13
Telex: 5231 DELCOMEU RC-
　BANGUI

Chad

Concession Caisse COTON
Route de Farcha
BP 552
N'Djamena

Telephone:
51 59 77/51 22 76
Telex: DELEGFED 5245 KD
N'DJAMENA TCHAD

Chile

1835 Avenida Américo
Vespucio
Santiago 9
Postal address: Casilla 10093
Telephone: 228 24 84/228 28 98
Telex: 340344 COMEUR CK
Telecopy: 228 25 71

China

Ta Yuan Diplomatic Offices
Building
Entrance No 2, 6th floor,
Apt. No 1
Liang Ma He Nan Lu 14
Beijing
Telephone: 532 44 43
Telecopy: 532 43 42

Comoros

BP 559
Moroni
Telephone: 73 19 81/73 03 06
Telex: 212 DELCEC KO

Congo

Avenue Lyautey (face à
l'ambassade d'Italie près de
l'hôtel Méridien)
BP 2149
Brazzaville
Telephone: 83 38 78/83 37 00
Telex: 5257 KG DELEFED-
BRAZZAVILLE

Costa Rica

Centro Calon
Apartado 836
1007 San José

Telephone: 33 27 55
Telex: 3482 CCE LUX
Telecopy: 21 08 93

Djibouti

11 boulevard du Maréchal
Joffre
BP 2477
Djibouti
Telephone: 35 26 15
Telex: 5894 DELCOM DJ

Egypt

6 rue Ibn Zanki
Zamalek Cairo
Telephone:
341 93 93/340 31 32/340
83 88
Telex: 94258 EUROP
UN-CAIRO
Telecopy: 340 03 85

Equatorial Guinea

BP 779
Malabo
Telephone: 2944/2945
Telex: 91 31 04 GE

Ethiopia

Tedla Desta Building, 1st Floor
Africa Avenue (Bole Road)
PO Box 5570
Addis Ababa
Telephone:
15 25 11/15 20 92/15 22
18/15 22 52/15 26 72
Telex: 21135 DELEGEUR-
ADDIS ABABA

Gabon

Quartier Batterie IV
Lotissement des Cocotiers
BP 321
Libreville

Telephone: 73 22 50
Telex: DELEGFED 5511 GO-
LIBREVILLE

Gambia

10 Cameron Street
PO Box 512
Banjul
Telephone:
277 77/287 69/268 60
Telex: DELCOM GV
2233-BANJUL

Ghana

PO Box 9505, Kotoka Airport
Accra
65 The Round House
Cantonments Road
Cantonments, Accra
Telephone:
77 42 01/77 42 02/77 49 04
Telex: 2069 DELCOM-
ACCRA

Grenada

PO Box 5
St George's Old Fort
St George's
Telephone: 440 35 61
Telex: 3431 CWBUR GA
Telecopy: 440 21 23 (Attention:
EEC Delegation)

Guinea Bissau

29 Rua Eduardo Mandlane
Caixa Postal 359
Bissau
Telephone: 21 33 60/21 28 78
Telex: 264 DELCOM-BI

Guinea Conakry

BP 730 Conakry
Corniche Sud, Madina
Dispensaire
Conakry

Telephone: 46 13 25/46 13 82
Telex: 22479 German Embassy
(Attention: EEC Delegation)

Guyana

64B Middle Street, South
Cummingsburg
PO Box 10847
Georgetown
Telephone:
626 15/640 04/654 24/639 63
Telex: 2258 DELEG GY

India

YMCA
Cultural Center Building
Jai Singh Road
New Delhi 110001
Telephone: 34 42 22/35 04 30
Telex: 31 61 315

Indonesia

Wisma Dharmala Sakti
Building, 16th floor
32 Jl, Jendral Sudirman
PO Box 55 JKPDS
Jakarta 10220
Telephone:
578 00 81/578 01 81/578
01 59
Telex: 62043 COMEUR IA
Telecopy: 578 00 72

Israel

'The Tower'
3 Daniel Frisch Street
Tel Aviv 64731
Telephone: 26 41 60,
26 41 66/7/8/9
Telex: 342 108 DELEG IL
Telecopy: 25 19 83

Ivory Coast

Immeuble 'Azur'
18 Boulevard Crozet
01 BP 1821
Abidjan 01
Telephone: 32 24 28/33 29 28
Telex: DELCE CI 23729
Telecopy: 32 40 89

Jamaica

Mutual Life Center, 2nd Floor
Oxford Rd/Old Hope Rd
PO Box 435, Kingston 5
  (Jamaica WI)
Telephone: 930 30/31/32
Telex: 2391 DELEGEC
  KINGSTON 5

Japan

Europa House
9–15 Sanbancho
Chiyoda-Ku
Tokyo 102
Telephone: 239 04 41
Telex: 28567 COMEUTOK J
    2325230 EURDOCG
  Domicile
Telecopy: 261 51 94

Jordan

Shmeisani-Wadi Sagra Circle
PO Box 926794
Amman
Telephone: 66 81 91/66 81 92
Telex: 22260 DELEUR JO
Telecopy: 68 67 46

Kenya

National Bank Building
Harambee Avenue
PO Box 45119
Nairobi
Telephone: 33 35 92
Telex: 22302 DELEUR KE
Telecopy: 72 55 03

Lebanon

Immeuble Duraffourd
Avenue de Paris
BP 11–4008
Beyrouth
Telephone:
  136 30 30/136 30 31/136
  30 32
Telex: DELEUR 23307-LE
  BEYROUTH

Lesotho

PO Box MS 518
Maseru 100, Lesotho
Telephone: 313 726
Telex: 4351 DELEGEUR LO
  MASERU

Liberia

34 Payne Avenue, Sinkor
PO Box 3049
Monrovia
Telephone: 26 22 78/26 26 87
Telex: 44358 DELEGFED LI-
  MONROVIA

Madagascar

Immeuble Ny Havana-67
  hectares
BP 746
Antananarivo
Telephone: 242 16/275 27
Telex: 22327 DELFED MG-
  ANTANANARIVO
Telecopy: 321 69

Malawi

Lingadzi House
PO Box 30102, Capital City
Lilongwe 3

Telephone:
 302 55/301 73/305 93
Telex: 4260 DELEGEUR MI-
 LILONGWE

Mali

Rue Guégau–Badalabougou
BP 115 Bamako
Telephone: 22 23 56/22 20 65
Telex: 2526 DELEGFED-
 BAMAKO
Telecopy: 22 36 70

Mauritania

Ilot V, Lot no. 24
BP 213
Nouakchott
Telephone: 527 24/527 32
Telex: 549 DELEG MTN-
 NOUAKCHOTT

Mauritius

61/63 route Floreal 'La
 Mauvraie' Vacoas
PO Box 10
Vacoas
Telephone: 50 61/50 62/50 63
Telex: 4282 DELCEC IW
 VACOAS
Telecopy: 6318

Morocco

4 Zankat Jaafar As Saadik
BP 1302
Rabat Agdal
Telephone: 742 95/739 15
Telex: 32620-RABAT
Telecopy: 798 00

Mozambique

1214 Avenida do Zimbabwe
CP 1306
Maputo

Telephone:
 44 73/40 92/40 93/40 94/18 66
Telex: 6–146 CCE MO

Netherlands Antilles

Mgr Kieckensweg 24
PO Box 822
Willemstad
Curaçao
Telephone: 62 50 84/62 64 33
Telex: 1089 DELEG NA-
 WILLEMSTAD
Telecopy: 962 32 81

Niger

BP 10388
Niamey
Telephone:
 73 23 60/73 27 73/73 48 32
Telex: 5267 NI DELEGFED-
 NIAMEY
Telecopy: 73 23 22

Nigeria

4 Idowu Taylor Street
Victoria Island
PM Bag 12767
Lagos
Telephone:
 61 78 52/61 72 40/61 08 57
Telex: 21868 DELCOM NG-
 LAGOS
Telecopy: 61 72 48

Norway

Haakon's VII Gate No 6
Oslo
Telephone: 33 10 40
Telecopy: 41 54 24

Pacific (Fiji)

Dominion House, 3rd Floor
Private Mail Bag, GPO
Suva
Fiji

Telephone: 31 36 33
Telex: 2311 DELECOM FJ-
  SUVA
Telecopy: 30 03 70

Pakistan

House No 8
Margalla Road
F6/3
Islamabad
Telephone: 82 18 28/82 26 04
Telex: 54044 COMEU PK
Telecopy: 82 26 04

Papua New Guinea

9th Floor
Pacific View Apartments, Lot 1,
  Section 84
Pruth Street, 3 Mile Hill,
  Korobosea
PO Box 1264
Boroko–Port Moresby
Telephone: 253 07
Telex: NE 22307 DELEUR
(Papua New Guinea)
Telecopy: 21 78 50

Rwanda

14 Avenue du Député
  Kamuzinzi
BP 515
Kigali
Telephone: 755 86/755 89
Telex: 515 DELCOMEUR
  RW-KIGALI

São Tomé and Principe

Boite postale 132
São Tomé
Telephone: 217 80
Telex: 224

Senegal

57 Avenue Pompidou (2e étage)
BP 3345
Dakar
Telephone:
  (221) 21 13 24/21 57 77/21
  79 75
Telex: 21665 DELEGSE-
  DAKAR
Telecopy: 21 78 85

Seychelles

PO Box 530
Victoria Mahé
Telephone: 239 40
Telex: 2213 DELCOM SZ

Sierra Leone

Wesley House
4 George Street
PO Box 1399
Freetown
Telephone: 239 75/230 25
Telex: 3203 DELFED SL-
  FREETOWN

Solomon Islands

NPF Plaza
PO Box 844
Honiaria
Telephone: 227 65/234 07
Telex: 66370 DELEG SI
Telecopy: 23318 (Telex
  DELEG SI)

Somalia

Via Makka Al Mukarram
  no. Z-A6/17
PO Box 943
Mogadiscio
Telephone:
  811 18/211 18/210 49
Telex: 628 EURCOM-SO

Sudan

No 11 Street 13, New
   Extension
PO Box 2363
Khartoum
Telephone:
   444 85/445 10/449 10/412 43
Telex: 24054 DELSU SD-
   KHARTOUM, SUDAN

Suriname

239 Dr S. Redmondstraat
PO Box 484
Paramaribo
Telephone: 993 22
Telex: 192 DELEGFED SN-
   PARAMARIBO

Swaziland

Dhlan'ubeka Building
3rd floor
Corner Walker and Tin Streets
PO Box A, 36
Mbabane
Telephone: 429 08/420 18
Telex: 2133 WD MBABANE

Switzerland

Case postale 195
37–39 rue de Vermont
CH-1211 Genève 20
Telephone: 34 97 50
Telex: 28261 or 28262 ECOM
   CH
Telecopy 34 23 31

Syria

73 rue Al Rachid
BP 11269
Damascus
Telephone: 24 76 40/24 76 41
Telex: DELCOM-SY 412919

Tanzania

Extelcoms House, 9th Floor
Samora Avenue
PO Box 9514
Dar es Salaam
Telephone:
   311 51/311 52/311 53
Telex: 41353 DELCOMEUR-
   DAR ES SALAAM
Telecopy: 385 75

Thailand

Thai Military Bank Bldg, 9th
   and 10th floors
34 Phya Thai Road
Bangkok
Telephone: 246 00 22
Telex: 086/82 764 COMEUBK
   TH
Telecopy: 246 10 54

Togo

Avenue Nicolas Grunitsky
BP 1657
Lomé
Telephone:
   21 36 62/21 08 32/21 77 45
Telex: 5267 DELFED TG-
   LOMÉ
Telecopy: 21 13 00

Tonga

Maila Taha
Taufa'ahau Road
Nuku-Alofa
Telephone: 21 820
Telex: 66207 DELCEC TS

Trinidad and Tobago

2 Champs Elysées
Long Circular
Maraval
PO Box 1144
Port of Spain

Telephone: 622 66 28/622 05 91
Telex: 22421 DELFED WG
  PORT OF SPAIN

Tunisia

avenue Jugurtha 21
BP 3
Bevédère–Tunis
Telephone: 78 86 00
Telex: 13596-TUNIS
Telecopy: 78 82 01

Turkey

Kuleli Sokak 15
Gazi Osman Pasa
Ankara
Telephone: 37 68 40/41/42/43
Telex: 44320 ATBE TR
Telecopy: 37 79 40

Uganda

Uganda Commercial Bank
  Building, Plot 12
Kampala Road, 5th Floor
PO Box 5244
Kampala
Telephone:
  23 33 03/23 33 04/24 27
  01/23 37 08
Telex: 61139 DELEGFED-
  UGA-KAMPALA
Telecopy: 23 37 08

United States

2100 M Street, NW (7th floor)
Washington, DC 20037
Telephone:
  862 9500/862 9501/862 9502
Telex: 64215 EURCOM UW
Telecopy: 429 17 66
44 Montgomery Street
Suite 2715
San Francisco, CA 94104

3 Dag Hammarskjöld Plaza
305 East 47th Street
New York, NY 10017
Telephone: 371 3804
Telex: EURCOM NY 012396
  EURCOM NY 661100
  EURCOM NY 668513
Telecopy: 758 27 18

Vanuatu

Pilioko House
1st Floor
Kumul Highway
PO Box 422
Port-Vila
Telephone: 25 01
Telex: 1093 DELCOM NH
Telecopy: 32 82

Venezuela

Calle Orinoco
Las Mercedes
Apartado 67076
Las Americas 1061A
Caracas
Telephone: 91 51 33
Telex: 27298 COMEU
Telecopy: 91 88 76

Western Samoa

Ioane Viliamu Building,
  4th floor
PO Box 3023
Apia
Telephone: 200 70
Telex: 204-CECOF-SX
Telefax: 246 22

Yugoslavia

29 Kablarsku
Senjak 11040
Beograd
Telephone: 64 86 66
Telex: 11949 COMEUR YU
Telecopy: 65 14 58

Zaire

71 avenue des Trois Z
BP 2000
Kinshasa
Telephone: 247 08
Telex: 21560 DECEKIN ZR-
  KINSHASA
Telecopy: 288 63

Zambia

Plot 4899
Brentwood Drive
PO Box 34871
Lusaka
Telephone:
  25 09 06/25 07 11/25 11 40
Telex: 40440 DECEC-ZA

Zimbabwe

NCR House 10th floor
65 Samora Machel Avenue
PO Box 4252
Harare
Telephone:
  70 71 20/70 71 43/70 71
  39/70 71 40/70 49 88
Telex: 4811-ZW-HARARE-
  ZIMBABWE
Telecopy: 72 53 60

To international organizations

Geneva

Case postale 195
37–39 rue de Vermont
CH-1211 Genève 20
Telephone: 34 97 50
Telex: 28261 and 28262
  ECOM CH
Telecopy: 34 22 36

New York

3 Dag Hammarskjöld Plaza
305 East 47th Street
New York, NY 10017
Telephone: 371 3804
Telex: EURCOM NY 012396
  EURCOM NY 661100
  EURCOM NY 668513
Telecopy: 758 27 18

Paris

61 rue des Belles-Feuilles
F-75782 Paris Cedex 16
Telephone:
  45 01 58 85/45 00 48 65
Telex: COMEUR 630176 F
Telecopy: 47 27 08 02

Vienna

Hoyosgasse 5
A-1040 Wien
Telephone:
  65 33 79/65 34 91/65 73
  35/65 74 52
Telex: 133152 EUROP A
Telecopy: 65 18 08

Sales Offices for EC Documentation

Office for Official Publications of the European Communities

2 rue Mercier
L-2985 Luxembourg

Telephone: 49 92 81
Telex: PUBOF LU 1324 b

SALES AGENTS

Belgium

Moniteur Belge
40–42 rue de Louvain
B-1000 Bruxelles

Telephone: 512 00 26

Sub-agents
Librairie européenne
B-1040 Bruxelles

CREDOC
34 rue de la Montagne
Bte 11
B-1000 Bruxelles

Canada

Renouf Publishing Co. Ltd.
61 Sparks Street
Ottawa
Ontario K1P 5R1

Telephone: Toll Free 1 (800) 267 4164
Telex: 053–4936

Denmark

Schultz EF-publikationer
Møntergade 19
DK-1116 København K

Telephone: (01) 14 11 95

France

Journal officiel
Service des Publications des Communautés européennes
26 rue Desaix
F-75727 Paris Cedex 15

Telephone: (1) 45 78 61 39

Federal Republic of Germany

Bundesanzeiger Verlag
Breite Strasse
Postfach 10 80 06
D-5000 Köln 1

Telephone: (02 21) 20 29–0

Greece

GC Eleftheroudakis SA
International Bookstore
4 Nikis Street
GR-10563 Athens

Telephone: 322 22 55
Telex: 219410 ELEF

Sub-agent
Molho's Bookstore
The Business Bookshop
10 Tsimiski Street
Thessaloniki

Telephone: 275 271
Telex: 412885 LIMO

Ireland

Government Publications Sales
  Office
Sun Alliance House
Molesworth Street
Dublin 2
Telephone: 71 03 09

or by post

Government Stationery Office:
  EEC Section
6th Floor
Bishop Street
Dublin 8
Telephone: 78 16 66
Telex: 93827

Italy

Licosa Spa
Via Lamarmora 45
Casella postale 552
I-50121 Firenze
Telephone: 57 97 51
Telex: 570466 LICOSA 1

Sub-agent
Libreria scientifica Lucio de
  Biasio-AEIOU
Via Meravigli 16
I-20123 Milano
Telephone: 80 76 79

Herder Editrice e Libreria
Piazza Montecitorio 117–120
I-00186 Roma
Telephone: 67 94 628/67 95 304

Libreria giuridica
Via 12 Ottobre 172/R
I-1621 Genova
Telephone: 59 56 93

Japan

Kinokuniya Company Ltd
17–7 Shinjuku 3-Chome
Shiniuku-ku
Tokyo 160–91
Telephone: (03) 354 0131

Journal department
PO Box 55 Chitose
Tokyo 156
Telephone: (03) 439 0124

Netherlands

Staatsdrukkeriji-en
  uitgeverijbedrijf
Christoffel Plantijnstraat
Postbus 20014
NL-2500 EA 's-Gravenhage
Telephone: (070) 78 98 80

Portugal

Imprensa Nacional
Casa da Molda, EP
Rua D, Francisco Manuel de
  Melo 5
P-1092 Lisboa Codex
Telephone: 69 34 14
Telex: 15328 INCM

Distribuidora Livros Bertrand
  Lda.
Grupo Bertrand, SARL
Rua das Terras dos Vales 4-A
Apart, 37
P-2700 Amadora Codex
Telephone: 493 90 50,
  494 87 88
Telex: 15798 BERDIS

Spain

Boletín Oficial del Estado
Trafalgar 27
28010 Madrid
Telephone: (91) 446 60 00

Mundi-Prensa Libros, SA
Castelló 37
28001 Madrid
Telephone: (91) 435 36 37
Telex: 49370-MPLI-E

Turkey

Dünya Süper Veb (DSV)
Narlibahçe Sokak 15
Cağaloğlu
Istanbul
Telephone: 5 12 01 90
Telex: 23 822 dsvo tr

United Kingdom

HMSO
Publications Centre, PC 16
51 Nine Elms Lane
London SW8 5DR

Telephone: (01) 873 9090

Sub-agent
Alan Armstrong and Associates
  Ltd,
2 Arkwright Road
Reading RG2 0SG
Telephone: (0734) 751769
Telex: 849937 AAALTD G
Fax: (0734) 755164

United States of America

European Community
  Information Service
2100 M Street NW
Suite 707
Washington, DC 20037
Telephone: (202) 862 9500

Non-EC Information Sources

Below is a selective list of information sources found useful by the author, published by non-EC organizations.

LEGISLATION, THE LEGISLATIVE PROCESS AND EC CASE-LAW

European Communities legislation: current status (Butterworths, 1988–)

A comprehensive chronological listing of EC secondary legislation from 1952 to date. Excludes legislation dealing with the daily running of the EC. Gives *Official Journal* references, New cumulative volume issued annually plus three supplements issued through the year. Reasonable subject index.

Encyclopaedia of European Community law (Sweet and Maxwell, 1974–)

A major legal encyclopaedia containing the text of much EC legislation with a fair index.

Guide to EC legislation (North-Holland, 1979–)

An index of EC legislation classified in a subject arrangement. Entries give a brief summary of the nature of the legislation and *Official Journal* references.

Halsbury's Laws of England (Butterworths, 4th edition, 1986 Vols 51/52)

A concise but comprehensive encyclopaedia of EC institutions, policies and laws with copious bibliographical references. The EC volumes can be purchased separately from the overall series.

Policy formation in the European Communities: a bibliographical guide to Community documentation 1958–1978 (Mansell, 1981)

A listing, with parallel descriptive essays, of the documentation of the legislative process.

Guide to EC Court decisions (North-Holland, 1982–)

An index to the judgments of the Court of Justice. In addition to bibliographical details brief summaries of the judgments are given.

Gazetteer of European law (European Law Centre, 1983)

An index to the judgments of the Court of Justice and national and international case law on EC matters for the period 1953–83.

STATISTICS

Eurostat index (Capital Planning Information 4th edition, 1989)

An authoritative index to the contents of Eurostat publications.

GRANTS AND LOANS

Guide to European Community grants and loans (Eurofi)

An annual looseleaf guide, with the option of buying supplements through the year. Eurofi also publish annual publications called *EEC contacts*, a directory of contacts in the EC and EC-related fields, and *Index to documents of the Commission of the European Communities*, an index to COM Documents. They also issue *EEC update*, a synopsis of current EC legislative proposals.

GENERAL

International organizations catalogue (HMSO, annual)

The annual catalogue of the publications from the international organizations for which HMSO are the United Kingdom sales agents. It contains a considerable number of EC titles. It is a cumulation of the titles from international organizations contained in the HMSO *Monthly Catalogue* and *Daily List*.

Weekly Information Bulletin (HMSO, weekly during the Parliamentary session)

Compiled in the Public Information Office of the Library of the House of Commons. In among its many non-EC features it lists recently received COM Documents and can be ahead of other sources in this respect. *The Weekly Information Bulletin* can also be useful to discover consultation papers issued by UK government departments in relation to proposed EC legislation. These are listed in the section called 'White Papers and Green Papers received since the last Bulletin'.

The European Community: bibliographical excursions (Frances Pinter, 1983)

Lists documentary sources on major EC policies and institutional developments.

Common Market digest: an information guide to the European Communities (The Library Association, 1983)

A well-structured introductory reference source to the EC institutions and policies with numerous bibliographical references.

Reports of the European Communities 1952–1977: an index to authors and chairmen (Mansell, 1981)

A listing of many reports difficult to track down elsewhere with a subject index.

European Access (Association of EDC Librarians – 1988; Chadwyck-Healey, 1989–)

A current awareness bulletin which seeks to bibliographically record all developments relating to the EC. Indexes EC documentation and much other material including academic monographs, academic, commercial and professional journals, pressure group material, UK official publications and newspapers. From 1989 each issue also contains a bibliographical review article surveying a major EC policy area of the 1980s, news of developments towards setting up the Single Market by 1992, R & D news, articles and other EC information developments.

The EEC: a guide to the maze (Kogan Page, 2nd edition, 1987)

A concise but very readable introduction to the EC with many practical pieces of advice and references.

EEC brief (Locksley Press, 1980–)

A looseleaf encyclopaedia to the EC updated annually.

Manual of law librarianship: the use and organization of legal literature (Gower, 2nd edition, 1987)

Contains a chapter on the legal literature of the European Communities.

How to use a law library (Sweet and Maxwell, 2nd edition, 1987)

Contains a chapter on the legal literature of the European Communities.

Basic sources for libraries and information units (Association of EDC Librarians, 1987)

A list of basic sources on EC information. Part of a series called European Communities Information of which this title is no. 11. Others in the series look at information sources about particular EC institutions and policies.

KEEPING UP TO DATE

It is impossible in a few lines to cover all the information sources available to trace very recent EC developments. There are many specialist sources which cover narrow policy areas or serve particular audiences. For general coverage the standard alerting agency bulletins are those published by Agence Europe (including their daily bulletin *Europe*) and European Information Service (including their biweekly *European Report*). Newspapers are the other major source for contemporary information – the *Financial Times* is the unrivalled leader for coverage of EC affairs and not just from a narrow business or financial perspective. Political, institutional, agricultural, regional and scientific perspectives, for example, are also covered. The leading specialist information source, *European Information Service (EIS)*, is published by the Local Government International Bureau, *EIS* is published ten times a year and, although intended primarily for local government, is of interest to a wider audience in its coverage of EC policies and proposals. Source references are given. For very recent bibliographical references, and from 1989 a related chronology of recent EC developments *European access*, published by Chadwyck-Healey, can be recommended.

APPENDIX 6

Euro Info Centres/EC Depository Libraries

In addition to Information Offices and the External Delegations as listed in Appendix 3 the EC have also created various other categories of information/documentation units.

EURO INFO CENTRES (EICs)

Thirty-nine EICs were set up in the member states during 1987–88 in the pilot phase of a new initiative. They are sometimes called European Business Information Centres or Euro-guichets. They are part of the attempt by the EC, through the SME Task Force, to help the small and medium-sized business sector. EICs provide an information service to the SME sector on EC and other matters and allow the Commission to discover the needs and concerns of SMEs. EICs have developed links across national boundaries with other EICs to create a novel feature of transnational information cooperation.

EICs are usually based in organizations with already well-established links with the SME sector. They are sent a certain amount of EC documentation which is deemed relevant to the business and industrial community. Documentation prior to their creation in 1987 is not usually available in EICs unless already taken by the parent body. EICs are expected to make considerable use of EC databases and have access to the Commission's electronic mail system, EUROKOM.

The Commission announced in 1988 that they wished to expand the number of EICs to 200 following an initial evaluation of the pilot centres. In November 1988 the Commission asked organizations interested in operating EICs to indicate their intentions prior to a formal call for applications in December 1988. For centres set up during the second phase contact the Information Offices in the appropriate country.

EUROPEAN DOCUMENTATION CENTRES (EDCs)

Approximately 300 EDCs exist throughout the world. They come under the aegis of the University Information section of DG X (Information,

Communication and Culture) of the Commission. They are based in academic institutions, and their primary function is to encourage the teaching and research of the EC in these academic institutions. Certain EDCs, most notably in the United Kingdom and Ireland, also attempt to offer a public information service.

EDCs traditionally have received a comprehensive range of EC documentation. In 1987–88 a rationalization exercise meant that henceforth certain EDCs receive only a selection of EC documentation, while the others will continue to receive a comprehensive supply.

EC DEPOSITORY LIBRARIES (DEPs)

DEPs are major collections of EC documentation intended primarily for the general public. They are to be found both in the member states and elsewhere and are usually, though not exclusively, based in national, state or parliamentary libraries. In the United States DEPs are found mostly in academic institutions.

EUROPEAN REFERENCE CENTRES (ERCs)

These are collections of basic EC documentation usually based in academic institutions. The range of material received by an ERC does not allow for an extensive EC information service to be provided unless the parent body supplements the material with further resources.

Below is a list of EICs, EDCs, DEPs and ERCs. The full address is given for the EICs, but the name of the parent institution and the town/ city is given in the case of EDCs, DEPs and ERCs. The rationalization exercise undertaken during 1987–88 of EDCs, DEPs and ERCs is taken into account. For the full address and names of librarians in charge contact the Information Offices of the Commission for the situation in particular countries or contact the University Information Section of DG X of the Commission (200 rue de la Loi, B-1049 Brussels, Belgium. Telephone: 235 11 11; Telex 21877 COMEU B).

EURO INFO CENTRES

(For EICs created in 1989–90 contact Offices of the Commission)

Belgium

Bureau Economique de la	2 avenue Sergent Vrithoff
Province de Namur	B-5000 Namur
Palais des Expositions	Telephone: 32/81/73.52.09

Kamervan Koophandel en
  Nijverheid
Markgravestraat 12
B-2000 Antwerpen
Telephone: 32/3/233.67.32

Denmark

Arhus Amtskommune
Haslegardvaenget 18–20
DK-8210 Århus
Telephone: 45/615.03.18

Odensen Erhvervsrad
Norregade 51
DK-5000 Odense C
Telephone: 45/912.61.21

France

Chambre de Commerce et
  d'Industrie de Comité
  d'Expansion Aquitaine
2 place de la Bourse
F-33076 Bordeaux Cedex
Telephone:
  33/56/52.65.47/52.98.94

Region Lorraine
1 place St Clement
BP 1004
F-57036 Metz Cedex 1
Telephone: 33/87/33.60.00

Chambre de Commerce et
  d'Industrie de Nantes
Centre des Salorges
BP 718
F-44027 Nantes Cedex 04
Telephone: 33/40/44.60.08

Chambre de Commerce et
  d'Industrie de Strasbourg et
  du Bas-Rhin
10 place Gutenberg
F-67081 Strasbourg Cedex
Telephone: 33/88/32.12.55

Chambre de Commerce et
  d'Industrie de Lyon
16 rue de la Republique
F-69289 Lyon Cedex 02
Telephone: 33/78/38.10.10

Federal Republic of Germany

ZENIT
Dohne 54
D-4330 Molheim
Telephone: 49/20.83.00.04

RKW
Heilwigstrasse 33
D-2000 Hamburg 20
Telephone: 49/40/460.20.87

DIHT
Adenauer Allee 148
Postfach 1446
D-5300 Bonn 1
Telephone: 49/228.10.40

Industrie- und Handelskammer
Martin Luther Strasse 12
D-8400 Regensburg
Telephone: 49/94.15.69.41

Handwerkskammer (DHKT)
Heilbronner Strasse 43
Postfach 2621
D-7000 Stuttgart 1
Telephone: 49/71.12.59.41

DHKT
Johanniterstrasse 1
Haus des Deutschen Hanwerks
D-5300 Bonn 1
Telephone: 49/228.54.51

Greece

Association of Industries of
  Northern Greece/Chamber of
  Commerce of Northern
  Greece
Place Morihovo 1
GR-54653 Thessaloniki
Telephone:
  30/31/53.98.17/53.96.82

EOMMEX
Rue Xenias 16
GR-11528 Athens
Telephone: 30/1/362.56.30

Ireland

Irish Export Board
Merrion Hall
PO Box 203
Strand Road
Sandymount
Dublin 4
Telephone: 353/1/69.50.11

One Stop Shop
The Granary
Michael Street
Limerick
Telephone: 353/61/407.77

Italy

Camera di Commercio
  Industria Artigianato e
  Agricoltura di Napoli
Corso Meridionale 58
I-80143 Napoli
Telephone: 39/81/28.53.22

Camera di Commercio
  Industria Artigianato e
  Agricoltura di Milano
Via Merivigli 9/b
I-20123 Milano
Telephone: 39/2/85151

Confartigianatoic
  NA/CLAAI/CASA
Via Milano 18
I-25126 Brescia
Telephone: 39/30/28.90.51

Confindustria
Viale dell'Astronomia 30
I-00144 Roma
Telephone: 39/6/59031

Ass. della Provincia di Bologna
Via San Domenico 4
I-40124 Bologna
Telephone: 39/51/52.96.11

Luxembourg

Chambre de
  Commerce/Chambre des
  Metiers/Federation des
  Industriels
7 rue Alcide de Gasperi.
BP 1503
L-2981 Luxembourg
Telephone: 352/43.58.53

Netherlands

CIMK–RIMK
Dalsteindreef – BP 112
NL-1112 XC Dimen-Suid
Telephone: 31/20/90.10.71

INDUMA/BOM/LIOF
Prins Hendriklann 21a
PO Box 995
NL-5700 AZ Helmond
Telephone: 31/49/203.40.35

Portugal

Associação Industrial
  Portuguesa
Exponsor
P-4100 Porto

Telephone:
351/2/68.48.14/67.32.20

Banco de Fomento Nacional
Avenida Casal Ribeiro 59
P-1000 Lisboa
Telephone:
351/1/56.10.71/56.20.21

Spain

CIDEM
Avenida Diagonal 403, 1
E-08008 Barcelona
Telephone: 34/3/217.20.08

Camara Oficial de Comercio,
Industria y Navegación
Avenida de Recalde 50
E-48008 Bilbao (Vizcaya)
Telephone: 34/4/444.50.54

Confederación de Empresarios
de Andalucía
Avenida. San Francisco Javier
s/n
Edificio Sevilla 2–9
E-41005 Sevilla
Telephone: 34/54/64.20.13

Confederación Española de
Organizaciones Empresariales
50 Diego de Leon
E-28006 Madrid
Telephone: 34/1/450.80.48

IMPI – INFE
141–2 Paseo de la Castellana
E-28046 Madrid
Telephone: 34/1/450.80.48

United Kingdom

Strathclyde Euro Info Centre
25 Bothwell Street
Glasgow G2 6 NR
Telephone: 44/41/221.0999

North of England Euro Info
Centre
Bank House
Carliol Square
Newcastle upon Tyne
NE1 6XE
Telephone: 44/91/261.5131

Birmingham European Business
Centre
Chamber of Commerce House
PO Box 360
75 Harborne Road
Birmingham B15 3DH
Telephone: 44/21/455.0268

Centre for European Business
Information
Small Firms Centre
Ebury Bridge House
2–18 Ebury Bridge Road
London SW1W 8QD
Telephone: 44/1/730.8115

EUROPEAN DOCUMENTATION CENTRES/EC DEPOSITORY LIBRARIES/EUROPEAN REFERENCE CENTRES

The following abbreviations are used:

EDC   European Documentation Centre receiving
comprehensive supply of EC documentation

EDC(S)	European Documentation Centre receiving basic EC documentation plus material from a selection of prechosen policy areas.
DEP	EC Depository Library
DEP(R)	EC Depository Library receiving a selection of EC documentation
ERC	European Reference Centre.

Member states

Belgium

Antwerp	Universiteit Antwerpen (UFSIA) – EDC(S)
	Europees Studie en Informatiecentrum – ERC
Arlon	La Maison de L'Europe du Luxembourg (CIFEL) – ERC
Bruges	College of Europe – EDC
Brussels	Royal Library – DEP
Brussels	Université Libre de Bruxelles – EDC
Brussels	Centre for European Policy Studies – EDC(S)
Brussels	Royal Institute of International Relations – EDC(S)
Brussels	Vrije Universiteit – EDC(S)
Ghent	Rijksuniversiteit Gent – EDC
Liège	Université de Liège – Facult de Droit – EDC(S)
Louvain	Université Catholique de Louvain – Institut d'Etudes Européennes — EDC
Louvain	Katholieke Universiteit Leuven – Universiteitsbibliotheek – EDC(S)
Louvain	Institut de Recherches (IRES) – EDC(s)
Mons	Université de L'Etat – ERC
Namur	Bibliothèque Universitaire Moretus Plantin – EDC(S)
Saint-Ghislain	Centre International de Formation Européenne (CIFE) – ERC

Denmark

Aalborg	Aalborg Universitetsbibliotek – EDC
Åarhus	Handelshojskolen i Åarhus – EF Biblioteket – EDC
Åarhus	Statsbiblioteket — EDC
Frederiksberg	Handelshojskolens Bibliotek – EDC
Copenhagen	Det Kongelige Bibliothek Kontoret for Internationale Publikationer – DEP

Copenhagen	Koebenhavns Universiteit – Institut for International Ret og Europaret – EDC
Odense	Odense Universitetsbibliotek – EDC

France

Aix en Provence	Faculté de Droit et de Science Politiques d'Aix-Marseille – EDC
Amiens	Université d'Amiens – Faculté d'Economie et Gestion – EDC(S)
Angers	Université d'Angers – Faculté de Droit et des Sciences Economies – EDC
Besançon	Université de Besançon – EDC
Brest	Université de Bretagne Occidentale – Faculté de Droit et Sciences Economiques – EDC(S)
Caen	Université de Caen – Faculté de Droit et des Sciences Politiques – EDC(S)
Clermont	Université de Clermont – Faculté de Droit – EDC
Dijon	Université de Dijon – Faculté de Droit et Science Politique – EDC(S)
Ecully	Groupe Ecole Supérieure de Commerce de Lyon – EDC(S)
Fontainebleau	Institut Européen d'Administration des Affaires – EDC(S)
Grenoble	Centre Universitaire de Recherche Européenne et Internationale – EDC
Lille	Université de Lille, Villeneuve – EDC
Limoges	Université de Limoges – EDC(S)
Lyons	Université Jean Moulin – EDC
Lyons	Université de Lyon – Institut d'Etudes Politiques – EDC(S)
Le Mans	Bibliothèque Universitaire du Maine – EDC(S)
Malakoff	Bibliothèque de l'Université Rene Descartes – EDC(S)
Montigny Le Brx	Manistel Management Info-Service Télématique – EDC
Montpellier	Université de Montpellier – EDC
Mont-St-Aignan	Faculté de Droit de Science Economies et de Gestion – EDC(S)
Nancy	Université de Nancy – EDC
Nanterre	Université de Paris-Nanterre – EDC(S)
Nantes	Université de Nantes – Faculté de Droit et des Sciences Politiques – EDC(S)

Nice	Université de Nice – Institut du Droit de la Paix et du Développement – EDC(S)
Orleans	Université d'Orleans – EDC(S)
Paris	Bibliothèque Nationale – DEP
Paris	Université de Paris – EDC
Paris	Université de Paris – Centre Universitaire d'Études des Communautés Européennes – EDC
Paris	Université de Paris-Nord, Villetaneuse – EDC(S)
Paris	Livres Hebdo/Livres de France – EDC
Paris	École Nationale d'Administration – EDC(S)
Paris	Université de Paris XII, La Varenne St Hilaire – Faculté Droit et Sciences Politiques et Economiques de St Maur – Maur – ERC
Paris	Palais de Justice – ERC
Pau	Université de Pau et des Pays l'Audour – Faculté de Droit et des Sciences Economiques – EDC(S)
Perpignan	CDRE Université – EDC(S)
Pessac	Université de Bordeaux – Faculté Droit et Sciences Economiques – EDC(S)
Poitiers	Université de Poitiers – Faculté Droit et Sciences Sociales – EDC
Rheims	UER Faculté de Droit et Sciences Economiques de Reims – EDC
Rennes	Facultés des Sciences Juridiques – EDC
Sceaux	Université de Paris – UER Sciences Juridiques et Economiques – EDC
Strasbourg	Université Sciences Juridiques, Politiques et Sociales de Strasbourg – EDC(S)
Strasbourg	Université Sciences Juridiques Politiques et Sociales – EDC(S)
Strasbourg	Chambre de Commerce et d'Industrie de Strasbourg et du Bas-Rhin – ERC
St Martin D'Heres	Université des Sciences Sociales de Grenoble – EDC(S)
Toulon	Bibliothèque de l'Université de Toulon – EDC(S)
Toulouse	Université Sciences Sociales Toulouse – EDC
Tours	Université François Rabelais de Tours – Faculté Science Juridiques et Economiques – EDC(S)

Federal Republic of Germany

Aachen	Aachener Zentrum für Europäische Studien – EDC
Augsburg	Universitätsbibliothek Augsburg – EDC(S)
Bamberg	Universitätsbibliothek Bamberg – ERC
Bayreuth	Universitätsbibliothek Bayreuth – EDC(S)
Berlin	Staatsbibliothek – DEP
	Freie Universität Berlin – Universitätsbibliothek – EDC
Berlin	Freie Universität Berlin – Fachbereich Politische Wissenschaften – EDC(S)
Berlin	Europäische Akademie – Bibliothek – EDC
Bielefeld	Universitätsbibliothek – EDC(S)
Bochum	Universität – Bibliothek – EDC(S)
Bonn	Deutscher Bundestag – Bibliothek – DEP
Bonn	Dokumentationsstelle der Deutschen Gesellschaft für Auswärtige Politik EV – EDC(S)
Bonn	Interdisziplinares Zentrum für Europäische Fragen und Lehrerausbildung – ERC
Bremen	Universität Bremen – Zentrum für Europäische Rechtspolitik – EDC
Cologne	see Köln
Darmstadt	TH Darmstadt – Fachbereich Gesellschafts – EDC(S)
Dortmund	Universität Dortmund – ERC
Duisburg	Universitätsbibliothek Duisburg – EDC
Ebenhausen	Stiftung Wissenschaft und Politik – EDC(S)
Emden	Fachhochschule Ostfriesland – ERC
Essen	Universitätsbibliothek – ERC
Flensburg	Pädagogische Hochschule Flensburg – ERC
Frankfurt	Deutsche Bibliothek – DEP
Frankfurt	Universität Frankfurt – Bibliothek – EDC(S)
Freiburg	Universität Freiburg – Institut für Öffentliches Recht – EDC(S)
Fulda	Fachhochschule – ERC
Giessen	Justus Liebig Universität – EDC
Göttingen	Universität Göttingen – Bibliothek – EDC(S)
Hamburg	HWWA – Institut für Wirtschaftsforschung, Hamburg – EDC
Hamburg	Universität Hamburg – Seminar für Öffentliches Recht abt Europarecht – EDC
Hamburg	Universität der Bundeswehr Hamburg – Bibliothek – ERC

Hanover	Fachbereichsbibliothek – EDC(S)
Heidelberg	Max-Planck Institut – EDC
Heidelberg	Institut für Ausländisches und Internationales – ERC
Kassel	Gesamthochschulbibliothek – ERC
Kiel	Institut für Weltwirtschaft an der Universität Kiel – Bibliothek – EDC
Koblenz	Fachhochschule des Landes Rheinland-Pfalz – Bibliothek – ERC
Köln (Cologne)	Universität Köln – EDC
Köln (Cologne)	Universität Köln – Institut für das Recht der Europäische Gemeinschaften – EDC(S)
Konstanz	Universität Konstanz – Bibliothek – EDC
Mainz	Gutenberg Universität Institut für Politikwissensch – EDC
Mainz	Universitätsbibliothek – ERC
Mannheim	Universität Mannheim – Europa Institut – EDC(S)
Marburg	Philipps-Universitat Marburg – EDC(S)
München (Munich)	Bayerische Staatsbibliothek – DEP
München (Munich)	Universität München – Institut Internationale Recht-Europäisches und Internationales Wirtschaftsrecht – EDC(S)
München (Munich)	Universität der Bundeswehr Munchen – Bibliothek – ERC
Munster	Westfälische Wilhelms Universität – Institut für Politikwissenschaft – EDC
Nurnberg (Nuremberg)	Universität Erlangen-Nurnberg – Gruppenbibliothek – EDC(S)
Oldenburg	Universität Oldenberg – ERC
Osnabrück	Universität Osnabrück – EDC
Osnabrück	Fachhochschule – ERC
Passau	Universität Passau – Lehrstuhl für Staats- und Verwaltungsrecht, Völkerrecht und Europarecht – EDC(S)
Pforzheim	Fachhochschule, Wirtschaft Pforzheim – ERC
Regensburg	Universitätsbibliothek Regensburg – EDC(S)
Reutlingen	Hochschulbibliothek Reutlingen – ERC
Saarbrucken	Universität des Saarlandes – Bibliothek – EDC
Siegen	Universitätsbibliothek – EDC(S)
Speyer	Hochschule für Verwaltungswissenschaften – EDC
Stuttgart	Universität Hohenheim – Institut für

	Agrarpolitik und landwirtschaftliche ... – EDC(S)
Stuttgart	Wurttembergische Landesbibliothek Zeitschriftenstelle – ERC
Trier	Universität Trier – Bibliothek – EDC
Tubingen	Universität Tubingen – Bibliothek – EDC
Worms	Fachhochschule des Landes Rheinland – Pfalz – ERC
Wurzburg	Universität Wurzburg – Institut für Europarecht – EDC

Greece

Athens	Spoudastirio Domiosio v Dikaio – Kentro Europaikis – EDC
Komotini	Université Demokritos de Thrace – Faculté de Droit – EDC
Thessaloniki	Centre de Droit Economique International et Européen – EDC

Ireland

Cork	University College – EDC
Dublin	Oireachtas Library – DEP
Dublin	National Library of Ireland – DEP
Dublin	University College – EDC
Dublin	Trinity College – EDC
Galway	University College – EDC(S)
Limerick	National Institute for Higher Education – EDC

Italy

Ancona	Università di Ancona – Facoltà di Economia e Commercio – Biblioteca – EDC(S)
Bari	Università di Bari – Facoltà di Giurisprudenza – EDC
Bergamo	Istituto Universitario di Bergamo – Biblioteca Economia e Commercio – ERC
Bologna	Università degli Studi di Bologna – EDC
Brindisi	Centro Informazioni e Studi sulle Comunità Europee – ERC
Cagliari	Università di Cagliari – Facoltà di Giurisprudenza – EDC
Campobasso	ASCOM Associazione dei Comuni Molisani – ERC
Castiglione Scalo	Università degli Studi della Calabria – ERC

Catania	Università di Catania – Facoltà Di Giurisprudenza – EDC
Cuneo	Biblioteca Civica – ERC
Ferrara	Università di Ferrara – Istituto di Economia e Finanza – EDC(S)
Firenze (Florence)	Biblioteca Nazionale Centrale – DEP
Firenze (Florence)	Dipartimento di Scienza Politica e Sociologia Politica – EDC
Firenze (Florence)	Istituto Universitario Europeo – Biblioteca – EDC
Firenze (Florence)	Istituto Universitario Europeo – Archivi – EDC
Genova (Genoa)	Università di Genova – Facoltà Economia e Commercio – EDC
Macerata	Università di Macerata – Istituto di Economia Finanza – ERC
Messina	Università di Messina – Facoltà di Economia e Commercio – Biblioteca – ERC
Milano (Milan)	Università degli Studi di Milano – EDC
Milano (Milan)	Centro Internazionale di Studi e Documentazione sulle Comunita Europee – EDC
Milano (Milan)	Università Commerciale Luigi Bocconi – Biblioteca – EDC
Milano (Milan)	Università Cattolica del Sacro Cuore – Biblioteca Centrale – ERC
Modena	Centro di Documentazione e Ricerche sulle Comunita Europee della Università degli Studi – EDC(S)
Napoli (Naples)	Biblioteca Nazionale – DEP
Napoli (Naples)	Società Italiana per l'Organizzazione Internazionale – EDC
Napoli (Naples)	Università di Napoli – Dipartimento de Economia e Politica Agraria – Biblioteca – EDC(S)
Napoli (Naples)	Università di Napoli – Istituto Sociologico Giuridico – EDC(S)
Nuoro	Biblioteca 'Sebastiano Satta' – ERC
Padova (Padua)	Università degli Studi di Padova – Centro di Studi Europei – EDC
Palermo	Università di Palermo – Facoltà di Lettere e Filosofia – Biblioteca – EDC(S)
Parma	Università di Parma – EDC
Parma	Collegio Europea di Parma – ERC

Pavia	Università degli Studi di Pavia – Centro Studi sulle Comunità Europee – EDC(S)
Perugia	Università di Perugia – Biblioteca Centrale – EDC(S)
Pescara	Università 'G. D'Annunzio' – Istituto di Studi Giuridici – EDC(S)
Pisa	Università di Pisa – Facoltà di Giurisprudenza – EDC(S)
Ragusa	Camera di Commercio, Industria Artigianato e Agricultura – ERC
Reggio Calabria	ISESP Istituto Superiore Europeo di Studi Politici – EDC(S)
Roma (Rome)	Società Italiana per l'Organizzazione Internazionale (SIOI) – Biblioteca – EDC
Roma (Rome)	Università di Roma – Facoltà di Economia e Commercio – EDC
Roma (Rome)	Centro Studi di Diritto Comunitario – EDC(S) and ERC
Roma (Rome)	Scuola Superiore della Pubblica Amministrazione – Biblioteca – ERC
Salerno	Università di Salerno – Facoltà di Economia e Commercio, Giurisprudenza – Biblioteca – ERC
Sassari	Università degli Studi di Sassari – Facoltà di Giurisprudenza – EDC
Sassari	Centro Studi e Informazione Europea – ERC
Siena	Università degli Studi di Siena – Biblioteca – EDC
Torino (Turin)	Università di Torino – Istituto Universitario di Studi Europei – EDC
Trieste	Università degli Studi – Facultà Giurisprudenza – EDC(S)
Trento	Libera Università degli Studi – Dipartimento di Economia – ERC
Trento	Ufficio Studi della Regione Trentino Alto Adige – ERC
Turin	see Torino
Urbino	Centro Alti Studi Europei – EDC
Verona	Università di Verona – Istituto di Scienze Economiche – EDC(S)

Luxembourg

Luxembourg	Bibliothèque Nationale – DEP
Luxembourg	Centre International d'Etudes et de

Recherches Européennes – Institut
Universitaire International – EDC

The Netherlands

Amsterdam	Universiteit van Amsterdam – Europa Instituut – EDC
Amsterdam	Vrije Universiteit – Economisch en Sociaal Instituut – EDC(S)
Delft	Technische Hogeschool – Bibliothek – EDC
Den Haag (The Hague)	TMC Asser Instituut – EDC
Enschede	Technische Hogeschool Twente – EDC
Groningen	Rijksuniversiteit Bibliothek – EDC
The Hague	see Den Haag
Leiden	Rijksuniversiteit te Leiden – Europa Instituut – EDC(S)
Maastricht	Raad der Europese Gemeenten en Regio's – EDC
Nijmegen	Katholieke Universiteit – Faculteit der Rechtsgeleerdheid – EDC(S)
Rotterdam	Erasmus Universiteit – Bibliothek – EDC(S)
Tilburg	Katholieke Hogeschool – Bibliothek Informatie – EDC(S)
Utrecht	Rijks Universiteit – Europa Instituut – EDC(S)
Wageningen	Agricultural University – Library – EDC(S)

Portugal

Braga	Universidade do Minho – EDC
Coimbra	Universidade de Coimbra – Centro Interdisciplinar de Estudos Juridico-Economicos – EDC
Lisboa (Lisbon)	Universidade Technica de Lisboa – Centro de Estudos e Documentação Europeia – EDC
Lisboa (Lisbon)	Universidade de Lisboa – Facultade de Economia – EDC(S)
Lisboa (Lisbon)	Universidade de Lisboa – Facultade de Diretto – EDC
Lisboa (Lisbon)	Universidade Catolica Portuguesa – Centro de Estados Europeus – EDC
Lisboa (Lisbon)	Colegio Iniversitario Pio XII – ERC
Oeiras	Instituto Nacional de Administração – Biblioteca – EDC
Ponta Delgada	Universidade dos Açores – EDC

Porto (Oporto)	Universidade do Porto – Centro de Documentação e Estudos Europeus – EDC

Spain

Alicante	Camara de Comercio – EDC
Badajoz	Universidad de Extremadura – EDC
Barcelona	Escuela Superior de Administracio de Empresas – EDC
Barcelona	Universidad Autonome de Barcelona – EDC
Bilbao	Universidad de Deusto – Instituto de Estudios Europeos – EDC
Bilbao	Universidad de Bilbao – EDC(S)
Córdoba	Universidad de Córdoba – Facultad de Derecho – EDC
Gijon	Universidad de Oviedo – Escuela Universitaria de Estudios Empresariales – ERC
Granada	Universidad de Granada
Granada	Economicas — EDC
Madrid	Biblioteca Nacional – DEP
Madrid	Universidad Politécnica de Madrid – EDC
Madrid	Universidad Autónoma de Madrid – Facultad de Ciencias Económicas – EDC
Madrid	Universidad Complutense – Facultad de Derecho – EDC
Madrid	Universidad de Alcala – Facultad de Económicas – EDC(S)
Madrid	Escuela Diplomatica Cursos sobre las Comunidades Europeas – ERC
Murcia	Universidad de Murcia – EDC
Oviedo	Universidad de Oviedo – EDC
Palma de Mallorca	Les Islas Baleares Centros de Documentación Europea – EDC
Pamplona	Universidad de Navarra – EDC
Salamanca	Universidad de Salamanca – EDC
San Sebastian	Empresariales (ESTE) – EDC
Santander	Universidad de Cantabria – EDC
Santiago de Compostela	Universidad de Santiago – Facultad de Economicas – EDC
Sevilla	Universidad de Sevilla – EDC
Tenerife	Universidad San Fernando de La Laguna – EDC
Toledo	Camera de Comercio y Industria – EDC
Valencia	Universidad de Valencia – Facultad de Economicas – EDC

Valladolid	Universidad de Valladolid – Facultad de Derecho – EDC
Zaragoza	Universidad de Zaragoza – Facultad de Derecho – EDC

United Kingdom

Aberdeen	Aberdeen University – EDC(S)
Aberystwyth	University College of Wales, Aberystwyth – ERC
Ashford	Wye College – EDC(S)
Bath	University of Bath – EDC
Belfast	Queen's University – EDC
Birmingham	City of Birmingham Polytechnic – EDC(S)
Birmingham	Birmingham University – EDC(S)
Boston Spa	British Library – DEP
Bradford	University of Bradford – EDC
Brighton	University of Sussex – EDC
Bristol	University of Bristol – EDC(S)
Cambridge	Cambridge University – EDC
Canterbury	University of Kent – EDC
Cardiff	University of Wales, College of Cardiff – EDC
Chalfont St Giles	Buckinghamshire College of Higher Education – ERC
Chelmsford	Chelmer Institute of Higher Education – ERC
Cleveland	Teesside Polytechnic – ERC
Colchester	University of Essex – EDC(S)
Coleraine	University of Ulster – EDC
Coventry	University of Warwick – EDC
Coventry	Lanchester Polytechnic – EDC(S)
Dundee	University of Dundee – EDC
Durham	University of Durham – EDC(S)
Edinburgh	University of Edinburgh – EDC
Edinburgh	National Library of Scotland – ERC
Exeter	Exeter University – EDC
Exmouth	Rolle College – ERC
Glasgow	University of Glasgow – EDC
Guildford	University of Surrey – EDC(S)
Halifax	Percival Whitley College of Further Education – ERC
Hatfield	Hatfield Polytechnic – ERC
Hull	University of Hull – EDC
Inverness	Highlands Regional Council, Library Service – ERC

Ipswich	Suffolk County Library – ERC
Keele	University of Keele – EDC(S)
Lancaster	University of Lancanster – EDC
Leeds	Leeds Polytechnic – EDC(S)
Leeds	University of Leeds – EDC(S)
Leicester	Leicester University – EDC
Liverpool	City of Liverpool Central Library – DEP
London	British Library – DEP
London	City of Westminster Library – DEP
London	Queen Mary College – EDC
London	British Library of Political and Economic Science – DEP
London	Polytechnic of North London – EDC
London	Royal Institute of International Affairs – EDC(S)
London	Ealing College of Higher Education – ERC
Loughborough	Loughborough University – EDC
Manchester	University of Manchester – EDC(S)
Newcastle upon Tyne	Newcastle Polytechnic – EDC
Northampton	Nene College – ERC
Norwich	University of East Anglia – EDC(S)
Nottingham	University of Nottingham – EDC
Oxford	Bodleian – EDC
Plymouth	College of St Mark and St John Foundation – ERC
Portsmouth	Portsmouth Polytechnic – EDC
Preston	Preston Public Library – ERC
Preston	Lancashire Polytechnic – ERC
Reading	University of Reading – EDC
Reading	Bulmershe College – ERC
Salford	University of Salford – EDC(S)
Sheffield	Sheffield Polytechnic – EDC
Sheffield	University of Sheffield – ERC
Southampton	University of Southampton – EDC(S)
Stirling	Stirling University – ERC
Swansea	University College of Swansea – ERC
Wolverhampton	Wolverhampton Polytechnic – EDC(S)
Wrexham	North East Wales Institute of Higher Education – ERC

Non-member states

Argentina

Buenos Aires	Universidad de Buenos Aires – ERC
Buenos Aires	Universidad Argentina de la Empresa – ERC

Buenos Aires	Eural – Centro de Investigaciones Europeo-Latinoamericana – ERC
Buenos Aires	Universidad del Salvador – ERC
Buenos Aires	Biblioteca del Congreso de la Nacion Argentina – ERC
Buenos Aires	Intal – Instituto para la Integración de América Latina – ERC
Buenos Aires	Instituto Torcuato di Tella – ERC
Cordoba	Universidad de Beunos Aires – ERC
Cordoba	Universidad Catolica – ERC
La Plata	Universita Nacional de la Plata – ERC
Mendoza	Universidad Nacional de Cuyo – ERC
Santa Fé	Universidad Nacional del Litoral – ERC

Australia

Bundoora	La Trobe University – EDC
Canberra	National Library of Australia – DEP(R)
Hobart	University of Tasmania – EDC(S)
Melbourne	State Library of Victoria – DEP(R)
Nedlands	University of Western Australia – ERC
Sydney	State Library of New South Wales – DEP
Sydney	University of Sydney – EDC(S)
Sydney	German–Australian Chamber of Industry and Commerce – ERC

Austria

Graz	Karl-Franzens Universität Graz – EDC(S)
Innsbruck	Leopold-Franzens Universität – EDC(S)
Wien (Vienna)	Zentrale Verwaltungsbibliothek und Dokumentation für Wirtschaft und Technik – DEP
Wien (Vienna)	Institut für Völkerrecht und Internationale Beziehungen – EDC(S)

Brazil

Bahia	Centro de Desenvoluimento de Administracio Publica – ERC
Belo Horizonte	Universidade Federal de Minas Gerais – ERC
Brasilia	Universidade de Brasilia – ERC
Porto Alegre	Universidade Federal do Rio Grande Sul – ERC
Rio de Janeiro	Fundação Gertulio Vargas – Biblioteca – ERC
Rio de Janeiro	Eciel – ERC

Rio de Janeiro	ILDES – ERC
Salvador, Bahia	Universidade Federal da Bahia – ERC
Salvador, Bahia	Centro de Estatistica e Informaçoes (CEI) – ERC
Santa Maria	Universidade Federal de Santa Maria – ERC

Botswana

Gaborone	University of Botswana – ERC

Bulgaria

Sofia	National Library – DEP(R)

Canada

Burnaby	Simon Fraser University – ERC
Charlottetown	University of Prince Edward Island – ERC
Downsview	York University – ERC
Edmonton	University of Alberta – ERC
Fredericton	University of New Brunswick – ERC
Halifax	Dalhousie University – EDC(S)
Kingston	Queen's University – EDC
Moncton	Université de Moncton – ERC
Montreal	McGill University – EDC (English)
Montreal	McGill University – EDC(S) (French)
Montreal	Université de Montréal – EDC(S)
Ottawa	Bibliothèque Nationale du Canada – DEP(R)
Ottawa	Carleton University – EDC
Ottawa	University of Ottawa – ERC
St Catharines	Brock University – ERC
St John's	Memorial University of Newfoundland – ERC
Saskatoon	University of Sakatchewan – ERC
Sherbrooke	University of Sherbrooke – ERC
Ste Foy	Université Laval
Sudbury	Université Laurentienne – ERC
Toronto	University of Toronto – EDC
Vancouver	University of British Columbia – ERC
Waterloo	Wilfried Laurier University – ERC
Waterloo	University of Waterloo – ERC
Winnipeg	University of Manitoba – EDC
Wolfville	Acadia University – ERC

Chile

Santiago	Biblioteca del Congreso Nacionalca del Hemeroteca Organismos Intern. – ERC

China

Beijing	National Library of China – DEP
Beijing	Chinese Academy of Social Sciences/Centre for EC Studies/Institute of Western European Studies – EDC
Beijing	Ministry of Foreign Affairs – ERC
Shanghai	Institute of World Economy – EDC
Sichuan	Sichuan University – EDC
Tianjin	Nan-Kai University – EDC(S)
Wuhan Hubei	Institute of the Study of Economy of Western Europe – EDC

Colombia

Bogotá	Universidad la Gran Colombia – ERC
Bogotá	Universidad de los Andes – ERC
Bogotá	Pontificia Universidad Javeriana – ERC
Cali	Universidad del Valle – ERC

Costa Rica

San José	Centro de Documentación, Facultad Latinoamericana de Ciencias Sociales – ERC
San José	ICAP: Instituto Centro-Americano de Administración Publica – ERC

Cuba

Havana	Universidad de la Habana – ERC

Ecuador

Quito	Universidad Central del Ecuador – ERC

Egypt

Cairo	Helwan University – ERC

El Salvador

San Salvador	Universidad Centroamericano 'José Siméon Cañas' – ERC

German Democratic Republic

Berlin	Institut für Internationale Politik und Wirtschaft der DDR – EDC
Leipzig	Deutsche Bücherei Abteilung Erwerbung – ERC

Guadeloupe

Basse-Terre	CCI de Basse-Terre – ERC
Pointe-à-Pitre	CCI de Pointe à Pitre – ERC
Pointe-à-Pitre	Université des Antilles et de La Guyane – ERC

Guatemala

Guatemala	SIECA – ERC

Guyana

Georgetown	University of Guyana – ERC

Guyane (French Guiana)

Cayenne	CCI de Guyane – ERC

Honduras

Tegucigalpa	Biblioteca Nacional – ERC

Hungary

Budapest	Institute of Economies, Hungarian Academy of Sciences – EDC(S)
Budapest	Eotvos Lorand University – EDC(S)

Iceland

Reykjavik	The University Library – ERC

India

Calcutta	National Library – DEP
New Delhi	Parliament Library – DEP
New Delhi	Indian Council of World Affairs – EDC
New Delhi	Jawaharlal Nehru University – ERC
Pune	Servants of India Society's Library – DEP(R)

Indonesia

Djakarta	ASEAN Secretariat – ERC
Djakarta	University of Indonesia – ERC
Djakarta	Atma Jaya Research Centre – ERC

Israel

Jerusalem	The Jewish National and University Library – EDC(S)
Tel Aviv	Tel Aviv University – EDC(S)

Jamaica

Mona Kingston	University of the West Indies – ERC

Japan

Fukuoka	Seinan Gakuin University – EDC
Fukuyama	Fukuyama University – EDC(S)
Hokkaido	Otaru University of Commerce – ERC
Ishikawa	Kanazawa University – EDC(S)
Kagawa	Kagawa University – EDC(S)
Kawauchi, Sendai	Tahoku University – EDC
Kyoto	Doshisha University – EDC
Nagoya	Nagoya University – EDC(S)
Nayoga	Nanzan University – ERC
Okinawa	University of the Ryukyus – EDC
Osaka	Kansai University – EDC(S)
Saitama	Saitama University – ERC
Sapporo	Hokkaido University – EDC(S)
Shizuoka-Ken	Nihon University – EDC(S)
Tokyo	National Diet Library – DEP
Tokyo	University of Tokyo – EDC
Tokyo	Chuo University – EDC
Tokyo	Keio University – EDC(S)
Tokyo	Sophia University – EDC(S)
Tokyo	Waseda University – EDC(S)

Kenya

Nairobi	University of Nairobi – ERC

Korea (South)

Seoul	Kyung Hee University – ERC

Lebanon

Beirut	Université Saint-Joseph – ERC
Beirut	Chambre de Commerce et d'Industre de Beyrouth – ERC

Malawi

Zomba	University of Malawi – ERC

Malaysia

Kuala Lumpur	University of Malaya – ERC

Malta

Valletta	University of Malta – EDC

Martinique

Fort-de-France	Chambre de Commerce et d'Industrie de la Martinique – ERC

343

Mexico

Mexico City	Universidad Nacional Autónoma de México – ERC
Mexico City	Colegio de México – ERC
Monterrey	Universidad del Nuevo Leon – ERC
San Jeronimo Lidice	Centro de Estudios Económicos y Sociales del Tercer Mundo – CEESTEM – ERC

Morocco

Rabat	Documentation Service of the Ministry of Information – ERC

New Zealand

Auckland	Auckland Public Library – DEP
Auckland	University of Auckland – EDC(S)
Christchurch	University of Canterbury – EDC
Wellington	Parliamentary Library – DEP(R)

Norway

Oslo	Det Norske Nobelinstitutt – DEP

Peru

Lima	Universidad de Lima – ERC
Lima	Pontificia Universidad Catolica del Peru – ERC

Papua New Guinea

Papua	University of Papua New Guinea – ERC

Paraguay

Asunción	University Católica 'Nuestra Señora de la Asunción' – ERC

Philippines

Quezon City	University of the Philippines – ERC

Poland

Poznań	Instytut Zachodni dzial Dokumentacji i Informacji – EDC(S)
Sopot	Uniwersytet Gdansky – EDC(S)
Warsaw	Polski Instytut Spraw Miedzynarodowych – EDC(S)
Warsaw	Central School of Planning and Statistics – EDC(S)

Réunion

St Denis   Chambre de Commerce et d'Industrie de la
                      Réunion – ERC

Romania

Bucharest   Biblioteca Centrala de Stat – DEP(R)

Saudi Arabia

Riyadh   The Cooperation Council for the Arab States
                      of the Gulf – ERC
Riyadh   Ministry of Planning – ERC
Riyadh   Riyadh University – ERC

Sierra Leone

Freetown   Fourah Bay College – ERC

Singapore

Singapore   National University of Singapore – ERC

South Africa

Cape Town   South African Library – DEP(R)
Johannesburg   City of Johannesburg Public Library –
                      DEP(R)
Pretoria   University of South Africa – ERC

Sweden

Lund   Lunds Universitet – EDC
Stockholm   Stockholms Universitet – EDC(S)

Switzerland

Basel   Universität Basel – EDC(S)
Bern   Universität Bern – EDC(S)
Fribourg   Université de Fribourg – EDC
Genève (Geneva)   Centre d'Études Juridiques Européennes –
                      EDC(S)
Genève (Geneva)   Institut Universitaire d'Études Européennes –
                      EDC(S)
Lausanne   Université de Lausanne – EDC
Neuchâtel   Université de Neuchâtel – EDC(S)
St Gallen   Institut für Europäisches und Internationales
                      Wirtschafts und Sozialrecht – EDC(S)
Zürich   Universität Zürich – EDC

Thailand
Bangkok   Thammasat University – ERC

Trinidad and Tobago
St Augustine   University of the West Indies – ERC

Tunisia
Tunis   Tunis Campus Universitaire – ERC

Turkey
Adana   Çukurova Üniversitesi – ERC
Ankara   Union of Chambers of Commerce, Industry
                        and Commodity Exchanges of Turkey –
                        DEP(R)
Bornova-Izmir   Ege University Ziraat – EDC(S)
Eskisehir   Anadolu Üniversitesi – EDC(S)
Istanbul   Iktisadi Kalkinma Vakfi – DEP
Istanbul   Avrupa Toplulugu Enstitüsu Marmara
                        Üniversitesi – EDC
Istanbul   Istanbul Üniversitesi – EDC

Union of Soviet Socialist Republics
Moscow   Institut Mirovoji Economiki i
                        Mezhdunarodnich – ERC

United States of America
Albany   State University of New York at Albany –
                        DEP
Albuquerque   University of New Mexico – DEP
Ann Arbor   University of Michigan – DEP
Atlanta   Emory University – DEP
Athens   University of Georgia – EDC(S)
Austin   University of Texas – DEP
Berkeley   University of California – DEP
Bloomington   Indiana University – DEP
Boulder   University of Colorado – DEP
Buffalo   State University of New York at Buffalo –
                        DEP
Cambridge   Harvard Law School – DEP
Champaign   University of Illinois – DEP
Charlottesville   University of Virginia – DEP
Chicago   Library of International Relations – DEP
Chicago   University of Chicago – DEP
Columbia   University of South Carolina – DEP

Columbus	Ohio State University – DEP
Durham (North Carolina)	Duke University – DEP
East Lansing	Michigan State University – DEP
Eugene	University of Oregon – DEP
Evanston	Northwestern University – DEP
Gainesville	University of Florida – DEP
Honolulu	University of Hawaii – DEP
Iowa City	University of Iowa – DEP
La Jolla	University of California – DEP
Lawrence	University of Kansas – DEP
Lexington	University of Kentucky – DEP
Lincoln	University of Nebraska – DEP
Little Rock	University of Arkansas – DEP
Los Angeles	University of Southern California – DEP
Los Angeles	University of California – DEP
Madison	University of Wisconsin – DEP
Minneapolis	University of Minnesota – DEP
New Haven	Yale University – DEP
New York	New York University – DEP
New York	New York Public Library – DEP
New York	Council on Foreign Relations – DEP
New Orleans	University of New Orleans – DEP
Norman	University of Oklahoma – DEP
Notre Dame (Indiana)	University of Notre Dame – DEP
Pennsylvania	Pennsylvania State University – DEP
Philadelphia	University of Pennsylvania – DEP
Pittsburgh	University of Pittsburgh – DEP
Portland	University of Maine – DEP
Princeton	Princeton University – DEP
Seattle	University of Washington – DEP
Salt Lake City	University of Utah – DEP
St Louis	Washington University – DEP
Stanford	Stanford University – DEP
Tucson	University of Arizona – DEP
Washington	The Library of Congress – DEP
Washington	The American University (CERDEC) – EDC

Uruguay

Montevideo	Biblioteca Nacional – ERC
Montevideo	Universidad de Montevideo – ERC

Venezuela

Caracas	Universidad Central de Venezuela – ERC
Merida	Universidad de los Andes – ERC

Yugoslavia

Belgrade	Institut de Politique et d'Economie Internationales – EDC
Zagreb	University of Zagreb – ERC

Zaire

Kinshasa	Université Nationale du Zaïre – ERC
Lubumbashi	Université Officielle du Zaïre – ERC

Zimbabwe

Harare	University of Zimbabwe – ERC

Index

Note: The index includes entries for names of organizations, titles of publications, and subjects. All series and periodicals are indexed under title and subject; individual monographs within series are indexed only under subjects. No cross-references are given from abbreviations to the full forms of bodies; see the list of abbreviations on pp. xi–xiv. Page numbers corresponding to principal references are indicated by the use of bold type.